The Date-A-Base Book

2025

The Date-A-Base Book

2025

Compiled by Dave Haslett

ideas4writers

Copyright © Dave Haslett 2022

First published in Great Britain in 2022 by
ideas4writers
19 Crow Green
Cullompton
Devon
EX15 1EW

The right of Dave Haslett to be identified as the author
of this work has been asserted by him in accordance with the
Copyright, Designs and Patents Act 1988.

All rights reserved.

No part of this publication may be stored, copied or reproduced
in any form without the express written permission of the publisher.

Ice hockey image by brapai
licensed for use under Creative Commons 2.0

If you would like this series to continue, please tell people about it.

Contents

Introduction 7

January 9

February 29

March 49

April 69

May 91

June 113

July 135

August 155

September 177

October 201

November 223

December 243

Introduction

Welcome to the eighteenth edition of *The Date-A-Base Book* series.

As always, every entry has been cross-checked with official sources and reputable websites. And, as always, this was not an easy process as there's an awful lot of 'disinformation' out there. Whenever there was any doubt, I tried to find the original source. Even so, you are advised to double-check each entry before using it, and satisfy yourself that it is 100% correct. If you come across any mistakes please let me know.

I'll post any corrections I hear about on our blog at ideas4writers.com

As far as possible, and where appropriate, I've used New Style (NS) dates from the Gregorian calendar.

With such a vast number of worthy people to choose from, I elected to list only those who are included in *Encyclopaedia Britannica*, or those I've heard of. I apologise if a few non-British household names didn't make the final cut.

I have not included any births of living people, except for royalty.

In the case of wars, it was impossible to include every significant event. I've chosen what I think are the main ones, but if I've left out something you think should have been included please let me know.

How to use this book

The **Ann.** column gives the anniversary of each entry, so 700 means the 700th anniversary of that event. The date on which the event took place is listed next, followed by a brief description.

The most obvious way to use this book is to choose the entries that interest you, then write news reports, newspaper and magazine articles, TV/radio features, short stories, novels, essays, stage plays, screenplays, poems, jokes, non-fiction books, guidebooks, biographies, and so on about them.

But how about thinking outside the box? For example, you might try to see the event through the eyes of someone who was there at the time. Or think about how the world might have been different if that person hadn't been born, or if he had done something else, or if the event hadn't taken place, or if it had happened in a different way or at a different time or to someone else.

You could also use an event, or a series of them, as background detail in a novel or screenplay. Perhaps your characters could think about the events, and discuss them. Perhaps they could influence an event, or be influenced by it.

What most editors, publishers, broadcasters and producers are looking for is something original; something that hasn't been done before. They don't (necessarily) want a summary of a person's life, or a history and timeline of an event. They can probably write that in-house anyway, using their own staff writers – though it's always worth enquiring, just in case they can't.

But you'll probably have more success if you provide them with something different, more compelling, a new angle; something that ties in with the date of the event, but which can run alongside the more general features.

If you're writing about a person, don't just focus on his accomplishments. Have a look at the other things going on in his life: problems, rivalries, disputes, legal issues, patent and copyright issues, interests, hobbies, associations, relatives and relationships, fans and detractors, and so on. See if you can tie that in with one of your own areas of interest. You probably already read publications and visit websites related to those interests, so those are good markets to aim for.

See if you can relate the item to something from your own life, or use it to trigger memories and reminiscences that might lead you to a new writing project.

If you haven't written much before, or if you've never had anything published, use the item as a starting point and write a letter about it, which you can send to your local newspaper or your favourite magazine. You'll find it much easier to get published if the item is relevant to the geographic area the publication covers. Perhaps the famous person was born there, or went to school there, or worked there, or spent his holidays there, or made his big discovery there. You don't have to live there yourself: pick items that interest you, search online for publications that cover those areas, and tailor your letters and articles for their readers.

After you've had a few letters published, see if can get the coveted 'star letter' slot in one of the publications. Then, once you've achieved that, try writing some short articles.

Don't limit yourself to printed publications. There are thousands upon thousands of online publications that need writers – and some of them will even pay you.

Similarly, don't limit yourself to your own country – there's a whole world out there that's keen to hear what you have to say.

Timing is important too, of course. You need to start work well in advance of the anniversary, so that your finished piece of writing appears in print – or on stage or screen or radio – at the time of the anniversary. That's where *The Date-A-Base Book* can help you.

It's also important to bear in mind that magazines work several months in advance. For example, most monthly publications prepare their Christmas issues during the summer so they can be sure everything is ready in time. If you're writing for the stage or screen you might need to have your script ready at least two years before the anniversary occurs. That will allow time for things like casting, rehearsals, set design and building, filming, editing, post-production, promotion, and so on. So you should look at getting the next edition of *The Date-A-Base Book* as soon as it becomes available!

The currently available books are listed at ideas4writers.com and can be purchased from there.

Dave Haslett

Contact me at: mail@ideas4writers.com

JANUARY 2025

Ann.	Date	Event
700	7 Jan 1325	Death of Denis, (the Farmer King / the Poet King), King of Portugal (1279–1325). Succeeded by his son, Alfonso IV.
500	21 Jan 1525	Swiss Anabaptistism was founded when Conrad Grebel baptised George Blaurock, who in turn baptised fourteen other Christian radicals who attended the meeting. They had all been baptised when they were infants.
400	13 Jan 1625	Death of Jan Brueghel the Elder, Flemish artist.
250	8 Jan 1775	Death of John Baskerville, English printer and type designer.
250	11 Jan 1775	British-born plantation owner Francis Salvador became the first Jew to hold an elected office in the American colonies when he took his seat in the South Carolina Provincial Congress. (In August 1776 he became the first Jew to be killed in the American Revolutionary War.)
250	15 Jan 1775	Death of Giovanni Battista Sammartini, Italian composer, organist, violinist, choirmaster and teacher.
250	20 Jan 1775	Birth of André-Marie Ampère, French physicist, mathematician and educator. One of the founders of electromagnetism. Inventor of the solenoid. The SI unit of electric current, the ampere, was named in his honour.
200	3 Jan 1825	The first technological university in the English-speaking world, Rensselaer Polytechnic Institute, opened in Troy, New York, USA (as Rensselaer School).
200	4 Jan 1825	Death of Ferdinand I, King of the Two Sicilies (1816–25). Succeeded by his son, Francis I.
200	8 Jan 1825	Death of Eli Whitney, American inventor of the cotton gin – one of the key inventions of the Industrial Revolution.
150	5 Jan 1875	The Palais Garnier (also known as the Opéra Garnier) opened in Paris, France. It is one of the world's most famous opera houses.
150	9 Jan 1875	Birth of Gertrude Vanderbilt Whitney, American sculptor, art collector and patron of the arts. Founder of the Whitney Museum of American Art in New York City.
150	14 Jan 1875	Birth of Albert Schweitzer, German theologian, philosopher, physician, musicologist, writer and humanitarian. Winner of the 1952 Nobel Peace Prize.
150	19 Jan 1875	American inventor Thomas Edison was granted a U.S. patent for the electromotograph. It converted friction to electromagnetism and enabled telegraph signals to be repeated more effectively than previous methods. (U.S. patent 158,787.)
150	22 Jan 1875	Birth of D. W. Griffith, American film director. Best known for *The Birth of a Nation* and *Intolerance*. Co-founder of United Artists.
150	23 Jan 1875	Death of Charles Kingsley, British priest, historian, educator, social reformer and novelist. Best known for his novel *Westward Ho!*

JANUARY 2025

Ann.	Date	Event
150	24 Jan 1875	The première of French composer Camille Saint-Saëns' tone poem *Danse macabre*. Today it regarded as a masterpiece, but at the time it was not well received – the screeching violin caused widespread anxiety.
150	26 Jan 1875	American dentist George F. Green was granted a U.S. patent for the first electric dental drill. (U.S. Patent 171,121.)
125	1 Jan 1900	The British protectorates of Northern Nigeria and Southern Nigeria were established. The two protectorates, together with Lagos Colony were unified in 1914, forming the Colony and Protectorate of Nigeria. Nigeria gained its independence from the UK in 1960.
125	1 Jan 1900	The Net Book Agreement came into effect in the UK. Booksellers could only sell new books at fixed prices determined by publishers – no discounting was allowed. In 1997, it was ruled to be against the public interest, and therefore illegal, and it was abandoned.
125	2 Jan 1900	The Chicago Sanitary and Ship Canal opened. It connects the Chicago River to the Des Plaines River in the American MidWest.
125	5 Jan 1900	Birth of Yves Tanguy, French surrealistic artist.
125	6 Jan 1900	Birth of Maria of Yugoslavia, Queen consort of Serbs, Croats and Slovenes (1922–29), Queen consort of Yugoslavia (1929–34). Wife of Alexander I. Mother of Peter II.
125	9 Jan 1900	Birth of Richard Halliburton, American travel writer and adventurer. He famously swam the length of the Panama Canal, and died in 1939 while attempting to sail a Chinese junk across the Pacific.
125	10 Jan 1900	Birth of Violette Cordery, British racing driver and long-distance driver.
125	14 Jan 1900	The première of Italian composer Giacomo Puccini's opera *Tosca*, in Rome, Italy.
125	20 Jan 1900	Birth of Colin Clive, British stage and film actor. Best known for his role as Henry Frankenstein, the creator of the monster, in the films *Frankenstein* and *Bride of Frankenstein*.
125	20 Jan 1900	Death of R. D. Blackmore, British novelist. Best known for *Lorna Doone*.
125	20 Jan 1900	Death of John Ruskin, British writer, art critic, educator and philosopher.
125	22 Jan 1900	Death of David Edward Hughes, British-American inventor and professor of music. Known for developing the printing telegraph and for his improvements to the microphone.
125	23 Jan 1900 to 24th	Second Boer War – the Relief of Ladysmith Campaign – the Battle of Spion Kop. Boer victory.
125	27 Jan 1900	Birth of Hyman Rickover, U.S. Navy admiral. The 'Father of the Nuclear Navy'. He directed the development of nuclear-powered ships and oversaw the development of the first commercial pressurised water reactor.
125	31 Jan 1900	Death of John Douglas, 9th Marquess of Queensberry, Scottish nobleman. Best known for the Marquess of Queensberry Rules – the basis of modern boxing. His dispute with the Irish writer Oscar Wilde led to an infamous trial in which Wilde was convicted of gross indecency and imprisoned.

JANUARY 2025

Ann.	Date	Event
100	1 Jan 1925	The city of Oslo in Norway returned to using its original name. It was known as Christiania from 1624 to 1876 and Kristiania from 1877 to 1924.
100	3 Jan 1925	Benito Mussolini declared himself dictator of Italy.
100	4 Jan 1925	French psychologist and self-help guru Émile Coué arrived in the USA. He immediately became a huge celebrity, founded self-help institutes, and his book *Self-Mastery Through Conscious Autosuggestion* became a bestseller. He is best known for encouraging people to repeat the phrase: 'Every day in every way I am getting better and better.'
100	5 Jan 1925	Nellie Tayloe Ross became Governor of Wyoming. She was the first female governor in the USA.
100	6 Jan 1925	Birth of John DeLorean, American automotive engineer and executive (General Motors and the DeLorean Motor Company). His career was tainted by drug trafficking and financial scandals. (Died 2005.)
100	7 Jan 1925	Birth of Gerald Durrell, Indian-born British naturalist, conservationist, zoo keeper, writer and television presenter. (Died 1995.)
100	8 Jan 1925	The first all-female state Supreme Court in the USA sat in Texas. They met for five months to hear a case involving a fraternal organisation that almost all of the male elected officials and lawyers in the state belonged to. The only way to ensure an impartial verdict was for women to decide the case.
100	9 Jan 1925	Birth of Lee Van Cleef, American film actor. Known for his Westerns and action movies (*High Noon*, *The Man Who Shot Liberty Valance*, *The Good, the Bad and the Ugly*, and more). (Died 1989.)
100	15 Jan 1925	Leon Trotsky was removed from his posts as Chairman of the Revolutionary Military Council of the Soviet Union and leader of the Red Army.
100	15 Jan 1925	Hans Luther became Chancellor of Germany.
100	16 Jan 1925	Austrian theoretical physicist Wolfgang Pauli announced his exclusion principle, which states that no two electrons in an atom can be in the same quantum state at the same time. He was awarded the 1945 Nobel Prize in Physics for his discovery.
100	19 Jan 1925	Birth of Nina Bawden, British novelist and children's writer. (Died 2012.)
100	26 Jan 1925 to 2 Feb	The serum run to Nome, Alaska, USA (also known as the Great Race of Mercy). With a diphtheria epidemic threatening the city of Nome and no planes available to carry an anti-toxin, dog-sledders worked in relays to carry a canister of serum 674 miles in five days. This event is now commemorated in the annual Iditarod Trail Sled Dog Race.
100	26 Jan 1925	Birth of Paul Newman, American film actor, director, entrepreneur and philanthropist (*The Hustler*, *Cool Hand Luke*, *Butch Cassidy and the Sundance Kid*, *The Sting*, and more). (Died 2008.)
100	30 Jan 1925	The Turkish government banished Ecumenical Patriarch Constantine VI of Constantinople and sent him into exile in Greece.

JANUARY 2025

Ann.	Date	Event
100	30 Jan 1925	Birth of Douglas Engelbart, American computer scientist, engineer and inventor. Best known for inventing the computer mouse. He also helped found the field of human-computer interaction and developed hypertext, computer networks, and early graphical user interfaces. (Died 2013.)
100	31 Jan 1925	Albania declared itself a republic and the First Albanian Republic was established with Ahmet Zogu as its President. The monarchy was restored in 1928 and the President became King Zog I.
90	1 Jan 1935	The Surname Law of 1934 came into effect in Turkey. All of its citizens were required to use fixed, hereditary Turkish surnames from this date. President Mustafa Kemal adopted the surname Atatürk (meaning Father of Turkey) which had been granted to him by the Turkish parliament. He was the only person allowed to use that surname.
90	1 Jan 1935	The Associated Press launched its AP Wirephoto service, which transmitted photographs to newspapers over regular telephone lines. The first photo showed the rescued survivors of a plane crash in the Adirondacks, taken on 31st December 1934.
90	1 Jan 1935	The first Orange Bowl college football game was held in Florida, USA, the first Sugar Bowl college football game was held in Louisiana, USA, and the first Sun Bowl college football game was held in Texas, USA.
90	2 Jan 1935 to 13 Feb	German immigrant Bruno Hauptmann went on trial in the USA for the murder of aviator Charles Lindbergh's infant son. He was found guilty and sentenced to death. He was executed in April 1936.
90	4 Jan 1935	Dry Tortugas National Park was established in Florida, USA (as Fort Jefferson National Monument).
90	4 Jan 1935	The Mosul–Haifa oil pipeline began operating, sending crude oil from Iraq to the Mediterranean port of Haifa (now in Israel, but then part of the British Mandate of Palestine). It was strategically important in WWII, providing fuel to British and U.S. forces in the Mediterranean.
90	4 Jan 1935	Bob Hope made his first appearance on national radio in the USA, as master of ceremonies on the show *The Intimate Revue*.
90	4 Jan 1935	Birth of Floyd Patterson, American world heavyweight boxing champion. (Died 2006.)
90	7 Jan 1935	The Italo–French agreements were signed in Rome by the Italian Prime Minister Benito Mussolini and the French Foreign Minister Pierre Laval. France granted Italy control of disputed territories and allowed Italy to invade Ethiopia without interference (the Second Italo–Ethiopian War). In exchange Italy agreed to support France against German aggression. (Mussolini broke the agreement and allied with Nazi Germany in 1939, in the lead-up to WWII.)
90	8 Jan 1935	American physicist Arthur C. Hardy was granted a patent for the first spectrophotometer. It is used to measure the transmission and absorption of light from a material.
90	8 Jan 1935	Birth of Elvis Presley, ('The King'), American rock and roll singer, guitarist and actor. (Died 1977.)

JANUARY 2025

Ann.	Date	Event
90	9 Jan 1935	Birth of Bob Denver, American film and television actor (*The Many Loves of Dobie Gillis, Gilligan's Island*). (Died 2005.)
90	10 Jan 1935	Death of Edwin Flack, Australian sprinter and tennis player. The first Australian Olympic champion. He was Australia's only competitor at the 1896 Olympics, where he won the gold medal in the 800 m and 1500 m, and took part in the tennis.
90	11 Jan 1935	American aviator Amelia Earhart became the first person to make a solo flight from Hawaii to California, USA.
90	13 Jan 1935	The Saar status referendum. The Territory of the Saar Basin held a referendum in which its citizens were given the option of unifying with either Germany or France or remaining under League of Nations administration. Over ninety percent voted to unify with Germany, and the region became the German state of Saarland.
90	16 Jan 1935	Death of Ma Barker, American criminal. Matriarch of a notorious gang of outlaws in the 1920s–30s. (Shot dead in a gun battle with the FBI.)
90	19 Jan 1935	Men's briefs (also known as Jockey shorts or Y-fronts) were first sold by Coopers, Inc. in Chicago, Illinois, USA. They went on sale in the UK in 1938.
90	21 Jan 1935	The Wilderness Society was founded in the USA.
90	24 Jan 1935	The first canned beer went on sale, in Virginia, USA. The beers were Krueger's Cream Ale and Krueger's Finest Beer. They were an immediate success.
90	28 Jan 1935	Iceland became the first Western country to legalise abortion.
80	1 Jan 1945	World War II – the Battle of the Bulge – Operation Bodenplatte. The German Luftwaffe launched a failed attempt to cripple Allied air power in the Low Countries in a single blow.
80	2 Jan 1945	World War II: the British RAF and U.S. Army Air Force bombed the city of Nuremburg, Germany, destroying ninety percent of its medieval centre within one hour.
80	2 Jan 1945 to 3rd	World War II – the Burma Campaign: the Allies landed on the west coast of Burma and occupied Akyab Island, which the Japanese had abandoned. They secured the entire southern coast by the end of the month.
80	3 Jan 1945	Death of Edgar Cayce, American psychic and faith healer.
80	6 Jan 1945	The cartoon character Pepé Le Pew made his first appearance, in the Warner Bros. cartoon *Odor-able Kitty*.
80	9 Jan 1945 to 15 Aug	World War II – the Battle of Luzon, Philippines. Allied victory.
80	11 Jan 1945	World War II: the Second Phase of the Greek Civil War ended. Kingdom of Greece victory. The third and final phase began in March 1946.
80	12 Jan 1945 to 2 Feb	World War II – the Eastern Front – the Vistula–Oder Offensive, central Poland and eastern Germany. A massive Red Army operation involving more than two million infantry. Soviet victory.

JANUARY 2025

Ann.	Date	Event
80	13 Jan 1945	The première of Russian composer Sergei Prokofiev's *Symphony No. 5* (Opus 100) in Moscow.
80	15 Jan 1945	World War II: the Soviet Red Army liberated the city of Krakow, Poland.
80	15 Jan 1945	Birth of Vince Foster, American lawyer. Deputy White House Counsel during the Clinton administration. He also worked with Hillary Clinton at Rose Law Firm in Arkansas. His suicide in 1993 led to five official investigations and several conspiracy theories.
80	16 Jan 1945	World War II: Adolf Hitler took up residence in the Führerbunker, a subterranean bunker complex in the garden of the Reich Chancellery in Berlin, Germany. It became the headquarters of the Nazi regime, and he remained there for the rest of his life. He committed suicide there in April.
80	17 Jan 1945	Holocaust: the Nazis began evacuating 58,000 prisoners from Auschwitz concentration camp as the Soviet Red Army closed in. Thousands died on the subsequent death march to Bergen–Belsen.
80	17 Jan 1945	World War II: the Soviet Red Army liberated Warsaw, Poland. The city had been almost completely destroyed by the Germans.
80	17 Jan 1945	World War II: the Soviet Red Army liberated Budapest, Hungary.
80	17 Jan 1945	Holocaust: Swedish diplomat and humanitarian Raoul Wallenberg, who rescued tens of thousands of Jews in Hungary during the Holocaust, was arrested for espionage by Soviet authorities. He was never seen again. He was reported to have died in a Soviet prison in July 1947, though this is disputed.
80	19 Jan 1945	World War II: the Soviet Red Army liberated the city of Łódź in Poland. Only five percent of the 230,000 Jews in the Łódź Ghetto had survived.
80	20 Jan 1945	Franklin D. Roosevelt was inaugurated as President of the United States for an unprecedented fourth term. He died in April.
80	20 Jan 1945	World War II: Hungary signed an armistice with the Allies in Moscow and officially dropped out of the war.
80	22 Jan 1945	World War II: the Allies reopened the Burma Road linking Myanmar and south-west China. It had been closed since 1942 after the Japanese occupied Myanmar, forcing the Allies to supply China by air. The first trucks loaded with supplies reached China on 28th January.
80	23 Jan 1945 to May	World War II – Operation Hannibal. Germany evacuated 1.8 million civilians and military personnel across the Baltic Sea from East Prussia and the neighbouring area as the Soviet Red Army advanced. It was one of the largest emergency evacuations by sea in history, with more than three times the number of people evacuated than from Dunkirk. (See also: 30th January 1945.)
80	24 Jan 1945 to 23 Feb	World War II: the Battle of Poznań, Poland. Soviet victory. The city was liberated but much of the older part was left in ruins.
80	25 Jan 1945	World War II: the Battle of the Bulge ended when Germany's Operation North Wind failed. Allied victory. This was Germany's last major offensive on the Western Front. The battle had begun on 16th December 1944.

JANUARY 2025

Ann.	Date	Event
80	25 Jan 1945 to 26th	Holocaust: The Nazis began evacuating Stutthof concentration camp in Poland. About 25,000 prisoners were sent on a ten-day march with only two days' food supply. Thousands died on the journey. On 31st January another 5,000 prisoners were forcibly marched into the Baltic Sea and machine-gunned.
80	25 Jan 1945	Grand Rapids, Michigan became the first city in the USA to fluoridate its drinking water to prevent tooth decay.
80	26 Jan 1945	Birth of Jacqueline du Pré, British cellist. (Died 1987.)
80	26 Jan 1945	Birth of David Purley, British racing driver. Best known for abandoning his race in the 1973 Dutch Grand Prix to help fellow driver Roger Williamson, whose car had crashed and caught fire. (Williamson suffocated in the fire.) (Died 1985 – plane crash, aged 40.)
80	27 Jan 1945	Holocaust: the Soviet Red Army liberated Auschwitz Concentration Camp in southern Poland. Auschwitz was the largest Nazi concentration camp and at least 1.1 million prisoners died there. Most of the camp's population had been sent on death marches to other camps in Germany and Austria as the Red Army approached. The day is now commemorated as International Holocaust Remembrance Day.
80	27 Jan 1945	World War II: Nazi occupiers blocked food transportation to the densely populated western Netherlands. It was already experiencing famine because of the severe winter, destroyed bridges and docks, and flooded farmland. Swedish Red Cross ships arrived on 28th January, bringing food for the starving people, but the Nazis refused to allow the food to be distributed until the end of February. Around 22,000 people died during the 'Hunger Winter'.
80	30 Jan 1945	World War II: the German ship *Wilhelm Gustloff*, packed with refugees during Operation Hannibal (see 23rd January above), was hit by a Soviet torpedo and sank in the Baltic Sea. More than 9,000 people were killed. It remains the largest loss of life in history from a single ship sinking.
80	30 Jan 1945	World War II – the Raid at Cabanatuan (also known as The Great Raid). More than 550 Allied prisoners-of-war were liberated from the Cabanatuan prisoner-of-war camp in the Philippines.
80	31 Jan 1945 to 21 Feb	World War II – the Battle of Bataan, Philippines. Allied victory. The strategically important peninsula was recaptured from the Japanese, who had held it since April 1942. This opened up additional supply lines to U.S. troops fighting in the Battle of Manila, which was won on 3rd March.
80	31 Jan 1945	Death of Eddie Slovik, U.S. Army soldier. (Executed for desertion.) He was the first and only American soldier to be executed for desertion since the American Civil War.
75	3 Jan 1950	The Memphis Recording Service was opened by Sam Phillips in Memphis, Tennessee, USA. Many famous artists made their first recordings there. In 1952 it became the recording studio for Sun Records, which Phillips also founded.

JANUARY 2025

Ann.	Date	Event
75	5 Jan 1950	Sverdlovsk plane crash, Soviet Union. The plane crashed during a heavy snowstorm on its fifth attempt to land at Koltsovo Airport. All nineteen people on board were killed, including eleven members of the Soviet Air Force's VVS Moscow ice hockey team, and their team doctor and masseur.
75	6 Jan 1950	The United Kingdom officially recognised the People's Republic of China and established diplomatic relations. The Republic of China (Taiwan) severed relations with the United Kingdom in response.
75	7 Jan 1950	Mercy Hospital fire, Davenport, Iowa, USA. A fire broke out in St. Elizabeth's ward, which housed 62 female patients. The doors were locked because it was a psychiatric ward, the windows were barred, there was no evacuation plan, and no sprinkler system in the 80-year-old building (though the fire department had recommended installing one for more than 25 years). 40 patients and a nurse were killed.
75	12 Jan 1950	The British submarine *HMS Truculent* sank in the mouth of the River Medway in south-east England after accidentally hitting a Swedish oil tanker. 63 men on board the submarine were killed – many of them escaped from the submarine but were swept away by the tide. Subsequently, all British submarines were fitted with 'Truculent Lights' to make them more visible.
75	14 Jan 1950	The Soviet Union's MiG-17 fighter jet made its first flight. It was used in the Second Taiwan Strait Crisis and the Vietnam War.
75	17 Jan 1950	The Great Brinks Robbery. Eleven thieves stole more than $2 million from an armoured car company's offices in Boston, Massachusetts, USA.
75	17 Jan 1950	The United Nations Security Council adopted Resolution 79 concerning the regulation and reduction of armaments.
75	18 Jan 1950	Birth of Gilles Villeneuve, Canadian racing driver. (Died 1982.)
75	19 Jan 1950	First Indochina War: China joined the Soviet Union in recognising Ho Chi Minh's communist North Vietnam.
75	21 Jan 1950	Former U.S. State Department official Alger Hiss, who was accused of being a Soviet spy, was sentenced to five years in prison for perjury after being convicted of lying to a grand jury. He served 3½ years.
75	21 Jan 1950	Death of George Orwell, British novelist, journalist and critic. Best known for his novels *Animal Farm* and *Nineteen Eighty-four*.
75	23 Jan 1950	Israel declared that Jerusalem was its capital city. Jerusalem's status is disputed, and Palestine also claims it as its capital.
75	24 Jan 1950	American physicist and inventor Percy Spencer, an employee of Raytheon, was granted a U.S. patent for the microwave oven. (U.S. Patent 2,495,429.)
75	26 Jan 1950	India became an independent republic. President Rajendra Prasad replaced King George VI as head of state. This day is now marked as Republic Day in India.
75	27 Jan 1950	Scientists working at the Pfizer pharmaceutical company in the USA announced a new type of antibiotic, Oxytetracycline. They had discovered it in soil samples near their laboratories, determined its chemical structure, and mass-produced it under the trade name Terramycin.

JANUARY 2025

Ann.	Date	Event
75	31 Jan 1950	U.S. President Harry S. Truman announced that he had ordered the Atomic Energy Commission to develop a hydrogen bomb. The first prototype, 'Ivy Mike', was detonated in November 1952.
70	2 Jan 1955	Death of José Antonio Remón, President of Panama (1952–55). (Assassinated). He was succeeded by José Ramón Guizado, who was swiftly deposed when it was discovered that he had been involved in the assassination.
70	7 Jan 1955	American contralto Marian Anderson became the first African American to perform at the Metropolitan Opera in New York City.
70	15 Jan 1955	Death of Yves Tanguy, French-born American surrealist artist.
70	19 Jan 1955	U.S. President Dwight D. Eisenhower gave the first televised presidential news conference. The conference was filmed in the morning and broadcast on television that evening. The first live conference was given by John F. Kennedy in January 1961.
70	19 Jan 1955	The board game Scrabble went on sale in the UK and Australia. It had been available in the USA since 1952.
70	21 Jan 1955	Death of Archie Hahn, American athlete and coach. One of the best sprinters of the 20th century. 3x gold medallist at the 1904 Olympics.
70	23 Jan 1955	Sutton Coldfield rail crash, Birmingham, UK. A passenger train travelling from York to Bristol derailed and crashed at Sutton Coldfield station. Seventeen people were killed and 25 injured. Cause: excessive speed on a curve – reason unknown.
70	25 Jan 1955	The Soviet Union ended its state of war with Germany, which had existed since 1941.
70	25 Jan 1955	The world's first accurate atomic clock was unveiled by scientists at the National Physical Laboratory in the UK. It measured time by counting the vibrations of caesium-133 atoms, and was accurate to one second every three hundred years.
70	26 Jan 1955	Birth of Eddie Van Halen, Dutch-born American rock guitarist and songwriter (Van Halen). Regarded as one of the greatest rock guitarists in history. (Died 2020.)
70	31 Jan 1955	RCA unveiled the first electronic music synthesizer.
65	1 Jan 1960	The Republic of Cameroon became independent from France and the UK.
65	4 Jan 1960	Death of Albert Camus, Algerian-born French writer and philosopher. Winner of the 1957 Nobel Prize in Literature. (Car crash, aged 46.)
65	12 Jan 1960	Death of Nevil Shute, British-born Australian novelist.
65	14 Jan 1960	The Reserve Bank of Australia was established. It is Australia's central bank and banknote issuing authority.
65	21 Jan 1960	Coalbrook mining disaster, Clydesdale Colliery, near Sasolburg, Free State, South Africa. 435 miners were killed when the mine collapsed due to pillar failure. It was the worst mining disaster in South African history.
65	22 Jan 1960	Birth of Michael Hutchence, Australian rock singer (INXS). (Died 1997.)

JANUARY 2025

Ann.	Date	Event
65	23 Jan 1960	The U.S. Navy's bathyscaphe *Trieste* descended to the deepest point in the Pacific Ocean – the Challenger Deep in the Mariana Trench near Guam. 35,797 feet (10,911 meters).
65	24 Jan 1960 to 1 Feb	Algerian war – the Siege of Algiers (also known as the week of barricades). Algerian protesters staged an insurrection against the French in Algiers. French victory.
65	25 Jan 1960	The Soviet Union abolished its Gulag system of forced labour camps. However, forced labour camps continued to be used for political prisoners and criminals until 1987.
65	25 Jan 1960	Payola scandal. The National Association of Broadcasters in the USA threatened to fine DJs who accepted money for playing particular records.
65	28 Jan 1960	The Moon Relay communications system was inaugurated in the USA. The U.S. Navy used it to transmit data between Hawaii and Washington, D.C. by bouncing radio waves off the Moon. It remained in use until the late 1960s, when it was superseded by satellite communication.
65	28 Jan 1960	The last regular episode of the radio comedy series *The Goon Show* was broadcast on the BBC Home Service in the UK. (Three special episodes were broadcast in 1968, 1972 and 2001.)
60	3 Jan 1965	American civil rights leader Martin Luther King Jr. began a drive to register black voters. Many of those who tried to register were arrested. It led to the signing of the landmark Voting Rights Act into law on 6th August, which prohibited racial discrimination in voting.
60	4 Jan 1965	U.S. President Lyndon Baines Johnson announced the details of his Great Society programme in his State of the Union Address. Its main goal was to eliminate poverty and racial injustice. The programmes included Medicare, Medicaid, Civil Rights, Voting Rights, Food Stamps, Public Broadcasting, Clean Air and Water Legislation, Consumer Protection, and several more.
60	4 Jan 1965	Death of T. S. Eliot, American-born British poet, playwright, literary critic and editor. Winner of the 1948 Nobel Prize for Literature.
60	5 Jan 1965	CBS purchased the Fender Electric Instrument Company for $13 million. Fender is best known for its solid-body electric guitars and bass guitars. Fender employees purchased the company from CBS in 1985 and renamed it the Fender Musical Instruments Corporation.
60	8 Jan 1965	The Star of India, a golf ball-sized sapphire, was found in a bus locker in Miami, Florida. It was returned to the American Museum of Natural History in New York City, from where it had been stolen in October 1964. It was found after a thief led police to it in a bid for leniency.
60	12 Jan 1965	Jackson Flats nuclear test, Nevada, USA. Scientists launched a nuclear rocket and vaporised its core to study the effect of radiation on the environment. The radioactive cloud spread downwind for 200 miles and reached Los Angeles and San Diego in California, where increased levels of radiation were detected in milk samples. Although the radiation level was within safe limits, details of the incident remained classified until 1994. It sparked considerable controversy when it came to light.

JANUARY 2025

Ann.	Date	Event
60	12 Jan 1965	Death of Lorraine Hansberry, American playwright. Known for *A Raisin in the Sun* – the first play by an African American woman to be produced on Broadway.
60	14 Jan 1965	Birth of Shamil Basayev, Chechen terrorist. He was responsible for numerous guerrilla attacks and hostage-takings, including the 2002 Moscow theatre crisis and the 2004 Beslan school siege. He was one of the world's most-wanted terrorists. (Died 2006.)
60	14 Jan 1965	Death of Jeanette MacDonald, American stage, film, radio and TV singer and actress. She starred in numerous musical films in the 1930s, and was one of the most influential operatic sopranos of the 20th century.
60	15 Jan 1965	British rock band The Who released their first UK single, *I Can't Explain*. (USA: December 1964.)
60	20 Jan 1965	Indonesia became the first country to unilaterally withdraw from the United Nations, as a result of the Indonesia–Malaysia confrontation. It resumed its membership in September 1966.
60	20 Jan 1965	Death of Alan Freed, American radio DJ who coined the term 'rock and roll'. His career was destroyed by the payola scandal, in which he was convicted of accepting bribes to play particular records. (Alcohol-related cirrhosis and uremia, aged 43.)
60	21 Jan 1965	Birth of Jam Master Jay, American rap musician, record producer and DJ (Run–D.M.C.). (Died 2002.)
60	24 Jan 1965	Death of Winston Churchill, British Prime Minister (1940–45, 1951–55). One of the greatest wartime leaders of the 20th century. Named 'the Greatest Briton of all time'. Winner of the 1953 Nobel Prize in Literature.
60	27 Jan 1965	Death of Hassan Ali Mansur, Prime Minister of Iran. (Shot and mortally wounded by an assassin in Tehran on 22nd January.)
60	28 Jan 1965	Death of Maxime Weygand, French Army officer. Chief of staff during WWI and commander-in-chief of the Allied armies in France during WWII.
50	1 Jan 1975	Watergate Scandal: former U.S. President Richard Nixon's senior aides were convicted of conspiracy, obstruction of justice and perjury. They included John Mitchell (Attorney General), John Ehrlichman (Domestic Affairs Advisor) and H.R. Haldeman (Chief of Staff).
50	1 Jan 1975	Ethiopia's military rulers nationalised all land, farms, financial institutions and insurance companies in the country.
50	2 Jan 1975	The Federal Rules of Evidence were adopted in the USA.
50	5 Jan 1975	Charlie Smalls' musical *The Wiz* opened on Broadway. It was a contemporary African American retelling of *The Wonderful Wizard of Oz*. It was first performed in Baltimore, Maryland, USA in October 1974.
50	6 Jan 1975	*AM America* was first broadcast on ABC television in the USA. It was not a success and was replaced by *Good Morning America* in November.
50	6 Jan 1975	The first episode of the television game show *Wheel Of Fortune* was broadcast on NBC in the USA.

JANUARY 2025

Ann.	Date	Event
50	7 Jan 1975	The musical *Shenandoah* by Gary Geld and Peter Udell opened on Broadway. It ran until August 1977.
50	8 Jan 1975	Ella T. Grasso became Governor of Connecticut. She was the first female governor in the USA to be elected in her own right rather than succeeding her husband.
50	14 Jan 1975	British heiress Lesley Whittle, aged seventeen, was kidnapped from her home in Shropshire by Donald Neilson ('the Black Panther'). He demanded a ransom of £50,000. The money was not delivered in time because of a series of errors by the police, and her body was found on 7th March. Neilson was arrested in December and imprisoned for life for killing her and for three earlier murders.
50	15 Jan 1975	The thirteen-year Angolan War of Independence ended with the signing of the Alvor Agreement in Portugal. Portugal agreed to grant Angola its independence from 11th November 1975.
50	15 Jan 1975	The original *Space Mountain* space-themed indoor roller coaster opened at Walt Disney World Resort in Florida, USA. Other versions have since opened at other Disney theme parks.
50	18 Jan 1975	The first episode of the television sitcom *The Jeffersons* was broadcast on CBS in the USA. It ran for eleven seasons until 1985. It was a spin-off series from the sitcom *All in the Family*, which was based on the British sitcom *Till Death Us Do Part*.
50	20 Jan 1975	Bob Dylan's album *Blood on the Tracks* was released.
50	22 Jan 1975	NASA launched the Earth Resources Technology Satellite *Landsat 2* to capture images of the Earth.
50	23 Jan 1975	The Philippine Basketball Association was founded. It is the first professional basketball league in Asia, and the world's second-oldest after the NBA in the USA. Its played its first games in April.
50	23 Jan 1975	The first episode of the police-based television sitcom *Barney Miller* was broadcast on ABC in the USA. It ran for eight seasons until 1982.
50	24 Jan 1975	Death of Larry Fine, American comedian and actor (The Three Stooges).
50	27 Jan 1975	The U.S. Senate established the Church Committee to investigate abuses by the FBI, CIA, NSA and IRS. It uncovered several shocking abuses, including Operation MKULTRA – the drugging and torture of unwitting people during experiments on mind control. It published its full report in April 1976.
50	30 Jan 1975	The Monitor National Marine Sanctuary was established as the first national marine sanctuary in the USA. It is the site of the wreck of the *USS Monitor*, which sank during the American Civil War off Cape Hatteras, North Carolina and became an artificial reef.
40	1 Jan 1985	The U.S. Department of Defense's Committee on the Atmospheric Effects of Nuclear Explosions published its report *The Effects on the Atmosphere of a Major Nuclear Exchange*. It confirmed the theory that an atomic war would reduce the amount of sunlight and cause a 'nuclear winter'.

JANUARY 2025

Ann.	Date	Event
40	1 Jan 1985	New York became the first U.S. state to introduce a mandatory seat-belt law. All car drivers, front-seat passengers and children under ten were required to wear them, or face a $50 fine.
40	1 Jan 1985	The first mobile phone call in the UK was made by comedian Ernie Wise. He called Vodafone's head office in Newbury, Berkshire from St. Katherine Docks in London.
40	1 Jan 1985	The television channel VH1 launched in the USA.
40	3 Jan 1985	405-line television transmissions were shut down in the UK (4th January in Scotland) after more than 48 years. All UK television channels had been broadcast in 625 lines since November 1969. The 405-line broadcasts were maintained as a legacy system until the vast majority of viewers could receive 625-line broadcasts.
40	4 Jan 1985	British surrogate mother Kim Cotton gave birth to a baby girl and was investigated by Scotland Yard over reports that she would receive £6,500 from a childless couple when she handed it over to them. Surrogacy is legal in the UK, but payment is not.
40	5 Jan 1985	Death of Robert L. Surtees, American cinematographer (*King Solomon's Mines, The Bad and the Beautiful, Ben-Hur, Mutiny on the Bounty, The Graduate, The Sting*, and more).
40	6 Jan 1985	Death of Robert W. Welch Jr., American businessman who founded and led the far-right anti-communist John Birch Society after his retirement.
40	7 Jan 1985	Japan launched its first interplanetary spacecraft, *Sakigake*, on an experimental mission to Halley's Comet. It was first deep-space probe launched by a country other than the USA or Soviet Union.
40	10 Jan 1985	Daniel Ortega was inaugurated as President of Nicaragua (until 1990). He became President again in 2007.
40	10 Jan 1985	The Sinclair C5 electric tricycle was launched in the UK. Immediate concerns were raised about its safety in traffic, and it was ridiculed in the media. It was not a commercial success.
40	13 Jan 1985	A passenger train derailed in Ethiopia, with four of its five carriages plunging into a ravine. Approximately 428 people were killed, making it the worst-ever railway disaster in Africa. In February 2002 a train caught fire in Egypt. The official death toll was 383 but media reports estimated it to be over 1,000 – if this is correct then it would be the worst-ever in Africa.
40	15 Jan 1985	Tancredo Neves was elected President of Brazil. He did not take office as he became severely ill on the eve of his inauguration and died in April. Vice-President José Sarney took office in his place.
40	17 Jan 1985	British Telecom officially retired Britain's iconic red telephone boxes.
40	18 Jan 1985	Death of Wilfrid Brambell, Irish film and television actor. Best known for his roles in the British TV series *Steptoe and Son* and the Beatles' film *A Hard Day's Night*.
40	21 Jan 1985	Death of James Beard, American chef and food writer. The first chef to demonstrate cooking on U.S. network television.

JANUARY 2025

Ann.	Date	Event
40	23 Jan 1985	A debate from Britain's House of Lords was televised live for the first time. It was an experimental broadcast, but it became permanent soon afterwards.
40	24 Jan 1985	Penny Harrington became the first female chief of the Portland Police Bureau in Oregon, and the first woman in the USA to head a major police department. However, her administration was reported to be a failure, and she resigned in 1986 – later saying that members of the police department had conspired to drive her out of office.
40	25 Jan 1985	South African President P. W. Botha opened the country's new three-chamber parliament. It had separate chambers for Whites, Asians/Indians, and Coloureds/Mixed Race – but not blacks.
40	26 Jan 1985	Death of James Cameron, British journalist and writer. A founding member of the Campaign for Nuclear Disarmament (CND). The annual James Cameron Memorial Lecture is given in his honour.
40	28 Jan 1985	The supergroup USA for Africa recorded the hit single *We Are the World* to raise money for famine relief in Ethiopia. The song was written by Michael Jackson and Lionel Richie and was released on 7th March. It raised over $63 million.
40	29 Jan 1985	Oxford University refused to award Prime Minister Margaret Thatcher an honorary doctorate after she cut funding for higher education.
40	31 Jan 1985	South African President P. W. Botha offered to free Nelson Mandela from prison if he unconditionally rejected violence as a political weapon. Mandela refused and remained in prison until 1990.
30	Jan 1995 and March	Some of the worst floods in the U.S. state of California's history killed 28 people and caused billions of dollars worth of damage.
30	1 Jan 1995	The World Trade Organisation was established.
30	1 Jan 1995	Fernando Henrique Cardoso became President of Brazil.
30	1 Jan 1995	The last *The Far Side* cartoon by Gary Larson was published. Larson then retired. *The Far Side* was first published in 1980.
30	1 Jan 1995	The History Channel (now known as History) launched in the USA. (UK: 11th November 1995.)
30	1 Jan 1995	Death of Fred West, British serial killer (found hanged in his prison cell).
30	2 Jan 1995	Death of Siad Barre, President of Somalia (1969–91).
30	3 Jan 1995	The World Health Organisation (WHO) reported that the cumulative total reported AIDS cases had passed the one million mark, with cases in 192 countries. (Including unreported cases, the total was estimated to be approximately 4.5 million.)
30	3 Jan 1995	Parkhurst Prison escape, Isle of Wight, UK. Three prisoners, including two convicted murderers and a blackmailer, escaped from the high-security prison. This caused the British government a great deal of embarrassment. The prisoners attempted to steal a plane, but failed, and spent four days living in a garden shed before being recaptured. Parkhurst's high-security status (Category A) was subsequently down-graded (to Category B).

JANUARY 2025

Ann.	Date	Event
30	4 Jan 1995	Newt Gingrich became Speaker of the U.S. House of Representatives.
30	6 Jan 1995	Death of Joe Slovo, Lithuanian-born South African lawyer and political activist. General secretary of the South African Communist Party (SACP). He fought against apartheid for more than 40 years.
30	7 Jan 1995	Death of Larry Grayson, British comedian and television game show host. Known for his camp humour and catchphrases ('Shut that door!', 'What a gay day!') and for hosting *The Generation Game*.
30	9 Jan 1995	Russian cosmonaut Valeri Poliakov became the first person to spend an entire year in space in a single mission. (His mission to the *Mir* space station lasted for a total of 437 days.)
30	9 Jan 1995	The first episode of the late-night television talk/variety show *The Late Late Show* was broadcast on CBS in the USA. The first host was Tom Snyder.
30	9 Jan 1995	Death of Peter Cook, British satirist, actor, writer and comedian. Known for his anti-establishment comedy and long comedy partnership with Dudley Moore.
30	9 Jan 1995	Death of Souphanouvong, President of Laos (1975–91).
30	11 Jan 1995	The WB Television Network was launched in the USA. It shut down in September 2006 and was replaced by The CW.
30	16 Jan 1995	The Troubles in Northern Ireland: the British Army ended daylight patrols of Belfast streets after 25 years.
30	16 Jan 1995	The first episode of the science fiction television series *Star Trek: Voyager* was broadcast on the UPN network in the USA. It ran for seven seasons.
30	17 Jan 1995	The Kobe earthquake (also known as the Great Hanshin earthquake), Japan, caused massive damage to the city and devastated the region's infrastructure and industry. More than 6,400 people were killed.
30	20 Jan 1995	Jean-Claude Juncker became Prime Minister of Luxembourg.
30	24 Jan 1995	Opening statements began in the O. J. Simpson murder trial in Los Angeles, California, USA. (He was acquitted in October.)
30	25 Jan 1995	Norwegian rocket incident. U.S. and Norwegian scientists launched a Black Brant XII sounding rocket over Svalbard, Norway to study the aurora borealis. The rocket's flight path resembled that of a Trident missile, and triggered a full-scale nuclear attack warning in Russia. Russia's military prepared for a possible nuclear retaliation, and President Boris Yeltsin activated his nuclear keys for the first time. Fortunately Russian observers tracking the rocket noted that it was moving away from Russian airspace and was not a threat. The scientists had notified Russia before the launch, but the information had not been relayed to radar technicians monitoring Russia's airspace.
30	25 Jan 1995	French football player Eric Cantona, playing for Manchester United at Crystal Palace, launched a kung fu-style attack on a fan who shouted abuse at him. On 27th January he was banned from playing football for eight months and fined £30,000.

JANUARY 2025

Ann.	Date	Event
30	26 Jan 1995 to 28 Feb	The Cenepa War between Ecuador and Peru. After a brief military conflict, the United Nations brokered a ceasefire, troops were withdrawn, and the disputed territory was recognised as Peruvian.
30	30 Jan 1995	The National Heart, Lung, and Blood Institute in the USA announced the first drug for the treatment of sickle-cell anaemia. The drug, hydroxyurea, had previously been used in chemotherapy.
30	30 Jan 1995	Death of Gerald Durrell, Indian-born British naturalist, conservationist, zoo keeper, writer and TV presenter.
30	31 Jan 1995	Mexican peso crisis: U.S. President Bill Clinton authorised a $20 billion loan to Mexico to help stabilise its economy after the Mexican government devalued the peso and caused an international financial crisis.
30	31 Jan 1995	Death of George Abbott, American theatre director, producer, playwright, actor and film director. He staged some of the most popular Broadway productions from the 1920s to the 1960s.
25	1 Jan 2000	The calendar switched over to the year 2000, with no major computer problems from the Y2K 'Millennium Bug'.
25	1 Jan 2000	Death of Victor Serebriakoff, British timber worker who made significant contributions to timber technology and, as an early member of Mensa (the society for the highly intelligent), helped develop and promote the organisation, designed IQ tests, wrote puzzle books, and became President of International Mensa.
25	3 Jan 2000	The last daily *Peanuts* comic strip was published. Its creator, Charles M. Schulz died a month later. Five Sunday strips were published after this, the last one appearing the day after Schulz's death. (See also: 12th February 2000.)
25	4 Jan 2000	The first British women to walk across Antarctica reached the South Pole. The group also included the first married couple to achieve the feat.
25	5 Jan 2000	Steve Jobs announced that he had become the CEO of Apple Computer. He had been ousted from the role in 1985.
25	9 Jan 2000	Death of Nigel Tranter, Scottish writer (Scottish history and architecture) and historical novelist.
25	11 Jan 2000	Death of Phil Carrick, British cricketer (Yorkshire 1970–93). (Leukaemia, aged 47.)
25	12 Jan 2000	The U.S. Supreme Court ruled that if someone flees at the mere sight of a police officer, then the police have reasonable justification to stop, question and search them. (Illinois v. Wardlow.)
25	13 Jan 2000	Bill Gates announced that he was stepping down as chief executive of Microsoft. Company president Steve Ballmer took over, while Gates remained as chairman and chief software architect.

JANUARY 2025

Ann.	Date	Event
25	14 Jan 2000	The United Nations International Criminal Tribunal for the Former Yugoslavia sentenced five Bosnian Croats to between 6 and 25 years in prison for killing more than 100 Bosnians in the Ahmići massacre in April 1993, during the Bosnian civil war. It was the first significant judgment on ethnic cleansing.
25	19 Jan 2000	Transmeta launched its first product, the Crusoe microprocessor. It emulated Intel's Pentium II processor using a software abstraction layer, and could be reprogrammed to emulate other processors and architectures, while using a fraction of the power of hardware processors. The processors were used in numerous devices. In 2007 the company switched from production to licensing its designs. It ceased operating in 2009.
25	19 Jan 2000	Death of Bettino Craxi, Prime Minister of Italy (1983–87). Noted for his assertive foreign policy. He was convicted of corruption and illegally financing the Italian Socialist Party.
25	19 Jan 2000	Death of Hedy Lamarr, Austrian-born American film actress and co-inventor of spread spectrum radio communication.
25	21 Jan 2000	The President of Ecuador, Jamil Mahuad, was forced to resign after a week of protests by indigenous groups and a military revolt. He was succeeded by Vice-President Gustavo Noboa.
25	22 Jan 2000	Death of Craig Claiborne, American restaurant critic (*The New York Times*), food writer and journalist.
25	22 Jan 2000	Death of Anne Hébert, Canadian writer and poet.
25	26 Jan 2000	Extensible HyperText Markup Language (XHTML) was released. It extended HTML, the language in which web pages are written, to make it more flexible. The latest version, XHTML5, is incorporated into HTML5.
25	26 Jan 2000	Death of A. E. van Vogt, Canadian science fiction writer.
25	31 Jan 2000	British family doctor Harold Shipman was sentenced to life in prison for murdering fifteen of his patients. He is thought to have killed at least 215 patients and possibly as many as 260, making him Britain's worst-ever serial killer.
20	1 Jan 2005	The Freedom of Information (FOI) Act came into effect in the UK, allowing the public to access documents about the workings of local and national government and other public bodies.
20	1 Jan 2005	Death of Shirley Chisholm, American politician. The first African American woman elected to the U.S. Congress.
20	1 Jan 2005	Death of Bob Matsui, American politician. Democratic congressman from California (1979–2005 – died in office).
20	2 Jan 2005	Death of Cyril Fletcher, British comedian. Known for his 'Odd Odes'.
20	5 Jan 2005	The dwarf planet Eris was discovered. It is the largest of the dwarf planets (27 percent more massive than Pluto). As a result of its discovery, the term 'planet' was redefined, and Pluto was designated a dwarf planet.

JANUARY 2025

Ann.	Date	Event
20	9 Jan 2005	The Comprehensive Peace Agreement (also known as the Naivasha Agreement) was signed by the Government of Sudan and the Sudan People's Liberation Movement. It marked the end of the Second Sudanese Civil War and led to South Sudan becoming an independent state.
20	12 Jan 2005	NASA launched the space probe *Deep Impact* to study the interior composition of comet 9P/Tempel. Its impactor collided with the comet on 4th July 2005 and the probe returned photographs of the resulting crater.
20	13 Jan 2005	Britain's Prince Harry was forced to apologise after being photographed at a costume party wearing a Nazi uniform. The photograph was published in *The Sun* newspaper.
20	14 Jan 2005	The European Space Agency's *Huygens* probe landed on Saturn's moon Titan and sent back the first detailed pictures of the surface, along with measurements of the environmental conditions there.
20	14 Jan 2005	U.S. Army Specialist Charles Graner Jr. was found guilty by a U.S. military court of leading the abuse of prisoners at Abu Ghraib prison in Iraq. He and ten others were convicted of war crimes. He was sentenced to ten years in prison. (Released 2011.) Another notable abuser was Private Lynndie England, to whom Graner was engaged. She was convicted in September 2005 and sentenced to three years in prison.
20	15 Jan 2005	Mahmoud Abbas became President of the Palestinian National Authority, succeeding Yasser Arafat who died in November 2004.
20	15 Jan 2005	The European Space Agency's *SMART-1* lunar orbiter detected the presence of chemical elements including calcium, aluminium, silicon, and iron on the surface of the Moon.
20	23 Jan 2005	Viktor Yushchenko became President of Ukraine (until 2010).
20	23 Jan 2005	Death of Johnny Carson, American comedian and television host (*The Tonight Show*).
20	25 Jan 2005	The social networking website Bebo was launched. It became one of the world's most popular social networks, especially in the UK. It was acquired by AOL in 2008, but sold in 2010 after most users had migrated to Facebook. It became bankrupt in 2013. In 2021 new owners announced plans to relaunch it.
20	26 Jan 2005	Condoleezza Rice became U.S. Secretary of State (until 2009). She was the first African American woman to hold the post.
20	30 Jan 2005	A general election was held in Iraq to elect a National Assembly. This was the first general election since the 2003 Invasion of Iraq, and the first free election for 50 years. More than 100 polling stations were attacked, and 44 people were killed.
15	4 Jan 2010	The Burj Khalifa in Dubai opened. It is the world's tallest structure, standing 2,722 feet (829.8 meters).

JANUARY 2025

Ann.	Date	Event
15	11 Jan 2010	Egypt displayed newly discovered tombs of workers who had helped build the Pyramids of Giza. They showed that the pyramids were built by free workers, not slaves. The fact that they were buried near the pyramids along with jars containing supplies for the afterlife showed they were much-respected workers. They would not have been given such honours if they had been slaves.
15	12 Jan 2010	Haiti earthquake. The capital, Port-au-Prince, was devastated and at least 100,000 people were killed and buried in mass graves. The official death toll of up to 316,000 is believed to have been deliberately inflated by the Haitian government.
15	27 Jan 2010	Porfirio Lobo Sosa became President of Honduras. Former president Manuel Zelaya had been ousted in a military coup in June 2009.
10	1 Jan 2015	The Eurasian Economic Union was established by Russia, Belarus and Kyrgyzstan. Armenia also joined the following day, and Kazakhstan joined in August.
10	3 Jan 2015 to 7th	2015 Baga massacre. Militants from the Boko Haram terrorist group attacked the town of Baga in north-east Nigeria. They forced thousands of residents out of the region and killed around 150 people. (Some sources say 2,000 were killed.)
10	7 Jan 2015	Charlie Hebdo shooting, Paris, France. Two Muslim brothers forced their way into the offices of the *Charlie Hebdo* satirical magazine and opened fire. Twelve people were killed and eleven injured. The brothers carried out further attacks in northern France on 8th and 9th January, and were shot dead by police. The magazine published images of the Islamic prophet Muhammad in 2011 and 2012, and its offices were firebombed in November 2011.
10	20 Jan 2015	Death of Edgar Froese, Russian-German musician and songwriter. Founder of the electronic music group Tangerine Dream.
10	21 Jan 2015	Death of Leon Brittan, British politician. He held numerous positions in Margaret Thatcher's cabinet, including Home Secretary (1983–85) and Secretary of State for Trade and industry (1985–86) – from which he resigned over the Westland affair. He later held various positions at the European Commission.
10	23 Jan 2015	Death of Abdullah, King of Saudi Arabia (2005–15). Succeeded by his half-brother Salman bin Abdulaziz.
10	25 Jan 2015	Death of Demis Roussos, Egyptian-born Greek singer, songwriter and musician. Known as a member of the prog rock band Aphrodite's Child and for his solo career. Best known for the song *Forever and Ever*.
10	30 Jan 2015	Death of Geraldine McEwan, British stage, film and television actress. Best known for her TV roles in *Oranges Are Not the Only Fruit* (1990) and as Miss Marple in *Marple* (2004–09).
10	31 Jan 2015	Death of Richard von Weizsäcker, President of West Germany (1984–90), President of Germany (1990–94).

FEBRUARY 2025

Ann.	Date	Event
750	26 Feb 1275	Death of Margaret of England, Queen consort of Scots (1251–75). Wife of King Alexander III.
600	27 Feb 1425	Death of Vasily I, Grand Prince of Moscow (1389–1425). Succeeded by his son, Vasily II.
500	24 Feb 1525	Italian War of 1521–1526 – the Battle of Pavia (Milan, Italy). The decisive battle of the war. Hapsburg victory over France.
500	24 Feb 1525	Death of Richard de la Pole, pretender to the English crown. The last Yorkist claimant to actively seek the English throne. (Killed in the Battle of Pavia, aged 44/45 – see above.)
500	27 Feb 1525	Death of Cuauhtémoc, the last Aztec Emperor (1520–21). (Executed.)
300	5 Feb 1725	Birth of James Otis Jr., American lawyer, political activist and patriot. A member of the Massachusetts provincial assembly. Noted for his Patriot views against the English parliament's policies, and his catchphrase, 'Taxation without representation is tyranny'.
300	8 Feb 1725	Death of Peter I, (Peter the Great), Tsar (Emperor) of Russia (1682–1725). (Bladder infection, aged 52.) Succeeded by his wife, Catherine I.
300	26 Feb 1725	Birth of Nicolas-Joseph Cugnot, French inventor. He designed and built the first full-size self-propelled vehicle – a steam-powered dray. He is recognised as the inventor of the world's first automobile.
250	6 Feb 1775	Death of William Dowdeswell, British politician. Chancellor of the Exchequer (1765–66).
250	9 Feb 1775	American Revolutionary War: the British Parliament declared that Massachusetts was in a state of rebellion. British soldiers were authorised to shoot suspected rebels on sight.
250	10 Feb 1775	Birth of Charles Lamb, British essayist and poet. Best known for *Essays of Elia* and *Tales from Shakespeare* (co-written with his sister Mary Lamb).
250	12 Feb 1775	Birth of Louisa Adams, First Lady of the United States (1825–29). Wife of U.S. President John Quincy Adams.
250	15 Feb 1775	Pius VI was elected Pope.
250	27 Feb 1775	John Adams, later President of the USA, first used the name 'United Colonies' in reference to the Thirteen Colonies that would later form the USA. The name was officially changed to the United States of America in September 1776. (The name United Colonies may have been used before this, but this is the first recorded usage.)
200	3 Feb 1825 to 5th	The February flood of 1825 (known as the Great Hallig Flood in Germany). The North Sea coasts of the Netherlands, Denmark and Germany flooded. Around 800 people were killed.
200	12 Feb 1825	The Second Treaty of Indian Springs (also known as the Treaty with the Creeks) was signed by the Muscogee and the USA. The Muscogee agreed to cede their lands to Georgia and Alabama and relocate west of the Mississippi. Their leader, William McIntosh, was executed by the Creeks in April, along with two other signatories, for ceding so much land and violating Creek law.

FEBRUARY 2025

Ann.	Date	Event
200	24 Feb 1825	Death of Thomas Bowdler, British editor, censor and physician. Best known for producing expurgated ('bowdlerised') versions of Shakespeare's plays to make them more suitable for a family audience.
200	28 Feb 1825	Great Britain and Russia signed the Treaty of Saint Petersburg, which established the border between Alaska and Canada. The border was further refined by arbitration between Britain and the USA in 1903 (the Hay–Herbert Treaty).
175	5 Feb 1850	American inventor Dubois D. Parmelee was granted the first U.S. patent for an adding machine operated by pushing keys. (U.S. Patent 7,074.) His 'calculating machine' was not commercially successful. The first successful calculator was invented by William Burroughs in 1885.
175	8 Feb 1850 to 17th	Ute Wars – the Battle at Fort Utah. Mormon settlers killed 100 members of the Native American Timpanogos tribe after renegade tribesmen took fifty of their cattle.
175	23 Feb 1850	Birth of César Ritz, Swiss hotelier. He founded several notable hotels including the Ritz and Carlton Hotels in London, UK, and the Hôtel Ritz in Paris, France.
175	28 Feb 1850	The University of Utah was established in Salt Lake City, Utah, USA.
150	4 Feb 1875	Birth of Ludwig Prandtl, German physicist, fluid dynamicist and aerospace pioneer. Regarded as the father of modern aerodynamics. He developed mathematical analyses of aerodynamics that form the basis of modern aerospace engineering.
150	21 Feb 1875	Birth of Jeanne Calment, French supercentenarian with the longest verified human lifespan. She died in 1997, aged 122.
150	24 Feb 1875	The Australian steamship SS Gothenburg hit the Great Barrier Reef and sank. Between 98 and 112 people were killed, including a number of dignitaries and senior civil servants.
150	25 Feb 1875	Guangxu became Emperor of China at the age of four. Empress Dowager Cixi acted as his regent until 1881. He died in 1908, aged 37, after being poisoned.
125	3 Feb 1900	Death of William Goebel, American politician. Governor of Kentucky (for four days). (Assassinated.) He was sworn in as Governor on his deathbed, and is the only Governor of a U.S. state to have been assassinated while in office. His assassin's identity remains unknown.
125	5 Feb 1900 to 7th	Second Boer War – the Battle of Vaal Krantz, South Africa. Boer victory. The British, led by General Redvers Buller, failed in their third attempt to reach Ladysmith to lift the siege.
125	7 Feb 1900 to 1904	Bubonic plague epidemic, San Francisco, California, USA. A Chinese immigrant who had recently landed in San Francisco was found to be suffering from an unidentified disease. He died four weeks later. The disease was later identified as bubonic plague, but the Governor of California denied its existence for more than two years. It was the first plague epidemic in the USA. There were 121 known cases and 119 people died.

FEBRUARY 2025

Ann.	Date	Event
125	8 Feb 1900	Kodak began selling the Brownie camera. It was a simple box camera made from leather-covered cardboard and cost $1. It used inexpensive film that was cheap to process, and made snapshot photography available to the mass market for the first time.
125	14 Feb 1900 to 27th	Second Boer War – the Battle of the Tugela Heights, South Africa. The British finally succeeded in fighting their way through to Ladysmith to lift the siege. (See also: 15th and 28th February 1900.)
125	15 Feb 1900	Second Boer War: the 124-day Siege of Kimberley was relieved by cavalry forces led by Lieutenant-General John French. British victory.
125	16 Feb 1900	The Tripartite Convention between the USA, UK and Germany came into effect. The UK renounced its claims to the Samoan islands, and they were partitioned into a U.S. territory and a German colony.
125	18 Feb 1900 to 27th	Second Boer War – the Battle of Paardeberg, South Africa. British victory.
125	20 Feb 1900	Death of Washakie, Native American leader of the Eastern Shoshone people.
125	22 Feb 1900	Birth of Luis Buñuel, Spanish-born Mexican film director.
125	24 Feb 1900	Birth of Irmgard Bartenieff, German-born American dancer, choreographer and physical therapist. A pioneer of dance therapy.
125	27 Feb 1900	The Labour Party was founded in the UK.
125	27 Feb 1900	The German football club FC Bayern Munich was founded.
125	27 Feb 1900	German chemist Felix Hoffman (working at Bayer) was granted a U.S. patent for Aspirin (acetyl salicylic acid). (U.S. Patent 644,077.) His claim to be the inventor of aspirin is disputed. Another Bayer employee, Arthur Eichengrün, claimed Hoffman used his process to synthesise it, and said he should be given the credit for its invention. Bayer denied this in a press release.
125	28 Feb 1900	Second Boer War: the 118-day Siege of Ladysmith was relieved by British forces led by Major Hubert Gough. (The first party of the relief column included Winston Churchill, later British Prime Minister.)
100	1 Feb 1925	Ahmet Zogu was inaugurated as the first President of Albania. (Albania's monarchy was established in 1928 and he became King Zog I.)
100	2 Feb 1925	Birth of Elaine Stritch, American stage, film and television actress. Known for her many Broadway and West End stage shows, as well as the British TV sitcom *Two's Company*, the TV series *Law & Order*, and the U.S. sitcom *30 Rock*. (Died 2014.)
100	3 Feb 1925	Death of Jaap Eden, Dutch world champion speed skater and cyclist (1893–96).
100	12 Feb 1925	The United States Federal Arbitration Act was signed into law by President Calvin Coolidge. It took effect on 1st January 1926.
100	20 Feb 1925	Birth of Robert Altman, American film director, producer and screenwriter. His films include *M*A*S*H*, *McCabe & Mrs. Miller*, and *Nashville*. (Died 2006.)

FEBRUARY 2025

Ann.	Date	Event
100	21 Feb 1925	The first issue of *The New Yorker* magazine was published.
100	21 Feb 1925	Birth of Sam Peckinpah, American film director and screenwriter. Noted for the violence of some of his films, which include *The Wild Bunch, Major Dundee, Straw Dogs,* and *Pat Garrett and Billy the Kid*. (Died 1984.)
100	22 Feb 1925	Birth of Edward Gorey, American writer, illustrator and poet. Noted for his unsettling Victorian- and Edwardian-style pen-and-ink drawings. (Died 2000.)
100	24 Feb 1925	The first recorded use of a thermite bomb. It was used to break up a 250,000-ton ice jam on the St. Lawrence River in New York state, USA.
100	25 Feb 1925	Birth of Shehu Shagari, President of Nigeria (1979–83). Nigeria's first democratically elected president. (Died 2019.)
100	25 Feb 1925	Glacier Bay National Monument (now Glacier Bay National Park and Preserve) was established in Alaska, USA.
100	26 Feb 1925 or 27th	Adolf Hitler re-established the Nazi Party in Munich, Germany after a ban on its existence was lifted.
100	28 Feb 1925	Charlevoix–Kamouraska earthquake, Canada. There was considerable damage near the epicentre along the St. Lawrence River.
100	28 Feb 1925	Birth of Harry H. Corbett, Burmese-born British film and television actor and comedian. Best known for his role as Harold Steptoe in the TV sitcom *Steptoe and Son*. (Died 1982.)
90	1 Feb 1935	The first *The March of Time* newsreel was shown in the USA. It was a companion to *The March of Time* radio series and was shown monthly in over 500 movie theatres until 1951.
90	2 Feb 1935	A lie detector (polygraph) machine was used in court for the first time. Its inventor, Leonarde Keeler, tested two suspects in a criminal case in Portage, Wisconsin, USA. The machine showed they were guilty, the court agreed to accept its results, and they were convicted.
90	3 Feb 1935	Death of Hugo Junkers, German aircraft designer. The first aircraft designer to use an all-metal skin (on the Junkers J-1).
90	6 Feb 1935	The board game Monopoly went on sale in the USA.
90	8 Feb 1935	Turkish General Election. Women were allowed to vote and stand for parliament for the first time – eighteen women were elected.
90	8 Feb 1935	Death of Max Liebermann, German artist and printmaker. The leading proponent of Impressionism in Germany.
90	11 Feb 1935	The lowest temperature ever recorded in Africa: -24°C (-11°F) in Ifrane, Morocco.
90	11 Feb 1935	Birth of Gene Vincent, American rock and roll/rockabilly singer and guitarist. Best known for the song *Be-Bop-A-Lula*. (Died 1971.)
90	12 Feb 1935	The American airship *USS Macon* crashed and sank in a storm off the coast of California. Two of the 76 crew were killed.
90	12 Feb 1935	Death of Auguste Escoffier, French chef, restaurateur and writer. A leader in the development of modern French cuisine. Known as 'the king of chefs and the chef of kings'.

FEBRUARY 2025

Ann.	Date	Event
90	13 Feb 1935	Bruno Hauptmann was found guilty of kidnapping and murdering American aviator Charles Lindbergh's infant son. He was sentenced to death and executed in April 1936.
90	15 Feb 1935	Birth of Roger Chaffee, American astronaut. (Killed in January 1967 during a pre-launch test for *Apollo 1*.)
90	16 Feb 1935	Birth of Sonny Bono, American singer, record producer and politician. Best known for his pop duo partnership with his then-wife Cher (Sonny and Cher). He later became a congressman for California. (Died 1998.)
90	20 Feb 1935	Caroline Mikkelsen of Denmark became the first woman to set foot on Antarctica.
90	21 Feb 1935	Birth of Mark McManus, Scottish television actor. Best known for his lead role in the crime drama series *Taggart*. (Died 1994.)
90	22 Feb 1935	U.S. President Franklin D. Roosevelt banned aircraft from flying over the White House – because the noise kept him awake. The ban remains in place today, mainly for security reasons.
90	26 Feb 1935	Nazi Germany reformed the Luftwaffe (military air force). It had been disbanded in 1920 under the terms of the Treaty of Versailles after WWI.
90	26 Feb 1935	British radio engineer Robert Watson-Watt demonstrated a working radar system for the first time, in Daventry, UK.
90	28 Feb 1935	Nylon was first produced by a team led by Wallace Carothers at DuPont's research station in Wilmington, Delaware, USA.
80	Feb 1945	Death of Anne Frank, Dutch Jewish diarist and Holocaust victim who died in Bergen–Belsen concentration camp, Germany at the age of 15, probably from typhus. Known for *The Diary of a Young Girl*.
80	3 Feb 1945	World War II – Operation Thunderclap. The U.S. 8th Air Force carried out a huge daytime bombing raid on the German capital, Berlin. Almost 1,000 B-17 bombers took part, causing massive destruction and a fire that burned for four days. The Allies carried out another significant bombing raid on Berlin on 26th February, which left 80,000 people homeless. The raids continued until April when the Soviet Red Army reached the city.
80	3 Feb 1945 to 3 Mar	World War II – the Battle of Manila, Philippines. The U.S./Philippines successfully recaptured the capital city from Japan and ended Japan's occupation of the Philippines. But the city was totally destroyed and over 100,000 civilians were killed.
80	4 Feb 1945 to 11th	World War II – The Yalta Conference, Crimea. U.S. President Franklin D. Roosevelt, British Prime Minister Winston Churchill, and Soviet leader Joseph Stalin met to plan the final defeat of Nazi Germany. Stalin also agreed to enter the war in the Pacific within three months of the war in Europe ending.
80	4 Feb 1945 to 13 May	World War II – the Battle of Pokoku and Irrawaddy River operations, central Burma. Allied victory.
80	6 Feb 1945 to 15th	World War II – the Mostar operation, Yugoslavia (now in Herzegovina). Yugoslav Partisans liberated the city from Axis forces.

FEBRUARY 2025

Ann.	Date	Event
80	6 Feb 1945	Birth of Bob Marley, Jamaican reggae/ska/rock steady singer, songwriter, musician and cultural icon. (Died 1981.)
80	8 Feb 1945 to 11 Mar	World War II – Operation Veritable. British and Canadian troops successfully cleared German forces from the area between the Rhine and the Maas rivers in the Rhineland, close to the German–Dutch border.
80	9 Feb 1945	World War II: the only submarine to sink another submarine while both were submerged. The British submarine *HMS Venturer* sank the German U-boat *U-864* off Norway.
80	13 Feb 1945 to 15th	World War II: the Bombing of Dresden, Germany. The Allies carried out four massive bombing raids, completely destroying the inner city and killing about 25,000 people.
80	13 Feb 1945	World War II: the Siege of Budapest in Hungary ended. The Soviet Red Army captured the city and the German and Hungarian forces surrendered unconditionally.
80	14 Feb 1945	World War II: the Bombing of Prague in Czechoslovakia. The U.S. 8th Air Force carried out a bombing raid on the city after mistaking it for Dresden in Germany (see 13th February above). 701 civilians were killed.
80	14 Feb 1945 to 15th	The Quincy Agreement: U.S. President Franklin D. Roosevelt and King Ibn Saud of Saudi Arabia made a secret agreement aboard the *USS Quincy*. The USA agreed to provide Saudi Arabia with military assistance and training in exchange for secure access to oil.
80	15 Feb 1945	World War II: Venezuela declared war on Germany. It had waited until late in the war to ensure its oil production facilities were not attacked. It did not engage in combat, but some of its merchant ships were sunk.
80	16 Feb 1945 to 26th	World War II – the Battle of Corregidor, Philippines. U.S. victory. The island was recaptured from the Japanese who had held it since May 1942.
80	16 Feb 1945	The Alaska Equal Rights Act of 1945 was signed into law. It was the first state anti-discrimination law in the USA. It prohibited racial discrimination against individuals in public areas.
80	16 Feb 1945	Birth of Jeremy Bulloch, British film and television actor. Best known for his role as Boba Fett in the Star Wars films *The Empire Strikes Back* and *Return of the Jedi*. (Died 2020.)
80	19 Feb 1945 to 26 Mar	World War II – the Battle of Iwo Jima, Japanese Volcano Islands. U.S. victory. The iconic photo of U.S. Marines raising the American flag on top of Mount Surabachi was taken on 23rd February.
80	21 Feb 1945	World War II: the Battle for the Recapture of Bataan (Philippines) ended. Allied victory.
80	21 Feb 1945	World War II – the Battle of Monte Castello (Italy) ended. Allied victory (Brazil and the USA).
80	21 Feb 1945	Death of Eric Liddell, Scottish athlete. Olympic gold medallist in 1924 (400 m). He withdrew from the 100 m heats because they were held on a Sunday, and entered the 400 m instead. The story is featured in the film *Chariots of Fire*. (Died in a WWII internment camp in China, aged 43.)

FEBRUARY 2025

Ann.	Date	Event
80	23 Feb 1945	World War II – the Battle of Reichswald – Operation Grenade. The U.S. 9th Army crossed the River Rur after a two-week delay caused by flooding when the Germans destroyed dams upstream.
80	23 Feb 1945	World War II: the British RAF destroyed the German town of Pforzheim. More than 17,000 people were killed.
80	23 Feb 1945	World War II: Los Baños internment camp in the Philippines was liberated by a combined U.S. and Filipino task force.
80	24 Feb 1945	World War II: Princess Elizabeth (later Queen Elizabeth II) joined the Women's Auxiliary Territorial Service as an honorary Second Subaltern. She trained as a driver and mechanic.
80	24 Feb 1945	World War II: Egypt declared war on Germany and Japan. (See also below.)
80	24 Feb 1945	Death of Ahmed Mahir Pasha, Prime Minister of Egypt. (Assassinated in parliament immediately after declaring war on Germany and Japan.)
80	26 Feb 1945	World War II: Syria declared war on Germany and Japan.
80	26 Feb 1945 to April	The U.S. government imposed a midnight curfew on all bars, nightclubs and entertainment venues to conserve fuel during the war. Newspaper reporters said it was more likely an attempt to direct the public's money into war bonds rather than spending it on 'fun'. The curfew was lifted in April, having saved little fuel.
80	27 Feb 1945	World War II: Lebanon declared war on Germany and Japan.
80	28 Feb 1945	Birth of Bubba Smith, American football player (Baltimore Colts, Oakland Raiders, Houston Oilers) and film and television actor. Best known for his role as Moses Hightower in the *Police Academy* series of comedy films, and for his appearances in a series of TV commercials for Miller Lite. (Died 2011.)
75	2 Feb 1950	The first episode of the television game show *What's My Line?* was broadcast on CBS in the USA.
75	3 Feb 1950	Death of Karl Seitz, President of Austria (1919–20).
75	6 Feb 1950	Birth of Natalie Cole, American R&B/pop singer, songwriter and actress. Daughter of the singer and jazz pianist Nat King Cole. (Died 2015.)
75	7 Feb 1950	Britain and the USA officially recognised Vietnam (South Vietnam) under Bao Dai's regime.
75	8 Feb 1950	Cold War: the Stasi – the East German secret police force – was established. It was dissolved in 1990. Numerous Stasi officials were subsequently prosecuted for their crimes. Millions of East German citizens were then allowed to see the extensive documentation the Stasi had compiled against them through their network of informants.
75	8 Feb 1950	The world's first payment by credit card. The founders of Diners Club (now Diners Club International) used it to pay their restaurant bill at Major's Cabin Grill in New York City, USA.

FEBRUARY 2025

Ann.	Date	Event
75	9 Feb 1950	Red Scare – the beginning. U.S. Senator Joseph McCarthy announced that he had a list of 'known communists' who worked in the U.S. State Department, fuelling Cold War tensions. He went on to make further sensational claims of communists, Soviet spies and sympathisers in the federal government, U.S. Army, and elsewhere – none of which he could substantiate. (His actions were condemned by the U.S. Senate in 1954 and his career was ruined. He died in 1957.)
75	12 Feb 1950	German physicist Albert Einstein warned that the USA's attempts to build a hydrogen bomb could lead to radioactive contamination of the atmosphere and the loss of all life on Earth. He gave his warning on the television show *Today with Mrs. Roosevelt*, hosted by former First Lady Eleanor Roosevelt. As a result, the FBI ordered a report on his background and activities, and the Immigration and Naturalization Service considered deporting him.
75	14 Feb 1950	China and the Soviet Union signed the Sino–Soviet Treaty of Friendship, Alliance and Mutual Assistance. (When it expired in 1979, China launched an immediate attack on Vietnam – a Soviet ally.)
75	14 Feb 1950	Death of Karl G. Jansky, American physicist and radio engineer. One of the founding fathers of radio astronomy. He was the first person to discover cosmic radio sources.
75	15 Feb 1950	The première of the Walt Disney film *Cinderella*, in Boston, Massachusetts, USA. (Released USA: 4th March. UK: 26th July.)
75	15 Feb 1950	The play *Come Back, Little Sheba* by William Inge opened on Broadway. It was his first play. It was adapted into a 1952 film, a 1974 stage musical, and a 1977 TV film.
75	18 Feb 1950	Birth of John Hughes, American film director, producer, and screenwriter. Best known for his teen movies and comedy films (*National Lampoon's Vacation, Weird Science, The Breakfast Club, Ferris Bueller's Day Off, Pretty in Pink*, and more). (Died 2009.)
75	20 Feb 1950	Birth of Tony Wilson, British record label owner (Factory Records), radio and television presenter, and nightclub owner (the Haçienda). He was associated with some of Manchester's most successful rock bands. (Died 2007.)
75	21 Feb 1950	The first International Pancake Race was held in Liberal, Kansas, USA between members of the local community and the people of Olney, Buckinghamshire, UK. The race continues to be contested each year.
75	22 Feb 1950	Birth of Genesis P-Orridge, British singer-songwriter, musician, poet and performance artist. Best known as a member of the industrial band Throbbing Gristle and the experimental pop/rock band Psychic TV. (Died 2020.)
75	23 Feb 1950	United Kingdom General Election. Prime Minister Clement Attlee (Labour Party) was re-elected, but his majority was reduced from 146 seats to just five. This was the first General Election where the results were covered by BBC TV. (Another election was held in 1951. It was won by the Conservatives.)

FEBRUARY 2025

Ann.	Date	Event
75	25 Feb 1950	The first episode of the television variety show *Your Show of Shows* was broadcast on NBC in the USA.
75	25 Feb 1950	Birth of Néstor Kirchner, President of Argentina (2003–07). (Died 2010.) Wife of Cristina Fernández de Kirchner, who was also President (2007–15).
75	26 Feb 1950	Death of Harry Lauder, Scottish music hall/vaudeville comedian and singer. The first British artist to sell one million records.
70	8 Feb 1955	Soviet Prime Minister Georgy Malenkov resigned after being accused by President Nikita Khrushchev of abusing his power and being responsible for the slow pace of reforms. He was succeeded by Nikolai Bulganin.
70	10 Feb 1955	Birth of Chris Adams, British wrestler and national judo champion. (Died 2001.)
70	15 Feb 1955	General Electric (GE) announced that they had created the first synthetic diamonds using a commercially reproducible process. The first diamonds were created by Tracy Hall at GE's Schenectady Laboratories in New York, USA on 16th December 1954. (In the 1980s it was revealed that Swedish researchers had created synthetic diamonds in February 1953, but they were very small and of poor quality.)
70	17 Feb 1955	Britain's Ministry of Defence announced that it was developing a hydrogen bomb. The first one was successfully tested in May 1957.
70	18 Feb 1955 to 15 May	Operation Teapot: the USA successfully detonated fourteen nuclear weapons at the Nevada Test Site, with the twin aims of improving nuclear weapons and establishing tactics for ground forces on a nuclear battlefield.
70	19 Feb 1955	The South East Asia Treaty Organization (SEATO) was established. Its primary objective was to prevent further communist gains in the region. It was dissolved in 1977.
70	19 Feb 1955	The synthetic chemical element Mendelevium (Md – atomic number 101) was created for the first time by a team led by Glenn T. Seaborg at the Lawrence Berkeley National Laboratory in Berkeley, California, USA. The discovery was formally announced in April.
70	22 Feb 1955	American tennis player Maureen ('Little Mo') Connolly was forced to retire at the age of nineteen after being injured in a horse-riding accident. She was regarded as one of the USA's greatest tennis stars.
70	24 Feb 1955	Turkey and Iraq formed the Baghdad Pact – a pact of mutual cooperation similar to NATO. The UK, Pakistan and Iran joined later that year. It became the Central Treaty Organisation (CENTO) in 1959 when Iraq withdrew. It was dissolved in 1979.
70	24 Feb 1955 to March	Britain's Big Freeze. Deep snow and freezing temperatures caused havoc, with many places cut off. The RAF dropped food and medical supplies to affected areas. Thousands of sheep died from exposure.
70	24 Feb 1955	Birth of Steve Jobs, American businessman and personal computer pioneer. Co-founder of Apple and NeXT. (Died 2011.)
70	25 Feb 1955	The British aircraft carrier *HMS Ark Royal* went into service with the Royal Navy. It was decommissioned in 1979.
70	26 Feb 1955	British biophysicist Rosalind Franklin's discovery of the complete structure of a virus (the tobacco mosaic virus) was published in *Nature* magazine.

FEBRUARY 2025

Ann.	Date	Event
65	1 Feb 1960	Four black students began a sit-in at a college in Greensboro, North Carolina, USA to protest against segregated lunch counters.
65	8 Feb 1960	The Hollywood Walk of Fame was established in Hollywood, California, USA. It consists of more than 2,700 stars embedded in the pavement that bear the names of notable figures from the entertainment industry.
65	8 Feb 1960	Queen Elizabeth II of the United Kingdom issued an Order-in-Council stating that she and her family would be known as the House of Windsor, and that her descendants would use the surname Mountbatten-Windsor.
65	8 Feb 1960	Birth of Benigno Aquino III, President of the Philippines (2010–16). (Died 2021.)
65	8 Feb 1960	Death of Sir Giles Gilbert Scott, British architect who designed Battersea Power Station, Liverpool Cathedral, and Britain's iconic red telephone boxes.
65	9 Feb 1960	Adolph Coors III, heir to the Coors Brewing Company empire, and grandson of the founder, was kidnapped near Morrison, Colorado, USA while driving to work. The kidnapper, an escaped murderer, demanded a ransom of $500,000 but failed to make contact when the money was offered. Coors's decomposed body was found on 11th September. He was probably shot dead at the time of the kidnapping.
65	12 Feb 1960	Death of Bobby Clark, American comedian, minstrel, vaudevillian and stage, film, television and circus performer. Known for his 36-year comedy partnership with Paul McCullough as Clark and McCullough. Noted for his painted-on glasses.
65	13 Feb 1960	France tested its first atomic bomb in the Sahara desert.
65	13 Feb 1960	Death of Barney Roos, American automotive engineer. Head of engineering at Studebaker (1926–36). He later helped design the British Humber, Hillman and Sunbeam-Talbot cars, and then returned to the USA to co-design the original Jeep.
65	18 Feb 1960 to 28th	The 1960 Winter Olympics were held in Squaw Valley, California, USA.
65	27 Feb 1960	Death of Adriano Olivetti, Italian businessman and engineer who developed his father's Olivetti company into Europe's largest manufacturer of office machines.
65	29 Feb 1960	Agadir earthquake, southern Morocco. The city was devastated and 12,000 people were killed.
65	29 Feb 1960	The first Playboy Club opened, in Chicago, Illinois, USA.
60	1 Feb 1965	NHS prescription charges were scrapped in England. They were reintroduced in June 1968.
60	1 Feb 1965	Peter Jennings became the youngest network news anchorman in the USA at the age of 26, hosting *Peter Jennings With the News* on ABC Television. He still holds the record.
60	1 Feb 1965	Joe Orton's play *Loot* was first performed, in Cambridge, England.

FEBRUARY 2025

Ann.	Date	Event
60	1 Feb 1965	Birth of Brandon Lee, American actor and martial artist. Son of martial arts film star Bruce Lee. (Died 1993.)
60	5 Feb 1965	The Beursschouwburg visual arts theatre and concert hall opened in Brussels, Belgium.
60	7 Feb 1965	Vietnam War – Operation Flaming Dart. The USA launched air strikes on targets in North Vietnam after the Viet Cong attacked several of its bases. This led to an escalation of the war. (See also: 2nd March 1965).
60	8 Feb 1965	The hit Motown song *Stop! In the Name of Love* by the Supremes was released.
60	15 Feb 1965	The current National Flag of Canada – the red-and-white maple leaf design – was adopted.
60	15 Feb 1965	The Beatles' song *Eight Days a Week* was released in the USA. It was not released as a single in the UK, but appeared on their album *Beatles for Sale*, released on 4th December 1964.
60	15 Feb 1965	Death of Nat King Cole, American jazz/swing/ballad singer and pianist.
60	16 Feb 1965	The chairman of the British Railways Board, Dr Richard Beeching, issued his second report (*The Development of the Major Railway Trunk Routes*) on the restructuring of British railways to prepare it for the next 25 years. He concluded that only 3,000 miles of Britain's 7,500 miles of track should be considered for future development.
60	16 Feb 1965	NASA launched the space probe *Pegasus 1* to study micrometeoroid impacts in Low Earth orbit. It remained in operation until August 1968 and re-entered the atmosphere in September 1978.
60	17 Feb 1965	NASA launched the space probe *Ranger 8* on a mission to take close-up photos of the surface of the Moon, ahead of a manned Apollo mission. After sending back more than 7,000 photographs it was deliberately crashed into the Moon on 20th February.
60	18 Feb 1965	The Gambia gained its independence from the UK.
60	19 Feb 1965	Death of Gheorge Gheorghiu Dej, Communist leader of Romania (1944–65). Succeeded by Nicolae Ceaușescu.
60	21 Feb 1965	Death of Malcolm X, African-American Muslim leader and human rights activist. (Assassinated.)
60	22 Feb 1965	Death of Felix Frankfurter, Associate Justice of the U.S. Supreme Court (1939–62).
60	23 Feb 1965	Death of Stan Laurel, British-born American comic actor and writer (Laurel and Hardy).
60	27 Feb 1965	The Dutch cabinet collapsed after failing to reach an agreement on commercial television broadcasting. Prime Minister Victor Marijnen announced his resignation and was succeeded by Jo Cals on 14th April.
60	28 Feb 1965	Death of Adolf Schärf, President of Austria (1957–65).
50	4 Feb 1975	Haicheng earthquake, China. More than 1,300 people were killed.

FEBRUARY 2025

Ann.	Date	Event
50	5 Feb 1975 to 6th	Limazo riots, Lima, Peru. The local police force went on strike after being offered a pay rise that was well below what they had asked for. They barricaded themselves into police stations. Students marched through the streets in support of the police, looting, setting fires, vandalising property, and causing more than $27 million worth of damage. The Peruvian military was sent in to quell the unrest. 100 people were killed, 500 injured, and 1,300 arrested.
50	11 Feb 1975	Margaret Thatcher became the first female leader of the Conservative Party in the UK. She became Britain's first female Prime Minister in 1979.
50	12 Feb 1975	Death of Carl Lutz, Swiss diplomat. Swiss Vice-Consul to Hungary (1942–45). He is credited with saving more than 62,000 Hungarian Jews by issuing protective documents and establishing safe houses. They were not deported to Nazi extermination camps because of his actions.
50	13 Feb 1975	British miners were awarded pay rises of up to 35 percent, averting a national strike. Coal prices rose by 22 percent (domestic) and 7 percent (industrial) from 1st March 1975 to cover the cost of the wage increases.
50	13 Feb 1975	A fire broke out on the 11th floor of One World Trade Center (the North Tower) in New York City, USA. It spread to nearby floors via a utility shaft, but did not cause any structural damage.
50	14 Feb 1975	Death of Sir Julian Huxley, British evolutionary biologist, philosopher, writer and educator. First Director of UNESCO. A founding member of the World Wildlife Fund.
50	14 Feb 1975	Death of P. G. Wodehouse, British-born American comic novelist, short story writer, lyricist and playwright. Best known as the creator of Jeeves.
50	21 Feb 1975	Watergate Scandal: the former U.S. Attorney General, John N. Mitchell, and former White House aides H. R. Haldeman and John D. Ehrlichman were each sentenced to 2½ to 8 years in prison for conspiracy and obstruction of justice.
50	23 Feb 1975	Daylight Saving Time began two months early in the USA to conserve energy during the oil crisis.
50	24 Feb 1975	Death of Nikolai Bulganin, Premier of the Soviet Union (1955–58). Minister of Defence (1953–55).
50	28 Feb 1975	Moorgate tube crash, London underground, UK. A train failed to stop at the end of the line and crashed into a wall, killing 43 people. (Cause: unknown, but probably a driver-related issue not a mechanical failure. A new train protection system was introduced as a result.)
40	3 Feb 1985	Death of Frank Oppenheimer, American particle physicist and educator. He conducted research on nuclear physics as part of the Manhattan Project and worked on uranium enrichment. He was later blacklisted from any physics or teaching position because of his connection with the American Communist Party. After the ban was lifted, he established the Exploratorium in San Francisco, California. Brother of the physicist J. Robert Oppenheimer.

FEBRUARY 2025

Ann.	Date	Event
40	6 Feb 1985	The co-founder of Apple Computer, Steve Wozniak, left the company to pursue other interests. However, he remains on the payroll as a part-time engineering consultant, remains a shareholder, and continues to appear at Apple events.
40	6 Feb 1985	Death of James Hadley Chase, British thriller novelist.
40	7 Feb 1985	The Mayor of New York City, USA, Ed Koch, adopted the song *New York, New York* by Frank Sinatra as the city's official anthem. (However, it was never written into law.)
40	7 Feb 1985	Death of Matt Monro, British singer.
40	8 Feb 1985	Death of Sir William Lyons, British motor vehicle manufacturer. Co-founder of Jaguar Cars Ltd.
40	11 Feb 1985	The Amman Agreement was signed by King Hussein of Jordan and Yasser Arafat, leader of the Palestine Liberation Organisation. They agreed to convene an international peace conference and to pursue a proposed confederation between the two states.
40	11 Feb 1985	Death of Ben Abruzzo, American businessman and hot-air balloonist. He made the first transpacific balloon flight and the longest non-stop balloon flight.
40	12 Feb 1985	Death of Nicholas Colasanto, American film and television actor and director. Best known for his role as Coach in the TV sitcom *Cheers*.
40	16 Feb 1985	The Islamic militant group and political party Hezbollah was founded in Lebanon.
40	16 Feb 1985	British civil servant Clive Ponting, an assistant secretary in the Ministry of Defence, resigned over the *Belgrano* affair. He had leaked a document revealing that the Argentine warship was outside the Falklands exclusion zone and sailing away from the Royal Navy task force when it was attacked and sunk. He was also charged with breaking the Official Secrets Act, but was acquitted on 11th February when a jury declared that the leak was in the public interest.
40	19 Feb 1985	The first episode of the BBC television soap opera *EastEnders* was broadcast in the UK.
40	19 Feb 1985	The Coca-Cola Company launched Cherry Coke (also known as Coca-Cola Cherry).
40	20 Feb 1985	The sale of contraceptives was legalised in Ireland following a highly controversial vote in the Irish parliament, and condemnation by the Catholic Church.
40	20 Feb 1985	Death of Clarence Nash, American voice actor. Best known as the voice of the Disney character Donald Duck.
40	25 Feb 1985	Edwin Meese became Attorney General of the United States. He resigned in 1988 over his involvement in the Wedtech scandal.
40	27 Feb 1985	Death of Ray Ellington, British singer, drummer and bandleader. He led the Ray Ellington Quartet, which regularly performed on *The Goon Show*.

FEBRUARY 2025

Ann.	Date	Event
40	28 Feb 1985	The Troubles in Northern Ireland: the IRA carried out a mortar bomb attack on a police station in Newry. Nine Royal Ulster Constabulary officers were killed – the RUC's highest loss of life in a single day.
30	1 Feb 1995	Welsh rock musician Richey Edwards, guitarist and lyrist with the band Manic Street Preachers, went missing from a hotel in London. There have been no confirmed sightings of him since then. His car was found abandoned near the Severn Bridge on 14th February. He was declared presumed dead in November 2008.
30	2 Feb 1995	The leaders of Egypt, Jordan, Israel and the Palestine Liberation Organisation held an emergency summit in Cairo, Egypt where they reaffirmed their commitment to the Middle East peace process. It was seen as a last-ditch attempt to salvage the failing peace process.
30	2 Feb 1995	Death of David Kindersley, British typeface designer and stone letter-carver. His work can be seen on many British churches and public buildings, including the gates of the British Library in London.
30	2 Feb 1995	Death of Fred Perry, British tennis player, commentator and co-founder of Fred Perry sportswear. World No. 1 for four years in the 1930s. He won Wimbledon three times in succession.
30	2 Feb 1995	Death of Donald Pleasence, British stage, film and television actor (*Halloween, You Only Live Twice, The Great Escape*, and many others). His career spanned more than fifty years.
30	3 Feb 1995	American astronaut Eileen Collins became the first woman to pilot a space shuttle. In 1999 she became the first woman to command a space shuttle.
30	4 Feb 1995	Death of Patricia Highsmith, American novelist and short story writer. Best known for her psychological thrillers, including *Strangers on a Train* (adapted into a Hitchcock film) and *The Talented Mr. Ripley*.
30	5 Feb 1995	Death of Doug McClure, American film and television actor (*The Virginian, At the Earth's Core, The Land That Time Forgot*, and more).
30	6 Feb 1995	Death of James Merrill, American poet. Known for his lyric and epic poems. Best known for *Divine Comedies* and *The Changing Light at Sandover*.
30	6 Feb 1995	Death of Art Taylor, American jazz drummer who played in many notable bands and helped define the sound of modern jazz drumming.
30	7 Feb 1995	Pakistani terrorist Ramzi Yousef was arrested in Pakistan. He was one of the main terrorists behind the 1993 World Trade Center bombing, the 1994 bombing of Philippine Airlines Flight 484, and the 1995 Bojinka plot. He was extradited to the USA, convicted on all charges, and sentenced to life in prison + 240 years.
30	7 Feb 1995	IBM discontinued its formal dress code in favour of casual wear. Many other U.S. companies followed suit.
30	9 Feb 1995	The first British-born astronaut to perform a spacewalk (Michael Foale) and the first African American astronaut to perform a spacewalk (Bernard A. Harris) spent more than four hours outside the space shuttle *Discovery*. They were testing modifications to their spacesuits that would keep them warm in the extreme cold of space. Both astronauts reported that they became very cold, and the spacewalk was cut short.

FEBRUARY 2025

Ann.	Date	Event
30	9 Feb 1995	Death of J. William Fulbright, American politician. Senator from Arkansas. Best known for creating the Fulbright scholarship – an international exchange programme for scholars. He also opposed U.S. military involvement in Vietnam.
30	12 Feb 1995	Death of Tony Secunda, British rock band manager (The Moody Blues, Procol Harum, The Move, T. Rex, Motörhead, Steeleye Span, Marianne Faithfull, The Pretenders).
30	14 Feb 1995	The sports radio station talkSPORT began broadcasting in the UK (as Talk Radio UK).
30	14 Feb 1995	Death of U Nu, Prime Minister of Burma/Myanmar (1948–56, 1957–58, 1960–62).
30	15 Feb 1995	American computer hacker Kevin Mitnick was arrested by the FBI. He was charged with numerous counts of wire fraud, computer fraud, breaking into federal computer systems and causing criminal damage, and cloning cell phones. He served five years in prison.
30	16 Feb 1995	The environmental campaign group Greenpeace discovered Shell's plan to dump its defunct *Brent Spar* oil rig in the Atlantic. It launched an international campaign objecting to it, which included a boycott of Shell's products. Activists also occupied the rig from 30th April. On 20th June Shell withdrew its plan. The rig was taken to Norway, where it remained in a fjord for several years. It was eventually dismantled and parts of it were used to extend a quay.
30	17 Feb 1995	American spree killer Colin Ferguson was convicted of six cases of murder and nineteen cases of attempted murder in the 1993 Long Island Rail Road shooting. His trial was unusual, as he represented himself and questioned his victims in court. He was sentenced to over 300 years in prison.
30	17 Feb 1995	Death of Thelma Hulbert, British artist. Noted for her landscapes and still lives.
30	21 Feb 1995	American businessman and adventurer Steve Fossett became the first person to fly solo across the Pacific Ocean in a hot air balloon. He landed in Saskatchewan, Canada having taken off from South Korea.
30	21 Feb 1995	Death of Robert Bolt, British playwright and screenwriter (*A Man for All Seasons*, *Lawrence of Arabia*, *Doctor Zhivago*).
30	22 Feb 1995	Death of Ed Flanders, American stage, film and television actor. Best known for his role as Dr Donald Westphall in the TV medical drama series *St. Elsewhere*.
30	23 Feb 1995	Death of Melvin Franklin, American bass singer (The Temptations).
30	23 Feb 1995	Death of James Herriot, British veterinary surgeon and writer who wrote semi-autobiographical stories about his experiences. Best known for the book *All Creatures Great and Small*, which was adapted into a popular television series.
30	26 Feb 1995	Barings Bank, the oldest merchant bank in London, collapsed after its chief trader in Singapore, Nick Leeson, lost £827 million ($1.4 billion) on unauthorised transactions.

FEBRUARY 2025

Ann.	Date	Event
30	28 Feb 1995	The Cenepa War between Peru and Ecuador officially ended with the signing of the Montevideo Declaration.
30	28 Feb 1995	Denver International Airport opened in Colorado, USA.
25	4 Feb 2000	The first version of the life-simulation video game *The Sims* was released. It became one of the best-selling video game series in history.
25	4 Feb 2000	Wolfgang Schüssel of the Austrian People's Party became Chancellor of Austria, leading a coalition government that included the far-right Freedom Party of Austria. The European Union imposed sanctions on Austria as a result.
25	4 Feb 2000	Death of Carl Albert, American politician. Speaker of the House of Representatives (1971–76).
25	4 Feb 2000	Death of Doris Coley, American pop singer (The Shirelles).
25	6 Feb 2000	Second Chechen War – the Battle of Grozny ended. Russian forces seized the capital city and raised the Russian flag over the city centre, and the separatist government fell. (Battles continued until May and fighting against insurgents continued until 2009.)
25	7 Feb 2000	Death of Doug Henning, Canadian magician.
25	11 Feb 2000 to 29 May	The British government suspended the Northern Ireland Assembly after it failed to strike a deal on decommissioning IRA weapons.
25	11 Feb 2000	Death of Roger Vadim, French film director Best known for *Barbarella*.
25	12 Feb 2000	Death of Tom Landry, American football coach (Dallas Cowboys).
25	12 Feb 2000	Death of Charles M. Schulz, American cartoonist. Creator of the *Peanuts* comic strip.
25	13 Feb 2000	The last *Peanuts* comic strip was published in Sunday newspapers, the day after cartoonist Charles M. Schulz's death. The last daily strip had been published on 3rd January 2000.
25	14 Feb 2000	NASA's *NEAR Shoemaker* became the first spacecraft to orbit an asteroid (Eros). It completed 230 orbits, then landed on Eros a year later, becoming the first spacecraft to land on an asteroid rather than crashing into it.
25	17 Feb 2000	Microsoft released Windows 2000 (aimed at business users).
25	22 Feb 2000	Cyclone Leon–Eline hit Mozambique. The country was already experiencing some of the worst flooding in its history. Up to 150 people had been killed by the floods, but this rose to 700 – 800 people after the cyclone. Around 463,000 people were displaced or made homeless.
25	23 Feb 2000	Death of Ofra Haza, Israeli singer. (AIDS, aged 42.)
25	23 Feb 2000	Death of Sir Stanley Matthews, British football player.
20	1 Feb 2005	King Gyanendra of Nepal dismissed the government and took direct control after it was unable to restore peace during the Nepalese Civil War. Parliament was restored in April 2006. The monarchy was abolished in May 2008 and Nepal became a republic.
20	1 Feb 2005	The first issue of *Make* magazine was published in the USA. It organised the first Maker Faire in April 2006.

FEBRUARY 2025

Ann.	Date	Event
20	5 Feb 2005	Death of Gnassingbé Eyadéma, President of Togo (1967–2005). Succeeded by his son, Faure Gnassingbé.
20	7 Feb 2005	British yachtswoman Ellen MacArthur broke the record for the fastest solo circumnavigation of the globe, gaining international renown. (Her record has since been broken.)
20	8 Feb 2005	Israel and the Palestinian Authority signed a truce at the Sharm el-Sheikh Summit, ending the four-year Second Intifada.
20	9 Feb 2005	Death of Robert Kearns, American engineer. Inventor of the intermittent windscreen wiper.
20	10 Feb 2005	Charles, Prince of Wales and Camilla Parker Bowles announced their engagement. They were married on 9th April 2005.
20	10 Feb 2005	North Korea confirmed it had nuclear weapons. It carried out its first nuclear test in October 2006.
20	10 Feb 2005	Death of Arthur Miller, American playwright. Best known for *All My Sons*, *Death of a Salesman*, *The Crucible*, *A View from the Bridge*, and *The Misfits*. Husband of Marilyn Monroe.
20	11 Feb 2005	Blizzard Entertainment released the massively multiplayer online role-playing game *World of Warcraft* in Europe. (North America/Australia: 23rd November 2004.) It remains the world's most-subscribed MMORPG.
20	13 Feb 2005	Death of Lúcia Santos, Portuguese Carmelite nun who claimed to witness a series of visions of the Virgin Mary at Fátima in 1917. It subsequently became one of the most famous shrines in the world.
20	14 Feb 2005	Valentine's Day bombings, Philippines. Eight people were killed and about 150 injured when an Islamist separatist group detonated bombs in the cities of Manila, Davao and General Santos.
20	14 Feb 2005	YouTube, the online video-sharing service, was founded. It was officially launched in November 2005 after several months of development and testing. It was purchased by Google in 2006.
20	14 Feb 2005	Death of Rafic Hariri, Prime Minister of Lebanon (1992–98, 2000–04). His assassination triggered massive political change in Lebanon, including the Cedar Revolution and the withdrawal of Syrian troops.
20	16 Feb 2005	The Kyoto Protocol came into effect. The international treaty obliges industrialised nations to reduce their greenhouse gas emissions.
20	16 Feb 2005	The National Hockey League (NHL) cancelled its entire 2004–05 season over a labour dispute. It was the first major sports league in North America to do so. (The ten-month dispute began on 16th September 2004, and the entire season was cancelled after last-ditch negotiations failed.)
20	16 Feb 2005	Death of Narriman Sadek, the last Queen consort of Egypt. Second wife of King Farouk. Mother of King Fuad II.
20	18 Feb 2005	Hunting wild mammals with dogs was banned in England and Wales. Hunting foxes with dogs had already been banned in Scotland.

FEBRUARY 2025

Ann.	Date	Event
20	19 Feb 2005	The submarine *USS Jimmy Carter* went into service with the U.S. Navy. It was the last of the Seawolf-class nuclear-powered attack submarines, and the only submarine to be named after a living U.S. President.
20	20 Feb 2005	Spain became the first country to hold a referendum on the ratification of the proposed Constitution of the European Union. Its citizens voted in favour of ratification, but turnout was low. France and the Netherlands rejected ratification in May and June, bringing the process to a halt.
20	20 Feb 2005	Death of Sandra Dee, American model and film actress. Popular in the 1960s. Wife of pop singer Bobby Darin.
20	20 Feb 2005	Death of John Raitt, American stage and film actor and singer. Known for his baritone voice and powerful stage presence. Best known for his performances in musical theatre. Father of the singer Bonnie Raitt.
20	20 Feb 2005	Death of Hunter S. Thompson, American journalist and writer. Creator of Gonzo journalism (where reporters get involved in the action themselves and become central figures in the stories).
20	22 Feb 2005	Death of Simone Simon, French film actress. Best known outside France for the film *Cat People*.
20	23 Feb 2005	New York City's Medical Examiner announced that the process of identifying the remains of people killed in the 9/11 World Trade Center terrorist attacks in 2001 had ended. All attempts had been exhausted, and 1,100 remains were still unidentified.
20	25 Feb 2005	American serial killer Dennis Rader (the 'BTK killer') was arrested in Wichita, Kansas. On 18th August 2005 he was sentenced to ten consecutive life terms in prison for torturing and killing ten people.
20	25 Feb 2005	Death of Peter Benenson, British lawyer and human rights activist. Founder of Amnesty International.
20	26 Feb 2005	The President of Egypt, Hosni Mubarak, ordered the Constitution to be amended to allow multi-candidate presidential elections. A referendum was held in May and the amendment was passed. A presidential election was held in September under the new rules and Mubarak was re-elected.
20	26 Feb 2005	Death of Jef Raskin, American computer scientist who pioneered the graphical user interface. He started the Macintosh project while working at Apple Computer, but left the company before it went on sale.
15	8 Feb 2010	Salang avalanches, Afghanistan. A freak storm in the Hindu Kush mountains triggered at least 36 avalanches that struck the southern approach road to the Salang Tunnel. 175 people were killed.
15	11 Feb 2010	The U.S. Air Force and U.S. Missile Defense Agency successfully shot down a ballistic missile using a laser beam for the first time. The laser was mounted inside the Boeing YAL-1 Airborne Laser (a modified Boeing 747 jumbo jet) and shot down the missile off the coast of California.
15	15 Feb 2010	Halle train collision, Belgium. Two trains crashed after a driver passed a red stop signal. The train was not fitted with a train protection system that could have prevented the crash. 19 people were killed and 171 injured.

FEBRUARY 2025

Ann.	Date	Event
15	12 Feb 2010	Death of Nodar Kumaritashvili, Georgian luger. (Crashed during a training run at the Winter Olympics in Vancouver, Canada, aged 21.)
15	18 Feb 2010	WikiLeaks published the first classified documents leaked by U.S. Army intelligence analyst Chelsea Manning. Manning had served in Iraq since October 2009, and the documents related to the Iraq War. In total, Manning sent WikiLeaks nearly 750,000 sensitive documents. She was arrested in May 2010, convicted of espionage, and sentenced to 35 years in prison. Her sentence was later commuted to seven years, and she was released in 2017. She was also jailed for a year in 2019–20 for refusing to testify against WikiLeaks founder Julian Assange.
15	25 Feb 2010	Victor Yanukovych became President of Ukraine (until 2014).
15	27 Feb 2010	2010 Chile earthquake and tsunami. 525 people were killed. The earthquake caused between $4 billion and $7 billion worth of damage. The tsunami crossed the Pacific and caused over $60 million worth of damage to the fisheries industry in Japan.
10	12 Feb 2015	Death of Steve Strange, Welsh pop/new wave/new romantic singer (Visage).
10	16 Feb 2015	Death of Lesley Gore, American pop singer, songwriter, actress and television personality. Best known for the song *It's My Party*. She also composed songs for the film *Fame*.
10	27 Feb 2015	Death of Leonard Nimoy, American actor and film director. Best known for his role as Spock in the *Star Trek* films and television series.

MARCH 2025

Ann.	Date	Event
400	27 Mar 1625	Death of James VI and I, King of England and Ireland (1603–25) as James I, King of Scotland (1567–1625) as James VI. Succeeded by Charles I.
300	20 Mar 1725	Birth of Abdul Hamid I, Sultan of the Ottoman Empire (1774–89).
300	24 Mar 1725	Birth of Thomas Cushing, American lawyer and politician. First Lieutenant Governor of Massachusetts (1780–88). Speaker of the Lower House of the Massachusetts provincial assembly (1766–74). The British considered him a dangerous radical, but he actually opposed American independence.
250	22 Mar 1775	American Revolution: British politician Edmund Burke gave a speech in the House of Commons in which he called for peace and reconciliation with the American colonies rather than civil war. He warned that the Americans would never back down in the face of force.
250	23 Mar 1775	American Revolution: Patrick Henry, a Founding Father of the United States, gave a famous speech at the Second Virginia Convention. He called for America's independence from Britain, saying: 'Give me liberty, or give me death!'
250	30 Mar 1775	American Revolution: Britain passed the New England Restraining Act, prohibiting its colonies in New England from trading with any country except Britain, Ireland and the British West Indies (from 1st July 1775). In April the Act was extended to include colonies outside of New England.
200	4 Mar 1825	John Quincy Adams was inaugurated as the 6th President of the United States. He was appointed President in a contingent election after no candidates won a majority in the 1824 presidential election.
200	29 Mar 1825	Death of Roberto Cofresí, Puero Rican pirate. One of the last successful pirates of the Caribbean. (Executed after being captured by the authorities and sentenced to death by a military tribunal, aged 33.) He became a legendary figure after his death.
175	5 Mar 1850	The Britannia Bridge, which links Anglesey and mainland Wales across the Menai Strait was officially opened. It was designed and built by the railway engineer Robert Stephenson. (This bridge was replaced with a new structure following a disastrous fire in 1970.)
175	13 Mar 1850	The Women's Medical College of Pennsylvania was founded in the USA (as the Female Medical College of Pennsylvania). It was the second female medical college in the world, after the New England Female Medical College, which was founded in 1848. It held its first classes in October 1850.
175	18 Mar 1850	American Express, the multinational financial services company, was founded in Buffalo, New York, USA.
175	30 Mar 1850	The Irish paddle steamship *RMS Royal Adelaide* sank off Margate, Kent, England. All 300 people on board were killed.
175	31 Mar 1850	Death of John C. Calhoun, Vice President of the United States (1825–32).
150	1 Mar 1875	The Civil Rights Act of 1875 was signed into law in the USA. The U.S. Supreme Court ruled in 1883 that the public accommodation sections were unconstitutional.

MARCH 2025

Ann.	Date	Event
150	3 Mar 1875	The première of Georges Bizet's opera *Carmen*, in Paris, France. He died three months later at the age of 36, unaware that his opera would become a huge international success.
150	3 Mar 1875	The first recorded indoor ice hockey game was played, at the Victoria Skating Rink in Montreal, Canada. It is now recognised by the International Ice Hockey Federation as the first organised ice hockey game.
150	4 Mar 1875	Birth of Mihály Károlyi, first and only President of the Hungarian People's Republic (1919). Prime Minister of the Hungarian People's Republic (1918–19).
150	7 Mar 1875	Birth of Maurice Ravel, French composer. Best known for *Boléro*.
150	15 Mar 1875	John McCloskey, the first American-born Archbishop of New York, became the first American cardinal.
150	26 Mar 1875	Birth of Syngman Rhee, first President of South Korea (1948–60).
150	27 Mar 1875	Death of Juan Crisóstomo Torrico, President of Peru (1842). Peru's youngest president. He assumed the presidency following a coup, and was ousted later that year in another coup.
150	29 Mar 1875	Birth of Lou Henry Hoover, First Lady of the United States (1929–33). Wife of U.S. President Herbert Hoover.
125	2 Mar 1900	Birth of Kurt Weill, German-born American composer. Best known for his collaborations with the playwright Bertolt Brecht, including *The Threepenny Opera*.
125	6 Mar 1900	Birth of Lefty Grove, American baseball pitcher (Philadelphia Athletics, Boston Red Sox). One of the greatest pitchers in history.
125	6 Mar 1900	Death of Gottlieb Daimler, German engineer, industrialist, designer and car manufacturer. Founder of Daimler Motors Corporation. Together with his business partner Wilhelm Maybach, he invented the high-speed internal combustion engine and the motorcycle.
125	7 Mar 1900	Second Boer War – the Battle of Poplar Grove, South Africa. British victory over the Boers, who were demoralised after the Relief of Kimberley and fled in panic when the British cavalry arrived. The battle was swiftly followed by the Battle of Driefontein on 10th March, which was also a British victory.
125	7 Mar 1900	The German transatlantic liner *SS Kaiser Wilhelm der Grosse* sent the first ship-to-shore wireless telegraph message. The message was picked up by a receiving station 35 miles away.
125	8 Mar 1900	Birth of Howard Aiken, American physicist and computer pioneer. He designed IBM's Automatic Sequence Controlled Calculators, including the Harvard Mark I computer.
125	10 Mar 1900	Birth of Violet Brown, Jamaican supercentenarian. The oldest Jamaican ever. At the time of her death, she was the oldest person in the world, and one of the last two living people born in the 19th century. (Died 2017, aged 117.)
125	12 Mar 1900	Birth of Gustavo Rojas Pinilla, President of Colombia (1953–57).

MARCH 2025

Ann.	Date	Event
125	13 Mar 1900	Second Boer War: British forces captured Bloemfontein, the capital of the Orange Free State Republic. They also built a concentration camp nearby to house Boer women and children.
125	13 Mar 1900	Birth of Giorgos Seferis, Turkish-born Greek poet and diplomat. Winner of the 1963 Nobel Prize in Literature. Greek Ambassador to the UK (1957–62).
125	14 Mar 1900	The Gold Standard Act was signed into law in the USA. It established gold as the only standard for redeeming paper money. (Before this, silver could also be exchanged.) The USA abandoned the gold standard domestically in 1933, and internationally in 1971.
125	17 Mar 1900	Birth of Alfred Newman, American film composer (*Wuthering Heights, The Hunchback of Notre Dame, The Mark of Zorro, How Green Was My Valley, All About Eve, Love is a Many Splendored Thing, How The West Was Won, The Greatest Story Ever Told, Airport*, and more). He also composed the fanfare that plays at the start of 20th Century Fox's productions, and won nine Academy Awards.
125	18 Mar 1900	The Dutch football club Ajax was founded in Amsterdam.
125	19 Mar 1900	Birth of Frédéric Joliot-Curie, French physicist. Joint winner of the 1935 Nobel Prize in Chemistry (with his wife, Irène Joliot-Curie) for discovering artificial radioactivity.
125	20 Mar 1900	Serbian-American inventor Nikola Tesla was granted a U.S. patent for the wireless transmission of electric power. (U.S. Patent 645,576.)
125	27 Mar 1900	Death of Joseph A. Campbell, American entrepreneur who founded the Campbell Soup Company.
125	28 Mar 1900	British archaeologist Arthur Evans began excavating the ancient city of Knossos, the capital of the Minoan civilisation, in Heraklion, Crete. Knossos is regarded as the oldest city in Europe. It was abandoned (for unknown reasons) over 3,000 years ago.
125	29 Mar 1900	Birth of John McEwen, Prime Minister of Australia (1967–68). He acted as interim Prime Minister following the disappearance of Harold Holt, who is thought to have drowned while swimming in the sea.
125	31 Mar 1900	The first advertisement for an automobile appeared in the USA. The W. E. Roach Company's advertisement in the *Saturday Evening Post* simply claimed that Roach automobiles 'give satisfaction'.
125	31 Mar 1900	Birth of Prince Henry, Duke of Gloucester. Third son of King George V. Governor-General of Australia (1945-47).
100	4 Mar 1925	Calvin Coolidge was inaugurated as President of the United States for a second term. In his first, partial, term he succeeded Warren G. Harding, who died in office in 1923. This was the first U.S. Presidential inauguration to be broadcast on the radio.
100	4 Mar 1925	Death of John Montgomery Ward, American baseball player, manager, executive, and union organiser.

MARCH 2025

Ann.	Date	Event
100	5 Mar 1925	Frank B. Kellogg became U.S. Secretary of State. He is best known for co-authoring the Kellogg–Briand Pact, in which signatory countries agreed to renounce war as a means of settling disputes or conflicts. He was awarded the 1929 Nobel Peace Prize.
100	6 Mar 1925	The Russian children's newspaper *Pionerskaya Pravda* was founded. It is one of the oldest children's newspapers in Europe.
100	7 Mar 1925	Birth of Richard Vernon, British film and television actor. He often played aristocratic roles in a wide range of productions. Best known for his role as Slartibartfast in *The Hitchhiker's Guide to the Galaxy* radio and TV series. (Died 1997.)
100	9 Mar 1925	Nazi Party leader Adolf Hitler was banned from speaking in public by the Government of Bavaria (and by several other German states shortly afterwards).
100	12 Mar 1925	Birth of Harry Harrison, American-born Irish science fiction writer and illustrator. Best known for his novel *Make Room! Make Room!*, which was adapted into the film *Soylent Green*, and for his character The Stainless Steel Rat. (Died 2012.)
100	12 Mar 1925	Death of Sun Yat-sen, Chinese politician. Known as the 'Father of the Nation' in the Republic of China (Taiwan). He played a leading role in overthrowing the Qing dynasty.
100	14 Mar 1925	Death of Walter Camp, ('the Father of American Football'), American football player, coach and sports writer.
100	16 Mar 1925	Dali earthquake, Yunnan, southern China. The city of Dali was severely damaged, around 5,000 people were killed, over 7,000 injured, and 76,000 homes were destroyed.
100	18 Mar 1925	The Tri-State Tornado hit Missouri, Illinois and Indiana in the USA. 695 people were killed. It remains the deadliest tornado in U.S. history.
100	18 Mar 1925	Birth of James Pickles, British judge and newspaper columnist. Noted for his controversial sentencing decisions and outspoken comments to the press. He was also known for supporting the legalisation of prostitution and cannabis. (Died 2010.)
100	20 Mar 1925	Death of George Curzon, 1st Marquess Curzon of Kedleston, British statesman. Governor-General of India (1899–1905), Foreign Minister (1919–24), Leader of the House of Lords (1924–25).
100	21 Mar 1925	The Butler Act was signed into law in Tennessee, USA. Tennessee became the first U.S. state to ban the teaching of the theory of evolution. It led to the Scopes Trial in July 1925.
100	21 Mar 1925	The President of the Provisional Government of the Republic of Korea, Syngman Rhee, was removed from office after being impeached for misuse of power. He became President of South Korea in 1948.
100	21 Mar 1925	Murrayfield Stadium in Edinburgh, Scotland was officially opened.
100	22 Mar 1925	Tokyo Broadcasting Station (now NHK) launched the first radio broadcasts in Japan.

MARCH 2025

Ann.	Date	Event
100	25 Mar 1925	Birth of Flannery O'Connor, American novelist, short story writer and essayist. Known for her Southern Gothic stories that were often violent. (Died 1964.)
100	27 Mar 1925	Death of Carl Neumann, German mathematician.
100	30 Mar 1925	Death of Rudolf Steiner, Austrian philosopher, esotericist, social reformer and spiritualist.
100	31 Mar 1925	Iran adopted the Solar Hijri calendar.
90	1 Mar 1935	Saar (also known as the Territory of the Saar Basin) was reincorporated into Germany as the federal state of Saarland following a referendum. It had been occupied and governed by the UK and France since 1920 under a League of Nations mandate.
90	6 Mar 1935	Death of Oliver Wendell Holmes Jr., Associate Justice of the U.S. Supreme Court (1902–32).
90	11 Mar 1935	The Bank of Canada began operating.
90	16 Mar 1935	Adolf Hitler ordered the rearming of Germany, violating the Treaty of Versailles. He also reintroduced conscription.
90	16 Mar 1935	Driving tests were introduced in Britain. They were voluntary until 1st June. From that date anyone who had started to drive on or after 1st April 1934 had to pass the test.
90	18 Mar 1935	A speed limit of 30 mph in built-up areas was introduced in the UK when the Road Traffic Act 1934 came into effect.
90	21 Mar 1935	Persia was renamed Iran.
90	21 Mar 1935	Birth of Brian Clough, British football player and manager. Best known as the manager of Nottingham Forest (1975–93). (Died 2004.)
90	22 Mar 1935	The first regular television broadcasts began in Germany. The world's first public television station, the Fernsehsender Paul Nipkow, operated in Berlin until 1944.
90	22 Mar 1935	Blood tests were first used to determine paternity cases in the USA.
90	24 Mar 1935	The first episode of the radio talent show *Major Bowes Amateur Hour* was broadcast on NBC in the USA. (It began in April 1934 as a New York-only show but was broadcast nationally on this date. It transferred to CBS in September 1936. There was also a television version from 1948.)
90	28 Mar 1935	The first rocket with a gyroscopic guidance system made a successful test flight. The system was designed by American engineer Robert H. Goddard, who also created the first liquid-fuelled rocket. NASA's Goddard Space Flight Center in Maryland, USA was named in his honour.
80	1 Mar 1945	World War II: Turkey declared war on Germany and Japan and joined the Allies. (No Turkish forces were involved in WWII combat.)
80	1 Mar 1945	World War II: Field Marshal Albert Kesselring succeeded Gerd von Rundstedt as commander of the German Armed Forces on the Western Front.
80	3 Mar 1945	World War II: U.S. and Filipino troops recaptured Manila, the capital of the Philippines, from the Japanese.

MARCH 2025

Ann.	Date	Event
80	3 Mar 1945	World War II: Finland declared war on Germany, its former Axis partner, after switching sides.
80	3 Mar 1945	World War II: due to navigational error the British RAF mistakenly bombed a heavily populated area of The Hague, Netherlands, killing 511 people. Their target was supposed to be a V-2 rocket installation in a nearby park.
80	6 Mar 1945	World War II: U.S. forces captured the German city of Cologne.
80	6 Mar 1945 to 15th	World War II – Operation Spring Awakening (western Hungary). Germany's last major offensive of the war. Soviet victory. The operation included the Battle of the Transdanubian Hills in Bulgaria (Soviet/Bulgarian victory).
80	6 Mar 1945	World War II: members of the Dutch resistance attacked and severely wounded German SS officer Hans Albin Rauter after hijacking his car. Germany launched an immediate reprisal, executing 117 political prisoners at the site of the attack, as well as 145 other prisoners in Amersfoort concentration camp, the Hague, and Rotterdam.
80	6 Mar 1945	Petru Groza became Prime Minister of Romania (until 1952). This marked the beginning of the Communist regime in Romania. He became President of Romania in 1952 (until 1958).
80	6 Mar 1945	World War II: Erich Honnecker (later Leader of East Germany) escaped from prison in Berlin during an Allied bombing raid. He had been sentenced to ten years for treason and falsifying documents in 1937. He handed himself back in a few days later, and was released in April when the Soviet Red Army liberated the prisons.
80	7 Mar 1945 to 25th	World War II – the Battle of Remagen, Germany. Allied victory. U.S. forces captured Ludendorff Bridge over the River Rhine and advanced into the rest of Germany. The bridge collapsed on 17th March after days of bombardment by the Germans as they tried to prevent the Americans from crossing it.
80	8 Mar 1945	Phyllis Mae Dailey became the first African American nurse in the United States Navy. She was inducted into the U.S. Navy Nurse Corps. African Americans had previously been excluded from the Nurse Corps.
80	9 Mar 1945 to 10th	World War II – Operation Meetinghouse (the Bombing of Tokyo, Japan). Considered to be the most destructive air raid in history. 330 U.S. B-29 bombers carried out low-altitude incendiary bomb attacks on Tokyo, destroying a quarter of the city and killing over 100,000 people.
80	11 Mar 1945	World War II: the Empire of Vietnam was established. It was a short-lived puppet state established by Japan. It was dissolved on 23rd August 1945.
80	11 Mar 1945	World War II – Operation Tan No. 2. The Imperial Japanese Navy launched a long-range kamikaze attack against the Allied fleet anchored at Ulithi atoll. Result: inconclusive.
80	12 Mar 1945	New York became the first U.S. state to ban discrimination against job applicants and employees on the basis of their race, religion or creed. (Ives–Quinn Anti-Discrimination Bill.)

MARCH 2025

Ann.	Date	Event
80	12 Mar 1945	Death of Friedrich Fromm, German Army officer. Commander in Chief of the Replacement Army. Executed for failing to stop the 20th July plot to assassinate Adolf Hitler in 1944.
80	13 Mar 1945	World War II: Queen Wilhelmina returned to the Netherlands. She had evacuated to the UK at the start of the war.
80	14 Mar 1945	World War II: the British RAF used its Grand Slam earthquake bomb for the first time. It caused a 100-yard (91-metre) stretch of the Schildesche viaduct to collapse, knocking out one of Germany's major rail routes. The earthquake bomb was invented by Barnes Wallis, best known for his 'Dam Busters' bouncing bombs.
80	15 Mar 1945	*Billboard* published the first album chart in the USA. The first #1 album was by The King Cole Trio.
80	16 Mar 1945	World War II: the British RAF bombed Würzburg in Germany, destroying 90 percent of the city in just seventeen minutes. 5,000 people were killed in the resulting fire-storm.
80	16 Mar 1945 to 15 Apr	World War II – the Vienna offensive. The Soviet Union launched an offensive to capture Vienna, Austria from the Germans. Soviet victory with the assistance of Romanian and Bulgarian forces.
80	18 Mar 1945	World War II: the U.S. Air Force launched its largest bombing raid on Berlin, Germany, using more than 1,200 bomber aircraft. German fighter jets intercepted them, and there was a massive air battle. More than half of the American planes sustained damage, but they still dropped more than 3,000 tons of bombs on the city, killing an estimated 3,000 people.
80	19 Mar 1945	World War II: Adolf Hitler issued his 'Nero Decree' – an order to destroy all German infrastructure and everything of value to prevent it from being used by the Allies. The German Minister of Armaments and War Production, Albert Speer, was so appalled by this that he requested sole responsibility for carrying out the order, and then deliberately ignored it.
80	19 Mar 1945	World War II: the U.S. aircraft carrier *USS Franklin* was bombed off the coast of Japan, killing 800 crew. It was the most heavily damaged U.S. aircraft carrier to survive the war.
80	21 Mar 1945	World War II: Operation Carthage (Copenhagen, Denmark). The British RAF destroyed the Danish headquarters of the Gestapo, but also hit a school, accidentally killing 125 civilians including 86 children. RAF leaders had initially turned down the operation because the building was in the crowded city centre and civilian deaths were a high risk.
80	21 Mar 1945	World War II: British troops liberated Mandalay, Burma.
80	22 Mar 1945	The Arab League (also called the League of Arab States) was established by Egypt, Iraq, Jordan, Lebanon, Saudi Arabia, and Syria. It currently has 22 members. (Syria's membership has been suspended since 2011.)
80	22 Mar 1945	Death of John Hessin Clarke, Associate Justice of the U.S. Supreme Court Justice (1916–22).
80	23 Mar 1945 to 2 Jul	World War II – the Battle of Okinawa, Japan. Allied victory. The largest amphibious assault in the Pacific Theatre of the war. Fighting was fierce, both sides lost considerable numbers of ships and aircraft, and there were around 160,000 casualties in total.

MARCH 2025

Ann.	Date	Event
80	24 Mar 1945	World War II – Operation Varsity (Wesel, Germany). Allied victory. The USA, Britain and Canada carried out the largest single-day airborne landing operation in history, involving more than 16,000 paratroopers and thousands of aircraft.
80	26 Mar 1945	Death of David Lloyd George, British Prime Minister (1916–22).
80	27 Mar 1945 to April	World War II – Operation Starvation (Japan). The USA mined vital ports and waterways in Japan to disrupt shipping. U.S. victory.
80	27 Mar 1945	Death of Vincent Hugo Bendix, American engineer, inventor, industrialist, and automotive and aviation pioneer. Founder of the Bendix Corporation.
80	28 Mar 1945	World War II: the last German V-2 rocket hit Britain, killing one person in Orpington, Kent.
80	29 Mar 1945	World War II: the last German V-1 flying bomb hit Britain (Datchworth, Hertfordshire). On the same day, the Allies captured the last German V-1 launch site, preventing any further attacks.
80	30 Mar 1945	World War II: the Soviet Red Army captured the city of Gdańsk (also known as Danzig), Poland from the Germans.
80	31 Mar 1945	World War II: a German test pilot defected and delivered an operational Messerschmitt Me 262A-1 to the Americans. It was the world's first jet-powered fighter aircraft. It was sent to the USA for testing.
80	31 Mar 1945	Tennessee Williams's play *The Glass Menagerie* opened on Broadway.
75	1 Mar 1950	A British court sentenced German-born nuclear physicist Klaus Fuchs to fourteen years in prison for passing vital American and British atomic research secrets to the Soviet Union. He served nine years, then returned to Germany to continue his scientific career.
75	1 Mar 1950	Chiang Kai-shek reassumed his position as President of the Republic of China. He had resigned in January 1949 after the communists refused to recognise his nationalist government, and he was forced to relocate to Taiwan in December 1949. He remained in office until 1975.
75	2 Mar 1950	Birth of Karen Carpenter, American singer and drummer (The Carpenters). (Died 1983.)
75	5 Mar 1950 to 1 May	Chinese Civil War – the Battle of Hainan Island (also called the Landing Operation on Hainan Island). The People's Liberation Army captured the island, forcing the Republic of China to retreat to Taiwan.
75	6 Mar 1950	Silly Putty went on sale in the USA.
75	8 Mar 1950	The U.S. Navy's first female doctor to serve at sea: Bernice Walters was assigned to the hospital ship *USS Consolation*. She served as an anaesthetist in the Korean War.
75	8 Mar 1950	Volkswagen launched the Type 2 Transporter van – also known as the VW Camper, Bus, microbus, or Kombi. It became the best-selling van in history, and early versions remain much-loved icons of the counterculture/hippie movement.

MARCH 2025

Ann.	Date	Event
75	12 Mar 1950	Llandow air disaster, Sigingstone, Wales. A privately hired plane stalled and crashed during a return flight from Ireland, killing 75 passengers and all five crew. Three passengers survived. It was the world's worst air disaster at that time.
75	12 Mar 1950	In a referendum the people of Belgium voted in favour of the return of King Leopold III from exile as their monarch. The ruling party's coalition partners and the opposition refused to accept this, as did a large section of the public, leading to the collapse of the government, a general strike, and violence. The King resumed his duties in April, but abdicated in August (effective from July 1951) in favour of his son, Baudouin.
75	14 Mar 1950	The FBI published its first list of the Ten Most-Wanted Fugitives.
75	16 Mar 1950	The National Book Awards were re-established in the USA, having been suspended since 1942.
75	17 Mar 1950	The creation of the chemical element Californium (Cf – atomic no. 98) was announced by scientists at the University of California, Berkeley, USA.
75	19 Mar 1950	Death of Edgar Rice Burroughs, American novelist. Best known for creating the character Tarzan.
75	23 Mar 1950	The World Meteorological Organisation (WMO) was established in Geneva, Switzerland.
75	23 Mar 1950	The first episode of the television game show *Beat the Clock* was broadcast on CBS in the USA.
75	26 Mar 1950	Birth of Teddy Pendergrass, American R&B/soul/disco/funk singer. Known as the lead singer with Harold Melvin & the Blue Notes, and for his successful solo career. Paralysed in a car crash in 1982. (Died 2010.)
75	30 Mar 1950	Bell Telephone Laboratories announced the invention of the photo-transistor, which operated by light rather than by electric current. It was invented by John N. Shive in 1948.
75	30 Mar 1950	Death of Léon Blum, Prime Minister of France (1936–37, 1938, 1946–47). Noted for his opposition to Vichy France, and for his trial for treason, in which he defended himself so expertly that the Germans cancelled the trial for fear of embarrassment. They imprisoned him in Buchenwald concentration camp until the end of the war.
70	2 Mar 1955	King Norodom Sihanouk of Cambodia abdicated and was succeeded by his father King Norodom Suramarit. Norodom Sihanouk became king for the second time in 1993.
70	3 Mar 1955	American singer Elvis Presley made his first television appearance, on the show *Louisiana Hayride*. It was broadcast in the Louisiana area only. His first national TV appearance was on 28th January 1956 on the Dorsey Brothers' variety series *Stage Show*.
70	4 Mar 1955	The first transcontinental radio fax transmission was sent across the USA.
70	7 Mar 1955	The first full-length Broadway musical to be broadcast on colour television in the USA: *Peter Pan* was broadcast on NBC as part of its *Producer's Showcase* series. It featured nearly all of the show's original cast.

MARCH 2025

Ann.	Date	Event
70	9 Mar 1955	Death of Matthew A. Henson, African American explorer. He accompanied Robert E. Peary on most of his expeditions, including the 1909 expedition when they became the first men to reach the North Pole.
70	11 Mar 1955	Death of Sir Alexander Fleming, Scottish bacteriologist. Joint winner of the 1945 Nobel Prize in Physiology or Medicine for discovering penicillin.
70	11 Mar 1955	Death of Oscar F. Mayer, German-born American founder of the Oscar Mayer processed meat company.
70	12 Mar 1955	Death of Charlie Parker, ('Bird', 'Yardbird'), American jazz saxophonist, composer and bandleader. One of the most important figures in jazz history.
70	13 Mar 1955	Death of Tribhuvan, King of Nepal (1911–50, 1951–55). Died in mysterious circumstances. Succeeded by Mahendra.
70	23 Mar 1955	Death of Artur Bernardes, President of Brazil (1922–26). He ruled under a state of siege for most of his time in office.
70	24 Mar 1955	The first seagoing oil rig went into service in the Gulf of Mexico. The *Scorpion* was a three-legged jack-up rig operated by the Zapata Offshore Company. Zapata's president was future U.S. President George H. W. Bush.
70	24 Mar 1955	Tennessee Williams's play *Cat on a Hot Tin Roof* opened on Broadway.
70	27 Mar 1955	NBC opened the world's first colour television studio facility 'Color City' in Burbank, California, USA.
70	30 Mar 1955	Birth of Randy VanWarmer, American singer and songwriter. Best known for the song *Just When I Needed You Most*. (Died 2004.)
70	31 Mar 1955	Chase National Bank and the Bank of Manhattan Company merged to form Chase Manhattan Bank (now known as Chase). It is the second-largest bank in the USA.
65	4 Mar 1960	The French freighter *La Coubre* exploded in Havana, Cuba. It was loaded with 76 tons of grenades and other munitions supplied by Belgium. Between 75 and 100 people were killed and more than 200 injured. Cuban leader Fidel Castro said the explosion was an act of sabotage by the USA, which did not want Cuba to receive the armaments. The USA denied any involvement. A witness reported hearing an anti-communist dockworker speak of his plan to blow up the ship.
65	5 Mar 1960	American rock and roll singer Elvis Presley was discharged from the U.S. Army and returned to civilian life after completing his two years' service.
65	9 Mar 1960	American physician Belding Hibbard Scribner implanted a Scribner shunt in a kidney dialysis patient for the first time. The shunt, which he developed with engineer Wayne Quinton, revolutionised haemodialysis. It enabled patients to receive regular dialysis treatment, and allowed many more patients to receive treatment.
65	10 Mar 1960	The UK's first Top 50 record chart was published by the music trade magazine *Record Retailer* (now *Music Week*).

MARCH 2025

Ann.	Date	Event
65	11 Mar 1960	NASA launched its *Pioneer 5* space probe. It was the USA's first successful deep space probe and operated until 30th April. It returned a wealth of data on cosmic radiation, electrical fields, and magnetic fields in the interplanetary space between the Earth and Venus.
65	15 Mar 1960	Key Largo Coral Reef Preserve was established in Florida, USA, as the first underwater state park. In 1963 it was renamed the John Pennekamp Coral Reef State Park and opened to the public.
65	16 Mar 1960	Kitt Peak National Observatory in Arizona, USA was officially dedicated. It was founded in 1958 and houses more than twenty optical and radio telescopes.
65	21 Mar 1960	Sharpeville Massacre, South Africa. Police opened fire on a group of black anti-apartheid demonstrators, killing 69 and wounding 180.
65	21 Mar 1960	Major League Baseball teams in the USA began displaying players' names on their jerseys to make them more easily identifiable to fans. The Chicago White Sox were the first team to adopt this. The New York Yankees were the last in 2017.
65	21 Mar 1960	Birth of Ayrton Senna, Brazilian racing driver. Formula One world champion in 1988, 1990 and 1991. (Died 1994.)
65	22 Mar 1960	The first laser was patented by American physicists Arthur Schawlow and Charles Townes of Bell Telephone Laboratories. (U.S. Patent 2,929,922.)
65	25 Mar 1960	The first guided missile to be launched from a nuclear-powered submarine: the U.S. Navy submarine *USS Halibut* successfully test-launched a Regulus cruise missile. The *Halibut* was the first submarine designed specifically to launch guided missiles.
65	28 Mar 1960	The first permanent star was installed on the Hollywood Walk of Fame in Los Angeles, California, USA. It honoured film director Stanley Kramer. Eight temporary stars, two of which honoured actress Joanne Woodward and actor Burt Lancaster, had been installed in 1958 to show what the Walk of Fame might eventually look like.
60	1 Mar 1965	Australian swimming champion Dawn Fraser was banned from competitive swimming for ten years and expelled from the Australian Amateur Swimming Association for misconduct at the 1964 Olympics in Tokyo, Japan. She announced her retirement the same day. She was banned because she marched in the opening ceremony (defying a team ban), and wore an outdated swimming costume.
60	2 Mar 1965 to 2 Nov 1968	Vietnam War – Operation Rolling Thunder. The U.S. Air Force, U.S. Navy and the South Vietnam Navy launched a sustained aerial bombardment campaign against North Vietnam. But North Vietnam, assisted by the Soviet Union, China and North Korea, established an effective air defence. Result: U.S. failure.
60	2 Mar 1965	The U.S. première of the film *The Sound of Music*. (UK: 29th March.)
60	5 Mar 1965 to Apr	March Intifada, Bahrain – a Leftist uprising against the British presence in Bahrain after hundreds of workers were laid off from the Bahrain Petroleum Company. Six people were killed in clashes with police.

MARCH 2025

Ann.	Date	Event
60	5 Mar 1965	American composer Walter Piston's *Symphony No. 8* was performed for the first time, in Boston, Massachusetts, USA.
60	5 Mar 1965	Death of Chen Cheng, Premier of the Republic of China (1950–54, 1958–63), Vice President of the Republic of China (1954–65).
60	6 Mar 1965	The first non-stop helicopter flight across the USA. U.S. Navy Commander James R. Willford and two crew-mates made the flight in a Sikorsky Sea King helicopter from an aircraft carrier off California to an aircraft carrier off Florida. They flew 2,105 miles in 16 hours and 52 minutes.
60	7 Mar 1965 to 25th	Selma to Montgomery civil rights protest marches, Alabama, USA. Martin Luther King Jr. made three attempts to lead a protest march to the state capitol in support of voting rights for African Americans. The third attempt succeeded, arriving on 25th March. The first attempt was marred by violence when marchers were attacked by state troopers – known as 'Bloody Sunday'. (See also: 25th March 1965.)
60	8 Mar 1965	Vietnam War: the first U.S. combat troops arrived in Vietnam. 3,500 U.S. Marines landed in Da Nang, joining the 23,000 military advisers who were already present. This marked the beginning of the USA's main involvement in the war. It followed General William Westmoreland's request for combat troops, which U.S. President Lyndon B. Johnson approved on 22nd February.
60	10 Mar 1965	Neil Simon's play *The Odd Couple* opened on Broadway.
60	15 Mar 1965	The first TGI Fridays restaurant opened in New York City, USA. It now has branches in around sixty countries, and was the first American restaurant to open in Russia.
60	17 Mar 1965	Death of Amos Alonzo Stagg, American athlete and coach, most notably in American football where he had the longest coaching career in the history of the sport (71 years).
60	18 Mar 1965	Soviet cosmonaut Aleksei Leonov became the first person to make a spacewalk.
60	18 Mar 1965	Death of Farouk I, the last King of Egypt (1936–52).
60	19 Mar 1965	Indonesia seized two U.S. oil companies and a British–Dutch oil company. As a result, the U.S. may have become involved in the ousting of Indonesia's President Sukarno in March 1967. (The USA's involvement is officially denied.)
60	19 Mar 1965	The wreck of the Confederate steamer *SS Georgiana* was discovered in Charleston harbor, South Carolina, USA after 102 years.
60	19 Mar 1965	Death of Gheorghe Gheorghiu-Dej, Communist leader of Romania (1947–65). Succeeded by Chivu Stoica on 24th March.
60	21 Mar 1965	NASA launched its *Ranger 9* spacecraft on a mission to crash into the Moon and send back live TV images as it made its final approach. It crashed into the Moon's surface as intended on 24th March, and the images were broadcast live across the USA to millions of viewers.

MARCH 2025

Ann.	Date	Event
60	22 Mar 1965	Vietnam War: the USA confirmed it had used chemical weapons against the Viet Cong, and had supplied the South Vietnamese armed forces with chemical weapons.
60	22 Mar 1965	The album *Bringing It All Back Home* by Bob Dylan was released. It is now widely acclaimed, but it alienated many of his fans at the time because his band played electric instruments rather than acoustic ones.
60	23 Mar 1965	NASA launched its *Gemini 3* spacecraft on the USA's first two-man space flight. The astronauts were Gus Grissom and John Young.
60	23 Mar 1965	Death of Mae Murray, ('The Girl with the Bee-Stung Lips', 'The Gardenia of the Screen'), American stage and silent film actress, dancer, screenwriter and producer.
60	24 Mar 1965	The world's first teach-in. Faculty members and 3,500 students at the University of Michigan at Ann Arbor in the USA cancelled regular classes and held a twelve-hour series of anti-war debates, lectures, film-screenings and musical events to protest against the Vietnam War.
60	25 Mar 1965	Martin Luther King Jr. led the Selma to Montgomery civil rights march in Alabama, USA. This was the third, and finally successful, attempt to march to the state capitol. The first attempt was aborted because mobs and police violently attacked the demonstrators (known as 'Bloody Sunday'). The second attempt was blocked by a court injunction.
60	28 Mar 1965	Death of Princess Mary, Princess Royal and Countess of Harewood. A member of the British royal family. Third child and only daughter of King George V.
60	30 Mar 1965	Vietnam War: U.S. Embassy bombing, Saigon, South Vietnam. The Viet Cong detonated a car bomb outside the embassy. Nineteen Vietnamese, two Americans, and one Filipino were killed and 183 people were injured. The embassy was rebuilt in a different location.
50	1 Mar 1975	All television stations in Australia began broadcasting in colour.
50	5 Mar 1975	The Homebrew Computer Club held its first meeting in Menlo Park, California, USA. It is considered to have started the personal computer revolution. Several notable computer pioneers and entrepreneurs were members, including the founders of Apple.
50	6 Mar 1975	The Zapruder film showing the assassination of U.S. President John F. Kennedy in Dallas, Texas in 1963 was shown on national television in the USA for the first time.
50	8 Mar 1975	Death of George Stevens, American film director, producer, screenwriter and cinematographer (*A Place in the Sun, Giant, Shane, The Diary of Anne Frank, The Greatest Story Ever Told*).
50	15 Mar 1975	The novelty pop song *The Funky Gibbon* by British comedians The Goodies was released.

MARCH 2025

Ann.	Date	Event
50	15 Mar 1975	Death of Aristotle Onassis, Greek shipping magnate. Husband of former U.S. First Lady Jacqueline Kennedy Onassis.
50	16 Mar 1975	Death of T-Bone Walker, American blues musician and songwriter. Regarded as one of the greatest guitarists of all time.
50	19 Mar 1975	The film *Tommy*, a musical based on The Who's rock opera album *Tommy*, was released in the USA. (UK: 26th March.)
50	21 Mar 1975	Ethiopia abolished its monarchy after 3,000 years.
50	25 Mar 1975	Death of Faisal, King of Saudi Arabia (1964–75). (Assassinated by his nephew, who was later beheaded.) Succeeded by King Khalid.
50	26 Mar 1975	The Biological Weapons Convention came into effect. The multilateral disarmament treaty banned the development, production and stockpiling of all biological and toxin weapons.
50	27 Mar 1975	Death of Sir Arthur Bliss, British composer and conductor. One of the leading composers of his era.
40	1 Mar 1985	Julio María Sanguinetti became President of Uruguay for the first time. He was President again from 1995 to 2000.
40	1 Mar 1985	Apple Computer launched the Apple LaserWriter laser printer. It was one of the first mass-market laser printers and helped launch the desktop publishing revolution.
40	2 Mar 1985	The U.S. Food and Drug Administration (FDA) approved a screening test for HIV/AIDS, allowing contaminated blood to be excluded from blood transfusions.
40	2 Mar 1985	The pop song *Crazy for You* by Madonna was released.
40	3 Mar 1985	Santiago earthquake, Chile. 177 people were killed, 2,575 injured and around 1 million left homeless.
40	3 Mar 1985	British miners voted to return to work after a year-long strike over pit closures and job losses.
40	3 Mar 1985	The first episode of the comedy-drama television series *Moonlighting* was broadcast on ABC in the USA. It ran for five seasons until 1989.
40	4 Mar 1985	The U.S, Environmental Protection Agency announced a virtual ban on leaded fuel. The permitted level of lead (1.1 grams per gallon) was cut to 0.5 grams per gallon from 1st July 1985 and 0.1 grams per gallon from 1st January 1986.
40	6 Mar 1985	American boxer Mike Tyson's first professional fight, at the age of 18. He knocked out Hector Mercedes in the first round.
40	7 Mar 1985	The charity single *We Are the World* by USA for Africa was released to raise money for famine relief.
40	8 Mar 1985	Beirut car bombing, Lebanon. Eighty people were killed and 200 injured in a failed assassination attempt on Shia cleric Sayyed Mohammad Hussein Fadlallah. There were further car bombings in May and August.
40	10 Mar 1985	Death of Konstantin Chernenko, Leader of the Soviet Union (1984–85). Succeeded by Mikhail Gorbachev.

MARCH 2025

Ann.	Date	Event
40	12 Mar 1985	Death of Eugene Ormandy, Hungarian-born American conductor and violinist. Best known for his work with the Minneapolis Symphony Orchestra and his 44 years with the Philadelphia Orchestra.
40	15 Mar 1985	The first .com internet domain name was registered (symbolics.com).
40	16 Mar 1985	American journalist Terry Anderson, chief Middle East correspondent for the Associated Press, was kidnapped in Beirut, Lebanon. (Released December 1991.)
40	18 Mar 1985	The first episode of the television soap opera *Neighbours* was broadcast in Australia.
40	20 Mar 1985	Libby Riddles became the first woman to win the Iditarod Trail Sled Dog Race.
40	21 Mar 1985	Death of Sir Michael Redgrave, British stage and film actor, writer and director. Father of the actresses Vanessa Redgrave and Lynn Redgrave.
40	23 Mar 1985	American singer and musician Billy Joel married supermodel Christie Brinkley. They divorced in 1994.
40	23 Mar 1985	The world première of *The Care Bears Movie*, in Canada. (U.S. première: 24th March, released 29th March. UK: 2nd August.)
40	23 Mar 1985	Death of Richard Beeching, Baron Beeching, Chairman of British Railways. Known for his controversial report *The Reshaping of British Railways*, which had far-reaching consequences for the British railway network, including the closure of thousands of miles of track.
40	23 Mar 1985	Death of Patricia Roberts Harris, American public official. The first African American woman to serve as a U.S. ambassador, and the first in the presidential cabinet.
40	28 Mar 1985	Death of Marc Chagall, Russian-born French artist, printmaker and designer.
40	29 Mar 1985	Death of Jeanine Deckers, ('The Singing Nun', 'Sister Smile'), Belgian nun, singer and songwriter. (Suicide, aged 51, due to financial problems.)
40	30 Mar 1985	Christos Sartzetakis became President of Greece (until 1990).
40	30 Mar 1985	Death of Harold Peary, American radio, film and television actor, comedian and singer (*Fibber McGee and Molly*, *The Great Gildersleeve*, *Blondie*).
40	31 Mar 1985	The World Wrestling Federation held the first WrestleMania, at Madison Square Garden in New York City, USA.
30	1 Mar 1995	Julio María Sanguinetti became President of Uruguay for the second time (until 2000). He was also President from 1985 to 1990.
30	1 Mar 1995	The European Parliament abandoned a controversial directive that would have allowed biotechnology companies to patent new life forms. Pressure groups had been lobbying and protesting against the directive for seven years.
30	1 Mar 1995	The internet search company Yahoo! was founded. Its search engine was launched on 5th March.
30	2 Mar 1995	The discovery of the top quark was announced by two teams of scientists working at Fermilab in Illinois, USA.

MARCH 2025

Ann.	Date	Event
30	2 Mar 1995	British 'rogue trader' Nick Leeson was arrested for his role in the collapse of Barings Bank. (See also: 6th March 1995.)
30	3 Mar 1995	The last United Nations peacekeeping troops left Somalia at the end of a two-year operation (UNOSOM II) aimed at creating a secure environment for humanitarian operations to begin.
30	3 Mar 1995	Death of Howard W. Hunter, President of The Church of Jesus Christ of Latter-day Saints (1994–95).
30	5 Mar 1995	Death of Vivian Stanshall, British rock singer, songwriter, musician, artist, actor, writer and poet. Best known for his work with the Bonzo Dog Doo-Dah Band, the comedy record *Sir Henry at Rawlinson End*, and for narrating Mike Oldfield's *Tubular Bells*.
30	6 Mar 1995	The Dutch bank ING purchased Britain's oldest merchant bank, Barings PLC, for the nominal price of £1 ($1.60) following its collapse.
30	7 Mar 1995	The pharmaceutical company Glaxo took over Wellcome to form Glaxo Wellcome. In December 2000 it merged with SmithKline Beechham to form GlaxoSmithKline (GSK).
30	9 Mar 1995	The Asian American sorority Kappa Phi Lambda was founded at Binghamton University, New York, USA.
30	9 Mar 1995	Death of Ian Ballantine, American publisher. Founder of Ballantine Books.
30	10 Mar 1995	Kostis Stephanopoulos became President of Greece (until 2005).
30	13 Mar 1995	Death of Odette Hallowes, French-born British WWII heroine. Noted for her work with the French Resistance. The only woman to receive the George Cross while still alive.
30	14 Mar 1995	The highest number of people in space at the same time: thirteen. Three on Russia's *Mir* space station, seven on the U.S. space shuttle *Endeavour*, and three on a Russian Soyuz TM21 travelling to *Mir*.
30	14 Mar 1995	Norman Thagard became the first American cosmonaut when he travelled on a Russian Soyuz launch vehicle to visit the *Mir* space station.
30	14 Mar 1995	Death of William Alfred Fowler, American nuclear physicist and astrophysicist. Joint winner of the 1983 Nobel Prize in Physics for his studies of how nuclear reactions in stars create heavier chemical elements.
30	16 Mar 1995	Mississippi finally ratified the Thirteenth Amendment to the U.S. Constitution, which abolished slavery. The Amendment had come into effect in December 1865 after 27 other states ratified it.
30	17 Mar 1995	The U.S. Food and Drug Administration (FDA) approved Varivax, the first vaccine against chicken pox.
30	17 Mar 1995	Death of Donald Baverstock, British television producer and executive. Director of Programmes at the BBC and Yorkshire TV. He played a key role in the creation of the TV series *Doctor Who*.
30	17 Mar 1995	Death of Ronnie Kray, British gangster (the Kray twins).
30	20 Mar 1995	The Japanese terrorist group Aum Shinrikyo released sarin nerve gas on the Tokyo underground in Japan. Twelve people were killed and thousands injured.

MARCH 2025

Ann.	Date	Event
30	22 Mar 1995	Russian cosmonaut Valeri Polyakov returned to Earth after spending 438 days on the *Mir* space station. This is the current record for the longest single space flight.
30	22 Mar 1995	Death of Peter Woods, British journalist and BBC television newsreader.
30	23 Mar 1995	Death of Alan Barton, British singer (Black Lace, Smokie). (Killed when Smokie's tour bus crashed in Germany, aged 41.)
30	24 Mar 1995	Death of Joseph Needham, British biochemist, sinologist and historian. Best known for his multi-volume work *Science and Civilisation in China*.
30	25 Mar 1995	Pope John Paul II condemned abortion and euthanasia as crimes that no human laws could legitimise.
30	25 Mar 1995	The first wiki (user-editable website) was launched: WikiWikiWeb. It was part of the Portland Pattern Repository – a repository for computer programming design patterns.
30	25 Mar 1995	Death of Warren E. Burger, Chief Justice of United States (1969–86).
30	26 Mar 1995	The Schengen Treaty came into effect in the European Union. Seven nations (Belgium, France, Germany, Luxembourg, the Netherlands, Portugal and Spain) eliminated their internal border controls and tightened their external borders.
30	26 Mar 1995	Death of Eazy-E, American rapper. Considered the godfather of gangsta rap. A founding member of N.W.A. (HIV/AIDS, aged 31.)
30	31 Mar 1995	Operation Uphold Democracy (the United States Intervention in Haiti) officially ended and was replaced by the United Nations Mission in Haiti. Over 2,000 U.S. troops remained in Haiti in support and peacekeeping roles under UN command.
30	31 Mar 1995	Death of Selena, American singer. (Shot by the founder of her fan club, aged 23.)
25	1 Mar 2000	Tarja Halonen became the first female President of Finland (until 2012).
25	4 Mar 2000	Sony's PlayStation 2 video game console was released in Japan. (North America: 26th October. Australia: 17th November. Europe: 24th November.)
25	5 Mar 2000	Death of Lolo Ferrari, French actress, singer, television presenter and porn star. Listed in *Guinness World Records* as 'the woman with the largest breasts in the world'. (Probable prescription drug overdose/suicide, aged 37. Her husband served 13 months for her murder, but he was later cleared.)
25	6 Mar 2000	Death of John Colicos, Canadian stage and television actor. He appeared in a wide range of roles, but is best known for playing the first Klingon ever seen in the Star Trek TV series, and for helping to design their appearance. He also played Count Baltar in the film and TV series *Battlestar Galactica*.
25	7 Mar 2000	Death of Charles Gray, British stage, film and television actor. Best known for his role as the villain Blofeld in the James Bond film *Diamonds Are Forever*. He also played the narrator in *The Rocky Horror Picture Show*.

MARCH 2025

Ann.	Date	Event
25	10 Mar 2000	The NASDAQ Composite stock index reached its peak during the dotcom boom. By 20th March it had fallen by ten percent as the bubble began to burst. By 2001 scores of online brands had gone out of business after burning through their venture capital without ever making a profit.
25	11 Mar 2000	Ricardo Lagos became President of Chile (until 2006).
25	17 Mar 2000	530 members of the Movement for the Restoration of the Ten Commandments of God died in Kanungu, Uganda. Initially thought to be a mass suicide, but now thought to be a mass murder by cult leaders who may still be alive. Mass deaths were also found at other sites in southern Uganda over the following days, taking the total to around 940.
25	17 Mar 2000	Jens Stoltenberg became Prime Minister of Norway after Kjell Magne Bondevik and his cabinet lost a vote of no confidence over the construction of gas-fired power stations. Stoltenberg lost the October 2001 election to Bondevik, but became Prime Minister again in 2005 (until 2013). He became Secretary General of NATO in 2014.
25	21 Mar 2000	The U.S. Supreme Court ruled that the U.S. Food and Drug Administration (FDA) did not have the authority to regulate tobacco products. (FDA v. Brown & Williamson Tobacco Corp.) The Family Smoking Prevention and Tobacco Control Act was signed into law in June 2009, granting the FDA the power to regulate the tobacco industry. It also banned flavoured tobacco products, required FDA approval for new products, and restricted advertising to minors.
25	26 Mar 2000	Death of Alex Comfort, British physician and writer. Best known for his book *The Joy of Sex*.
25	27 Mar 2000	Death of Ian Dury, British punk/new wave singer, songwriter and actor. Best known as the lead singer of Ian Dury and the Blockheads.
25	28 Mar 2000	Death of Anthony Powell, British novelist. Best known for the twelve-volume *A Dance to the Music of Time*.
25	30 Mar 2000	Death of Rudolf Kirchschläger, President of Austria (1974–86).
20	1 Mar 2005	The U.S. Supreme Court abolished the death penalty for criminals who were under 18 years old when they committed their offence. (Roper v. Simmons.)
20	3 Mar 2005	The Mayerthorpe tragedy, Alberta, Canada. Four Royal Canadian Mounted Police (RCMP) officers were shot and killed by a criminal (James Roszko) when they raided his property. Roszko then killed himself. This was the RCMP's worst one-day loss of life since the North-West Rebellion of 1885.
20	3 Mar 2005	American businessman and adventurer Steve Fossett made the first solo flight around the world without landing or refuelling.
20	3 Mar 2005	Margaret Wilson became Speaker of New Zealand's House of Representatives. From this date until 23rd August 2006, all of New Zealand's highest political offices were filled by women – including Queen Elizabeth II as Head of State. This was the first time this occurred.

MARCH 2025

Ann.	Date	Event
20	6 Mar 2005	Death of Tommy Vance, British radio DJ who championed hard rock and heavy metal music.
20	8 Mar 2005	Death of Aslan Maskhadov, President of Chechnya (1997–2005). Killed during a raid by Russian forces.
20	10 Mar 2005	The first Chief Executive of Hong Kong, Tung Chee Hwa, announced his resignation after widespread protests over his poor governance. He was succeeded by Donald Tsang.
20	10 Mar 2005	Death of Dave Allen, Irish comedian.
20	11 Mar 2005	The Nintendo DS dual-screen portable video games console was released in Europe. (North America: 21st November 2004. Japan: 2nd December 2004.)
20	14 Mar 2005 to 27 Apr	Cedar Revolution, Lebanon. A series of massive demonstrations were held (particularly in Beirut) to demand the withdrawal of Syrian troops, following the assassination of former Lebanese Prime Minister Rafik Hariri. Syrian troops withdrew on 27th April.
20	15 Mar 2005	Bernard Ebbers, the former CEO of WorldCom, was convicted of securities fraud and conspiracy. On 13th July he was sentenced to 25 years in prison. He is regarded as one of the most corrupt CEOs in U.S. history.
20	16 Mar 2005	A Los Angeles jury acquitted American actor Robert Blake of murdering his wife, Bonnie Lee Bakley. On 18th November 2005 a civil jury found him liable for her death and ordered him to pay $30 million.
20	19 Mar 2005	Death of John DeLorean, American motor vehicle engineer and executive. He developed the Pontiac GTO, Firebird and Grand Prix, and the Chevrolet Vega for General Motors. He also founded the DeLorean Motor Company. His career was tainted by drug trafficking and financial scandals.
20	21 Mar 2005	Red Lake Senior High School shooting, Minnesota, USA (also known as the Red Lake massacre). A former student shot and killed nine people (including five students) and wounded five others before committing suicide.
20	22 Mar 2005 to 11 Apr	Tulip Revolution, Kyrgyzstan. President Askar Akayev was ousted in a coup on 24th March after revolutionaries declared the recent parliamentary elections corrupt. An interim parliament was installed on 11th April. Kurmanbek Bakiyev became acting-president, and officially took office on 14th August.
20	22 Mar 2005	Death of Kenzo Tange, Japanese architect. One of the most important architects of the 20th century. Known for combining traditional Japanese styles with Modernism.
20	24 Mar 2005	The Sony PlayStation Portable (PSP) hand-held games console was released in North America. (Japan: 12th December 2004. Europe: 1st September 2005.)

MARCH 2025

Ann.	Date	Event
20	26 Mar 2005	Death of James Callaghan, British Prime Minister (1976–79).
20	26 Mar 2005	Death of Paul Hester, Australian drummer (Split Enz, Crowded House). (Suicide, aged 46.)
20	28 Mar 2005	Sumatra earthquake. Around 1,300 people were killed, mostly on the island of Nias where there was extensive damage.
20	28 Mar 2005	Death of Dame Moura Lympany, British concert pianist.
20	29 Mar 2005	Death of Johnnie Cochran, American lawyer. Best known for his successful defence of the former football star and actor O. J. Simpson in his 1994 double murder trial.
20	29 Mar 2005	Death of Mitch Hedberg, American stand-up comedian. (Drug overdose, aged 37.)
20	31 Mar 2005	Death of Terri Schiavo, American brain damage victim who was the subject of a lengthy legal battle between her husband and parents over her right to die.
15	11 Mar 2010	Sebastián Piñera became President of Chile (until 2014). He became President again in 2018.
15	23 Mar 2010	The Affordable Care Act (also known as the Patient Protection and Affordable Care Act, or Obamacare) came into effect in the USA.
15	29 Mar 2010	Moscow Metro bombings, Russia. Two female Islamic terrorists carried out suicide bombings at Lubyanka station and Park Kultury station during the morning rush hour. Forty people were killed and 102 injured. The two women were members of the militant Caucasus Emirate group, which demanded independence for Muslim states in the North Caucasus region.
10	12 Mar 2015	Death of Terry Pratchett, British fantasy novelist. Best known for his *Discworld* series. (Alzheimer's disease, aged 66.)
10	20 Mar 2015	Death of Malcolm Fraser, Prime Minister of Australia (1975–83).
10	24 Mar 2015	Germanwings Flight 9525 crashed in the French Alps. All 150 people on board were killed. An investigation found that co-pilot deliberately caused the crash. He had been declared unfit for work by his doctor because of his suicidal tendencies, but he reported for duty anyway.

APRIL 2025

Ann.	Date	Event
1900	30 Apr 125	Death of An, Emperor of China (106–125).
1000	18 Apr 1025 ?	The coronation of Bolesław I the Brave, the first king of Poland. His coronation is commonly believed to have taken place on this date (Easter Sunday) although some historians believe it took place on 24th December 1024. (He died a few weeks later, on 17th June.)
750	13 Apr 1275	Death of Eleanor of England, Countess of Leicester. Youngest child of King John.
400	13 Apr 1625	German scientist Giovanni Faber invented the word 'microscope'. Galileo had developed a compound microscope, but he called it the occhiolino ('little eye').
300	2 Apr 1725	Birth of Giacomo Casanova, Italian adventurer and writer. Noted for his many affairs with women.
300	30 Apr 1725	The First Treaty of Vienna (the Peace of Vienna) was signed by the Habsburg Monarchy, the Holy Roman Empire, and Bourbon Spain. It was the first of four treaties these parties signed in 1725, and marked the founding of the Austro–Spanish Alliance. Great Britain, France, Hanover and Prussia formed their own alliance in September in response.
250	7 Apr 1775	Birth of Francis Cabot Lowell, American businessman. He established the first integrated textile mill in the USA in Boston, Massachusetts, and helped bring the Industrial Revolution to the USA.
250	14 Apr 1775	The Pennsylvania Abolition Society was established in the USA (as the Society for the Relief of Free Negroes Unlawfully Held in Bondage). It was the first abolition society in North America.
250	18 Apr 1775	American Revolutionary War: American silversmith and folk hero Paul Revere made his famous midnight ride on horseback from Charleston to Lexington to warn residents that the British were about to attack. (Numerous other riders also helped spread the word.)
250	19 Apr 1775 to 3 Sep 1783	The American Revolutionary War. American victory, as a result of which Britain ceded all of its North American territories to the USA.
250	19 Apr 1775 to 17 Mar 1776	American Revolutionary War: the Siege of Boston. As the war began, the Americans successfully prevented the British, stationed in Boston, from proceeding any further. The British were forced to abandon Boston after eleven months and relocate to Nova Scotia.
250	23 Apr 1775	Birth of J. M. W. Turner, British artist. Known for his landscapes and turbulent marine paintings.
175	4 Apr 1850	The city of Los Angeles, California, USA was incorporated. Its population at that time was 1,610. It is now around 3.9 million.
175	8 Apr 1850	Birth of William H. Welch, ('the Dean of American Medicine'), American physician and pathologist. Co-founder of Johns Hopkins Hospital and Johns Hopkins University School of Medicine in Baltimore, Maryland.

APRIL 2025

Ann.	Date	Event
175	15 Apr 1850	The city of San Francisco, California, USA was incorporated. Its population at that time was about 25,000. It is now around 875,000.
175	16 Apr 1850	Death of Marie Tussaud, French artist known for her wax sculptures. Founder of Madame Tussauds wax museum in London. There are now Madame Tussauds wax museums in many other cities.
175	20 Apr 1850	Birth of Daniel Chester French, American sculptor. Best known for his statue of U.S. President Abraham Lincoln in the Lincoln Memorial in Washington D.C. He also created numerous other notable sculptures, monuments and memorials.
175	23 Apr 1850	Death of William Wordsworth, British Romantic poet. Poet Laureate (1843–50).
150	1 Apr 1875	Birth of Edgar Wallace, British writer, playwright and journalist. Best known for creating King Kong. One of the most prolific thriller writers of the 20th century, he wrote more than 170 novels, 957 short stories and eighteen plays, as well as poetry, screenplays and historical non-fiction.
150	2 Apr 1875	Birth of Walter Chrysler, American automobile pioneer and executive. Founder of the Chrysler Corporation.
150	6 Apr 1875	Scottish-born inventor Alexander Graham Bell was granted a U.S. patent for the harmonic telegraph (or multiple telegraph), which allowed two telegraph signals to be sent along the same wire at the same time by transmitting them at different frequencies. (U.S. Patent 161,739.)
150	8 Apr 1875	Birth of Albert I, King of Belgium (1909–34).
150	17 Apr 1875	The game of snooker was invented by British Army officer Sir Neville Chamberlain while he was stationed in India.
150	25 Apr 1875	Death of the 12th Dalai Lama of Tibet (Trinley Gyatso). He died from a mysterious illness, aged 18. Succeeded by the 13th Dalai Lama (Thubten Gyatso).
125	3 Apr 1900	Birth of Camille Chamoun, President of Lebanon (1952–58).
125	4 Apr 1900	Assassination attempt on the Prince of Wales (later King Edward VII). A fifteen-year-old boy shot at him as he was travelling through Belgium, in protest against the Second Boer War. The prince was not injured. The boy was acquitted because he was a juvenile. This worsened the already-poor relations between Britain and continental Europe.
125	5 Apr 1900	British archaeologist Arthur Evans and his team discovered a large cache of clay tablets in Knossos, Crete. They were inscribed with Greek hieroglyphic writing, which is now known as Linear B. The text was translated between 1951 and 1953 and published in 1956.
125	5 Apr 1900	Birth of Spencer Tracy, American stage and film actor. One of the greatest Hollywood actors.
125	11 Apr 1900	The U.S. Navy acquired its first modern submarine, the *USS Holland*. It was commissioned on 12th October and remained in service until July 1905. It could hold a crew of six, and was armed with three torpedoes and a gun.

APRIL 2025

Ann.	Date	Event
125	14 Apr 1900 to 12 Nov	The Exposition Universelle of 1900, a World's Fair, also known as the 1900 Paris Exposition, was held in Paris, France. Nearly 50 million people visited it. It featured numerous innovations, including the first commercial escalator, which was designed by American engineer Charles Seeberger and the Otis elevator company.
125	15 Apr 1900 to 19th	Philippine–American War – the Siege of Catubig, Philippines. Filipino guerrillas launched a surprise attack on a U.S. infantry detachment. Filipino victory, but at a heavy cost.
125	16 Apr 1900	The United States Post Office issued its first booklets of postage stamps. Each booklet held 12, 24 or 48 two-cent stamps.
125	17 Apr 1900	The Treaty of Cession of Tutuila was signed by the USA and the chiefs of the island of Tutuila. The island became a U.S. territory and part of American Samoa.
125	23 Apr 1900	The word 'hillbilly' first appeared in print, in an article in the *New York Journal* in the USA.
125	25 Apr 1900	Birth of Wolfgang Pauli, Austrian theoretical physicist. A pioneer of quantum physics. Winner of the 1945 Nobel Prize in Physics for discovering the Exclusion Principle.
125	26 Apr 1900	Birth of Charles Francis Richter, American seismologist and physicist. Best known for creating the Richter scale which measured the magnitude of earthquakes. The Richter scale was superseded by the moment magnitude scale in 1979.
125	28 Apr 1900	Birth of Jan Oort, Dutch astronomer. A pioneer of radio astronomy. He made many important contributions to our understanding of the Milky Way galaxy. The Oort cloud (the theoretical cloud at the boundary of our solar system where comets originate) is named in his honour.
125	30 Apr 1900	Hawaii became an organised incorporated territory of the USA. It became a U.S. state in 1959.
125	30 Apr 1900	Death of Casey Jones, American locomotive engineer. Known for his heroic actions in saving his passengers' lives in a train crash in which he was killed.
100	1 Apr 1925	Danmarks Radio (now DR), the Danish Broadcasting Corporation, was founded.
100	1 Apr 1925	The Hebrew University of Jerusalem was officially opened in Israel.
100	2 Apr 1925	Birth of George MacDonald Fraser, British historical novelist, short story writer and screenwriter. Best known for the *Flashman* series of novels. (Died 2008.)
100	3 Apr 1925	Birth of Tony Benn, British Labour politician. Secretary of State for Industry (1974–75), Secretary of State for Energy (1975–79). President of the Stop the War Coalition (2001–14). (Died 2014.)
100	4 Apr 1925	The Schutzstaffel (SS) (meaning 'Protection Squadron') was founded in Germany. It became one of the most powerful paramilitary organisations in Nazi Germany.

APRIL 2025

Ann.	Date	Event
100	6 Apr 1925	Imperial Airways introduced in-flight movies on scheduled flights. The first film shown was *The Lost World* on a flight from London to Paris. (The first in-flight movie was shown in the USA when Aeromarine Airways passengers flying around Chicago, Illinois were shown a film called *Howdy Chicago*.)
100	10 Apr 1925	The city of Tsaritsyn in Russia was renamed Stalingrad. (It was renamed Volgograd in 1961. Campaigners are now trying to get the name changed back to Stalingrad.)
100	10 Apr 1925	F. Scott Fitzgerald's novel *The Great Gatsby* was published.
100	12 Apr 1925	Birth of Oliver Postgate, British animator, puppeteer and writer. He co-founded Smallfilms with Peter Firmin, and created, wrote and narrated several popular children's television shows including *Bagpuss*, *Noggin the Nog*, *Ivor the Engine*, *The Clangers*, and *Pogles' Wood*. (Died 2008.)
100	14 Apr 1925	Birth of Rod Steiger, American stage, film and television actor (*On the Waterfront*, *Oklahoma!*, *Doctor Zhivago*, *In the Heat of the Night*, and more). (Died 2002.)
100	14 Apr 1925	Death of John Singer Sargent, Italian-born American artist who spent most of his life in Europe. Renowned for his portraits.
100	17 Apr 1925	Paul Painlevé became Prime Minister of France (for the second time) after Édouard Herriot's government collapsed. He remained in office until 28th November.
100	18 Apr 1925	The International Amateur Radio Union was founded in Paris, France.
100	18 Apr 1925	Death of Charles Ebbets, American sports executive. Owner and President of the Brooklyn Dodgers (now the Los Angeles Dodgers). Ebbets Field baseball stadium in Brooklyn, New York was named in his honour. It was demolished in 1960.
100	22 Apr 1925	Birth of Aaron Spelling, American film and television producer. The leading TV producer of his era (*Charlie's Angels*, *T. J. Hooker*, *The Love Boat*, *Fantasy Island*, *Hart to Hart*, *Beverly Hills 90210*, *Melrose Place*, *Charmed*, and more).
100	29 Apr 1925	Birth of John Compton, first Prime Minister of Saint Lucia (1979, 1982–96, 2006–07 – died in office).
90	2 Apr 1935	British radio engineer Robert Watson-Watt was granted a patent for his radar system.
90	5 Apr 1935	Birth of Peter Grant, British rock band manager and record company executive (The Yardbirds, Led Zeppelin, Bad Company, and others). (Died 1995.)
90	13 Apr 1935	Birth of Lyle Waggoner, American film and television actor. Best known for *The Carol Burnett Show* and for his role as Steve Trevor in the TV series *Wonder Woman*. He later founded Star Waggons, which rented luxury trailers to film and television studios. (Died 2020.)

APRIL 2025

Ann.	Date	Event
90	14 Apr 1935	Black Sunday – the worst dust storm of the Dust Bowl occurred in Kansas, USA.
90	16 Apr 1935	The first episode of the radio comedy series *Fibber McGee and Molly* was broadcast on NBC in the USA. It ran until 1959.
90	17 Apr 1935	Sun Myung Moon (aged 15) claimed that Jesus appeared before him and asked him to complete the work he left unfinished when he was crucified – specifically his failure to marry. He founded the Unification Church, known for its mass blessing ceremonies, in South Korea in 1954.
90	19 Apr 1935	Birth of Dudley Moore, British actor, comedian, musician and composer. Best known for the films *10* and *Arthur* and for his comedy partnership with Peter Cook (Pete and Dud/Derek and Clive). (Died 2002.)
90	20 Apr 1935	The first episode of *Your Hit Parade* was broadcast on NBC radio in the USA. It ran until 1953. A television version ran from 1950 to 1959.
90	21 Apr 1935	King Boris of Bulgaria banned all opposition political parties and ruled the country himself until 1943 using puppet prime ministers.
90	24 Apr 1935	Nazi Germany ordered all publishers and newspaper editors to prove their own (and their spouses') Aryan descent dating back to 1800.
90	25 Apr 1935	The first round-the-world telephone call: the president and vice president of AT&T spoke to each other from separate rooms at the Long Lines Department office in New York City, USA. They were connected via 25,000 miles of wire and radio channels that travelled all the way around the world.
90	25 Apr 1935	The Oregon State Capitol building in Salem, Oregon, USA was destroyed by fire.
90	27 Apr 1935 to 6 Nov	The Brussels International Exposition, a World's Fair, was held in Belgium. 20 million visitors attended. The theme was colonisation.
80	1 Apr 1945 to 22 Jun	World War II – the Battle of Okinawa, Japan (also known as Operation Iceberg). The largest amphibious assault in the Pacific War. Allied victory. U.S. forces occupied Okinawa until 1972.
80	1 Apr 1945 to 4th	World War II: U.S forces captured the city of Kassel, Germany. Much of the city had already been destroyed by Allied bombing, and this attack caused further destruction. Most of the city was rebuilt after the war.
80	2 Apr 1945 to 13th	World War II – the Vienna Offensive, Austria. The Soviet Red Army captured the Austrian capital from the Germans on 13th April after an eleven-day siege. They then pushed further into Austria.
80	4 Apr 1945	World War II: the Soviet Red Army expelled the last German forces from Hungary, and the country was liberated. This paved the way for the Soviet occupation of Hungary, and it became a Communist country and part of the Eastern Bloc until 1989.)
80	4 Apr 1945	Holocaust: U.S. forces liberated Ohrdruf concentration camp in Germany.

APRIL 2025

Ann.	Date	Event
80	5 Apr 1945	World War II: Yugoslav Partisan leader Josip Broz Tito met Soviet leader Joseph Stalin in Moscow. They signed a friendship treaty that granted Soviet troops the temporary right to enter Yugoslav territory. Under the terms of the agreement, Soviet forces would leave once they had completed their operation. Stalin tried to maintain a Soviet military presence in Yugoslavia after the war, but Tito prevented it.
80	6 Apr 1945 to 2 May	World War II: the Spring Offensive in Italy. Allied victory. All German forces in Italy surrendered.
80	6 Apr 1945	World War II: the liberation of Sarajevo, Yugoslavia.
80	7 Apr 1945	World War II: the Prime Minister of Japan, Kuniaki Koiso, resigned. He was succeeded by Kantarō Suzuki.
80	7 Apr 1945	World War II: the Japanese battleship *Yamato* was sunk by U.S. bombers near Okinawa. The *Yamato* and sister ship *Musashi* (sunk in October 1944) were the heaviest and most powerfully armed battleships ever constructed.
80	7 Apr 1945	Birth of Gerry Cottle, British circus owner, and owner of Wookey Hole Caves in Somerset. (Died 2021)
80	8 Apr 1945	Holocaust: the Celle massacre, Prussian Hanover. A train transporting about 4,000 concentration camp internees to Bergen–Belsen stopped next to an ammunition train that was hit by an Allied air raid. The ammunition train exploded, most of the wagons carrying the internees were destroyed, and many people were killed. Others died of illness or malnutrition during the journey. Between 200 and 300 survivors of the explosion fled, but they were pursued, caught and executed. Only 487 internees reached Bergen–Belsen.
80	9 Apr 1945	World War II – the Battle of Königsberg (Germany) ended. Soviet victory. The battle began in January. (Königsberg is now Kaliningrad in Russia.)
80	9 Apr 1945	The German pocket battleship *Admiral Scheer* was sunk by the British RAF during an air raid on Kiel harbour, Germany. The *Admiral Scheer* was one of Germany's most successful ships of WWII in terms of the number of ships it sank or captured.
80	9 Apr 1945	World War II: the American Liberty ship *SS Charles Henderson* exploded in Bari, Italy, while its cargo of 500-pound bombs was being unloaded. 523 people were killed and 1,800 injured. Buildings along the waterfront were destroyed, and nearby ships were severely damaged.
80	11 Apr 1945	Holocaust: U.S. forces liberated Buchenwald concentration camp in Germany. (See also: 13th April 1945.)
80	12 Apr 1945	Holocaust: Canadian forces liberated Westerbork transit camp in the Netherlands. (Jewish diarist Anne Frank was an inmate at this camp in August–September 1944 before she was transferred to Bergen–Belsen.)
80	12 Apr 1945	Death of Franklin D. Roosevelt, President of the United States (1933–45). Succeeded by Vice-President Harry S. Truman who pledged to continue Roosevelt's WWII policies for war and peace.

APRIL 2025

Ann.	Date	Event
80	13 Apr 1945	Holocaust: the Gardelegen massacre, Germany. More than 1,000 prisoners who had been transported from the Mittelbau–Dora labour camp (part of Buchenwald concentration camp) were forced into a barn, which was then barricaded and set on fire. Those who tried to escape were shot.
80	15 Apr 1945	Holocaust: British and Canadian forces liberated Bergen–Belsen concentration camp in Germany.
80	16 Apr 1945 to 2 May	World War II – the Battle of Berlin, Germany. Soviet victory resulting in the surrender of German forces in the city, Hitler's suicide, and the end of WWII in Europe on 8th May. Soviet forces captured the Reichstag (parliament building) on 30th April.
80	16 Apr 1945 to 20th	World War II – the Battle of Nuremberg, Germany. Allied victory, and the city of Nuremberg was liberated. This was a major loss for Germany, as Nuremberg was one of the main centres of the Nazi regime. The four-day battle devastated the city.
80	16 Apr 1945	World War II: U.S. forces liberated Colditz Castle in Germany (officially known as Oflag IV-C), a high-security prisoner-of-war camp for officers.
80	16 Apr 1945	World War II: the German transport ship *MV Goya* was torpedoed by a Soviet submarine and sank in the Baltic Sea. The overcrowded ship was carrying about 7,000 wounded troops and civilians fleeing from the advancing Soviet forces. Only 183 of them survived. It was one of the biggest maritime losses in history.
80	17 Apr 1945 to 27th	World War II: the Alsos Mission (a British–U.S. mission to uncover enemy scientific developments) located 1,000 tons of uranium ore that had been hidden in the Soviet occupation zone in Germany. Mission leader Boris T. Pash commandeered it, and it was transported to the UK to prevent the Soviets from using it to develop an atomic bomb.
80	18 Apr 1945	World War II: nearly 1,000 Allied bombers attacked the German island of Heligoland in the North Sea, completely destroying the town. All survivors were evacuated the following day. (From 1945 to 1952 the British used it as a bombing range. It was then handed back to Germany.)
80	18 Apr 1945	Death of John Ambrose Fleming, British electrical engineer and physicist. He invented the first vacuum tube (thermionic valve) and designed the radio transmitter used for the first transatlantic radio transmission.
80	18 Apr 1945	Death of Ernie Pyle, American journalist and broadcaster. Killed by Japanese gunfire while working as a war correspondent during the Battle of Okinawa.
80	19 Apr 1945	World War II: U.S. forces captured the city of Leipzig, Germany. They handed it over to the Soviet Union in July, and it became one of the major cities of East Germany.
80	19 Apr 1945	The Rodgers and Hammerstein musical *Carousel* opened on Broadway.
80	20 Apr 1945	World War II: Soviet forces captured the headquarters of the Supreme High Command of the German Army at Zossen near Berlin. Soviet forces then used it as their headquarters in Germany until 1994.

APRIL 2025

Ann.	Date	Event
80	21 Apr 1945 to 30th	World War II – the Battle of Bautzen, Germany. A local victory for Germany, which allowed troops and refugees to escape to the west and surrender to the Allies. This was one of the last battles on the Eastern Front, one of Germany's last successful tank battles, and one of Poland's bloodiest battles of the war, though it had little impact on the war overall.
80	21 Apr 1945	World War II: the city of Stuttgart in Germany was captured by French forces who continued to occupy it until 1946 (the Stuttgart Crisis) when it was handed over to U.S. control.
80	22 Apr 1945	World War II: Hitler admitted defeat. After learning that the Soviet Red Army had taken the German town of Eberswalde without resistance, German leader Adolf Hitler admitted to those in his underground bunker that the war was lost and suicide was his only option. He committed suicide on 30th April.
80	22 Apr 1945	Holocaust: Soviet and Polish forces liberated Sachsenhausen concentration camp in Germany.
80	22 Apr 1945	Holocaust: 600 prisoners at the Jasenovac concentration camp in Croatia revolted. 520 were killed and 80 escaped. Following the revolt, all remaining prisoners were killed, the buildings were destroyed, and the camp was abandoned.
80	23 Apr 1945	World War II: After hearing that Adolf Hitler intended to commit suicide, his designated successor, Hermann Göring, sent him a telegram asking for his permission to assume control of the Third Reich. Hitler considered this an act of treason, fired him from all of his positions, ordered his arrest, and (on 26th April) appointed Karl Dönitz as his successor instead.
80	23 Apr 1945	Holocaust: U.S. forces liberated Flossenbürg concentration camp in Germany.
80	24 Apr 1945	Newly installed U.S. President Harry S. Truman was given a comprehensive briefing on the Manhattan Project's progress towards creating the first atomic bomb. After learning that the project was proceeding well, he had to decide whether to use the bomb against Japan. (See also: 6th and 9th August 1945.)
80	25 Apr 1945	World War II: Elbe Day. An important milestone near the end of the war in Europe. U.S. forces advancing from the west and Soviet forces advancing from the east met at the River Elbe, effectively cutting Nazi Germany in two.
80	25 Apr 1945	World War II: Liberation Day in Italy. The cities of Milan and Turin were liberated from the Nazis.
80	25 Apr 1945	World War II – the Lapland War ended in Finland. Finnish victory. The last German forces retreated into Norway on 27th April, which is now celebrated in Finland as National Veterans' Day.
80	25 Apr 1945 to 26 Jun	The United Nations Conference on International Organization (UNCIO) was held in San Francisco, California, USA. Representatives from fifty nations met to create the United Nations Charter.
80	26 Apr 1945	World War II – the Burma Campaign – the Japanese army abandoned their Burmese headquarters in Rangoon.

APRIL 2025

Ann.	Date	Event
80	27 Apr 1945	World War II: Austria seceded from the Third Reich (Germany) and became an independent state again – the Second Republic of Austria. It was occupied by the Allies until 1955.
80	28 Apr 1945	Death of Benito Mussolini, Prime Minister/fascist dictator of Italy (1922–43). (Executed by partisans, along with his mistress, Clara Petacci.)
80	29 Apr 1945	German dictator Adolf Hitler married his long-term partner Eva Braun in his bunker in Berlin. They both committed suicide the following day.
80	29 Apr 1945	Holocaust: U.S. forces liberated Dachau concentration camp in Germany.
80	29 Apr 1945	World War II: German forces in Italy signed a surrender agreement (effective from 2nd May).
80	29 Apr 1945 to 7 May	World War II – Operation Manna. The British RAF dropped thousands of tons of food into the German-occupied Netherlands to help feed starving civilians. The U.S. Air Force also took part – Operation Chowhound. Both operations proved insufficient and were supplemented by Operation Faust, in which 1,000 tons of food per day were sent by truck from the non-occupied section of the Netherlands.
80	29 Apr 1945	World War II: British and New Zealand forces liberated Venice and Mestre in Italy.
80	29 Apr 1945	Birth of Tammi Terrell, American R&B/soul singer and songwriter. A Motown star of the 1960s, she performed several notable duets with Marvin Gaye, including *Ain't No Mountain High Enough*. She died from a brain tumour in 1970, aged 24.
80	30 Apr 1945	World War II: Stalag Luft I prisoner-of-war camp in Germany was liberated by Soviet forces. 9,000 American, British and Canadian airmen were released.
80	30 Apr 1945	World War II: the Nazi Party's official newspaper *Völkischer Beobachter* (People's Observer) ceased publication. The final issue was printed on this date, but it was not distributed to readers.
80	30 Apr 1945	The first episode of the radio show *Arthur Godfrey Time* was broadcast on CBS in the USA. It ran until 1972.
80	30 Apr 1945	Birth of Michael J. Smith, American astronaut. Pilot of the space shuttle *Challenger* which exploded in 1986.
80	30 Apr 1945	Death of Adolf Hitler, Austrian-born German Nazi Party leader, Chancellor of Germany (1933–45) and dictator (1934–45). (Committed suicide, along with his wife Eva Braun.) He was succeeded as President of Germany by Karl Dönitz.
75	1 Apr 1950	Death of Charles R. Drew, American surgeon and medical researcher. He developed improved methods for storing blood for transfusion, and created the first large-scale blood banks during WWII, which saved the lives of thousands of Allied forces. (Car crash, aged 45.)
75	3 Apr 1950	Death of Kurt Weill, German-born American composer. Best known for his collaborations with the playwright Bertolt Brecht, including *The Threepenny Opera*. (Heart attack, aged 50.)

APRIL 2025

Ann.	Date	Event
75	7 Apr 1950	Cold War: U.S. President Harry S. Truman received a copy of National Security Council Paper Number 68 (NSC 68). The top-secret document formed the basis for the USA's Cold War military policy from 1950 until the early 1990s.
75	7 Apr 1950	Death of Walter Huston, Canadian actor and singer. Best known for the films *Yankee Doodle Dandy* and *The Treasure of the Sierra Madre*. Father of the film director John Huston. Grandfather of the actors Anjelica Huston, Danny Huston and Tony Huston, and the writer Allegra Huston.
75	8 Apr 1950	India and Pakistan signed the Delhi Pact (also called the Liaquat–Nehru Pact). It called for a peaceful resolution to difficulties, and protected the rights of minorities.
75	8 Apr 1950	Death of Vaslav Nijinsky, Russian ballet dancer and choreographer. His career was ended by schizophrenia.
75	9 Apr 1950	Bob Hope's first television special, *The Bob Hope Show*, was broadcast on NBC in the USA. 272 episodes were broadcast between 1950 and 1996.
75	12 Apr 1950	Birth of David Cassidy, American teen idol, actor, singer, songwriter and musician. Best known for his role as Keith Partridge in the TV musical sitcom *The Partridge Family*. (Died 2017.)
75	14 Apr 1950	The first issue of the British children's comic *Eagle* was published. It is best known for the character Dan Dare, Pilot of the Future. It ran until 1959 when it was taken over by its rival *Lion*. It was re-launched in 1982 and ran until 1994.
75	16 Apr 1950	Birth of David Graf, American film and television actor. Best known for his role as Eugene Tackleberry in the *Police Academy* series of films. (Died 2001.)
75	18 Apr 1950	The first international jet plane to reach the USA. An Avro Canada jetliner flew from Toronto to New York City in 58 minutes, carrying three crew, three passengers and 15,000 airmail letters.
75	20 Apr 1950	The newly rebuilt and expanded Memorial Stadium in Baltimore, Maryland, USA opened. Construction work was still in progress, and was not completed until 1954. It closed in 1997 and was demolished in 2001–02. It was the home of the Baltimore Orioles baseball team and the Baltimore Colts football team.
75	24 Apr 1950	Leonard Bernstein's musical adaptation of J. M. Barrie's play *Peter Pan* opened on Broadway. It ran until January 1951 (321 performances).
75	27 Apr 1950	Apartheid in South Africa. The Group Areas Act was passed, formally segregating races and barring people from living, operating businesses or owning land outside the areas designated for their race.
70	1 Apr 1955 to Dec 1959	EOKA rebellion, Cyprus. EOKA, a Greek-Cypriot nationalist paramilitary group launched a campaign of violence against British targets in Cyprus, demanding an end to British rule. (Cyprus gained its independence in August 1960.)
70	3 Apr 1955	Guadalajara train disaster, Mexico. An overnight express train derailed and fell into a canyon. About 300 people were killed.

APRIL 2025

Ann.	Date	Event
70	5 Apr 1955	British Prime Minister Winston Churchill announced his retirement because of his failing health. He was succeeded by Anthony Eden on 7th April.
70	5 Apr 1955	The UK joined the Baghdad Pact, a defensive organisation whose main purpose was to prevent communist incursions and to foster peace in the Middle East. It was renamed the Central Treaty Organisation (CENTO) in 1959 when Iraq withdrew. It was dissolved in 1979.
70	7 Apr 1955	Death of Theda Bara, ('The Vamp'), American stage and silent film actress. One of cinema's first sex symbols.
70	10 Apr 1955	British nightclub hostess Ruth Ellis shot and killed her lover, David Blakely. On 13th July she was hanged at Holloway Prison – the last woman to be executed in the UK.
70	11 Apr 1955	Air India's plane *Kashmir Princess* crashed in the South China Sea after a bomb exploded on board. Sixteen people were killed. It was a failed assassination attempt on the Chinese Prime Minister Zhou Enlai, who missed the flight as he was having an emergency appendectomy. Some commentators say he did not have an appendectomy but delayed his flight by three days because he knew about the plot to kill him.
70	12 Apr 1955	American virologist Jonas Salk's polio vaccine was publicly announced, following extensive testing that proved it was safe and effective.
70	15 Apr 1955	American fast-food pioneer Ray Kroc opened his first McDonald's franchise in Des Plaines, Illinois.
70	15 Apr 1955	Birth of Dodi Fayed, Egyptian businessman and film producer. Son of Harrods department store owner Mohamed Al-Fayed. (Killed in a car crash in Paris in 1997, along with Diana, Princess of Wales.)
70	17 Apr 1955	Birth of Pete Shelley, British pop/punk/new wave singer, songwriter and guitarist (Buzzcocks). (Died 2018.)
70	18 Apr 1955 to 24th	The first Asian-African Conference (also known as the Bandung Conference) was held in Bandung, Indonesia.
70	18 Apr 1955	The first 'Walk/Don't Walk' street crossing signals were installed at intersections in New York City, USA.
70	18 Apr 1955	Death of Albert Einstein, German-born American theoretical physicist. Considered the most influential physicist of the 20th century. Known for developing the special and general theories of relativity. Winner of the 1921 Nobel Prize in Physics for his services to physics and his work on the photoelectric effect.
70	19 Apr 1955	Death of Jim Corbett, British-Indian army officer, hunter, animal tracker and naturalist. He gained a reputation for killing man-eating tigers and leopards in India that were preying on people. He later called for the protection of India's wildlife and wrote books recounting his experiences.
70	25 Apr 1955	Death of Constance Collier, British stage and film actress and voice/acting coach.

APRIL 2025

Ann.	Date	Event
70	30 Apr 1955	The State Bank of India was established when the Imperial Bank of India (the oldest and largest commercial bank in India) was nationalised.
65	1 Apr 1960	The USA launched the world's first weather satellite, *Tiros I*.
65	1 Apr 1960	Dr Martens boots went on sale in the UK.
65	4 Apr 1960	U Nu became Prime Minister of Burma (for the third and final time).
65	4 Apr 1960	The pop song *Cathy's Clown* by The Everly Brothers was released. It became a worldwide hit in May.
65	8 Apr 1960	West Germany agreed to pay the Netherlands 280 million Deutsche Marks (£121 million/$166 million) in compensation for 26 square miles of land that the Netherlands annexed from Germany in 1949 and returned in 1957.
65	8 Apr 1960	Project Ozma, the world's first search for signs of extra-terrestrial intelligence, was launched in the USA. It ran for four months and used the National Radio Astronomy Observatory's Howard Tatel radio telescope. No recognisable signs were detected.
65	13 Apr 1960	The USA launched *Transit 1B*, the first successful satellite in the world's first satellite navigation system. The *Transit* system was mainly used by the U.S. Navy from 1964 to 1996. (*Transit 1A* was launched in September 1959, but failed to reach orbit.)
65	16 Apr 1960	The Student Nonviolent Coordinating Committee was formed. It was one of the major U.S. Civil Rights Movement organisations of the 1960s. It was disbanded in 1976.
65	17 Apr 1960	Death of Eddie Cochran, American rock and roll musician. Known for his hit songs *C'mon Everybody*, *Summertime Blues* and *Three Steps to Heaven*. (Car crash, aged 21.)
65	21 Apr 1960	Brasilia became the capital city of Brazil, replacing Rio do Janeiro.
65	24 Apr 1960	Fars earthquake, Iran. 420 people were killed. Earthquakes are frequent in Iran as major fault lines cover more than ninety percent of the country.
65	25 Apr 1960	Death of Amanullah Khan, Emir of Afghanistan (1919–26), King of Afghanistan (1926–29). In 1929 he abdicated because of the Afghan Civil War and went into exile in Italy.
65	26 Apr 1960	April Revolution: the President of South Korea, Syngman Rhee, was forced to resign after nationwide student-led protests over a rigged election. He was succeeded by Yun Posun on 13th August.
65	27 Apr 1960	French Togoland became independent as the Republic of Togo.
65	28 Apr 1960	Birth of John Cerutti, American baseball pitcher and broadcaster (Toronto Blue Jays). (Died 2004.)
65	28 Apr 1960	Birth of Jón Páll Sigmarsson, Icelandic strongman, powerlifter and bodybuilder. The World's Strongest Man (1984, 1986, 1988, 1990). (Died 1993 – ruptured aorta while lifting weights, aged 32.)
60	1 Apr 1965	Death of Henry ('Harry') Crerar, Canada's leading field commander in WWII.

APRIL 2025

Ann.	Date	Event
60	1 Apr 1965	Death of Helena Rubinstein, Polish-born American businesswoman. Founder of the Helena Rubinstein cosmetics company. One of the richest women in the world.
60	2 Apr 1965	Birth of Rodney King, American victim of police brutality. His videotaped beating by LAPD officers in 1991, and the officers' acquittal, led to the 1992 Los Angeles riot. Two of the officers were found guilty in a subsequent trial in 1993, and Mr King was awarded $3.8 million in damages. (Died 2012 – accidental drowning.)
60	3 Apr 1965	The USA launched *SNAP-10A*, the first nuclear-powered satellite. It stopped working after 43 days when a non-nuclear electrical component failed. It was the only spacecraft with a nuclear-fission reactor that the USA has launched into space, but the Soviet Union launched more than 30.
60	6 Apr 1965	The USA launched *Intelsat I* (also known as Early Bird). It was the first communications satellite to be placed into geosynchronous orbit. It went into service on 28th June and operated for four years, handling television, phone and fax transmissions between North America and Europe. It remains in orbit.
60	9 Apr 1965	The Houston Astrodome (now the NRG Astrodome) opened in Texas, USA. It was originally called the Harris County Domed Stadium.
60	9 Apr 1965	The Beatles' song *Ticket to Ride* was released in UK. (USA: 19th April.)
60	11 Apr 1965 to 12th	Palm Sunday tornado outbreak, American Midwest. 47 tornadoes hit six U.S. states. 271 people were killed and 1,500 injured.
60	12 Apr 1965	The American folk-rock band The Byrds released their first single *Mr. Tambourine Man*. It initiated the folk-rock boom of the mid-1960s.
60	19 Apr 1965	Moore's Law: in an article published in *Electronics Magazine* in the USA, Gordon Moore, the Head of Research and Development at Fairchild Semiconductor, predicted that the number of transistors on an integrated circuit would double every year for the next ten years. His prediction proved correct, and the number continues to double roughly every two years.
60	19 Apr 1965	The first all-news radio station in the USA was launched: WINS 1010 AM in New York City. The station began broadcasting in 1924, and broadcast rock and roll from 1953 until April 1965.
60	21 Apr 1965	Death of Sir Edward Victor Appleton, British physicist and educator. Winner of the 1947 Nobel Prize in Physics for discovering the Appleton layer of the ionosphere, which reflects radio waves and is useful in communication.
60	23 Apr 1965	The Soviet Union launched its first successful communications satellite, *Molniya-1*. It was used for military communications.
60	23 Apr 1965	Death of George Adamski, Polish-born American ufologist and writer. He showed photos that he claimed were of alien spacecraft, claimed to have met aliens, and said they had taken him to the Moon and other planets on their spacecraft. He later wrote three books about his experiences.

APRIL 2025

Ann.	Date	Event
60	24 Apr 1965 to 3 Sep	Dominican Civil War, Santo Domingo, Dominican Republic. CEFA/U.S. victory. On 28th April, U.S. forces occupied the Dominican Republic (Operation Powerpack) to prevent a communist coup. They remained there until July 1966.
60	24 Apr 1965	Death of Louise Dresser, American stage and film actress. Best known for playing the wife of actor Will Rogers in numerous films.
60	27 Apr 1965	Death of Edward R. Murrow, American broadcast journalist. He was highly influential and esteemed, and was considered one of journalism's greatest figures.
50	1 Apr 1975	The President of the Khmer Republic, Lon Nol, fled Cambodia and went into exile in Indonesia, and later in the USA after the Khmer Rouge took over the country and stated that it intended to execute him.
50	3 Apr 1975 to 26th	Vietnam War: Operation Babylift. The USA evacuated more than 3,300 orphaned children from South Vietnam to the USA, Canada, Australia, France and West Germany, where they were adopted. The first mission, on 4th April, crashed shortly after take-off when the locks on the loading bay door failed, causing explosive decompression. 138 people were killed, including 78 children.
50	3 Apr 1975	Soviet chess player Anatoly Karpov became world champion by default after the reigning champion, Bobby Fischer of the USA, resigned after refusing to adhere to FIDE rules and defend his title.
50	3 Apr 1975	Death of Mary Ure, Scottish stage and film actress (*Sons and Lovers*, *Where Eagles Dare*, and more). Her career (and life) were cut short by alcoholism. (Died aged 42.)
50	4 Apr 1975	Microsoft, the computer software/hardware company, was founded by Bill Gates and Paul Allen in Albuquerque, New Mexico, USA.
50	5 Apr 1975	Death of Chiang Kai-shek, Chairman of the Nationalist government in China (1928–41, 1943–48). President of the Republic of China (Taiwan) (1948–49, 1950–75).
50	10 Apr 1975	Death of Marjorie Main, American stage and film actress and singer. Best known for her role as Ma Kettle in the *Ma and Pa Kettle* series of films.
50	12 Apr 1975	Vietnam War – Operation Eagle Pull. The USA admitted defeat in Cambodia and, with the communist Khmer Rouge forces closing in for their final assault, evacuated its remaining personnel from the U.S. Embassy in Phnom Penh.
50	13 Apr 1975 to Oct 1990	The Lebanese Civil War.
50	13 Apr 1975	Death of Larry Parks, American stage and film actor and singer. Best known for playing Al Jolson in *The Jolson Story* and *Jolson Sings Again*.
50	13 Apr 1975	Death of François (N'Garta) Tombalbaye, first President of Chad (1960–75). (Killed in a coup.)
50	17 Apr 1975	The Cambodian Civil War ended after eight years. Khmer Rouge victory.
50	17 Apr 1975	Death of Sarvepalli Radhakrishnan, President of India (1962–67).
50	18 Apr 1975	The disco song *The Hustle* by Van McCoy was released.

APRIL 2025

Ann.	Date	Event
50	19 Apr 1975	India launched its first satellite, *Aryabhata*. (It failed after four days due to a power failure and re-entered the Earth's atmosphere in February 1992.)
50	21 Apr 1975	Vietnam War: the President of South Vietnam, Nguyen Van Thieu, announced his resignation after losing the confidence of his closest allies. He was succeeded by Duong Van Minh, who surrendered to the communist People's Army of Vietnam after two days in office.
50	23 Apr 1975	Vietnam War: U.S. President Gerald Ford gave a televised speech in which he announced that the USA's involvement in the war was over, and all U.S. aid to South Vietnam had ended. The war ended on 30th April when North Vietnamese forces captured the South Vietnamese capital, Saigon.
50	23 Apr 1975 to 1 Nov	Vietnam War: Operation New Life. The USA transported more than 111,000 South Vietnamese refugees to Guam, where they were processed for resettlement. Most of them resettled in the USA, while some chose to live in other countries. About 1,600 asked to return to Vietnam, and they were repatriated on 16th October. On reaching Vietnam, the ship's Vietnamese captain and his crew were imprisoned or sent to re-education camps.
50	23 Apr 1975	Death of William Hartnell, British stage, film and television actor. Best known as the first incarnation of The Doctor in the TV series *Doctor Who*.
50	24 Apr 1975	The Red Army Faction (also known as the Baader–Meinhof Gang) attacked the West German embassy in Stockholm, Sweden, taking eleven (or thirteen) hostages, including the West German Ambassador. Two hostages were killed, and two gang members died when they detonated explosives and set the building on fire.
50	24 Apr 1975	Death of Pete Ham, Welsh rock singer, songwriter and guitarist (Badfinger). (Suicide, aged 27.)
50	25 Apr 1975	The Portuguese Constituent Assembly election was held – the first free election in Portugal for fifty years. The assembly's main role was to produce a new constitution, ahead of a legislative election in April 1976.
50	29 Apr 1975 to 30th	Vietnam War – Operation Frequent Wind. The USA evacuated its civilian personnel and South Vietnamese refugees from Saigon ahead of the takeover of the city by the North Vietnamese (see 30th April below).
50	30 Apr 1975	The Vietnam War ended with the fall of Saigon. South Vietnam surrendered to the North. North Vietnam established the Republic of South Vietnam. Vietnam was reunified as a communist state on 2nd July 1976.
40	6 Apr 1985	The President of Sudan, Jaafar Nimeiry, was ousted in a coup and replaced by field marshal Abdel Rahman Swar al-Dahab.
40	11 Apr 1985	Death of Enver Hoxha, Communist leader/dictator of Albania (1944–85). Succeeded by Ramiz Alia.
40	12 Apr 1985	U.S. Senator Jake Garn from Utah became the first public official to fly into space, aboard the space shuttle *Discovery*.

APRIL 2025

Ann.	Date	Event
40	14 Apr 1985	Death of Noele Gordon, British stage, film and television actress. Best known for her role as Meg Richardson/Mortimer in the TV soap opera *Crossroads*.
40	19 Apr 1985	The far-right American militant organisation The Covenant, The Sword, and the Arm of the Lord was dissolved after law enforcement officials raided their compound in Arkansas for weapons violations and terrorist acts, and arrested their leaders.
40	21 Apr 1985	Brazilian racing driver Ayrton Senna won the Portuguese Grand Prix – the first of his 41 Formula One wins.
40	21 Apr 1985	Death of Rudi Gernreich, Austrian-born American avant-garde fashion designer.
40	21 Apr 1985	Death of Tancredo Neves, President-elect of Brazil. He became seriously ill on the eve of his inauguration and never took office. Vice-President-elect José Sarney became President in his place.
40	22 Apr 1985 to 9 Dec	The Trial of the Juntas, Argentina. Leaders of the military government which ruled Argentina from 1976 to 1983 went on trial for their role in the 'dirty war' in which thousands of people 'disappeared'. Two received life sentences, three received shorter sentences, and four were acquitted. They were all pardoned by President Carlos Menem in 1989–90.
40	23 Apr 1985	The Coca-Cola Company changed the formula of Coca-Cola and launched it onto the market as New Coke. Public response was overwhelmingly negative and the original formula was restored within three months.
40	23 Apr 1985	Death of Samuel (Sam) J. Ervin, American politician. Senator from North Carolina. Chairman of the committee that investigated the Watergate scandal, which led to U.S. President Richard Nixon's resignation.
40	25 Apr 1985	West Germany revised its libel and slander laws, making it illegal to deny the holocaust.
30	2 Apr 1995	The New York City Transit Police was dissolved. It became the Transit Bureau of the New York City Police Department (NYPD).
30	2 Apr 1995	The longest strike in Major League Baseball history ended after 232 days. The strike began in August 1994 after a collective bargaining agreement expired and team owners proposed a salary cap clause in the next agreement. The remainder of the 1994–95 season, the entire postseason, and the World Series were cancelled.
30	4 Apr 1995	Death of Kenny Everett, British radio DJ, comedian and television entertainer (*The Kenny Everett Video Show* and *The Kenny Everett Television Show*). Known for his zany humour, characters and sketches.
30	10 Apr 1995	The UK National DNA Database was launched. It was the world's first national DNA database. It holds DNA samples collected from crime scenes and taken from police suspects. Samples from those who are not charged or convicted are deleted.
30	10 Apr 1995	New York City banned smoking in the indoor dining areas of restaurants with more than 35 seats. The ban was gradually extended and by July 2003 it included all enclosed workplaces in the entire state, including all bars, restaurants and construction sites.

APRIL 2025

Ann.	Date	Event
30	14 Apr 1995	Death of Burl Ives, American stage, film and television actor and folk singer.
30	16 Apr 1995	Canada and Spain ended the 'Turbot War', a long-running dispute over fishing rights in the north-west Atlantic, and agreed to provide for the conservation of fish stocks.
30	16 Apr 1995	Death of Arthur English, British radio, film and television actor and variety comedian. Best known for his roles in the TV comedy series *Are You Being Served?*, *In Sickness and in Health*, and *Till Death Us Do Part*.
30	18 Apr 1995	*The Houston Post* newspaper in Texas, USA ceased publication after 115 years. Its assets were purchased by the *Houston Chronicle*.
30	18 Apr 1995	Death of Arturo Frondizi, President of Argentina (1958–62).
30	19 Apr 1995	Oklahoma City bombing. A truck bomb exploded outside the Alfred P. Murrah Federal Building in Oklahoma City, Oklahoma, USA, killing 168 people and injuring 500. Timothy McVeigh was arrested on 21st April, convicted of the bombing, and executed in June 2001. Terry Nichols and Michael Fortier were convicted as conspirators and received prison sentences.
30	19 Apr 1995	A terrorist group released poisonous phosgene gas on a crowded train at Yokohama railway station, Japan, injuring about 370 people.
30	20 Apr 1995	Death of Robert (Rob) Wyatt, British cricketer. Captain of the England national team (1933–35).
30	22 Apr 1995	Whitewater affair: special prosecutor Kenneth Starr separately interviewed U.S. President Bill Clinton and First Lady Hillary Clinton about their involvement in the Whitewater Development Corporation.
30	25 Apr 1995	Death of Ginger Rogers, American dancer and actress. Known for her on-screen partnership with Fred Astaire.
30	26 Apr 1995	Coors Field baseball stadium opened in Denver, Colorado, USA. It is the home of the Colorado Rockies team.
30	27 Apr 1995	Death of Willem Frederik Hermans, Dutch satirical novelist, short story writer, playwright, poet, essayist and photographer. Regarded as one of the most important post-war Dutch authors.
30	27 Apr 1995	Death of Peter Wright, British MI5 counter-intelligence officer. Author of the controversial memoir/exposé *Spycatcher*, which the British government attempted to ban.
30	28 Apr 1995	Daegu gas explosion, South Korea. Workers constructing a new metro line accidentally drilled into a gas pipeline, causing gas to leak into the metro tunnel and through a sewer. A fire (cause unknown) ignited the gas, causing an explosion. 101 people were killed, including 42 students at Yeongnam Middle School. 202 people were injured.
30	30 Apr 1995	Death of Maung Maung Kha, Prime Minister of Burma (1977–88).
25	1 Apr 2000	Japanese Prime Minister Obuchi Keizo suffered a fatal stroke and fell into a coma from which he never regained consciousness. He died on 14th May. He was succeeded by Mori Yoshiro on 5th April.

APRIL 2025

Ann.	Date	Event
25	1 Apr 2000	A rare Enigma machine, used by the Germans to encrypt messages in WWII, was stolen from Bletchley Park, UK. It was posted to BBC television presenter Jeremy Paxman in October. Antiques dealer Dennis Yates was arrested in November and sentenced to ten months in prison.
25	3 Apr 2000	U.S. federal judge Thomas Penfield Jackson ruled that Microsoft had violated U.S. antitrust laws, had a monopoly in the personal computer market, and kept an 'oppressive thumb' on its competitors. In June, the court ordered Microsoft to be broken up into separate operating system and applications divisions. Microsoft appealed and the break-up order was rescinded. The case was settled in November 2001 when Microsoft agreed to share its application programming interfaces (APIs) with third-party companies for five years.
25	5 Apr 2000	UEFA Cup semi-final violence, Istanbul, Turkey. Two fans of the English football club Leeds United were stabbed to death by four fans of the Turkish team Galatasaray. The Turks were arrested, and Turkish fans were banned from attending the second leg of the semi-final in England.
25	5 Apr 2000	Death of Lee Petty, American NASCAR racing driver.
25	6 Apr 2000	Death of Habib Bourguiba, first President of Tunisia (1957–87).
25	7 Apr 2000	The Senior Citizens Freedom to Work Act of 2000 was signed into law in the USA. It allowed senior citizens to continue working between the ages of 65 and 69 with significantly fewer penalties on their retirement benefit. Previously, heavy penalties (introduced during the Great Depression) discouraged people from working beyond the age of 65.
25	10 Apr 2000	Death of Peter Jones, British actor, playwright and broadcaster. Best known as the narrator and voice of The Book in *The Hitchhiker's Guide to the Galaxy*, and for his lead role in the television series *The Rag Trade*.
25	10 Apr 2000	Death of Larry Linville, American stage, film and television actor. Best known for his role as Major Frank Burns in the TV series M*A*S*H.
25	12 Apr 2000	Queen Elizabeth II awarded the Royal Ulster Constabulary the George Cross in recognition of its collective and sustained bravery during the Troubles in Northern Ireland.
25	13 Apr 2000	The American rock band Metallica filed a lawsuit against Napster, Inc., a file-sharing company that distributed MP3 music files online. The band claimed that Napster was guilty of copyright infringement and racketeering. Napster lost the case and shut down its network in July 2001. It was also ordered to pay $26 million to copyright holders. In early 2002, it attempted to launch a subscription-based model, but it was unable to secure licensing deals with record companies. A takeover by German media firm Bertelsmann was also blocked, and Napster was forced into liquidation in September 2002. Its brand and logo were sold at auction, and the current Napster has no connection with the original company.
25	14 Apr 2000	British gangster Kenneth Noye ('The M25 killer') was sentenced to life in prison after being convicted of killing motorist Stephen Cameron in a road-rage incident near Swanley, Kent in May 1996.

APRIL 2025

Ann.	Date	Event
25	14 Apr 2000	Russia ratified the second Strategic Arms Reduction Treaty (START II) after five years of deadlock. It withdrew from the treaty in June 2002 after the USA withdrew from the Anti-Ballistic Missile Treaty (the ABM Treaty), and START II was never implemented. It was replaced by the Strategic Offensive Reductions Treaty (SORT) which came into effect in 2003 and was superseded by New START in 2011.
25	14 Apr 2000	Death of Phil Katz, American computer programmer. Creator of the ZIP file format for data compression, and PKZIP, one of the most successful shareware programs of all time. (Chronic alcoholism, aged 37.)
25	15 Apr 2000	Giant Sequoia National Monument was established in California, USA.
25	15 Apr 2000	Death of Edward Gorey, American writer, illustrator and designer. Known for his macabre illustrated books.
25	21 Apr 2000	The Children's Online Privacy Protection Act came into effect in the USA. It prohibits U.S.-based companies from collecting personal information from children aged under thirteen without their parents' permission.
25	22 Apr 2000 to 23rd	Sri Lankan Civil War – the Second Battle of Elephant Pass. The Tamil rebels captured the strategically important military base and held it until January 2009, when it was recaptured by the army.
25	22 Apr 2000	The U.S. Border Patrol's SWAT team raided a house in Florida and seized six-year-old Cuban boy Elián González. He had been staying with relatives after his mother drowned while trying to reach the USA from Cuba. His father in Cuba sought custody and there was a heated international custody dispute. The Attorney General ruled that he had to be returned to his father, but his relatives refused to hand him over. Four hours after he was seized in the raid, he was reunited with his father.
25	22 Apr 2000	'The Big Number' change took place on the UK's telephone system. Many area codes were updated or replaced, and new ones created for mobile, freephone, local rate, national rate, and premium rate services.
25	28 Apr 2000	A District Court in New York, USA ruled that the music distribution website MP3.com was guilty of the unauthorised duplication of CDs. The service enabled users to access their music collections online, from the company's servers, provided they could prove they already owned the music on CD. MP3.com was fined over $53 million. This caused the company severe financial hardship, and it was acquired by Vivendi Universal in 2001. The company was shut down in 2003 and its logo and brand name were acquired by CNET. (UMG Recordings, Inc. v. MP3.com, Inc.)
25	28 Apr 2000	Death of Penelope Fitzgerald, British novelist and biographer.
25	29 Apr 2000	Death of Phạm Văn Đồng, Prime Minister of Vietnam (1976–87), Prime Minister of North Vietnam (1955–76).
25	30 Apr 2000	Death of Poul Hartling, Prime Minister of Denmark (1973–75).
20	2 Apr 2005	James Stewart Jr. became the first African American to win a major motorsports event – the supercross motorcycle racing event at Texas Stadium. He was World Supercross Champion in 2006, 2007 and 2009.

APRIL 2025

Ann.	Date	Event
20	2 Apr 2005	Death of Pope John Paul II. Succeeded by Pope Benedict XVI on 19th April.
20	5 Apr 2005	American television news anchorman Peter Jennings, the host of ABC's *World News Tonight*, announced in a taped message that he had lung cancer. This was his final TV appearance. He died on 7th August.
20	5 Apr 2005	Death of Saul Bellow, Canadian-born American novelist. Winner of the 1976 Nobel Prize in Literature.
20	5 Apr 2005	Death of Dale Messick, American comic strip artist. Best known as the creator of *Brenda Starr, Reporter*.
20	6 Apr 2005	Death of Prince Rainier III of Monaco. Husband of Princess Grace (formerly the American actress Grace Kelly). Succeeded by Prince Albert II.
20	7 Apr 2005	Jalal Talabani became President of Iraq (until 2014). He was the first non-Arab president.
20	9 Apr 2005	Charles, Prince of Wales married Camilla Parker Bowles, who gained the title the Duchess of Cornwall.
20	9 Apr 2005	Death of Andrea Dworkin, American feminist and writer. Best known for her criticism of pornography.
20	10 Apr 2005	Death of Iakovos, Primate of the Greek Orthodox Archdiocese of North and South America (1956–96).
20	13 Apr 2005	Eric Rudolph pleaded guilty to carrying out the bomb attack at the 1996 Atlanta Olympics which killed two people and injured 111, as well as three other bombings. In July–August 2005 he was sentenced to life imprisonment without parole, having made a plea bargain to avoid the death penalty.
20	18 Apr 2005	Physicists from the Brookhaven National Laboratory in the USA announced that they had created a new state of hot, dense matter that behaved like an almost-perfect liquid. They said they believed this was the state of matter that existed in the universe in the first few milliseconds after the Big Bang.
20	19 Apr 2005	Death of Niels-Henning Ørsted Pedersen, Danish jazz double bassist and composer.
20	21 Apr 2005	John Negroponte became the first Director of National Intelligence in the USA.
20	22 Apr 2005	Death of Philip Morrison, American physicist and educator. He helped build the atomic bomb that was dropped on the Japanese city of Nagasaki in WWII. He subsequently became an advocate for arms control, and was Professor of Physics Emeritus at MIT.
20	23 Apr 2005	The first video was uploaded to the video-sharing website YouTube. 'Me at the zoo' was uploaded by the site's co-founder Jawed Karim. YouTube was officially launched on 15th December 2005.
20	23 Apr 2005	Death of Sir John Mills, British stage, film and television actor whose career spanned seven decades (*In Which We Serve, Waterloo Road, Great Expectations, Hobson's Choice, Gandhi*, and more).

APRIL 2025

Ann.	Date	Event
20	24 Apr 2005	Birth of Snuppy, the world's first cloned dog, at Seoul National University, South Korea.
20	24 Apr 2005	Death of Ezer Weizman, President of Israel (1993–2000).
20	26 Apr 2005	Following demonstrations and international pressure, Syria withdrew the last of its military forces from Lebanon, ending its 29-year presence there.
20	27 Apr 2005	The world's largest passenger airliner, the Airbus A380, made its first test flight. It went into service in October 2007. In its typical configuration it can carry 525 passengers, with a maximum capacity of 853. Many airports had to upgrade their facilities to accommodate it.
20	28 Apr 2005	The Patent Law Treaty went into effect in ten countries. (UK: 22nd March 2006. Australia: 16th March 2009. Ireland: 27th May 2012. USA: 18th December 2013.)
20	30 Apr 2005	Death of Ron Todd, British trade union leader. General Secretary of the Transport and General Workers Union (TGWU) (1985–1992).
15	3 Apr 2010	Apple released its first iPad tablet computer.
15	10 Apr 2010	Death of Lech Kaczyński, President of Poland (2005–10) Killed in a plane crash in Russia, along with his wife and dozens of senior officials. Succeeded by Bronisław Komorowski.
15	14 Apr 2010	Yushu earthquake, Qinghai, China. 2,698 people were killed and more than 12,000 injured.
15	15 Apr 2010 to 21st	Iceland's Eyjafjallajokull volcano erupted explosively, sending a plume of volcanic ash across north-west Europe. Air travel was disrupted for six days.
15	20 Apr 2010	BP's *Deepwater Horizon* oil platform in the Gulf of Mexico exploded, killing 11 workers. Crude oil began spewing from the well, and continued until it was eventually sealed in September, after several failed attempts. Around 210 million U.S. gallons were spilled in total, causing an environmental disaster. In July 2015, BP was fined $18.7 billion – the largest settlement in U.S. corporate history. It also paid $43.8 billion in criminal and civil penalties, clean-up costs, and compensation.
15	21 Apr 2010	Russia and Ukraine signed the Kharkiv Pact (The Agreement between Ukraine and Russia on the Black Sea Fleet in Ukraine). Russia's lease on naval facilities in Crimea was extended until 2042 in return for Russia providing Ukraine with discounted natural gas. Russia terminated the agreement in March 2014 after it annexed Crimea.
10	2 Apr 2015 to 6th	Hatton Garden Safe Deposit burglary, London. Six elderly burglars entered the underground safe deposit facility via a lift shaft and spent the entire Easter weekend drilling through the walls of the vault. They stole valuables worth around £14 million, of which only £4.3 million was recovered. They were arrested on 19th May, pleaded guilty, and received prison sentences. Hatton Garden Safe Deposit Ltd. went into liquidation in September. The story was adapted into three films and a television series.

APRIL 2025

Ann.	Date	Event
10	10 Apr 2015	Death of Richie Benaud, Australian cricketer and commentator.
10	14 Apr 2015	Death of Percy Sledge, American R&B/soul/gospel singer. Best known for the song *When a Man Loves a Woman*.
10	25 Apr 2015	Gorkha earthquake, Nepal. Nearly 9,000 people were killed, 22,000 injured and 3.5 million were made homeless.
10	30 Apr 2015	Death of Ben E. King, American soul/R&B singer and record producer. Best known for the song *Stand by Me*. He was also a member of The Drifters.

MAY 2025

Ann.	Date	Event
1700	20 May 325 to Aug	The First Council of Nicaea was held in what is now İznik, Turkey. It was the first ecumenical council of the Christian Church.
1300	26 May 725	Death of The Venerable Bede (Saint Bede the Venerable), English Benedictine monk, historian, linguist, translator and teacher. 'The father of English history.' He helped popularise the idea of dating years from the birth of Christ (Anno Domini – A.D.).
900	23 May 1125	Death of Henry V, King of Germany (1099–1125), Holy Roman Emperor (1111–25).
700	12 May 1325	Birth of Rupert II, Elector Palatine of the Rhine (1390–98).
600	29 May 1425	Death of Hongxi Emperor, Emperor of China (1424–25).
500	5 May 1525	Death of Frederick III, Elector of Saxony (1486–1525).
500	14 May 1525 to 15th	German Peasants' War – the Battle of Frankenhausen. Princely victory against the peasants.
300	9 May 1725	Dummer's War – Father Rale's War – the Battle of Pequawket (now Fryeburg in Maine, USA). A group of British colonial scalp hunters fought (and massacred) members of the Abenaki tribe in the last major engagement of the war. British colonial victory.
300	14 May 1725	Birth of Ludovico Manin, the last Doge (leader) of Venice (1789–97).
250	10 May 1775 to 1 Mar 1781	The Second Continental Congress met in Philadelphia, Pennsylvania. It took charge of the war effort against Great Britain (the American Revolutionary War) and declared independence in July 1776. It also began printing its own paper money, known as 'Continental currency', to fund the war effort.
250	10 May 1775	American Revolutionary War – the Capture of Fort Ticonderoga, New York. The Green Mountain Boys militia led by Ethan Allen and Benedict Arnold seized Fort Ticonderoga and Fort Crown Point, and captured the British forces defending them.
250	10 May 1775	Death of Caroline Matilda of Great Britain. Queen consort of Denmark and Norway (1766–72). Wife of King Christian VII. Youngest daughter of Frederick, Prince of Wales (born after his death).
250	20 May 1775	American Revolutionary War: representatives from North Carolina reportedly signed the Mecklenburg Declaration of Independence, declaring the colony's independence from Great Britain. The authenticity of the document is disputed, and the text was not published until 1819.
200	4 May 1825	Birth of Thomas Huxley, British naturalist, biologist and anthropologist. Noted for his public support and advocacy for Charles Darwin's theory of evolution, which gained him the nickname 'Darwin's Bulldog'.
200	7 May 1825	Death of Antonio Salieri, Italian composer, conductor and educator. He helped develop opera, and taught composers including Liszt, Schubert, Beethoven, and Mozart. He was rumoured to have poisoned his 'bitter rival' Mozart, but this was later proven to be false.
200	20 May 1825	Birth of Antoinette Brown Blackwell, the first woman in the USA to be ordained as a mainstream Protestant minister.

MAY 2025

Ann.	Date	Event
200	26 May 1825	The American Unitarian Association was founded. In 1961 it merged with the Universalist Church of America and became the Unitarian Universalist Association.
200	29 May 1825	The coronation of King Charles X of France.
175	4 May 1850	The Second Great Fire of San Francisco, California, USA. Three blocks in the city centre were destroyed. It was thought to be an arson attack and several people were arrested, but no trial took place. (The First Great Fire occurred in December 1849, and there were further major fires on 14th June and 17th September and 14th December that year, and others in 1851. The city's hospital was destroyed by fire on 31st October 1850 – also thought to be an arson attack.)
175	12 May 1850	Birth of Henry Cabot Lodge, American politician and historian. Senator from Massachusetts (1893–1924). Senate Majority Leader (1918–24).
175	15 May 1850	The Bloody Island Massacre, Clear Lake, California, USA. Two American settlers who had enslaved a number of Pomo Indians were murdered by their captives. The U.S. Cavalry killed at least sixty Pomo in revenge.
175	21 May 1850	Birth of Giuseppe Mercalli, Italian priest and volcanologist. Best known for devising the Mercalli intensity scale, which measures the intensity of earthquakes. (He died in suspicious circumstances in 1914 at the age of 63.)
150	1 May 1875	Alexandra Palace in London, England officially opened. It originally opened in 1873 but burnt down two weeks later. It became the home of BBC Television in 1935, and the world's first high-definition (405-line) broadcasts were made from there in 1936.
150	6 May 1875	Birth of William Leahy, American fleet admiral. The most senior U.S. military officer who served in WWII. Chief of Staff to the Commander in Chief (1942–49). Chief of Naval Operations (1937–39), Governor of Puerto Rico (1939–40), U.S. Ambassador to France (1941–42).
150	17 May 1875	The first Kentucky Derby horse race was held, at Churchill Downs in Louisville, Kentucky, USA.
150	17 May 1875	Death of John C. Breckinridge, Vice President of the United States (1857–61), Confederate States Secretary of War (1865).
150	18 May 1875	Cúcuta earthquake, Venezuela and Colombia. The catastrophic earthquake destroyed towns and cities and killed an estimated 10,000 people. (Casualty figures vary.)
150	20 May 1875	The International Bureau of Weights and Measures was formed in Paris, France.
125	1 May 1900	The Scofield Mine disaster, Utah, USA. At least 200 miners were killed in an explosion, or by asphyxiation. It was one of the worst mining accidents in U.S. history. (Cause: kegs of black powder detonated and ignited coal dust, killing many miners instantly. Others who tried to escape took the most direct route and walked into a cloud of poisonous gas, as they were unaware of where the explosion had originated.)

MAY 2025

Ann.	Date	Event
125	5 May 1900	*Billboard* magazine (founded in 1894 as the monthly *Billboard Advertising*) was relaunched as a weekly publication focused on entertainment news.
125	11 May 1900 to 26th	Thousand Days War – the Battle of Palonegro, Colombia. Conservative victory.
125	14 May 1900 to 28 Oct	The 1900 Summer Olympics were held in Paris, France.
125	17 May 1900	Second Boer War: the 217-day Siege of Mafeking was relieved by 2,000 British forces and South African volunteers led by Colonel B. T. Mahon. Colonel Robert Baden-Powell led the forces who successfully defended Mafeking throughout the siege. He became a national hero and later founded the Scouting movement.
125	17 May 1900	The children's novel *The Wonderful Wizard of Oz* by L. Frank Baum was published. It was adapted into the musical fantasy film, *The Wizard of Oz*.
125	17 May 1900	Birth of Ruhollah Khomeini, commonly known as Ayatollah Khomeini, 1st Supreme Leader of Iran (1979–89). Founder of the Islamic Republic of Iran. Leader of the 1979 Iranian Revolution in which the last Shah of Iran was overthrown.
125	18 May 1900	Tonga became a British protectorate. It gained its independence in 1970.
125	23 May 1900	William Harvey Carney, a former slave, became the first African American to be awarded the Medal of Honor. He received it for his heroism in saving the American flag in the Battle of Fort Wagner during the American Civil War in 1863.
125	28 May 1900	Second Boer War: Britain occupied the Orange Free State. It annexed it on 6th October and established it as the Orange River Colony in May 1902. It was disestablished in 1910 and incorporated into South Africa.
125	31 May 1900	Second Boer War: British forces captured and occupied Johannesburg.
100	1 May 1925	Cyprus became a British Crown Colony.
100	1 May 1925	The All-China Federation of Trade Unions was founded. It is the world's largest trade union, with more than 300 million members.
100	1 May 1925	Birth of Scott Carpenter, American astronaut, naval aviator and aquanaut. One of the original Mercury Seven astronauts. The second American to orbit the Earth. The fourth American in space. (Died 2013.)
100	5 May 1925	Scopes Trial: American science teacher John Scopes was arrested and charged with teaching the theory of evolution at a high school in Dayton, Tennessee, in violation of the Butler Act. (See also: 10th July 1925.)
100	5 May 1925	Men aged 25 and over were granted the right to vote in Japan.
100	5 May 1925	Afrikaans became an official language of South Africa, alongside English and Dutch.
100	7 May 1925	Death of William Lever, 1st Viscount Leverhulme, British businessman, politician and philanthropist. He co-founded Lever Brothers (with his brother James), which was one of the first commercial manufacturers of soap from vegetable oil. (It is now part of Unilever).

MAY 2025

Ann.	Date	Event
100	12 May 1925	Paul von Hindenburg took office as President of Germany (until 1934 when he was succeeded by Adolf Hitler).
100	12 May 1925	Birth of Yogi Berra, American baseball player, manager and coach. (Died 2015.)
100	13 May 1925	The Gold Standard Act was passed. Britain returned to the gold standard, which had been suspended since the outbreak of WWI. (Britain abandoned the gold standard permanently in 1931.)
100	14 May 1925	The novel *Mrs Dalloway* by British writer Virginia Woolf was published.
100	14 May 1925	Death of Sir H(enry) Rider Haggard, British novelist. Known for his adventure stories set mainly in Africa. Best known for *King Solomon's Mines*.
100	19 May 1925	Birth of Pol Pot, Cambodian communist revolutionary and brutal dictator. Leader of the Khmer Rouge. Responsible for the deaths of up to three million people. (Died 1998.)
100	19 May 1925	Birth of Malcolm X, controversial African American Muslim leader and human rights activist. (Assassinated in 1965.)
100	20 May 1925	Birth of Alexei Tupolev, Russian aircraft designer. Best known for leading the development of the Tupolev Tu-144, the first supersonic passenger jet (which closely resembled the Anglo–French Concorde), and for helping to design the Buran space shuttle (which closely resembled the U.S. space shuttle). (Died 2001.)
100	20 May 1925	Death of Joseph Howard, first Prime Minister of Malta (1921–23).
100	21 May 1925	Prohibition: the sale of beer was legalised in Canada.
100	24 May 1925	Birth of Mai Zetterling, Swedish actress and film director. (Died 1994.)
100	25 May 1925	The National Forensics League was founded in the USA. It encourages high school students to participate in public speaking, debate, and interpretation.
100	30 May 1925	May Thirtieth Incident, Shanghai, China. Police opened fire on demonstrators who were protesting against Japanese-run industries, and killed several of them. This led to the founding of the May Thirtieth Movement – a major trade union and anti-imperialist organisation.
90	2 May 1935	Birth of Faisal II, the last King of Iraq (1939–58). (Killed in a coup in 1958.)
90	6 May 1935	New Deal: the Works Progress Administration was established in the USA. It employed millions of unemployed workers on public works projects during the Great Depression. It operated until 1943.
90	8 May 1935	Birth of Jack Charlton, British football player (Leeds United, England) and manager. A member of the England national team that won the World Cup in 1966. (Died 2020.)
90	9 May 1935	Birth of Roger Hargreaves, British children's writer and illustrator who created the *Mr Men* and *Little Miss* series. (Died 1988.)

MAY 2025

Ann.	Date	Event
90	11 May 1935	Birth of Doug McClure, American film and television actor (*The Virginian, At the Earth's Core, The Land That Time Forgot*, and more). (Died 1995.)
90	15 May 1935	The first section of the Moscow Metro opened to the public. It was the first underground railway system in the Soviet Union.
90	17 May 1935	Birth of Dennis Potter, British television dramatist and screenwriter (*The Singing Detective, Brimstone and Treacle, Lipstick on Your Collar, Gorky Park*, and more). (Died 1994.)
90	17 May 1935	Death of Paul Dukas, French composer. Best known for *The Sorcerer's Apprentice*.
90	19 May 1935	Death of T. E. Lawrence, ('Lawrence of Arabia'), British Army officer, military strategist, archaeologist and writer. Best known for his activities in the Middle East during WWI and for his autobiographical account *The Seven Pillars of Wisdom*. (Fatally injured in a motorcycle accident, aged 46.)
90	21 May 1935	Death of Jane Addams, American social worker, reformer and women's rights campaigner. The first American woman to win the Nobel Peace Prize (1931).
90	21 May 1935	Death of Hugo de Vries, Dutch botanist and geneticist who suggested the concept of genes, rediscovered the laws of heredity, and developed the mutation theory of evolution.
90	24 May 1935	The first night game in Major League Baseball in the USA was played, at Crosley Field in Cincinnati, Ohio.
90	25 May 1935	American athlete Jesse Owens set three world records (long jump, 220-yard sprint and 220-yard hurdles) and equalled the record for the 100-yard dash (all in just 45 minutes) at the Big Ten meet in Ann Arbor, Michigan.
90	25 May 1935	Death of Sir Frank Watson Dyson, British Astronomer Royal (1910–33) He introduced the Greenwich time signal ('pips') and helped prove Einstein's theory of general relativity during observations of a solar eclipse.
90	30 May 1935	American baseball legend Babe Ruth played his final game.
90	31 May 1935	Balochistan earthquake, British India. The city of Quetta (now in Pakistan) was destroyed and between 40,000 and 60,000 people were killed. It was the deadliest earthquake in Southern Asia until the Kashmir earthquake in 2005.
90	31 May 1935	Holocaust: Jews were banned from serving in the German armed forces.
80	1 May 1945	German radio announced the death of Adolf Hitler. It reported that he had died a hero's death fighting to his last breath. The true nature of his death (suicide) emerged on 20th June.
80	1 May 1945 to 21 Jun	World War II – the Battle of Tarakan. The first stage of the Borneo Campaign. The Allies captured the airfield, which was their main aim, but it was heavily damaged during the battle and was unusable for later phases of the campaign.
80	1 May 1945	World War II: Trieste in Italy was liberated by Yugoslav partisans.

MAY 2025

Ann.	Date	Event
80	1 May 1945 to 8th	World War II – Operation Chowhound. The U.S. Air Force dropped thousands of tons of food into German-occupied Netherlands to help feed starving civilians. (See also: 29th April 1945.)
80	1 May 1945	Death of Joseph Goebbels, German politician. Nazi Minister of Propaganda (1933–45). He was deeply anti-Semitic and was responsible for presenting a positive image of the Nazi regime to the German people. He served as Chancellor of Germany for one day following Hitler's death, then he and his wife, Magda, killed their children and committed suicide by taking cyanide.
80	2 May 1945	World War II: the Battle of Berlin, Germany ended. Allied victory which led to the surrender of all German forces outside Berlin by 9th May, and the end of the war in Europe. Soviet forces took control of the Reichstag (parliament building) and raised the Soviet flag.
80	2 May 1945	World War II: German forces in Italy surrendered unconditionally and laid down their arms.
80	2 May 1945	Holocaust: U.S. forces liberated Wöbbelin concentration camp in Germany.
80	2 May 1945	World War II: Allied forces captured Rangoon, Burma from the Japanese.
80	2 May 1945	Death of Martin Bormann, German Nazi official. Hitler's private secretary. He was rumoured to have fled to South America after WWII, and there were several unconfirmed sightings. But his remains were found in Berlin in 1972, and positively identified by DNA testing in 1998.
80	3 May 1945	World War II: three German ships (*Cap Arcona*, *Thielbek* and *Deutschland*) were sunk by the British RAF who believed they were carrying SS personnel to Norway. In fact, they were prison ships transporting thousands of inmates from Neuengamme concentration camp (It is believed that the Germans may have been planning to scuttle the ships with the inmates still on board.) The British Army liberated Neuengamme concentration camp on 4th May.
80	4 May 1945	World War II: all German forces in north-west Germany, the Netherlands, Denmark and Norway surrendered, effective from 5th May.
80	5 May 1945	World War II: the Battle of Castle Itter, Austria. Allied victory. In the strangest battle of WWII, Americans and Germans (as well as some recently freed French prisoners) fought on the same side to successfully defend the castle against attacking Nazi forces.
80	5 May 1945 to 6th	Holocaust: the U.S. Army liberated Mauthausen–Gusen concentration camp in Germany.
80	5 May 1945 to 8th	World War II: the Prague Uprising, Czechoslovakia. The Czech resistance attempted to liberate Prague from the Nazis. The uprising ended in a ceasefire and the liberation of Prague when WWII ended on 8th May.
80	5 May 1945	World War II: a Japanese balloon bomb exploded in eastern Oregon, USA, killing six people – the only WWII casualties in the contiguous U.S. states.

MAY 2025

Ann.	Date	Event
80	6 May 1945 to 11th	World War II – the Prague Offensive (Czechoslovakia). Allied victory. This was the last major battle on the Eastern Front and the last major Soviet operation of the war.
80	6 May 1945	World War II: Nazi German military leader Hermann Göring was captured by the U.S. Army. During the Nuremberg Trials he was convicted of war crimes and sentenced to death, but he committed suicide on 15th October 1946 – the night before he was due to be executed.
80	6 May 1945	World War II: 'Axis Sally' (Mildred Gillars) made her last German propaganda radio broadcast to U.S. troops stationed in Europe. She was arrested in March 1946 and convicted of treason in March 1949. She was fined $10,000 and served twelve years in prison.
80	7 May 1945	World War II: Germany signed the official unconditional surrender document in Reims, France (and again the following day in Berlin, Germany – see 8th May below), ending the war in Europe. The document stated that all hostilities would cease as of 12:01 am on 9th May.
80	7 May 1945 to 8th	Halifax VE-Day riots, Nova Scotia, Canada. A celebration of the end of WWII in Europe turned into a riot when thousands of servicemen, seamen and civilians rampaged through the city and looted it.
80	8 May 1945	World War II: VE day (Victory in Europe) – celebrated as a public holiday.
80	8 May 1945	World War II: Soviet leader Joseph Stalin refused to recognise Germany's surrender document signed in Reims, France the previous day, so a second surrender ceremony was held in Berlin, Germany.
80	8 May 1945	Setif massacre, Algeria. French police opened fire on demonstrators, leading to riots and reprisal attacks in which approximately 6,000 people were killed. (Casualty estimates range from 1,020 to 45,000.)
80	9 May 1945	World War II: the Channel Islands of Jersey and Guernsey were liberated by British forces. (German forces on Alderney surrendered on 16th May.)
80	9 May 1945	World War II: Vidkun Quisling, Minister President of Norway, was arrested after handing himself in to police. In September he was convicted of embezzlement, murder and treason. He was executed on 24th October.
80	11 May 1945	World War II: the U.S. aircraft carrier *USS Bunker Hill* was badly damaged by Japanese kamikazes off the coast of Okinawa. 346 servicemen were killed, 43 were declared missing, and 264 were wounded. The ship resumed active service in September after repairs.
80	12 May 1945	Birth of Alan Ball, British football player and manager. The youngest member of England's World Cup-winning team in 1966. (Died 2007.)
80	14 May 1945 to 15th	World War II – the Battle of Poljana, Yugoslavia (now in Slovenia). Anglo–Partisan victory. Considered to be the final battle of WWII in Europe.
80	14 May 1945	Death of Heber J. Grant, President of The Church of Jesus Christ of Latter-day Saints (1918–45).
80	17 May 1945	Death of Sokei-an, Japanese Buddhist monk. Founder of the Buddhist Society of America (now the First Zen Institute of America).

MAY 2025

Ann.	Date	Event
80	23 May 1945	British Prime Minister Winston Churchill resigned and formed a National Government, which ran the country until the general election on 5th July. The election was won by Clement Attlee's Labour Party.
80	23 May 1945	World War II: German President Karl Dönitz was arrested by British forces, and the German government was dissolved. Following the Nuremberg Trials, he was imprisoned for ten years.
80	23 May 1945	Death of Heinrich Himmler, German Nazi officer. Head of the SS. (Committed suicide while in British custody following WWII.)
80	24 May 1945 and 26th	World War II: the USA dropped incendiary bombs on urban and industrial areas of Tokyo, Japan, south of the Imperial Palace. A second massive firebomb raid on 26th May targeted the same area.
80	25 May 1945	British science fiction writer Arthur C. Clark privately circulated a document in which he proposed using geostationary satellites as telecommunications relays. (His idea was first made public in the October 1945 issue of *Wireless World* magazine. The first commercial geostationary communications satellite, *Intelsat I*, was launched in April 1965.)
80	28 May 1945	World War II: American-born Nazi propaganda broadcaster William Joyce ('Lord Haw-Haw') was captured near the Danish border and taken to Britain to face trial, as he had a British passport. He was convicted of treason against the British Crown, and was sentenced to death on 19th September. He was hanged on 3rd January 1946, and was the last person to be executed for treason in Britain.
75	1 May 1950	Gwendolyn Brooks became the first African American to win a Pulitzer Prize for poetry.
75	3 May 1950	The British aircraft carrier *HMS Ark Royal* was launched. It was the fourth ship to bear the name. It was in service from 1955 until 1979. A fifth *Ark Royal* was launched in 1981 and decommissioned in 2011.
75	5 May 1950	The Coronation of King Rama IX of Thailand.
75	6 May 1950	British-American actress Elizabeth Taylor married her first husband, Conrad 'Nicky' Hilton Jr., heir to the Hilton Hotels chain. They divorced after eight months. Taylor was married eight times.
75	9 May 1950	French Foreign Minister Robert Schuman presented his proposal for the creation of an organised Europe. The Schuman Declaration is now celebrated annually in the European Union as 'Europe Day'.
75	9 May 1950	American writer and Scientology founder L. Ron Hubbard published his book *Dianetics: The Modern Science of Mental Health*.
75	10 May 1950	One of the first British computers, the Pilot ACE, ran its first program, at the National Physical Laboratory. The ACE (Automatic Computing Engine) was designed by Alan Turing.
75	12 May 1950	The American Bowling Congress (ABC) ended its white-males-only rule and allowed African American males to join (with effect from 1st August). Women were not allowed to join until 1993. They had their own Women's International Bowling Congress, which merged with the ABC in 2005.

MAY 2025

Ann.	Date	Event
75	13 May 1950	The first Formula One World Championship race was held, at Silverstone, England. (This race is also known as the 1950 British Grand Prix.)
75	19 May 1950	South Amboy munitions explosion, New Jersey, USA. Dockworkers were transferring ammunition from a freight train onto barges when the train exploded. 36 people were killed and more than 350 injured. Hundreds of buildings were damaged.
75	21 May 1950	The BBC's Lime Grove studios in London opened. The complex was originally built as a Gaumont film studio in 1915. The BBC used it until 1991. It was demolished in 1993.
75	22 May 1950	American chemist Harry Gold was arrested by the FBI and confessed to being a courier who had passed nuclear secrets to the Soviet Union on behalf of several espionage rings. His interrogation and testimony led to the arrest and conviction of spies including Klaus Fuchs, David Greenglass, and Julius and Ethel Rosenberg. He was sentenced to thirty years in prison.
75	23 May 1950	Birth of Martin McGuinness, Irish republican politician. A prominent member of Sinn Féin, and a former leader in the IRA. Deputy First Minister of Northern Ireland (2007–17 – died in office).
75	25 May 1950	The Brooklyn–Battery Tunnel opened in New York City, USA. It is officially called the Hugh L. Carey Tunnel and is commonly known as the Battery Tunnel.
75	26 May 1950	Fuel rationing ended in the UK, five years after the end of WWII.
75	27 May 1950	Celâl Bayar became President of Turkey. He was ousted in a coup in 1960.
75	29 May 1950	The Royal Canadian Mounted Police schooner *St. Roch* arrived in Halifax, Nova Scotia, becoming the first ship to completely circumnavigate North America. (It completed the route in several separate voyages.)
75	29 May 1950	The first (pilot) episode of the British radio soap opera *The Archers* was broadcast on the BBC Home Service (Midlands region only). It was broadcast nationally from 1st January 1951 and is still running.
70	4 May 1955	Death of Louis-Charles Bréguet, French aircraft builder and designer whose planes set several world records. Founder of Air France.
70	4 May 1955	Death of George Enescu, Romanian violist, composer and teacher.
70	5 May 1955	West Germany was granted the full authority of a sovereign state – although it didn't become fully sovereign until March 1991.
70	9 May 1955	West Germany joined NATO.
70	9 May 1955	The first television appearance of Jim Henson and the Muppets, in the series *Sam and Friends*, broadcast in the Washington D.C. area of the USA.
70	9 May 1955	Birth of Kevin Peter Hall, American film and television actor. Noted for his height (7' 2") which often led to him playing monsters. Best known for his roles in the films *Predator* and *Predator 2* and the TV series *Harry and the Hendersons*. (Died 1991.)
70	9 May 1955	Death of Kate Booth, British Salvation Army officer. Eldest daughter of Salvation Army founders William and Catherine Booth. She spread the Salvation Army to Europe, North America and Australia.

MAY 2025

Ann.	Date	Event
70	10 May 1955	Death of Tommy Burns, Canadian world heavyweight boxing champion.
70	11 May 1955	Giovanni Gronchi became President of Italy (until 1962).
70	14 May 1955	The Warsaw Pact was established. It was a Soviet-led mutual defence treaty between eight communist European states during the Cold War. It was disestablished in December 1991.
70	15 May 1955	The Austrian State Treaty was signed. It re-established Austria as an independent sovereign state. (Effective from 27th July.)
70	15 May 1955	The first successful ascent of Makalu, the world's fifth-highest mountain, by French climbers Lionel Terray and Jean Couzy.
70	18 May 1955	Partition of Vietnam: Operation Passage to Freedom ended and the border between North Vietnam and South Vietnam was sealed. The USA and France transported up to one million civilians and soldiers from North Vietnam to South Vietnam during the 300-day operation.
70	18 May 1955	The Hindu Marriage Act (1955) was passed in India. It included provision for Hindu divorce for the first time.
70	18 May 1955	Death of Mary McLeod Bethune, American educator, civil rights activist and presidential advisor to Franklin D. Roosevelt. Founder of Bethune-Cookman University in Daytona Beach, Florida.
70	22 May 1955	The oldest person to drive in a Formula One Grand Prix race: Louis Chiron (aged 55) from Monaco drove in the 1955 Monaco Grand Prix. He finished sixth.
70	25 May 1955 to 26th	Great Plains tornado outbreak, USA. At least 46 tornadoes struck seven states. The city of Udall in Kansas was particularly affected, with every building in the city damaged or destroyed. 80 people were killed and 273 injured. It was the worst tornado in Kansas's history.
70	25 May 1955	The first successful ascent of Kangchenjunga, the world's third-highest mountain, by British climbers Joe Brown and George Band.
70	25 May 1955	Birth of John McGeoch, Scottish post-punk/new wave guitarist (Siouxsie and the Banshees, Visage, Magazine, Public Image Ltd.) (Died 2004.)
70	26 May 1955	British General Election. The Conservative Party increased its majority and party leader Anthony Eden remained Prime Minister after taking over from Winston Churchill in April. The BBC covered the election results extensively, making it the biggest broadcast in its history at that time. It also used a computer to analyse the results and predict the winner for the first time.
70	26 May 1955	Death of Alberto Ascari, Italian racing driver. Formula One world champion in 1952 and 1953. Killed in a crash while testing at Monza.
70	31 May 1955	The U.S. Supreme Court ordered the desegregation of schools 'with all deliberate speed'.
65	1 May 1960	Bombay State in India was split into two separate states: Gujarat and Maharashtra.

MAY 2025

Ann.	Date	Event
65	1 May 1960	The Soviet Union shot down an American U-2 spy plane near the Russian city of Sverdlovsk (now Yekaterinburg) and captured pilot Gary Powers, sparking a diplomatic crisis. In August, he was sentenced to ten years in prison. He was released in 1962 in exchange for a Soviet spy.
65	3 May 1960	The European Free Trade Association was established.
65	3 May 1960	The Off-Broadway musical comedy *The Fantasticks* opened in New York City, USA. It became the longest-running musical of all time, with 17,162 performances in nearly 42 years.
65	3 May 1960	The Anne Frank House opened in Amsterdam, Netherlands. It is now a museum which preserves the building where Jewish diarist Anne Frank and her family hid from the Nazis during WWII.
65	6 May 1960	The Civil Rights Act of 1960 came into effect in the USA. It was designed to eliminate discrimination in voting rights, and made it an offence to obstruct someone from registering to vote. It was considered ineffective, and failed to legislate for those of different nationalities. It was succeeded by the more effective Civil Rights Act of 1964 and the Voting Rights Act of 1965.
65	6 May 1960	Britain's Princess Margaret married photographer Anthony Armstrong Jones at Westminster Abbey in London. It was the first royal wedding to be televised. (They divorced in 1978.)
65	7 May 1960	Leonid Brezhnev became Leader of the Soviet Union (until 1982).
65	9 May 1960	The U.S. Food and Drug Administration (FDA) approved the first birth-control pill.
65	10 May 1960	The American nuclear-powered submarine *USS Triton* completed the first submerged circumnavigation of the Earth. It had departed on 15th February.
65	11 May 1960	Death of John D. Rockefeller Jr., American businessman and philanthropist. Heir to the Rockefeller oil fortune. He built the Rockefeller Center in New York City.
65	13 May 1960	The first successful ascent of Dhaulagiri, the world's seventh-highest mountain, by a Swiss/Austrian/Nepali expedition led by Max Eiselin.
65	14 May 1960	The Soviet Union launched *Sputnik 4*. The unmanned self-sustaining capsule carried a life-sized human dummy and tested life-support systems, flight stresses, telemetry systems and communication systems ahead of the human space flights that followed.
65	16 May 1960	The first working laser was demonstrated by Theodore Maiman at Hughes Research Laboratories in Malibu, California, USA.
65	17 May 1960	The Kariba Dam, on the Zambia–Zimbabwe border, was officially opened. The hydroelectric dam supplies power to both countries.
65	21 May 1960	Birth of Jeffrey Dahmer, American serial killer. (Beaten to death in prison in 1994.)
65	22 May 1960	The Great Chilean Earthquake (also called the Valdivia earthquake). The most powerful earthquake ever recorded. 2,000 – 6,000 people were killed.

MAY 2025

Ann.	Date	Event
65	23 May 1960	Israel announced that it had captured former Nazi officer Adolf Eichmann in Argentina. He was responsible for organizing the mass extermination of Jews in WWII. Following a trial, he was sentenced to death, and executed on 1st June 1962.
65	23 May 1960	Death of Georges Claude, French engineer and inventor. Best known for inventing neon lighting. He also worked on generating energy from seawater, and the liquefaction of air. Some people call him 'the Edison of France'. During WWII he collaborated with the German occupiers, for which he was later imprisoned and stripped of all his honours.
65	27 May 1960	The President of Turkey, Celâl Bayar, was ousted in a military coup, along with the rest of his democratic government. He was succeeded by the Commander of the Turkish Army, Cemal Gürsel.
65	30 May 1960	Death of Boris Pasternak, Russian writer and poet. Best known for his novel *Doctor Zhivago*. He was awarded the 1958 Nobel Prize in Literature, but refused it because of opposition from the Soviet Union.
65	31 May 1960	Death of Walther Funk, German economist and Nazi politician. Reich Minister for Economic Affairs (1938–45), President of the Reichsbank (1939–45). He was closely involved in the seizure of property from Jews during WWII. He was convicted of war crimes and crimes against humanity by the Nuremberg Tribunal and sentenced to life in prison.
60	1 May 1965	Chinese Civil War – the Battle of Dong-Yin (a naval conflict). Both sides claimed victory.
60	1 May 1965	Death of Spike Jones, American musician and bandleader (Spike Jones and His City Slickers). Known for his satirical/novelty arrangements of popular songs.
60	3 May 1965	Vietnam War: the first major U.S. Army ground combat unit arrived in South Vietnam – the 173rd Airborne Brigade.
60	9 May 1965	The Soviet Union launched *Luna 5*. It was intended to be the first spacecraft to achieve a soft landing on the Moon, but due to a guidance system failure and engine failure it crashed into the lunar surface on 12th May.
60	9 May 1965	Death of Leopold Figl, Chancellor of Austria (1945–53).
60	11 May 1965	Bengal Cyclone I, India. A second cyclone hit the same region on 1st June. The two cyclones killed a total of about 47,000 people.
60	12 May 1965	West Germany and Israel established diplomatic relations. Most Arab nations immediately broke off relations with West Germany as a result.
60	14 May 1965	Death of Frances Perkins, U.S. Secretary of Labor (1933–45). The first woman appointed to a U.S. Cabinet post.
60	15 May 1965	The Canadian Football League Players' Association was established.
60	16 May 1965	SpaghettiOs first went on sale in the USA.
60	18 May 1965	Dolby Laboratories was founded in London, England. The company specialises in audio noise reduction and audio encoding/compression.

MAY 2025

Ann.	Date	Event
60	19 May 1965	Death of Maria Dąbrowska, Polish novelist, essayist, journalist, playwright and critic. One of the major Polish writers of the 20th century. Best known for her four-volume novel *Nights and Days*.
60	20 May 1965	The British government announced that police would be armed with tear gas guns and grenades for use against armed or dangerous individuals. Tear gas was used in the Northern Ireland Troubles of the 1970s, and CS gas was used against rioters on the British mainland in 1981, but it has rarely been used since then.
60	21 May 1965	Death of Sir Geoffrey de Havilland, British aircraft designer and engineer.
60	22 May 1965	Death of Christopher Stone, the first radio DJ in the UK (1927).
60	28 May 1965	Dhanbad coal mine disaster, India. A methane gas explosion and fire at the Dhori colliery killed 268 miners.
50	4 May 1975	Death of Moe Howard, American actor and comedian (The Three Stooges).
50	6 May 1975	Death of József Mindszenty, Hungarian cardinal. Prince Primate and Archbishop of Esztergom. Leader of the Catholic Church in Hungary (1945–73).
50	7 May 1975	U.S. President Gerald Ford announced that the Vietnam Era had ended.
50	10 May 1975	Sony launched the Betamax video cassette recorder in Japan. (USA: November.) It lost the videotape format war to its rival, VHS, though Betamax recorders remained on sale until 2002.
50	12 May 1975	Birth of Jonah Lomu, New Zealand rugby player. (Died 2015.)
50	13 May 1975	Death of Bob Wills, ('King of Western Swing'), American musician, songwriter and bandleader. Co-founder of Western swing music.
50	15 May 1975	American obstetrics nurse Norma Armistead killed Kathryn Viramontes and cut her unborn baby from her womb. The following day she checked into Kaiser Hospital in Los Angeles, California, claiming that the baby was hers and she had given birth at home. When doctors examined her, they found she had not been pregnant. When the murdered women's body was found, Armistead was arrested, convicted, and sentenced to life in prison.
50	16 May 1975	Sikkim became a state of India following a referendum, and its monarchy was abolished.
50	16 May 1975	Junko Tabei of Japan became the first woman to reach the summit of Mount Everest.
50	20 May 1975	Death of Dame Barbara Hepworth, British modernist sculptor.
50	21 May 1975	The Stammheim Trial began in Stuttgart, Germany. Four members of the Red Army Faction (also known as the Baader–Meinhof Gang) were charged with murder and forming a terrorist organisation. One defendant committed suicide in prison during the trial. The other three were found guilty and sentenced to life imprisonment.
50	22 May 1975	Death of Lefty Grove, American baseball player (Philadelphia Athletics, Boston Red Sox). Regarded as one of the greatest pitchers in history.
50	23 May 1975	The soft rock song *I'm Not in Love* by 10cc was released.

MAY 2025

Ann.	Date	Event
50	26 May 1975	American stuntman Evel Knievel attempted to jump over thirteen buses on a motorcycle at Wembley Station in London, England. He crashed, broke his pelvis, and announced his retirement. He changed his mind about retiring after recovering from the injury, and began performing stunts again in October.
50	27 May 1975	Dibble's Bridge coach crash, Hebden, North Yorkshire, UK. 32 people were killed and 13 injured when a coach's brakes failed on a steep hill. It remains the worst road accident in the UK, by fatalities.
50	28 May 1975	The Economic Community of West African States was founded.
50	28 May 1975	Death of Ezzard Charles, ('the Cincinnati Cobra'), American world middleweight, light-heavyweight and heavyweight boxing champion.
50	30 May 1975	The European Space Agency (ESA) was founded when the European Space Research Organisation (ESRO) merged with the European Launch Development Organisation (ELDO).
40	1 May 1985	U.S. President Ronald Reagan announced an embargo against Nicaragua, prohibiting all trade between the two countries in an attempt to undermine the Sandanista government. (Embargo lifted March 1990.)
40	1 May 1985	Death of Denise Robins, British romantic novelist and short story writer. She also wrote under the pen names Denise Chesterton, Hervey Hamilton, Francesca Wright, Ashley French, Harriet Gray and Julia Kane. First President of the Romantic Novelists' Association (1960–66).
40	2 May 1985	Death of Larry Clinton, American trumpet player and bandleader.
40	5 May 1985	U.S. President Ronald Reagan visited Bergen–Belsen concentration camp and a war cemetery in Bitburg, Germany. The visit was condemned because 49 of the 2,000 German soldiers buried at the cemetery were members of the Waffen-SS and regarded as war criminals.
40	5 May 1985	Death of Sir Donald Bailey, British civil engineer. Inventor of the Bailey bridge – a portable, pre-fabricated truss bridge used extensively by the British and U.S. during WWII.
40	11 May 1985	Bradford City stadium fire, UK. 56 football fans were killed and at least 265 injured when a flash fire swept through the main stand during a match against Lincoln City.
40	11 May 1985	Death of Chester Gould, American cartoonist who created the *Dick Tracy* comic strip.
40	12 May 1985	Amy Eilberg of Pennsylvania, USA became the first female rabbi to be ordained in Conservative Judaism.
40	13 May 1985	Police armed with explosives stormed the headquarters of the radical group MOVE, in Philadelphia, Pennsylvania, USA. Eleven members of the group were killed, including the group's leader (two members survived). Sixty other homes were destroyed when the entire city block burnt down, leaving 250 people homeless.
40	13 May 1985	The pop rock album *Brothers in Arms* by Dire Straits was released. It became the world's most successful album released on compact disc (CD) and the first CD album to sell over a million copies.

MAY 2025

Ann.	Date	Event
40	16 May 1985	Death of Margaret Hamilton, American actress. Best known for her role as the Wicked Witch of the West in the film *The Wizard of Oz*.
40	20 May 1985	Radio Martí, a U.S.-government-funded Spanish-language radio station, began broadcasting anti-Castro propaganda to Cuba. In March 1990 it also launched a television station.
40	22 May 1985	The U.S. première of the James Bond film *A View to a Kill*. (Released: 24th May. UK première: 12th June, released: 13th June.)
40	24 May 1985	Bangladesh was hit by a tropical cyclone. More than 10,000 people were killed.
40	24 May 1985	The birth of AOL. Quantum Computer Services was founded in the USA from the remnants of an earlier company, Control Video Corporation, which was founded in 1983. The company changed its name to America Online (AOL) in 1989, and later became one of the world's largest internet service providers.
40	27 May 1985	The Sino–British Joint Declaration came into effect following an exchange of ratifications. Britain agreed to return Hong Kong to China in 1997.
40	29 May 1985	Heysel Stadium disaster, Brussels, Belgium. 39 football fans were crushed to death during rioting at the European Cup Final between Liverpool and Juventus. All English football clubs were subsequently banned from playing in European competitions until 1990.
40	31 May 1985	United States–Canada tornado outbreak. A series of 41 tornadoes hit Ohio, Pennsylvania and New York, USA, and Ontario, Canada, killing 76 people and injuring hundreds.
30	1 May 1995 to 3rd	Croatian War of Independence – Operation Flash. Croatian victory. Croatia regained territory from the self-proclaimed Republic of Serbian Krajina.
30	1 May 1995	The World Health Organisation (WHO) published its first annual survey of global health.
30	2 May 1995	Death of Sir Michael Hordern, British stage, film and television actor and voiceover artist. Known for his wide range, distinctive voice, wry humour and 60+ year career. He also narrated the BBC TV children's series *Paddington*.
30	4 May 1995 to July	1995 Kikwit Ebola virus outbreak, Zaire (now the Democratic Republic of the Congo). The virus affected 315 people, of whom 254 died. The first case is believed to have appeared in January. It was identified as Ebola on 10th May.
30	5 May 1995 to 6th	Mayfest Storm, Fort Worth, Texas, USA. A supercell storm hit Fort Worth and Tarrant County, with flash flooding, lightning strikes, and hailstones up to 4 inches (10 cm) in diameter. At least 13 people were killed and more than 100 injured. It caused over $2 billion in damage.
30	5 May 1995	The first person to be banned from the internet: 24-year-old American computer hacker Chris Lamprecht (aka 'Minor Threat') was sentenced to 70 months in prison for laundering the proceeds from the sale of stolen circuit boards. He was also banned from accessing the internet until 2003.

MAY 2025

Ann.	Date	Event
30	5 May 1995	Death of Sir Alastair Pilkington, British industrialist who developed the float glass process used to manufacture high quality flat glass. Chairman of Pilkington Glass (1973–85). Director of the Bank of England.
30	8 May 1995	Death of Teresa Teng, Taiwanese pop singer. She was immensely popular throughout East Asia.
30	10 May 1995	More than 100 workers were killed at Anglo–American Corp's Vaal Reefs gold mine in South Africa when an underground train plunged down a shaft and crashed onto an elevator.
30	10 May 1995	Terry Lynn Nichols was formally charged with being an accomplice in the Oklahoma City bombing of 19th April. In December 1997 he was convicted of involuntary manslaughter and sentenced to life imprisonment.
30	10 May 1995	The British Minister for Northern Ireland, Michael Ancram, met representatives of Sinn Fein. It was their first formal meeting in 23 years, after a ban was lifted.
30	11 May 1995	The Nuclear Nonproliferation Treaty was extended indefinitely. (Full title: The Treaty on the Non-Proliferation of Nuclear Weapons.)
30	11 May 1995	The first Electronic Entertainment Expo (E3) was held in Los Angeles, California, USA. The annual event showcases the latest video games, consoles, accessories and game-related merchandise. It was an industry-only event until 2017, when it was opened to the public.
30	11 May 1995	The Sega Saturn video games console was released in the USA. (Japan: 22nd November 1994. Europe: 8th July 1995.) It was succeeded by the Dreamcast in 1998.
30	13 May 1995	British mountaineer Alison Hargreaves became the first woman to reach the summit of Mount Everest unaided (i.e. without the use of bottled oxygen or Sherpas). She died in August when she was hit by a storm while attempting to climb K2.
30	14 May 1995	Gedhun Choekyi Nyima (aged 6) was named the 11th Panchen Lama by the Dalai Lama. Three days later he was detained by Chinese authorities and has not been seen since. On 8th December China named Gyaincain Norbu (aged 5) the 11th Panchen Lama, but most Tibetan Buddhists refuse to accept him.
30	15 May 1995	Death of Eric Porter, British stage, film and television actor (*The Jewel in the Crown*, *The Forsyte Saga*).
30	17 May 1995	Jacques Chirac became President of France (until 2007).
30	18 May 1995 ?	Death of Alexander Godunov, Russian-born American ballet dancer. (Found dead on this date, but he had not been seen for several days.)
30	18 May 1995	Death of Elizabeth Montgomery, American film and television actress. Best known for her role as Samantha in the TV series *Bewitched*.

MAY 2025

Ann.	Date	Event
30	19 May 1995	The world's youngest doctor: Indian-born American ophthalmologist Balamurali Ambati, aged 17, became the youngest person in the world to graduate as a doctor. He graduated at Mount Sinai School of Medicine in New York City, USA.
30	21 May 1995	U.S. President Bill Clinton closed the two-block stretch of Pennsylvania Avenue in front of the White House as a temporary security measure following the Oklahoma City bombing. Pedestrians and cyclists were permitted but all motor vehicles were banned. The closure was made permanent following the 9/11 terrorist attacks in 2001.
30	23 May 1995	The first version of the computer programming language Java was released.
30	23 May 1995	The first version of the open-source relational database management system MySQL was released.
30	24 May 1995	Death of Harold Wilson, British Prime Minister (1964–70, 1974–76).
30	26 May 1995	Microsoft's CEO Bill Gates issued a memo entitled *The Internet Tidal Wave*. He said Microsoft had underestimated the importance of the internet. He called it the most important single development since the IBM personal computer, and said it was critical to every part of Microsoft's business. He also identified Netscape as a new competitor. In August, Microsoft launched MSN (Microsoft Network) as a direct competitor to America Online (AOL).
30	26 May 1995	Death of Friz Freleng, American cartoon animator, director and producer. Known for his work on the *Looney Tunes* and *Merrie Melodies* series. He created or developed characters including Bugs Bunny, Porky Pig, Sylvester and Tweety Pie, Yosemite Sam, and Speedy Gonzales.
30	27 May 1995	American *Superman* actor Christopher Reeve was paralysed from the neck down when he was thrown from his horse during an equestrian competition in Virginia. (Died 2004.)
30	28 May 1995	An earthquake destroyed the town of Neftegorsk on Sakhalin Island, eastern Russia. Approximately 2,000 people were killed.
30	28 May 1995	Death of Jean Muir, British dress designer.
30	29 May 1995	Death of Margaret Chase Smith, American politician. The first woman to serve in both houses of the U.S. Congress.
30	30 May 1995	Death of Lofty England, British engineer and businessman. Chairman and chief executive of Jaguar Cars. Manager of the Jaguar sports car racing team during the 1950s.
25	1 May 2000	May Day riot, London, UK. Hundreds of anti-capitalist protestors fought with police, defaced the Cenotaph and a statue of Winston Churchill, and ransacked a McDonald's restaurant. More than 5,000 police officers were on duty in the biggest police operation in London for thirty years. The following year there were more than 6,000 officers on duty. Civil rights activists claimed the authorities were being too heavy-handed.
25	2 May 2000	The U.S. government stopped deliberately degrading the Global Positioning System (GPS) signals available to the public, immediately making the system around ten times more accurate.

MAY 2025

Ann.	Date	Event
25	3 May 2000	The Pan Am Flight 103 (Lockerbie) bombing trial opened. The 36-week trial was held at a specially convened Scottish Court on a disused U.S. Air Force base in the Netherlands. At the end of the trial in January 2001, Abdelbaset al-Megrahi was convicted and sentenced to life imprisonment, while his co-defendant, Lamin Khalifah Fhimah, was found not guilty.
25	3 May 2000	The sport of geocaching began, the day after the more accurate GPS system was made available to the public (see 2nd May above). The first cache was hidden by Dave Ulmer in Beavercreek, Oregon, USA.
25	3 May 2000	Death of John O'Connor, Archbishop of New York (1984–2000 – died in office). Succeeded by Edward Egan.
25	4 May 2000	Ken Livingstone became the first mayor of London.
25	5 May 2000	The ILOVEYOU computer virus infected millions of Windows personal computers around the world. It was the fastest-spreading and most widespread virus ever seen at that time. (The Sobig worm of 2003 and the Mydoom worm of 2004 were worse.)
25	7 May 2000	Vladimir Putin was inaugurated as President of Russia. He had been acting-president since 31st December 1999.
25	7 May 2000 to Sept	Operation Pallister – the British military intervention in the Sierra Leone Civil War. British training teams remained until September 2001 and were then replaced by an international force. The war ended in January 2002 – Commonwealth victory.
25	7 May 2000	Death of Douglas Fairbanks Jr., American film actor (*The Mark of Zorro*, *The Three Musketeers*, *The Thief of Bagdad*), television producer, and highly decorated WWII naval officer.
25	12 May 2000	The Tate Modern art gallery opened in London.
25	12 May 2000	Death of Adam Petty, American NASCAR racing driver. The first fourth-generation sportsperson in the history of U.S. professional sports. (Killed in a practice session when his throttle stuck open, aged 19.)
25	13 May 2000	Death of Paul Bartel, American actor, writer, and director. Best known for his black comedy film *Eating Raoul*.
25	17 May 2000	Two Royal Marine commandos, Alan Chambers and Charlie Paton, became the first Britons to reach the geographic North Pole without outside support.
25	17 May 2000	Death of Donald Coggan, Archbishop of Canterbury (1974–80).
25	18 May 2000	Boo.com, a short-lived high-profile British online fashion retailer went into receivership. It had burnt through more than £125 million of venture capital in just six months, and is regarded as one of the greatest failures of the dot-com bust. Its failure was attributed to excessive marketing costs, over-ambitious growth plans, and its complicated website that took several minutes to load. It also had a much higher than anticipated rate of product returns.
25	21 May 2000	Death of Dame Barbara Cartland, British author of more than 700 romantic novels.

MAY 2025

Ann.	Date	Event
25	21 May 2000	Death of Sir John Gielgud, British actor, producer and director. One of the greatest Shakespearean actors of his generation.
25	21 May 2000	Death of Mark R. Hughes, American businessman who founded Herbalife. (Toxic combination of alcohol and antidepressants, aged 44.)
25	25 May 2000	Liberation Day in Lebanon. Israel withdrew its troops from South Lebanon, ending 22 years of occupation.
25	31 May 2000	Death of Tito Puente, 'King of Mambo', American mambo/Latin jazz musician, songwriter and record producer.
20	1 May 2005	The Chinese computer manufacturer Lenovo acquired IBM's personal computer division.
20	2 May 2005	Death of Wee Kim Wee, President of Singapore (1985–93).
20	7 May 2005	The first Time Traveller Convention was held, at the Massachusetts Institute of Technology (MIT) in the USA. Organiser Amal Dorai hoped to attract and make contact with time travellers from the future. There is no record that any time travellers attended, but the time and location of the event are still publicised so future time travellers will be aware of it and have the opportunity to attend.
20	8 May 2005	The new Canadian War Museum opened in Ottawa, Ontario. The original museum was established in 1942.
20	10 May 2005	The national Holocaust Memorial in Berlin, Germany was dedicated. (Official name: the Memorial to the Murdered Jews of Europe.) It opened to the public on 12th May.
20	12 May 2005	The U.S. première of the epic space opera film *Star Wars: Episode III – Revenge of the Sith*. (Released: 19th May. UK première: 16th May, released: 19th May.)
20	13 May 2005	Andijan Massacre, Uzbekistan. Government troops fired into a crowd of protesters, killing 187 people (official figure). Other sources estimate that the number killed was 'several hundred', and perhaps as many as 1,500.
20	16 May 2005	Kuwait granted women the right to vote and stand for election. Women had originally been granted the right to vote in 1985, but it was quickly suspended.
20	18 May 2005	Pluto's second and third moons, Nix and Hydra, were discovered from photos taken by the Hubble Space Telescope. Its first moon, Charon, was discovered in 1978. Its fourth moon, Kerberos, was discovered in 2006, and its fifth moon, Styx, in 2012.
20	19 May 2005	Scientists at the University of Newcastle in England announced that they had successfully cloned human embryos from stem cells. It was later revealed that the embryos had developed to the blastocyst stage – a mass containing a few hundred cells that forms five to nine days after fertilisation – but they did not develop any further.
20	21 May 2005	The world's tallest roller coaster, Kingda Ka, opened at Six Flags Great Adventure in Jackson, New Jersey, USA. Height: 456 feet (139 metres). It is also the world's second-fastest roller coaster. Speed: 128 mph (206 km/h).

MAY 2025

Ann.	Date	Event
20	25 May 2005	Death of Graham Kennedy, Australian actor, entertainer, talk show host and game show host. Known as the 'King of Television'.
20	25 May 2005	Death of Ismail Merchant, Indian film producer, director and writer. Known for his collaborations with the American film director James Ivory as Merchant Ivory Productions.
20	29 May 2005	In a referendum to approve the Constitution of the European Union, French voters rejected it. Dutch voters also rejected it on 1st June. It was eventually abandoned and replaced by the Lisbon Treaty.
20	31 May 2005	Mark Felt, the former Associate Director of the FBI, admitted that he was the Watergate Scandal whistleblower known as 'Deep Throat' who provided information to the *Washington Post* that led to the downfall of U.S. President Richard Nixon.
15	2 May 2010	Greek debt crisis: the European Union, European Central Bank and International Monetary Fund authorised a three-year €110 billion ($143 billion) bailout loan to Greece. The loan was given on condition that Greece imposed a wide range of austerity measures. Greece complied with the measures, but there were widespread public protests.
15	6 May 2010	British general election. Result: hung parliament. A coalition government was formed on 11th May by the Conservative Party and the Liberal Democrats. Conservative Party leader David Cameron became Prime Minister and Liberal Democrat leader Nick Clegg became Deputy Prime Minister.
15	20 May 2010	Scientists from the J. Craig Venter Institute in the USA announced that they had created the world's first artificial lifeform. It was a modified version of the bacterium *Mycoplasma mycoides* with the minimum viable genome. They transplanted their synthesised genome into an existing cell.
15	23 May 2010	Cash for access scandal. The Duchess of York, Sarah Ferguson, was caught on film asking an undercover reporter for £500,000 in exchange for access to her former husband, Prince Andrew, Duke of York. The reporter was posing as an Indian businessman. She later apologised for the 'serious lapse in judgement' and said her financial situation was 'under stress'. She said the Duke was not aware of the discussions.
10	2 May 2015	Death of Ruth Rendell, British novelist. Known for her psychological thrillers and murder mysteries. Best known for creating the character Chief Inspector Wexford.
10	3 May 2015	Death of Danny Jones, Welsh rugby player. (Cardiac arrest during a match, aged 29.)
10	6 May 2015	Death of Jim Wright, American politician. Speaker of the U.S. House of Representatives (1987–89). House Majority Leader (1977–87).
10	13 May 2015	Death of Earl Averill Jr., American baseball player.
10	14 May 2015	Death of B.B. King, American blues/R&B/rock and roll singer, songwriter, guitarist, and record producer.

MAY 2025

Ann.	Date	Event
10	19 May 2015	Refugio oil spill, Refugio State Beach, Santa Barbara, California, USA. A ruptured pipeline leaked 142,800 U.S. gallons (3,400 barrels/540,000 litres) of crude oil onto one of the most biologically diverse coastlines of the U.S. west coast. Hundreds of animals were covered in oil, and many died. Clean-up costs were an estimated $96 million, and the legal settlement is expected to be around $257 million.
10	22 May 2015	The Republic of Ireland became the first country to hold a referendum (the Marriage Equality referendum) on whether same-sex marriage should be legalised. Its citizens voted to approve it, and same-sex marriage became legal in Ireland from 16th November 2015.

JUNE 2025

Ann.	Date	Event
1000	17 Jun 1025	Death of Bolesław I the Brave, the first King of Poland (992–1025). Succeeded by Mieszko II Lambert.
500	13 Jun 1525	German Protestant Reformer Martin Luther married Katharina von Bora, a nun whom he had helped to escape from a convent. He had previously sworn to remain single – mainly because he thought he could be killed at any moment. As a result of his marriage, members of the Protestant clergy were also allowed to marry.
400	8 Jun 1625	Birth of Giovanni Domenico Cassini, Italian-born French astronomer, astrologer and engineer. He discovered four of Saturn's moons, and the divisions in Saturn's rings. The Cassini Division in the rings was named in his honour, as was the U.S.-European-Italian space mission *Cassini-Huygens*, which reached Saturn in 2004.
250	11 Jun 1775 to 12th	American Revolutionary War – the Battle of Machias. The first naval engagement of the war. Patriot forces captured a small British ship, the *HMS Margaretta*.
250	12 Jun 1775	American Revolution: British general Thomas Gage declared an amnesty and pardon to all colonists who laid down their arms and demonstrated their loyalty to the British Crown (except for Samuel Adams and John Hancock, who would be executed if they were captured). His amnesty had the opposite effect of that intended, as it fired up the colonists with rage and determination. He was recalled to Britain in September.
250	14 Jun 1775	American Revolutionary War: the Second Continental Congress established the Continental Army. It later became the United States Army. On 15th June, George Washington, who would become the first President of the USA, became the Army's Commander-in-Chief.
250	17 Jun 1775	American Revolutionary War – the Battle of Bunker Hill. The British captured Charlestown Peninsula in Massachusetts – though the Americans scored a moral victory as they had fewer casualties.
250	17 Jun 1775	American Revolution: the Second Continental Congress commissioned Horatio Gates as the first Adjutant General of the Continental Army (and of the U.S. Army). In July he declared that negros should not be recruited into the Army, because if they were armed they might cause slave rebellions. Despite his order, blacks were admitted into the Army, with many joining regular units – although there were some segregated units.
250	20 Jun 1775	Thomas Jefferson (the main author of the Declaration of Independence, and the third President of the United States) became a delegate to the second Continental Congress, representing Virginia.
250	23 Jun 1775	The first Thames Regatta was held in London, England.
250	23 Jun 1775	The first book to be printed and published in America: *The Impenetrable Secret*. It was published by Story and Humphreys and advertised in the *Pennsylvania Mercury* newspaper. The author is unknown and no copies survive.

JUNE 2025

Ann.	Date	Event
250	27 Jun 1775 to Oct 1776	American Revolutionary War: the Invasion of Quebec (now in Canada). The newly formed Continental Army attempted to take control of the British Province of Quebec, but were unable to overcome the British. This may have been the first use of biological warfare: the British sent smallpox-infected prostitutes and civilians to the American front lines. At least 5,000 Americans were infected and many died.
200	7 Jun 1825	Birth of R. D. Blackmore, British novelist. Best known for *Lorna Doone*.
200	11 Jun 1825	Death of Daniel D. Tompkins, Vice President of the USA (1817–25). Governor of New York (1807–17). He was in poor physical and financial health, became an alcoholic, and died shortly after completing his second term as Vice President.
175	5 Jun 1850	Birth of Pat Garrett, American lawman, bartender and customs agent of the Old West. Best known for killing Billy the Kid.
175	24 Jun 1850	Birth of Herbert Kitchener, 1st Earl Kitchener, Irish-born British Army officer and politician. Secretary of War during WWI – he appeared on an iconic poster asking people to join the army. Consul-General in Egypt (1911–14). (Killed in 1916 when his ship was hit by a German mine and sank while he was travelling to Russia for negotiations with Tsar Nicholas II.)
150	2 Jun 1875	James Augustine Healey became Bishop of Portland in Maine, USA. He is regarded as the first Black Catholic priest and bishop in the USA. (He was actually mixed race and identified as a Caucasian.)
150	3 Jun 1875	Death of Georges Bizet, French Romantic composer. Best known for his opera *Carmen*. (Heart attack, aged 36.)
150	6 Jun 1875	The Netherlands adopted the gold standard.
150	19 Jun 1875 to 1878	The Herzegovinian uprising against the Ottoman Empire. The uprising led to the Serbian–Ottoman War and the Montenegrin–Ottoman War, which led to the Russo–Turkish War and the Great Eastern Crisis.
150	29 Jun 1875	Death of Ferdinand I, Emperor of Austria (1835–48 – abdicated). King of Hungary, Croatia and Bohemia (1830–48). President of the German Confederation. King of Lombardy–Venetia (now part of Italy).
125	3 Jun 1900	Death of Mary Kingsley, British ethnographer, explorer and travel writer in West Africa. (Typhoid, aged 37.)
125	5 Jun 1900	Second Boer War: British forces captured Pretoria, the capital of the Transvaal.
125	5 Jun 1900	Birth of Dennis Gabor, Hungarian-born British electrical engineer and physicist. Winner of the 1971 Nobel Prize in Physics for inventing holography.
125	5 Jun 1900	Death of Stephen Crane, American poet, novelist, and short story writer. Best known for his Civil War novel *The Red Badge of Courage*. (Tuberculosis, aged 28.)
125	6 Jun 1900	Birth of Arthur Askey, British comedian and actor. He frequently appeared on radio and television, appeared in several comedy films during WWII, and was known for his novelty record *The Bee Song*.

JUNE 2025

Ann.	Date	Event
125	9 Jun 1900	Birth of Fred Waring, American musician, bandleader, and radio and television personality. Known as 'the man who taught America how to sing'. He also backed and promoted the Waring Blendor – the first modern electric blender. It was widely used in hospitals and was used to develop the polio vaccine.
125	10 Jun 1900	Boxer Rebellion – the Eight Nation Alliance invaded northern China to relieve foreign legations that were besieged by the Boxer rebels. The Alliance was made up of around 45,000 troops from Austria-Hungary, Britain, France, Germany, Italy, Japan, Russia and the USA. They remained in China until September 1901 when the rebellion ended and the Boxer protocol was signed. Allied victory.
125	11 Jun 1900 to 12th	Second Boer War – the Battle of Diamond Hill, Pretoria, South Africa. British victory.
125	14 Jun 1900	Germany passed the Second German Naval Law. It doubled the size of the Imperial German Navy, turning it from a coastal defence force into a powerful battle fleet that posed a serious threat to the British Royal Navy.
125	17 Jun 1900	Birth of Martin Bormann, German Nazi Party official. Adolf Hitler's private secretary. He was convicted of war crimes by the Nuremberg trials, and sentenced to death – though he had already committed suicide. (His body was not found and formally identified until 1973.)
125	19 Jun 1900	Serbian-born American inventor Mihajlo Pupin (also known as Michael Pupin) was granted a U.S. patent for his invention of pupinisation. His system greatly extended the range of long-distance telephone communication by placing loading coils (inductors) at regular intervals along the transmitting wire. (U.S. Patent 652,230.)
125	20 Jun 1900 to 14 Aug	Boxer Rebellion – the Siege of the International Legations, Peking (now Beijing), China. 900 foreign troops and 2,800 Chinese Christians sheltered in the Peking Legation Quarter and survived a 55-day siege by the Qing Army and Boxers. The siege was relieved by an international military force (the Eight-Nation Alliance) and the entire Imperial court was forced to retreat. Allied victory.
125	20 Jun 1900	Estonian explorer and geologist Baron Eduard von Toll led the Russian Polar Expedition of 1900–02 on a mission to find the legendary Sannikov Island off Russia's Arctic coast. The ship *Zarya* departed from Saint Petersburg on this date. It became trapped in ice near Bennett Island in October 1902, and Toll and a small party set off on foot. They were never seen again. The other members of the crew returned to Russia. (It is unknown whether Sannikov Island ever existed. It may have been destroyed by erosion.)
125	21 Jun 1900	Boxer Rebellion: Empress Dowager Cixi of China declared war on the invading powers.
125	25 Jun 1900	The Dunhuang manuscripts were discovered in the Mogao Caves in Dunhuang, China by Taoist monk Wang Yuanlu. The manuscripts are of great historical significance. They cover history, mathematics, folk songs, dance and religion from the late 4th century to the early 11th century.

JUNE 2025

Ann.	Date	Event
125	25 Jun 1900	Birth of Louis Mountbatten, 1st Earl Mountbatten of Burma, British admiral and politician. Governor-General of India (1947–48), First Sea Lord (1955–59), Chief of the Defence Staff (1959–65). Assassinated in 1979 by an IRA bomb planted on his fishing boat.
125	30 Jun 1900	Hoboken Docks fire, New Jersey, USA. Cotton bales stored at the Norddeutscher Lloyd (NDL) shipping company's wharf caught fire and set fire to barrels of oil and turpentine stored nearby. Several warehouses were destroyed, as were three of NDL's transatlantic liners and numerous smaller boats. At least 326 people were killed.
100	1 Jun 1925	Death of Thomas R. Marshall, Vice President of the USA (1913–21). Governor of Indiana (1909–13).
100	3 Jun 1925	The Goodyear airship *Pilgrim* made its first flight. It became the first Goodyear Blimp (i.e. used for promotional purposes rather than pleasure cruising). It was the first Goodyear airship to use helium, and the first with an enclosed cabin.
100	3 Jun 1925	Birth of Tony Curtis, American film and television actor. His best-known films include *The Defiant Ones*, *Some Like It Hot*, and *Spartacus*. He also starred in the action-comedy TV series *The Persuaders!* Husband of the actress Janet Leigh. Father of the actress Jamie Lee Curtis. (Died 2010.)
100	6 Jun 1925	The Chrysler Corporation was founded in the USA.
100	8 Jun 1925	Birth of Barbara Bush, First Lady of the United States (1989–93). Wife of U.S. President George H. W. Bush. (Died 2018.)
100	10 Jun 1925	The United Church of Canada was established.
100	11 Jun 1925	Birth of William Styron, American novelist and essayist. Known for his novels *Lie Down in Darkness*, *The Confessions of Nat Turner* and *Sophie's Choice*, and for his memoir *Darkness Visible*. (Died 2006.)
100	13 Jun 1925	American engineer Charles F. Jenkins gave a public demonstration of his mechanical television system, which could transmit moving images made up of 48 lines with synchronised sound. On 30th June he was granted a U.S. Patent (#1,544.156) for his invention. Like John Logie Baird's similar invention, his mechanical system was quickly superseded by electronic television.
100	14 Jun 1925	Birth of Pierre Salinger, American journalist, writer, politician and ABC news correspondent. Press secretary for U.S. Presidents John F. Kennedy and Lyndon B. Johnson. (Died 2004.)
100	15 Jun 1925	Birth of Richard Baker, British broadcaster. Best known as a BBC newsreader – he was the first person to read the *BBC Television News* in 1954 (which was only in voiceover at that time). He also presented radio and TV programmes on classical music, as well as several other radio shows, and he narrated the animated children's TV series *Mary, Mungo and Midge*. (Died 2018.)
100	16 Jun 1925	Artek, the Soviet Union's best-known Young Pioneer camp, was established in Crimea, Ukraine. It is now an international children's centre.

JUNE 2025

Ann.	Date	Event
100	17 Jun 1925	The Geneva Protocol (The Protocol for the Prohibition of the Use in War of Asphyxiating, Poisonous or other Gases, and of Bacteriological Methods of Warfare) was signed in Geneva, Switzerland. It came into effect in February 1928.
100	19 Jun 1925	Birth of Charlie Drake, British slapstick comic and actor. Known for his catchphrase 'Hello, my darlings!' (Died 2006.)
100	20 Jun 1925	Birth of Audie Murphy, American soldier and actor. He used falsified documents to enlist in the U.S. Army after the attack on Pearl Harbor, as he was underage. He then became one of the most-decorated combat soldiers of WWII and was awarded the Medal of Honor. After the war he became an actor and songwriter, and appeared in numerous westerns. (He died in a plane crash in 1971, aged 45.)
100	23 Jun 1925	The first successful ascent of Mount Logan, the highest mountain in Canada and the second-highest in North America, by an international team organised by the Alpine Club of Canada.
100	23 Jun 1925	Birth of Art Modell, American businessman and sports promoter. Owner of the Cleveland Browns NFL football team (1961–95), founder and owner of the Baltimore Ravens (1996–2004). He made several controversial decisions during his ownership of the Cleveland Browns. (Died 2012.)
100	25 Jun 1925	Theodoros Pangalos became President/dictator of Greece after seizing power in a bloodless coup.
100	25 Jun 1925	The Vitaphone Company was founded by Warner Brothers and Western Electric to develop sound-on-disc technology for cinemas. The first Vitaphone film was *Don Juan*, which was released on 5th August 1926. It had a musical score and sound effects, but no dialogue.
100	26 Jun 1925	The Hollywood première of Charlie Chaplin's comedy film *The Gold Rush*. (New York première: 15th August. UK première: 14th September.)
100	27 Jun 1925	Birth of Doc Pomus, American blues singer and songwriter. He co-wrote numerous hit records including *A Teenager in Love, Save The Last Dance For Me, Sweets For My Sweet, Can't Get Used to Losing You*, and many more. (Died 1991.)
100	29 Jun 1925	Canada House opened in London, England.
90	1 Jun 1935	Driving tests became compulsory for all new drivers in Britain. Anyone who had started driving on or after 1st April 1934 had to pass the test.
90	1 Jun 1935	Birth of Reverend Ike, American clergyman who preached the concepts of prosperity and material satisfaction on his radio and television shows and in books, magazines and videos – and became a multimillionaire. (Died 2009.)
90	2 Jun 1935	American baseball star Babe Ruth announced his retirement, aged 40.
90	2 Jun 1935	Birth of Carol Shields, American-born Canadian writer. Best known for her novel *The Stone Diaries*. (Died 2003.)
90	6 Jun 1935	Death of Julian Byng, Viscount Byng, British field marshal, Governor-General of Canada (1921–26), Commissioner of London police (1928–31).

JUNE 2025

Ann.	Date	Event
90	7 Jun 1935	Stanley Baldwin became British Prime Minister for the third time (until May 1937).
90	7 Jun 1935	Pierre Laval became Prime Minister of France for the second time (until January 1936). He was also Prime Minister twice during the Vichy regime of WWII, for which he was convicted of treason and executed in 1945.
90	10 Jun 1935	Alcoholics Anonymous was founded in Akron, Ohio, USA.
90	11 Jun 1935	American inventor Edwin Armstrong gave the first public demonstration of FM radio, in Alpine, New Jersey.
90	12 Jun 1935	The Chaco War between Bolivia and Paraguay ended in a truce.
90	13 Jun 1935	Birth of Christo and Jeanne-Claude, husband and wife environmental artists who wrapped large-scale natural and man-made structures in fabric and plastic. (Jeanne-Claude died in 2009, Christo died in 2020.)
90	13 Jun 1935	Birth of Samak Sundaravej, Prime Minister of Thailand (2008). (Died 2009.)
90	21 Jun 1935	Birth of Françoise Sagan, French novelist, playwright and screenwriter. Best known for her novel *Bonjour Tristesse*. (Died 2004.)
90	23 Jun 1935 to 24th	British Foreign Secretary Anthony Eden attempted to broker a peace agreement to resolve the Abyssinia Crisis. It failed. On 25th July Britain imposed an embargo on the sale of arms to Italy and Ethiopia, and on 3rd October the Second Italo–Ethiopian War broke out.
90	28 Jun 1935	Birth of John Inman, British stage, film and television comedy actor, singer and pantomime dame. Best known for his role as Mr Humphries in the sitcom *Are You Being Served?* and his catchphrase 'I'm free!' (Died 2007.)
80	1 Jun 1945 to 15th	World War II – the Philippines Campaign – the Battle of Bessang Pass, Luzon. Allied victory.
80	5 Jun 1945	World War II: the Allied Control Council was established in Berlin, Germany to oversee the division of Germany into four occupation zones: American, British, French, and Soviet.
80	7 Jun 1945	King Haakon VII and the Norwegian Royal Family returned to Norway after five years in exile during WWII.
80	7 Jun 1945	Benjamin Britten's opera *Peter Grimes* was first performed, in London, UK.
80	8 Jun 1945	U.S President Harry S. Truman issued Executive Order 9568. This permitted the release of scientific information from previously top-secret WWII documents. Truman hoped that releasing the information would help stimulate the USA's post-war economy.
80	11 Jun 1945	*The Franck Report* was signed by several prominent nuclear physicists. It recommended that the USA should not use the atomic bomb against Japan. U.S. President Harry S. Truman appointed a committee to examine the points made in the report, but the committee concluded that the bombing should go ahead – which it did in August.
80	13 Jun 1945	World War II: Australian forces captured Brunei from the Japanese after three days of bombing and heavy fighting.
80	15 Jun 1945	The General Dutch Youth League (ANJV) was founded in Amsterdam, Netherlands. It was dissolved in 2005.

JUNE 2025

Ann.	Date	Event
80	22 Jun 1945	World War II – the Battle of Okinawa in Japan ended after 82 days. This battle saw the highest number of casualties in the Pacific Theatre of the war, with more than 12,000 Allied forces, 110,000 Japanese forces, and 140,000 civilians killed. (Some sources give different figures.)
80	22 Jun 1945 to 1947	World War II: Operation Paperclip. The USA recruited 1,600 – 1,800 German scientists, engineers and technicians, plus 3,700 family members, and took them to the USA. They would work on government projects that would give the USA an advantage over the Soviet Union in fields such as space exploration. The first recruits left Germany for the USA on this day.
80	25 Jun 1945	Seán T. O'Kelly became the second President of Ireland (until 1959).
80	26 Jun 1945	The United Nations Charter was signed in San Francisco, California, USA by representatives from fifty countries. The United Nations was established on 24th October.
80	27 Jun 1945	Death of Emil Hácha, President of Czechoslovakia (1938–39).
80	28 Jun 1945	The Provisional Government of National Unity was established in Poland by Polish Communists and the Soviet Union. It was not recognised by the Polish government-in-exile.
80	30 Jun 1945	The first description of the logical design for an electronic, digital, stored-program computer was published by Hungarian-American physicist John von Neumann. His document, *The First Draft of a Report on the EDVAC*, described what is now known as the von Neumann architecture.
75	1 Jun 1950 to Sep	Chinchaga fire, British Columbia and Alberta, Canada. The largest recorded fire in North American history. It destroyed between 3.5 million and 4.2 million acres of forest. The 'Great Smoke Pall' could be seen as far away as Europe, though only as a haze in the upper atmosphere.
75	3 Jun 1950	The first successful ascent of Annapurna in the Himalayas, by a French expedition led by Maurice Herzog. This was the first successful ascent of a mountain over 8,000 meters. Annapurna is the tenth highest mountain in the world.
75	8 Jun 1950	Sir Thomas Blamey became the only Australian to achieve the rank of field marshal.
75	17 Jun 1950	The first human kidney transplant was performed by Dr Richard H. Lawler at the Little Company of Mary Hospital, Evergreen Park, Chicago, Illinois, USA.
75	17 Jun 1950	Egypt, Lebanon, Saudi Arabia, Syria and Yemen signed a Collective Security Pact in Alexandria, Egypt.
75	19 Jun 1950	The first drag strip in the USA opened: the Santa Ana Drags at the Orange County Airport (now John Wayne Airport) in California. It operated until 1959.
75	20 Jun 1950	The Standards Eastern Automatic Computer (SEAC) went into service in Washington D.C. It was the first fully operational stored-program electronic computer in the USA, and the first all-diode computer.

JUNE 2025

Ann.	Date	Event
75	22 Jun 1950	The UK première of Walt Disney's live-action adventure film *Treasure Island*. (U.S. release: 19th July.)
75	24 Jun 1950	Apartheid: South Africa passed the Group Areas Act. It established separate residential and business sections in urban areas for the different racial groups, and prohibited non-whites from living in the most-developed areas. (Effective from 30th March 1951.)
75	25 Jun 1950 to 27 Jul 1953	The Korean War. Result: military stalemate. North Korean and Soviet troops invaded South Korea. They were successfully repelled in 1953 with help from the USA, and the Korean Demilitarised Zone was established at the border. The USA entered the war on 27th June 1950 following a UN Security Council recommendation that member nations should help South Korea. North Korea captured Seoul, the capital of South Korea, on 28th June, in the First Battle of Seoul.
75	25 Jun 1950	The USA beat England 1 – 0 in a FIFA World Cup first round match in Brazil. It is regarded as one of the biggest upsets in World Cup history and became known as the 'Miracle Match' or the 'Miracle on Green'. It was England's first World Cup match, as it had boycotted the previous three tournaments.
75	28 Jun 1950	Korean War – the Bodo League massacre. The President of South Korea, Syngman Rhee, ordered the execution of communist members of the Bodo League and the South Korean Workers Party. Between 60,000 and 200,000 people were killed.
75	28 Jun 1950	Korean War – the Seoul National University Hospital massacre. The North Korean People's Army (KPA) killed between 700 and 900 doctors, nurses, and patients – including civilians and around 100 wounded South Korean soldiers.
70	2 Jun 1955	The Soviet Union established Baikonur Cosmodrome in Kazakhstan. It was initially a test centre for intercontinental ballistic missiles, but it was soon expanded to include launch facilities for space flights.
70	2 Jun 1955	The Soviet Union and Yugoslavia signed the Belgrade declaration, restoring diplomatic relations after seven years.
70	6 Jun 1955	Dwight D. Eisenhower became the first U.S. President to appear on colour television. He was filmed at the U.S. Military Academy at West Point for his class's 40th reunion.
70	6 Jun 1955	Birth of Sam Simon, American television writer, director and producer, poker player, and philanthropist. He co-developed the TV series *The Simpsons*, and wrote and produced episodes of *Cheers* and *It's Garry Shandling's Show*. (Died 2015.)
70	7 Jun 1955	The first episode of the television quiz show *The $64,000 Question* was broadcast on CBS in the USA. It was based on the radio quiz show *Take It or Leave It*, which began in April 1940.
70	11 Jun 1955	Le Mans disaster: a car span off the track during the Le Mans 24 Hour race in France. The driver, Pierre Levegh, and 83 spectators were killed and more than 100 were injured. It was the greatest loss of life in the history of motorsport.

JUNE 2025

Ann.	Date	Event
70	13 Jun 1955	Soviet geologists discovered diamond-bearing deposits in Eastern Siberia. The Soviet Union's first and largest diamond mine, the Mir mine, opened there in 1957. It is also the world's second-largest excavated hole.
70	15 Jun 1955	Argentine President Juan Perón was excommunicated by Pope Pius XII after he expelled two catholic bishops (see 16th June 1955 below).
70	16 Jun 1955	Attempted coup against Argentine President Juan Perón. Navy fighter jets bombed the Plaza de Mayo, Buenos Aires while Perón was holding a support rally there. 364 people were killed. Another coup in September was successful and Perón was forced into exile until 1973.
70	16 Jun 1955	The U.S. première of Walt Disney's animated film *Lady and the Tramp*. (Released USA: 22nd June. UK: 16th August.) It was the first animated film released in CinemaScope.
70	26 Jun 1955	The South African Congress Alliance adopted the Freedom Charter, which included equal rights for all South Africans.
70	30 Jun 1955	The first episode of *The Johnny Carson Show* was broadcast on CBS television in the USA. Although it was short-lived, many of its sketches were later adapted for *The Tonight Show*.
65	1 Jun 1960	Television broadcasts began in New Zealand.
65	5 Jun 1960	The Lake Bodom murders, Finland. Two fifteen-year-old girls and an eighteen-year-old man were killed and another eighteen-year-old man was injured while they were camping at the lake. They were stabbed and hit with a blunt instrument. The perpetrator remains unknown. The man who survived was arrested and tried in 2005, but he was acquitted.
65	8 Jun 1960 to 12th	Typhoon Mary caused massive damage in Hong Kong and China. More than 1,600 people were killed.
65	11 Jun 1960	The first Single-handed Trans-Atlantic Race began. It was the first single-handed ocean yacht race. Five sailors entered the race from Plymouth, England to New York City, USA. It was won by British sailor Francis Chichester in *Gipsy Moth III*, who finished in 40 days. The race is now known as the Transat.
65	14 Jun 1960	The former king of Cambodia, Prince Norodom Sihanoek, was appointed Head of State.
65	16 Jun 1960	The U.S. première of Alfred Hitchcock's suspense film *Psycho*. (Released 8th September. UK première: 4th August, released 15th September.)
65	20 Jun 1960	The Mali Federation gained its independence from France. In August it split into the republics of Mali and Senegal.
65	22 Jun 1960	The USA launched its first successful intelligence satellite, *GRAB 1* (Galactic Radiation and Background). Its primary mission was to map Soviet air defence radar systems. It remained classified until 1968.
65	23 Jun 1960	The Treaty of Mutual Cooperation and Security Between the United States and Japan came into effect.

JUNE 2025

Ann.	Date	Event
65	23 Jun 1960	The U.S. Food and Drugs Administration (FDA) approved the first combined oral contraceptive pill, Enovid. The first pill was a higher-dose pill intended to relieve menstrual disorders, but the FDA also approved its use as a contraceptive (though it was never marketed for this purpose). The manufacturer, Searle, began marketing a lower-dose version intended for use as a contraceptive in July 1961.
65	26 Jun 1960	Madagascar gained its independence from France.
65	26 Jun 1960	British Somaliland gained its independence from the UK. On 1st July it united with the former Italian Somaliland to form Somalia.
65	27 Jun 1960	Death of Lottie Dod, British sportswoman. Five times winner of Wimbledon, women's golf champion, Olympic medallist in archery, and founder of the England women's field hockey team.
65	28 Jun 1960	Cuba confiscated and nationalised all U.S.-owned oil refineries after they refused to process a shipment of Soviet crude oil.
65	28 Jun 1960	Six Bells Colliery disaster, Monmouthshire, Wales. 45 coal miners were killed by a gas explosion.
65	29 Jun 1960	The BBC Television Centre opened in Shepherd's Bush, west London. The building was closed and sold to developers in 2013.
65	30 Jun 1960	The Belgian Congo (now the Democratic Republic of the Congo) gained its independence from Belgium.
60	1 Jun 1965	Bengal Cyclone II, India. The second cyclone to strike the region in less than a month (see also: 11th May 1965). The two cyclones killed a total of 47,000 people.
60	1 Jun 1965	Yamano coal mine disaster, Fukuoka, Japan. 236 (or 237) miners were killed when a pocket of methane gas exploded.
60	1 Jun 1965	Death of Earl ('Curly') Lambeau, American football coach. Founder of the Green Bay Packers.
60	2 Jun 1965	Vietnam War: the first battalion of Australian combat troops arrived in South Vietnam following a request for more military assistance.
60	3 Jun 1965	NASA launched *Gemini 4*, its tenth manned space mission. The four-day mission included the USA's first spacewalk (by astronaut Edward Higgins White) and several scientific experiments were conducted for the first time.
60	5 Jun 1965	The rock song *(I Can't Get No) Satisfaction* by the Rolling Stones was released in the USA. (UK: 20th August.)
60	7 Jun 1965	King Hassan II of Morocco suspended the constitution, dissolved parliament, and ruled directly.
60	7 Jun 1965	The U.S. Supreme Court ruled that married couples had a right to privacy. This effectively legalised the use of contraception by married couples in states where it was outlawed. (Griswold v. Connecticut.)

JUNE 2025

Ann.	Date	Event
60	7 Jun 1965	Death of Judy Holliday, American stage and film actress. Known for her 'dumb blonde' comedy roles (*Born Yesterday*, *The Solid Gold Cadillac*, *It Should Happen to You*, *Bells Are Ringing*, and more).
60	8 Jun 1965	The Soviet Union launched its *Luna 6* unmanned space probe. It was meant to land on the Moon, but a mid-course correction failed and it missed the Moon by nearly 100,000 miles.
60	8 Jun 1965	Birth of Rob Pilatus, American-born German model, dancer and entertainer. A member of the disgraced pop duo Milli Vanilli, who were forced to return their Grammy Award when it was revealed they did not sing any of the songs on their album. (Died 1998.)
60	9 Jun 1965 to 13th	Vietnam War: the Battle of Đồng Xoài. Viet Cong victory in one of the biggest battles in the war.
60	9 Jun 1965	Franz Jonas became President of Austria (until 1974).
60	11 Jun 1965	The Beatles were awarded MBEs (Member of the Order of the British Empire). They were presented by Queen Elizabeth II on 26th October. John Lennon returned his in September 1969 in a protest against war and for the banning of one of his songs which contained drug references.
60	11 Jun 1965	Death of José Mendes Cabeçadas, President of Portugal (1926).
60	12 Jun 1965	Astronomers from Mount Wilson and Palomar Observatories in California, USA announced the discovery of blue galaxies. They said this supported the Big Bang theory of the creation of the universe, and suggested that the universe was a finite, closed system that pulsed every 82 billion years.
60	12 Jun 1965	American pop duo Sonny and Cher made their television debut on *American Bandstand*.
60	14 Jun 1965	Nguyễn Văn Thiệu became Prime Minister of South Vietnam after Phan Khắc Sửu resigned. He became President in 1967.
60	14 Jun 1965	The Beatles released the album *Beatles VI* in North America, and later also in New Zealand.
60	18 Jun 1965	Vietnam War: The U.S. Air Force launched its first B-52 bombing raid against Viet Cong guerrillas in South Vietnam. By August 1973 they had flown more than 126,000 B-52 missions in South-East Asia.
60	19 Jun 1965	The President of Algeria, Ahmed Ben Bella, was deposed in a bloodless coup and held under house arrest until 1979. He was succeeded by Houari Boumediene.
60	20 Jun 1965	Death of Bernard Baruch, American financier, presidential advisor and philanthropist.
60	21 Jun 1965	The Byrds' debut album *Mr. Tambourine Man* was released. It helped popularise the folk-rock music genre.
60	22 Jun 1965	Death of Joseph Auslander, American poet, anthologist, novelist and translator. The first Poet Laureate Consultant in Poetry to the Library of Congress (1937–41).
60	22 Jun 1965	Death of David O. Selznick, American film producer (*Gone With the Wind*, *Rebecca*, *The Third Man*, and more).

JUNE 2025

Ann.	Date	Event
60	26 Jun 1965	Death of Reginald Beckwith, British film and television character actor and playwright (*Thunderball*, *The Day the Earth Caught Fire*, *The 39 Steps*, and many more.)
60	27 Jun 1965	Vietnam War: the first U.S. forces in Vietnam began their first combat operation. 3,000 troops from the 173rd Airborne Brigade joined 800 Australian forces and a South Vietnamese airborne unit to attack Viet Cong forces in War Zone D.
60	30 Jun 1965	Gyula Kállai became Premier of Hungary (until 1967).
50	1 Jun 1975	The Patriotic Union of Kurdistan (PUK), a nationalist political party, was founded in Iraqi Kurdistan. Two of its founders, Jalal Talabani and Fuad Masum, became Presidents of Iraq in 2006–14 and 2014–18 respectively.
50	1 Jun 1975	Drivers and front seat passengers in cars in the Netherlands were required to wear seatbelts if their vehicles were fitted with them.
50	2 Jun 1975	The last time widespread snow fell in Britain during the month of June. It was also thought to be the first widespread snowfall in June since the beginning of the 19th century.
50	3 Jun 1975	The original Broadway production of the musical *Chicago* opened.
50	3 Jun 1975	Death of Ozzie Nelson, American film, radio and television actor, director, producer, screenwriter, musician, composer, conductor and bandleader. Best known for co-creating and starring in the radio and TV series *The Adventures of Ozzie and Harriet* with his wife Harriet and their two sons.
50	3 Jun 1975	Death of Eisaku Satō, Prime Minister of Japan (1964–72). Joint winner of the 1974 Nobel Peace Prize for his work on nuclear disarmament.
50	4 Jun 1975	The California Agricultural Labor Relations Act of 1975 was signed into law. California became the first U.S. state to give farm-workers collective bargaining rights.
50	5 Jun 1975	The first UK-wide referendum was held, with voters asked to decide whether Britain should remain in the European Economic Community (EEC). 67 percent voted in favour.
50	5 Jun 1975	The Suez Canal opened for the first time in eight years. It was closed by an Egyptian blockade following the end of the Arab–Israeli War (also known as the Six Day War) in 1967.
50	7 Jun 1975	Sony released the Betamax video cassette recorder in the USA. (Japan: 10th May 1975. Europe: 1978.) JVC released its competing (and more popular) VHS system a year later.
50	7 Jun 1975 to 21st	The first Cricket World Cup was held, in England.
50	8 Jun 1975	The Soviet Union launched its *Venera 9* space probe on a mission to Venus. In October it became the first spacecraft to orbit Venus and its lander became the first spacecraft to return an image from the surface of another planet. *Venera 10* was launched on 14th June and also reached Venus in October.

JUNE 2025

Ann.	Date	Event
50	9 Jun 1975	The first live radio broadcast of proceedings from Britain's House of Commons.
50	10 Jun 1975	The disco/funk song *That's the Way (I Like It)* by KC and the Sunshine Band was released.
50	11 Jun 1975	A U.S. federal interagency task force released a report, *Fluorocarbons and the Environment*. It recommended that fluorocarbons, used as propellants in aerosol spray cans, should be banned because of the damage they cause to the Earth's ozone layer. The U.S. government instituted the world's first ban on chlorofluorocarbons (CFCs) in 1978.
50	12 Jun 1975	Indian Prime Minister Indira Gandhi was found guilty of electoral corruption and barred from holding office for six years. She refused to resign. On 26th June she declared a State of Emergency, allowing her to suspend elections, curb civil liberties and rule by decree. She remained in office until March 1977, and became Prime Minister again in January 1980.
50	18 Jun 1975	The first North Sea oil was pumped ashore in Britain.
50	18 Jun 1975	NBC in the USA launched the NBC News and Information Service for local radio stations that wanted to provided an all-news service. Dozens of radio stations signed up as subscribers, but it never made a profit. It was discontinued in May 1977.
50	18 Jun 1975	Death of Faisal bin Musaid Al Saud, Saudi Arabian prince. Nephew and assassin of King Faisal of Saudi Arabia. (Executed by public beheading, aged 31.)
50	19 Jun 1975	British peer Lord Lucan was convicted in his absence of murdering his children's 29-year-old nanny, Sandra Rivett, in November 1974. He disappeared after the murder and has never been seen since.
50	20 Jun 1975	The film *Jaws* was released in the USA. (UK: 25th December.)
50	21 Jun 1975	British rock guitarist Ritchie Blackmore announced that he had left the band Deep Purple. He formed the supergroup Rainbow with American singer Ronnie James Dio and British musicians Graham Bonnet, Don Airey and Roger Glover.
50	24 Jun 1975	Eastern Air Lines Flight 66 crashed on approach to John F. Kennedy International Airport in New York City, USA. 113 of the 124 people on board were killed. (Cause: wind shear – the airport and flight crew also failed to recognise the potential hazard.)
50	25 Jun 1975	Mozambique gained its independence from Portugal.
50	26 Jun 1975	Pine Ridge Shootout, Pine Ridge Indian Reservation, South Dakota, USA. Two FBI agents and a member of the American Indian Movement (AIM) were killed in an armed confrontation between AIM activists and the FBI. One of the activists, Leonard Peltier, was later convicted of murdering the FBI agents. He was sentenced to two consecutive life terms in 1977.
50	26 Jun 1975	Death of Saint Josemaría Escrivá, Spanish Roman Catholic priest. Founder of Opus Dei. Canonised in 2002.
50	28 Jun 1975	Death of Rod Serling, American television scriptwriter, producer and narrator. Best known for *The Twilight Zone*.

JUNE 2025

Ann.	Date	Event
40	Jun 1985	The Atari ST personal computer was released. The first model was the 520ST. It was the first personal computer with a colour graphical user interface. It was followed by the 1040ST in 1986.
40	1 Jun 1985	Death of Richard Greene, British film and television actor. Best known for the TV series *The Adventures of Robin Hood*.
40	2 Jun 1985	American serial killer Leonard Lake was arrested in San Francisco, California. He and his accomplice Charles Ng had raped, tortured and murdered between 11 and 25 people. While he was in custody, he swallowed cyanide capsules he had hidden in his clothing. He died on 6th June. Ng was imprisoned in Canada after being convicted of robbery and weapons charges. He was later extradited to the USA, convicted of eleven murders, and sentenced to death (effectively life imprisonment, as there have been no executions in California since 2006).
40	2 Jun 1985	UEFA banned all English football clubs from playing in European competitions following the Heysel Stadium disaster of 28th May. On 6th June FIFA extended the ban to cover all worldwide competitions except friendly matches. It did not apply to the England national team. The ban was lifted after five years.
40	4 Jun 1985	Birth of Ana Carolina Reston, Brazilian fashion model. (Died from anorexia in 2006.)
40	6 Jun 1985	The grave of 'Wolfgang Gerhard' was exhumed in Embu das Artes, Brazil. The remains were later confirmed to be those of Josef Mengele, the Nazi doctor who conducted medical experiments on inmates at Auschwitz concentration camp during WWII. He had died in February 1979 after suffering a stroke while swimming.
40	7 Jun 1985	The comedy adventure film *The Goonies* was released in the USA and Canada. (UK: 29th November.)
40	9 Jun 1985	American educator Thomas Sutherland, Dean of Agriculture at the American University of Beirut, Lebanon, was kidnapped by Islamic Jihad. He was released in November 1991, and was later awarded a $35 million settlement.
40	11 Jun 1985	The Soviet space probe *Vega 1* flew past Venus and dropped a lander onto the planet, which sent back details of the atmosphere and surface. (The main probe continued on to Halley's Comet, arriving in June 1986.)
40	11 Jun 1985	Death of Karen Ann Quinlan, American woman who was the subject of a right-to-die controversy. She lapsed into a persistent vegetative state in 1975 after taking Valium and alcohol while on a crash diet. Her doctors refused to disconnect her ventilator. Her parents eventually won a legal appeal to disconnect it themselves. She continued to live for a further nine years before succumbing to respiratory failure caused by pneumonia, aged 31.

JUNE 2025

Ann.	Date	Event
40	14 Jun 1985	TWA Flight 847 was hijacked by Lebanese Shiite Muslim extremists after taking off from Athens, Greece. It was forced to fly between Beirut and Algiers a number of times, with hostages gradually being freed, and eventually halted in Beirut. The remaining hostages were held in Beirut until 30th June. One passenger was killed. The hijackers demanded the release of 700 prisoners held by Israel – the prisoners were released shortly afterwards, though Israel denied it had any connection with the hijacking.
40	17 Jun 1985	Sultan Salman Al Saud of Saudi Arabia became the first Arab, the first Muslim, and the first member of a royal family to fly in space. He was a payload specialist on board the U.S. space shuttle *Discovery*.
40	17 Jun 1985	Mexico's first satellite, *Morelos I*, was launched. It operated until 1998, providing telephone, data and television services.
40	17 Jun 1985	Death of John Boulting, British film director who worked in partnership with his twin brother Roy (*Brighton Rock*, *Private's Progress*, *Lucky Jim*, *I'm All Right, Jack*, *There's a Girl in My Soup*, and many more).
40	21 Jun 1985	The science-fiction comedy-drama film *Cocoon* was released in the USA and Canada. (UK: 13th September.)
40	21 Jun 1985	Death of Hector Boyardee, (Ettore Boiardi), Italian-born American chef. Founder of the Chef Boyardee brand of canned pasta products.
40	21 Jun 1985	Death of Tage Erlander, Prime Minister of Sweden (1946–69).
40	23 Jun 1985	Air India Flight 182 exploded over the Atlantic Ocean near Ireland, killing all 329 people on board. (Cause: bomb planted by terrorists.)
40	27 Jun 1985	The USA's historic Route 66 highway was decertified and removed from the U.S. Highway System. It had been replaced along its entire length by the Interstate Highway System.
40	30 Jun 1985	Death of James Dewar, American baker who invented the Twinkie.
40	30 Jun 1985	Death of Haruo Remeliik, first President of Palau (1981–85). (Assassinated.) Succeeded by Alfonso Oiterong (until October).
30	1 Jun 1995	The world's first DAB digital radio station began broadcasting: NRK Klassisk in Norway.
30	3 Jun 1995	Death of J. Presper Eckert, American electrical engineer and computer pioneer. Co-inventor of the first general-purpose electronic computer.
30	5 Jun 1995	Bose-Einstein condensate was created for the first time by a team led by Eric Cornell and Carl Wieman at the University of Colorado, Boulder.
30	8 Jun 1995	The first version of the PHP programming language was released by Greenlandic-Canadian programmer Rasmus Lerdorf. It was originally a scripting language for web development, but it has since evolved into a general-purpose programming language.
30	8 Jun 1995	Death of Juan Carlos Ongania, President of Argentina (1966–70).
30	9 Jun 1995	Andrew Richards became the first man in Britain to be charged with the attempted rape of another man. He was later sentenced to life imprisonment.

JUNE 2025

Ann.	Date	Event
30	12 Jun 1995	Death of Arturo Benedetti Michelangeli, Italian pianist. One of the greatest pianists of the 20th century.
30	14 Jun 1995 to 19th	Budyonnovsk hospital hostage crisis, Russia. A group of Chechen separatists stormed the city of Budyonnovsk. After encountering Russian forces, they retreated to the city's hospital, shooting 100 civilians on the way, and took up to 2,000 people hostage. On 18th June Russia agreed to halt its military actions in Chechnya, the hostages were released, and the rebels were allowed to go free.
30	14 Jun 1995	Pauline Clare was appointed Chief Constable of Lancashire Constabulary, becoming the first female Chief Constable in Britain.
30	14 Jun 1995	Death of Rory Gallagher, Irish blues/rock guitarist, singer and songwriter. (Complications following a liver transplant, aged 47.)
30	14 Jun 1995	Death of Roger Zelazny, American science fiction and fantasy writer.
30	15 Jun 1995	An infamous moment during the O. J. Simpson murder trial: Simpson struggled to don a blood-stained leather glove that had been found at the murder scene. Defence lawyer Johnnie Cochran quipped to the jury: 'If it doesn't fit, you must acquit.'
30	15 Jun 1995	Death of John Vincent Atanasoff, American physicist and computer pioneer. Inventor of what is now recognised as the first electronic digital computer (the Atanasoff–Berry Computer), which was successfully tested in 1942.
30	17 Jun 1995	Pride Scotland, the first Pride march in Scotland, took place in Edinburgh.
30	19 Jun 1995	Death of Peter Townsend, British equerry to King George VI and Queen Elizabeth II. Best known for his romance with Princess Margaret.
30	21 Jun 1995	A Japanese man hijacked an All Nippon Airways flight and forced it to land at Hakodate airport, Hokkaido, Japan. He demanded the release of Shoko Asahara, leader of the religious cult responsible for the sarin gas attack on the Tokyo subway system in March. All hostages were released unharmed. Shoko Asahara remained in prison.
30	22 Jun 1995	British Prime Minister John Major resigned as leader of the Conservative Party after three years of attacks by critics. He told his critics to 'put up or shut up' and invited them to stand against him in a leadership election. He beat John Redwood in the election and remained PM until May 1997.
30	22 Jun 1995	The U.S. première of the space drama film *Apollo 13*. (Released: 30th June. UK: 22nd September.)
30	22 Jun 1995	Death of Yves Congar, French Dominican cardinal. One of the most important Roman Catholic theologians of the 20th century.
30	23 Jun 1995	Death of Jonas Salk, American medical researcher who developed the first safe and effective polio vaccine.
30	25 Jun 1995	Death of Warren E. Burger, Chief Justice of the United States (1969–86).
30	25 Jun 1995	Death of Ernest Walton, Irish physicist. The first person to split an atom. Joint winner of the 1951 Nobel Prize in Physics for developing the first particle accelerator.

JUNE 2025

Ann.	Date	Event
30	27 Jun 1995	Hamad bin Khalifa Al Thani became Emir of Qatar after deposing his father Khalifa bin Hamad Al Thani in a bloodless coup.
30	27 Jun 1995	British actor Hugh Grant was arrested in Los Angeles, California, USA for engaging in lewd behaviour in a public place (a rented car) with a prostitute. On 10th July he appeared on *The Tonight Show* and host Jay Leno famously asked him, 'What the hell were you thinking?'
30	29 Jun 1995	The Sampoong Department Store in the Seocho-gu district of Seoul, South Korea collapsed. 502 people were killed and 937 injured – the largest peacetime disaster in South Korean history.
30	29 Jun 1995	The U.S. space shuttle *Atlantis* docked with Russia's *Mir* space station – the first time the two nations' spacecraft had docked in orbit for 20 years.
30	29 Jun 1995	Lisa Clayton became the first British woman to sail single-handed and non-stop around the world.
30	29 Jun 1995	Death of Lana Turner, American film actress (*The Postman Always Rings Twice*, *The Bad and the Beautiful*, *Peyton Place*, and more).
30	30 Jun 1995	Death of Phyllis Hyman, American jazz/R&B singer, songwriter and actress. (Suicide.)
30	30 Jun 1995	Death of Sicco Mansholt, Dutch politician. One of the founding fathers of what would become the European Union. European Commissioner for Agriculture (1958–72). President of the European Commission (1972–73).
30	30 Jun 1995	Death of Barney Simon, South African theatre director and playwright. Co-founder of the Market Theatre in Johannesburg – the first multi-racial theatre in South Africa.
25	1 Jun 2000	The Patent Law Treaty was signed by 53 countries and the European Patent Organisation. It harmonised the procedures for filing patent applications.
25	1 Jun 2000	Death of Tito Puente, American Latin jazz/mambo musician, songwriter and record producer. He helped popularise Latin dance music and jazz in the USA.
25	5 Jun 2000 to 10th	Second Congo War – the Six-Day War, Kisangani, Democratic Republic of the Congo. Rwandan victory over Ugandan forces. A large part of the city was destroyed.
25	7 Jun 2000	United States District Judge Thomas Penfield Jackson ordered that Microsoft should be broken up into two separate companies: one to develop operating systems and one to develop other applications. Microsoft appealed the decision, and it was later overturned. (United States v. Microsoft Corp.)
25	10 Jun 2000	The Millennium Bridge opened in London, UK. It closed two days later when it was found to sway uncomfortably when people walked in step. (It reopened in February 2002 after dampers were fitted to eliminate the problem.)
25	10 Jun 2000	Death of Hafez al-Assad, President of Syria (1971–2000).
25	10 Jun 2000	Death of Brian Statham, British cricketer (Lancashire 1950–68, England 1951–65). A renowned fast bowler.

JUNE 2025

Ann.	Date	Event
25	13 Jun 2000	The first North-South Korean summit (the Inter-Korean Summit) was held. (South Korean President Kim Dae-jung was awarded the Nobel Peace Prize for his efforts to ease tensions between the two countries.)
25	20 Jun 2000	British Telecom (BT) ordered internet service providers (ISPs) to pay it a licensing fee for the use of hyperlinks on websites. All of the ISPs it contacted refused to pay, and BT attempted to sue Prodigy, the oldest ISP in the USA. BT's claim to own the rights to hyperlinks, which dated from 1989, was rejected by a judge in August 2002. The earliest known mention of hyperlinks dates from 1965.
25	20 Jun 2000	Peter Houghton, a British heart patient, became the first person in the world to receive a permanent artificial heart. He received a Jarvik 2000 heart pump at John Radcliffe Hospital in Oxford and lived until November 2007. With the artificial heart, he completed a 91-mile charity walk; hiked, travelled and lectured extensively; and published two books.
25	21 Jun 2000	Section 28 of the Local Government Act 1988 was repealed in Scotland. (It was also repealed in England and Wales in 2003.) The clause had prohibited the 'promotion of homosexuality' and had forced many LGBT+ support groups, especially those for students, to close down or limit their activities.
25	24 Jun 2000	U.S. President Bill Clinton gave the first Presidential webcast. He announced a new website where citizens would be able to access government services online, and pledged to spend billions of dollars on increasing electronic access to more services.
25	24 Jun 2000	Death of David Tomlinson, British stage, film and television actor. Best known for his film roles in *Mary Poppins*, *Bedknobs and Broomsticks* and *The Love Bug*. A Disney Legend.
25	25 Jun 2000	Rival scientific teams from the Human Genome Project and Celera Genomics Corp. jointly announced that they had completed the first rough draft of the human genome.
25	28 Jun 2000	The U.S. Supreme Court ruled that laws which banned partial birth abortions were unconstitutional if they did not take into account the mother's welfare or if they could be construed as applying to other methods of abortion. The case particularly referred to a Nebraska law, but several other states had similar laws. (Stenberg v. Carhart.)
25	30 Jun 2000	The U.S. communications company Verizon was created when Bell Atlantic merged with GTE.
25	30 Jun 2000	The E-Signature Bill (the Electronic Signatures in Global and National Commerce Act) was enacted in the USA. It recognised electronic signatures as having the same legal validity as those signed in ink.
25	30 Jun 2000	American brothers Alan and Vincent Chow announced that they had invented and implanted artificial silicon retinas in blind patients, restoring some of their vision. The 2-mm diameter chip sits behind the retina and contains 3,500 photodiodes which convert light into electrical impulses.

JUNE 2025

Ann.	Date	Event
20	1 Jun 2005	The Netherlands held a referendum on the Constitution of the European Union. 61 percent of voters rejected it, and the Constitution was abandoned. It had already been rejected by France on 29th May. It was replaced by the Lisbon Treaty – a series of amendments to existing treaties, which contained much of the same material but did not require ratification. It was signed on 13th December 2007 and came into effect on 1st December 2009.
20	2 Jun 2005	Death of Melita Norwood, British civil servant and Soviet spy. She leaked secret project details to the Soviet Union while working as a secretary for the British Non-Ferrous Metals Research Association. She was never prosecuted for her activities.
20	6 Jun 2005	The United States Supreme Court ruled that Congress could ban the use of cannabis even if states allowed it to be used for medicinal purposes. (Gonzales v. Raich.) In practice, most authorities turn a blind eye to its use for medicinal purposes, and there are calls for the ruling to be revisited.
20	6 Jun 2005	Death of Anne Bancroft, American stage, film and television actress (*The Graduate, The Pumpkin Eater, The Turning Point, Agnes of God, 84 Charing Cross Road*, and more). Wife of the director Mel Brooks – she also appeared in several of his films.
20	11 Jun 2005	G8 finance ministers agreed to write off the entire $40 billion debt owed by eighteen of the world's poorest countries.
20	13 Jun 2005	American pop singer Michael Jackson was cleared of all ten charges of child molestation that had been made against him, after a four-month trial.
20	20 Jun 2005	Death of Jack Kilby, American electrical engineer. Co-inventor of the integrated circuit (microprocessor). Inventor of the hand-held calculator and thermal printer. Joint winner of the 2000 Nobel Prize in Physics.
20	21 Jun 2005	Former Ku Klux Klan organiser Edgar Ray Killen was convicted of the 1964 murder of three civil rights activists. He had been tried unsuccessfully in 1964. In 2004 a group of citizens launched an appeal for information and succeeded in launching a new prosecution. He was found guilty of manslaughter and sentenced to sixty years in prison. He died in prison in 2018.
20	21 Jun 2005	Donald Tsang became Chief Executive of Hong Kong.
20	21 Jun 2005	Death of Jaime Cardinal Sin, Filipino Roman Catholic cleric. Archbishop of Manila (1974–2003).
20	24 Jun 2005	Death of Paul Winchell, American ventriloquist, voice actor (most notably of Tigger in the *Winnie The Pooh* cartoons) and inventor of the first mechanical heart that could be implanted in a patient's chest.
20	25 Jun 2005	Death of John Fiedler, American stage, film, television and radio actor. Best known for his roles as Juror #2 in the film *12 Angry Men* and as the voice of Piglet in Walt Disney's *Winnie the Pooh* productions. He also voiced characters in numerous other Disney features and made many guest appearances on TV.
20	26 Jun 2005	Death of Richard Whiteley, British television presenter. Best known for hosting the word/number puzzle game show *Countdown*.

JUNE 2025

Ann.	Date	Event
20	27 Jun 2005	Dennis Rader, 'the BTK Killer', admitted torturing and killing ten people in Wichita, Kansas, USA between 1974 and 1991. In August he was sentenced to ten consecutive life terms.
20	27 Jun 2005	The U.S. Supreme Court ruled that companies which facilitate the infringing of copyrights can be sued by copyright holders. The case referred to the peer-to-peer file-sharing service Grokster. It shut down on 7th November 2005 and reached a settlement with the plaintiffs in 2006. (MGM Studios, Inc. v. Grokster, Ltd.)
20	27 Jun 2005	Death of Domino Harvey, British-born American bounty hunter. (Drug overdose, aged 35.) The 2005 film *Domino* is based on her life.
15	5 Jun 2010	Same-sex marriage was legalised in Portugal.
15	13 Jun 2010	The Japanese spacecraft *Hayabusa*, launched in May 2003, returned to Earth with samples collected from the asteroid 25143 Itokawa. It had collected 1,500 grains of rock, which were analysed by scientists. Their findings were published in *Science* magazine on 26th August 2011.
15	15 Jun 2010	The Saville Report, an enquiry into Bloody Sunday in Northern Ireland in 1972, was published. It found that British paratroopers had fired the first shot, without warning; had fired at unarmed civilians as they fled the scene; and had shot and killed a man who was already wounded. Prime Minister David Cameron apologised on behalf of the British government.
15	16 Jun 2010	Bhutan banned the cultivation, harvesting, production, and sale of tobacco and tobacco products. Smoking is permitted in a few designated areas, for people who import tobacco for their personal consumption, but the amount a person can own is restricted. Anyone found in possession of more than 300 cigarettes can be fined.
15	24 Jun 2010	Julia Gillard became the first female Prime Minister of Australia.
15	24 Jun 2010	Apple released the iPhone 4.
15	27 Jun 2010	The first round of the 2010 Guinea presidential election was held. It was the first free national election in Guinea since it gained its independence in 1958. A second round was held on 7th November. Alpha Condé was the winner, and took office on 21st December.
15	28 Jun 2010	The U.S. Supreme Court ruled that American citizens have the right to own a gun, regardless of which state they live in. The right was protected by the Second and Fourteenth Amendments to the U.S. Constitution, and could not be infringed by local or state authorities. (McDonald v. City of Chicago.)
15	30 Jun 2010	Benigno Aquino III became President of the Philippines (until 2016).
10	1 Jun 2015	A river cruise ship, the *Dongfang zhi Xing*, capsized and sank on the Yangtze River in Jianli, Hubei Province, China during a thunderstorm. 442 people were killed. Twelve were rescued.
10	1 Jun 2015	Death of Charles Kennedy, Scottish politician. Leader of the Liberal Democrats (1999–2006). (Alcohol-related haemorrhage, aged 55.)

JUNE 2025

Ann.	Date	Event
10	1 Jun 2015	Death of Nicholas Liverpool, President of Dominica (2003–12).
10	5 Jun 2015	Death of Tariq Aziz, Deputy Prime Minister of Iraq (1979–2003), Minister of Foreign Affairs (1983–91). A close advisor of President Saddam Hussein. He was arrested after the 2003 Invasion of Iraq, and later sentenced to death by the Iraqi High Tribunal. Iraqi President Jalal Talabani refused to sign his execution order, and his sentence was commuted to life imprisonment. He died in prison, aged 79.
10	11 Jun 2015	Death of Ron Moody, British stage and film actor and singer. Best known for his role as Fagin in *Oliver!*
10	17 Jun 2015	Death of Süleyman Demirel, President of Turkey (1993–2000).
10	17 Jun 2015	Death of Roberto M. Levingston, President of Argentina (1970–71). He staged a military coup in 1970, deposed President Juan Carlos Onganía, and seized the presidency. He was deposed in another military coup in 1971.
10	25 Jun 2015	Death of Patrick Macnee, British film and television actor. Best known for his role as John Steed in *The Avengers* and *The New Avengers*.
10	26 Jun 2015	The U.S. Supreme Court ruled that same-sex couples have the right to marry. All fifty states were required to perform and recognise same-sex marriages on the same terms and conditions as opposite-sex marriages. (Obergefell v. Hodges.) All states complied with the ruling by 2020, though some counties in Alabama, Kentucky and Texas resisted for several years.

JULY 2025

Ann.	Date	Event
600	21 Jul 1425	Death of Manuel II Palaiologos, Byzantine emperor (1391–1425). Succeeded by his son John VIII Palaiologos.
500	19 Jul 1525	German Reformation: the League of Dessau was founded by Catholic rulers in northern Germany. They aimed to halt the rebellion and stop the spread of the Martin Luther's teachings. They failed to persuade the rulers of southern Germany to join, and the Protestants formed their own rival league, so it had little effect.
400	27 Jul 1625	Birth of Edward Montagu, 1st Earl of Sandwich. British military officer, politician and diplomat. He is frequently mentioned in the diaries of Samuel Pepys. He was killed in the Anglo–Dutch War in 1672.
300	1 Jul 1725	Birth of Jean-Baptiste Donatien de Vimeur, comte de Rochambeau, French general and nobleman. Commander-in-chief of the French Expeditionary Force that helped the American Continental Army win the American Revolutionary War against the British.
250	1 Jul 1775	American Revolution: the New England Restraining Act came into effect. The British Parliament forbade its North American colonies from trading with anyone other than Britain, Ireland and the British West Indies. It also prohibited the colonies from fishing in the Atlantic without authorisation.
250	1 Jul 1775	American Revolution: the Second Continental Congress resolved to recruit Native American tribes to their cause as their dispute with the British escalated.
250	5 Jul 1775	American Revolution: the Second Continental Congress adopted the Olive Branch Petition, which was signed on 8th July. It was a direct appeal to King George III, reaffirming the colony's allegiance to Britain, and a last-ditch chance to avoid war. The King refused to look at the petition and declared the American colonies to be in open rebellion, and the British government rejected it. (See also: 6th July 1775.)
250	6 Jul 1775	American Revolution: the Second Continental Congress issued the Declaration of the Causes and Necessity of Taking up Arms. It listed the Thirteen Colonies' grievances, but denied any intent to become independent.
250	26 Jul 1775	American Revolution: the Second Continental Congress established the United States Post Office, headed by Benjamin Franklin. After the American Revolution, the official United States Post Office Department was established in 1792.
250	27 Jul 1775	The U.S. Army Medical Department was established by the Second Continental Congress (as the Army Hospital).
250	30 Jul 1775	British explorer Captain James Cook arrived home from his Second Voyage – a fruitless search for the mythical Terra Australis. During the voyage he mapped the east coast of Australia, discovered the South Sandwich Islands, and almost reached mainland Antarctica. He set off on his third, and last, voyage a year later, in search of the Northwest Passage between the Atlantic and Pacific Oceans.

JULY 2025

Ann.	Date	Event
200	29 Jul 1825	Birth of George Pendleton, American politician and diplomat. Senator from Ohio (1879–85). U.S. Ambassador to Germany (1885–89). He wrote and helped pass the Pendleton Civil Service Act of 1883 – though Ohio opposed it and it cost him his Senate seat.
175	2 Jul 1850	Benjamin Lane of Cambridge, Massachusetts, USA was granted a U.S. patent for the self-contained air-supplying gas mask (also known as a respirator). He called it 'Lanes Pneumatic Life Preserver'. (U.S. Patent 7,476.)
175	2 Jul 1850	Death of Robert Peel, British Prime Minister (1834–35, 1841–46). He founded the Metropolitan Police Service and is regarded as the father of modern British policing.
175	9 Jul 1850	Death of the Báb, Persian/Iranian prophet. Founder of Babism. One of the central figures of the Bahá'í Faith. (Executed, aged 30.)
175	9 Jul 1850	Death of Zachary Taylor, 12th President of the United States (1849–50 – died in office). (Stomach disorder, aged 65.) Succeeded by Vice President Millard Fillmore.
175	14 Jul 1850	American physician John Corrie gave the first public demonstration of ice made by refrigeration. He was awarded a British patent on his invention in August 1850 and a U.S. patent in 1851 (U.S. Patent 8,080) but it failed as a business venture and he died in poverty in 1855. French inventor Ferdinand Carre developed a more practical and successful version in 1860.
175	15 Jul 1850	Birth of Saint Francesca Xavier Cabrini (also called Mother Cabrini), the first American saint.
175	17 Jul 1850	The first photo of a star (Vega) was taken by William Bond and John Adams Whipple at Harvard College Observatory in the USA.
175	23 Jul 1850	Daniel Webster became U.S. Secretary of State for the second time. He helped pass the Compromise of 1850 in September, which postponed the American Civil War until 1861.
150	8 Jul 1875	Death of Francis Preston Blair Jr., American politician. Member of the House of Representatives (1857–59, 1860, 1861–64) and Senator (1871–73) from Missouri. He played a key role in the American Civil War and prevented Missouri from joining the Confederacy at the start of the war.
150	10 Jul 1875	Birth of Mary McLeod Bethune, American educator, writer, philanthropist, civil rights leader and humanitarian. She was the daughter of two slaves. She founded and/or led several organisations for African American women, was Presidential adviser to Franklin D. Roosevelt, and founded a private school for African Americans that later became Bethune-Cookman University.
150	11 Jul 1875	The Native Sons of the Golden West (NSGW) was founded in California, USA. The fraternal organisation documents and preserves historic structures and places in the state, and places historical plaques and markers. U.S. President Richard Nixon and Chief Justice Earl Warren were both presidents of the NSGW.

JULY 2025

Ann.	Date	Event
150	23 Jul 1875	Death of Isaac Singer, American inventor and businessman. He designed an improved sewing machine that could be adapted for home use, and founded the Singer Sewing Machine Company.
150	26 Jul 1875	Birth of Carl Jung, Swiss psychiatrist and psychoanalyst. The founder of analytical psychology.
150	27 Jul 1875	American electrical engineer Elisha Gray was granted a U.S. patent for acoustic telegraphy (an Electric Telegraph for Transmitting Musical Tones). It enabled multiple telegraph messages to be sent along the same line at the same time, reducing the cost of telegraphy. (U.S. Patent 166,095.) It was also a key invention that led to the invention of the telephone. Other inventors including Alexander Graham Bell and Thomas Edison developed their own versions of acoustic telegraphy.
150	31 Jul 1875	Death of Andrew Johnson, 17th President of the United States (1865–69). He was Vice-President to Abraham Lincoln and assumed the presidency after Lincoln was assassinated.
125	2 Jul 1900	The Zeppelin *LZ 1* made its first flight over Lake Constance in southern Germany. It was the world's first rigid airship. On this first test flight it flew 3.7 miles before one of its engines failed and it had to make an emergency landing for repairs.
125	2 Jul 1900	The première of Finnish composer Jean Sibelius's tone poem *Finlandia* (Opus 26) in Helsinki. It was often performed under alternative names to avoid Russian censorship.
125	2 Jul 1900	Birth of Tyrone Guthrie, British theatrical director. He founded the Stratford Festival of Canada, the Guthrie Theater in Minneapolis, Minnesota, USA, and the Tyrone Guthrie Centre in County Monaghan, Ireland. He later became Chancellor of Queen's University in Belfast, Northern Ireland.
125	6 Jul 1900	Death of Warren Earp, American frontiersman and lawman. The youngest of the Earp brothers. (Shot dead in an argument in a saloon in Arizona, aged 45.)
125	8 Jun 1900	Birth of George Antheil, American avant-garde composer, pianist, writer and inventor. Co-inventor (with the actress Hedy Lamarr) of spread spectrum communications.
125	10 Jul 1900	Emile Berliner, the inventor of the gramophone, trademarked British artist Francis Barraud's 1898 painting 'His Master's Voice'. It became the corporate logo for the Consolidated Talking Machine Company, which later became the Victor Talking Machine Company, and RCA Victor. It is currently the logo of the British music and film retailer HMV.
125	19 Jul 1900	The Paris Métro in France began operating.
125	27 Jul 1900	Kaiser Wilhelm II of Germany gave his infamous 'Hun' speech. He was addressing German forces that were setting off to help suppress the anti-Western Boxer Rebellion in China, and compared the German forces to the fearless Huns that were led by Attila the Hun a thousand years earlier. Anti-German propaganda used the term 'Hun' as a disparaging name for Germans for many years afterwards.

JULY 2025

Ann.	Date	Event
125	27 Jul 1900	Birth of Charles Vidor, Hungarian-born American film director (*The Tuttles of Tahiti, The Desperadoes, Gilda, Hans Christian Andersen, A Farewell to Arms*, and many more).
125	29 Jul 1900	Death of Umberto I, King of Italy (1878–1900). (Assassinated by an anarchist, aged 56.) Succeeded by his son, Victor Emmanuel III.
100	1 Jul 1925	Death of Erik Satie, French composer, pianist and writer.
100	2 Jul 1925	Birth of Medgar Evers, American civil rights activist who campaigned to end segregation and improve opportunities for African Americans in Mississippi and the South. (Assassinated in 1963, aged 37.)
100	2 Jul 1925	Birth of Patrice Lumumba, first Prime Minister of the Democratic Republic of the Congo (1960). (Assassinated/executed in 1961.)
100	4 Jul 1925	The Pickwick Club, a nightclub based in the former Hotel Dreyfus in Boston, Massachusetts, USA, collapsed during a Fourth of July party. 44 people were killed.
100	6 Jul 1925	Birth of Merv Griffin, American television talk show host, producer and entrepreneur. Host of *The Merv Griffin Show* and creator of the game shows *Jeopardy!* and *Wheel of Fortune*. He went on to establish a multi-million-dollar business empire, which included hotels, resorts and casinos. (Died 2007.)
100	6 Jul 1925	Birth of Bill Haley, American rock and roll singer (Bill Haley and His Comets). Best known for the songs *Rock Around the Clock, See You Later, Alligator* and *Shake, Rattle and Roll*. (Died 1981.)
100	10 Jul 1925 to 21st	The Scopes Trial, Dayton, Tennessee, USA. High school science teacher John Scopes was charged with teaching the theory of evolution, in violation of a Tennessee state law (the Butler Act). He was found guilty and fined $100, but the conviction was later overturned by the Court of Appeal and the trial was declared void. Scopes had agreed to be tried for violating the act. The trial was organised as a publicity stunt to gain attention for the town of Dayton, and was funded by the American Civil Liberties Union. The Butler Act was repealed in 1967.
100	10 Jul 1925	Indian spiritual master Meher Baba began maintaining his silence. He never said another word for the rest of his life. He died in 1969, having been silent for 44 years.
100	18 Jul 1925	The first volume of Adolf Hitler's autobiographical manifesto *Mein Kampf* (My Struggle) was published.
100	21 Jul 1925 to Jun 1927	The Great Syrian Revolt. French victory.
100	21 Jul 1925	British racing driver Malcolm Campbell became the first person to travel over 150 mph. He set a new land speed record of 150.87 mph at Pendine Sands in Wales in a Sunbeam 350HP. He also broke the 250 mph and 300 mph records, in 1932 and 1935.
100	23 Jul 1925	Birth of Tajuddin Ahmad, first Prime Minister of Bangladesh (1971–72). (Assassinated in 1975, aged 50.)

JULY 2025

Ann.	Date	Event
100	25 Jul 1925	TASS, the official news agency of the Soviet Union, was established. It was a successor of the Commercial Telegraph Agency, which was established in 1902.
100	26 Jul 1925	Death of Antonio Ascari, Italian racing driver. Killed in the French Grand Prix, aged 36. Father of the Formula One World Champion Alberto Ascari.
100	26 Jul 1925	Death of William Jennings Bryan, U.S. Secretary of State (1913–15).
100	30 Jul 1925	Birth of Stan Stennett, Welsh comedian, actor and jazz musician. (Died 2013.)
90	1 Jul 1935	Grant Park Music Festival began in Chicago, Illinois. It is the only free classical music concert series in the USA.
90	1 Jul 1935	Birth of David Prowse, British actor and bodybuilder. Best known for his role as Darth Vader in the *Star Wars* films, and as the Green Cross Man in children's road safety films in the UK. (Died 2020.)
90	3 Jul 1935	Death of André Citroën, French engineer and industrialist. Founder of the Citroën car company. He introduced Henry Ford's mass production systems to Europe.
90	6 Jul 1935	1935 Yangtze River flood, China. 145,000 people were killed. Millions were displaced and suffered from food shortages and famine.
90	6 Jul 1935	The National Labor Relations Act came into effect in the USA. It guarantees the basic rights of private sector employees.
90	9 Jul 1935	Birth of Wim Duisenberg, Dutch economist. First president of the European Central Bank (1998–2003). He oversaw the introduction of the euro. (Died 2005.)
90	9 Jul 1935	Birth of Michael Williams, British stage, film, television and radio actor. A noted Shakespearean actor but best known for the TV sitcom *A Fine Romance* which he starred in with his wife Dame Judi Dench. (Died 2001.)
90	12 Jul 1935	Death of Alfred Dreyfus, French military officer whose conviction for treason led to the Dreyfus Affair – a twelve-year political scandal concerning miscarriage of justice. (He was eventually exonerated.)
90	15 Jul 1935	Birth of Ken Kercheval, American actor. Best known for his role as Cliff Barnes in the television series *Dallas*. (Died 2019.)
90	16 Jul 1935	The world's first parking meter was installed in Oklahoma City, USA.
90	17 Jul 1935	Death of George William Russell, ('AE'), Irish nationalist, poet, artist and mystic.
90	20 Jul 1935	Birth of Ted Rogers, British comedian and television presenter. Best known for hosting the game show *3-2-1*. (Died 2001.)
90	24 Jul 1935	Greetings telegrams were introduced in Britain. They were an instant success, with 25,000 sent in the first week.
90	24 Jul 1935	The world's first children's railway opened in Tbilisi, Georgia.
90	25 Jul 1935	Abyssinia Crisis: Britain imposed an embargo on the sale of arms to Italy and Ethiopia.

JULY 2025

Ann.	Date	Event
90	25 Jul 1935	Birth of Gilbert Parent, Speaker of the House of Commons of Canada (1994–2001). (Died 2009.)
90	28 Jul 1935	The first flight of the Boeing B-17 Flying Fortress, in Seattle, Washington, USA.
90	28 Jul 1935	Birth of Simon Dee, British disc jockey and television talk show host. The first DJ on Radio Caroline (pirate radio) and one of the first on BBC Radio 1. (Died 2009.)
90	28 Jul 1935	Death of Meletius Metaxakis, Greek Eastern Orthodox bishop. Primate of the Church of Greece (1918–20 as Meletius III), Ecumenical Patriarch of Constantinople (1921–23 as Meletius IV), Greek Patriarch of Alexandria (1926–35 as Meletius II).
90	30 Jul 1935	The first ten Penguin paperbacks were published in the UK.
80	1 Jul 1945	The New York State Commission Against Discrimination (now the New York State Division of Human Rights) was established. It was the first permanent state agency in the USA to enforce legislation prohibiting discrimination in employment based on race, creed, colour, and national origin. It was later expanded to cover other forms of discrimination.
80	3 Jul 1945	Birth of Michael Martin, Speaker of the British House of Commons (2000–09). He resigned over his role in the parliamentary expenses scandal. (Died 2018.)
80	5 Jul 1945	World War II: the liberation of the Philippines. Allied forces recaptured the Philippines from the Japanese, although fighting continued until Japan surrendered in September.
80	5 Jul 1945	British General Election. WWII leader Winston Churchill was expected to remain Prime Minister, but he was defeated by Clement Atlee's Labour Party. (The result was declared on 26th July.)
80	5 Jul 1945	Death of John Curtin, Prime Minister of Australia (1941–45).
80	6 Jul 1945	U.S. President Harry S. Truman established the Medal of Freedom (now known as the Presidential Medal of Freedom). It honours civilians whose actions aid the war efforts of the USA and its allies.
80	11 Jul 1945	Cold War: the Soviet Union agreed to hand over all control of West Berlin in Germany to British and U.S. Forces. The handover took place the following day.
80	14 Jul 1945	World War II: U.S. Navy warships began bombarding the main Japanese islands for the first time.
80	16 Jul 1945	The USA detonated the world's first nuclear weapon ('Fat Boy') at the Trinity Site, White Sands Missile Range, New Mexico.
80	17 Jul 1945 to 2 Aug	World War II: the Potsdam Conference, Germany. Allied leaders met to discuss the fate of the defeated Germany and the terms for Japanese surrender (or its destruction if it did not surrender).
80	18 Jul 1945	Cold War: the U.S. House Military Affairs subcommittee's chief counsel, H. Ralph Burton, named sixteen Army officers who he said had Communist backgrounds. The Army investigated and found that none of the officers named were 'disaffected or disloyal'.

JULY 2025

Ann.	Date	Event
80	23 Jul 1945	(Henri) Philippe Pétain, the Chief of State of Vichy France during WWII, went on trial for treason. He was found guilty and sentenced to life imprisonment. He died in prison in 1951.
80	26 Jul 1945	Clement Attlee became British Prime Minister after defeating Winston Churchill in the General Election held on 5th July.
80	26 Jul 1945	World War II: the last British ship lost in the war, *HMS Vestal*, was critically damaged in a Japanese kamikaze attack, and was scuttled off Thailand. The Royal Navy minesweeper was the only British ship lost in a kamikaze attack.
80	28 Jul 1945	A U.S. Army B-25 Mitchell bomber crashed into the Empire State Building in New York City, USA in thick fog. All three people on the plane and eleven people in the building were killed.
80	29 Jul 1945	The BBC Light Programme radio station was launched in the UK. It broadcast mainstream light entertainment and music. It became BBC Radio 2 in 1967.
80	30 Jul 1945	World War II: the U.S. Navy heavy cruiser *USS Indianapolis* was torpedoed and sunk by a Japanese submarine after delivering key components of the Hiroshima atomic bomb to the Pacific island of Tinian. About 300 of the 1,196 crew were killed immediately, while almost 600 more died over the following days from dehydration, exposure, salt water poisoning or shark attacks while awaiting rescue. 317 survived.
75	1 Jul 1950	Korean War: the first American ground troops, Task Force Smith, arrived in South Korea. Their mission was to engage with the advancing North Korean army and delay them until more U.S. forces arrived. Most members of the task force were teenagers with only eight weeks of basic training and no combat experience. Their first battle was the Battle of Osan on 5th July, which saw the first American fatalities of the war.
75	4 Jul 1950	Cold War: Radio Free Europe made its first broadcast (to Czechoslovakia). Its aim was to bring about the peaceful demise of the Communists.
75	5 Jul 1950	The Law of Return was passed in Israel. It granted all Jews the right to immigrate to Israel.
75	6 Jul 1950	The Treaty of Zgorzelec was signed by Poland and East Germany. It recognised the Oder–Neisse line as the border between the two countries. The border was established by the Potsdam Agreement in 1945.
75	8 Jul 1950	Korean War: American General Douglas MacArthur was appointed commander-in-chief of the United Nations forces.
75	9 Jul 1950	Birth of Gwen Guthrie, American R&B/soul/pop singer, songwriter and pianist. She sang backing vocals for numerous artists including Aretha Franklin, Billy Joel, Madonna, and Stevie Wonder, and had a hit in her own right with the song *Ain't Nothin' Goin' on But the Rent*. (Died 1999.)
75	10 Jul 1950	The first episode of the television music show *Your Hit Parade* was broadcast on NBC in the USA. (It ran until 1959, transferring to CBS in 1958. The radio version ran from 1935 to 1953.)
75	11 Jul 1950	The first episode of the BBC children's television show *Andy Pandy* was broadcast in the UK.

JULY 2025

Ann.	Date	Event
75	14 Jul 1950 to 21st	Korean War – the Battle of Taejon (South Korea). This was a tactical win for North Korea, but it delayed them while U.S. forces established a 140-mile defensive line around Pusan (now Busan). (See also: 4th August 1950.)
75	16 Jul 1950	Korean War – the Chaplain-Medic massacre. The Korean People's Army (KPA) of North Korea killed thirty unarmed injured U.S. soldiers and a chaplain who were stranded on a mountain during the Battle of Taejon (see 14th July).
75	22 Jul 1950	King Leopold III of Belgium returned to the throne after more than five years in exile. His return was marked by violent protests and a general strike, and on 1st August he announced his abdication. He officially abdicated on 16th July 1951 and was succeeded by his son Baudouin on 17th July.
75	22 Jul 1950	Death of William Lyon Mackenzie King, Prime Minister of Canada (1935–48).
75	24 Jul 1950	The first rocket to be launched from Cape Canaveral, Florida, USA: the *Bumper 2*. Its first stage was a captured German V-2 rocket, and its upper stage was a U.S. Army WAC Corporal rocket. It reached a height of 25 miles.
75	26 Jul 1950	Vietnam War: U.S. military involvement in Vietnam began when President Harry S. Truman authorised $15 million of military aid to the French.
75	26 Jul 1950 to 29th	Korean War – the No Gun Ri massacre, South Korea. The U.S. Army 7th Cavalry Regiment killed at least 163 South Korean civilian refugees on a railway bridge. Some sources claim about 400 refugees were killed.
75	26 Jul 1950	The Royal Netherlands East Indies Army (KNIL) was disbanded.
70	2 Jul 1955	The first network broadcast of the television variety series *The Lawrence Welk Show*, on ABC in the USA. It began as a local show in Los Angeles, California in 1951. It ran until 1982.
70	4 Jul 1955	The first network broadcast of the children's television series *The Soupy Sales Show*, on ABC in the USA. It began as a local show, *Lunch with Soupy Sales*, in Detroit, Michigan, in 1953. It ran until 1966, and was followed by *The New Soupy Sales Show* (1978–79).
70	9 Jul 1955	*The Russell–Einstein Manifesto* was released by Bertrand Russell in London. It called on world leaders to seek peaceful resolutions to conflicts and highlighted the dangers of nuclear weapons. (See also: 15th July 1955.)
70	9 Jul 1955 or 10th	E. Frederic Morrow became the first African American executive to serve on the White House staff when he was appointed Administrative Officer for Special Projects.
70	11 Jul 1955	The U.S. Congress passed a resolution stating that the phrase 'In God We Trust' should be added to all U.S. Currency. It began appearing on banknotes from 1957.

JULY 2025

Ann.	Date	Event
70	11 Jul 1955	The U.S. Air Force Academy officially opened and the first cadets were sworn in. The Academy was initially housed in temporary quarters at Lowry Air Force Base, Denver, Colorado. The permanent site at Colorado Springs was completed in August 1958.
70	13 Jul 1955	Death of Ruth Ellis, British nightclub owner and convicted murderer. The last woman to be executed in the UK. Hanged for killing her boyfriend, David Blakely.
70	15 Jul 1955	The Mainau Declaration against nuclear weapons was signed in Germany by eighteen Nobel Prize laureates. 52 had signed it within a year.
70	16 Jul 1955	Stirling Moss became the first British driver to win the British Grand Prix.
70	17 Jul 1955	The first Disneyland theme park opened, in Anaheim, California, USA.
70	17 Jul 1955	The town of Arco, Idaho, USA became the first community in the world to be powered entirely by nuclear energy – though only for one hour.
70	20 Jul 1955	Death of Calouste Gulbenkian, Turkish-born Armenian businessman and philanthropist. He helped make Middle Eastern oil reserves available to the West, became one of the richest people in the world, and amassed one of the world's greatest private art collections.
70	21 Jul 1955	The *USS Seawolf* was launched in Connecticut, USA. It was the only U.S. submarine to be powered by a liquid metal (sodium) cooled nuclear reactor. The reactor proved difficult to maintain and was replaced by a pressurised water reactor after three years. The *Seawolf* was decommissioned in 1987.
70	23 Jul 1955	British racing driver Donald Campbell broke the world water speed record and became the first person to break the 200-mph barrier (202.32 mph) at Ullswater in Cumbria, UK.
70	23 Jul 1955	Death of Cordell Hull, U.S. Secretary of State (1933–44). Winner of the 1945 Nobel Peace Prize for his role in establishing the United Nations.
70	27 Jul 1955	El Al Flight 402, an international passenger flight from London, UK to Tel Aviv, Israel, was shot down by two Bulgarian jet fighters after straying into Bulgarian air space. All 51 passengers and seven crew were killed.
70	27 Jul 1955	The Allied occupation of Austria during/after WWII ended and Austria regained full independence.
65	1 Jul 1960	British Somaliland and Italian Somaliland were unified to form the new independent nation of Somalia.
65	1 Jul 1960	Ghana became a republic. Kwame Nkrumah became its first president.
65	4 Jul 1960	The current fifty-star Flag of the United States was flown for the first time. It had been updated to include Hawaii.
65	4 Jul 1960	Birth of Roland Ratzenberger, Austrian racing driver. (Died 1994.)
65	5 Jul 1960	Congo crisis, Democratic Republic of the Congo. Shortly after gaining its independence from Belgium, Congo was plunged into a series of civil wars. The crisis ended when Joseph-Désiré Mobutu (known as Mobutu Sese Seko from 1972) seized power and formed a corrupt military dictatorship, noted for its widespread human rights violations, which lasted until 1997.

JULY 2025

Ann.	Date	Event
65	6 Jul 1960	Death of Aneurin ('Nye') Bevan, British politician. Minister of Health (1945–51) who led the establishment of the National Health Service.
65	7 Jul 1960	The supernatural horror film *The Brides of Dracula* was released in the UK. (USA: 5th September.)
65	9 Jul 1960	Cold War: U.S. President Dwight D. Eisenhower and Soviet leader Nikita Khrushchev traded threats over Cuba. Khrushchev said the Soviet Union was prepared to use nuclear missiles to protect Cuba from U.S. intervention, and said the USA was no longer an unreachable target. Eisenhower said the USA would not countenance the establishment of a communist regime in the West. The two leaders continued to exchange charges and counter-charges in a bitter war of words.
65	11 Jul 1960	Harper Lee's novel *To Kill a Mockingbird* was published.
65	12 Jul 1960	Orlyonok Young Pioneer camp was established in Russia on the shore of the Black Sea. It is now a federal children's camp.
65	12 Jul 1960	The Etch-A-Sketch children's toy first went on sale.
65	14 Jul 1960	British primatologist Jane Goodall arrived in Gombe Stream National Park in Tanzania to begin her study of chimpanzees in the wild. She spent many years there, and discovered that, contrary to long-held beliefs, chimpanzees were not wholly vegetarian, and they used tools.
65	15 Jul 1960	Congo Crisis: the first United Nations troops arrived in the Republic of Congo to restore order after the country had descended into chaos and disorder following its independence from Portugal in June. UN forces remained in Congo until June 1964.
65	16 Jul 1960	Death of Albert Kesselring, German field marshal in the Luftwaffe during WWII. He was subsequently convicted of war crimes and sentenced to death – later commuted to life imprisonment. He was released following a political and media campaign in 1952.
65	20 Jul 1960	The world's first female head of state in modern times. Sirimavo Bandaranaike became Prime Minister of Ceylon (now Sri Lanka) following her husband's assassination.
65	20 Jul 1960	The first Polaris missile was successfully test launched from a submerged submarine, the *USS George Washington*, off Cape Canaveral, Florida, USA.
65	29 Jul 1960	Death of Richard Simon, American publisher. Co-founder of the publishing house Simon and Shuster. Father of the singer and songwriter Carly Simon.
60	3 Jul 1965	Death of Trigger, American golden palomino horse. He co-starred with the singer and actor Roy Rogers in over 100 Western films and *The Roy Rogers Show* television series.
60	7 Jul 1965	Death of Moshe Sharett, Prime Minister of Israel (1953–55).
60	8 Jul 1965	British Great Train Robber Ronnie Biggs escaped from Wandsworth Prison in London. He lived in Brazil until 2001 when he returned to the UK and was re-imprisoned. Released July 2009. Died December 2013.

JULY 2025

Ann.	Date	Event
60	9 Jul 1965	The song *I Got You Babe* by Sonny & Cher was released.
60	14 Jul 1965 to 15th	NASA's *Mariner 4* spacecraft flew past Mars and sent back the first close-up photos of another planet.
60	14 Jul 1965	Death of Adlai Stevenson, American politician and presidential candidate (1952, 1956). Governor of Illinois (1949–53). U.S. Ambassador to the United Nations (1961–65).
60	16 Jul 1965	The Mont Blanc Tunnel in the Alps was inaugurated. It links France and Italy. It opened to traffic on 19th July.
60	18 Jul 1965	The Soviet Union launched its *Zond 3* spacecraft. It flew past the Moon on 20th July and sent back several high-quality photos.
60	19 Jul 1965	The Beatles' song *Help!* was released in the USA. (UK: 23rd July.)
60	19 Jul 1965	Death of Syngman Rhee, first President of South Korea (1948–60). Died in exile in Hawaii, USA.
60	20 Jul 1965	Bob Dylan's song *Like a Rolling Stone* was released.
60	22 Jul 1965	Former British Prime Minister Alec Douglas-Home, the leader of the Conservative Party and leader of the Opposition, announced his resignation as leader. Following a leadership contest, Shadow Chancellor Edward Heath was elected as the new leader on 28th July. He became Prime Minister in 1970.
60	22 Jul 1965	The pilot episode of the television sitcom 'Till Death Us Do Part was broadcast on BBC 1 in the UK as an episode of *Comedy Playhouse*. The first series began in June 1966, and it ran until 1975. It was succeeded by *In Sickness and in Health*, which ran from 1985 to 1992.
60	25 Jul 1965	Bob Dylan went electric. The American folk musician performed at the Newport Folk Festival in Rhode Island, USA with the Paul Butterfield Blues Band, using electric guitars. Folk music purists and festival organisers reacted with hostility, and some of the audience booed him for abandoning his folk music roots. This performance signalled a major change in both folk music and rock.
60	26 Jul 1965	The Maldives gained its independence from the UK.
60	28 Jul 1965	Vietnam War: U.S. President Lyndon B. Johnson announced that he was significantly increasing the number of U.S. troops in South Vietnam. By the end of the year over 180,000 U.S. troops were stationed there.
60	29 Jul 1965	The Beatles' film *Help!* was released in the UK. (USA: première: 9th and 11th August, released 25th August.)
60	30 Jul 1965	The Social Security Act of 1965 came into effect in the USA, and Medicare and Medicaid were established.
60	30 Jul 1965	Death of Jun'ichiro Tanizaki, Japanese novelist. One of the major writers of modern Japanese literature.
50	1 Jul 1975	Microsoft's first product was released: the BASIC programming language for the MITS Altair 8800 computer. It was hugely popular with computer enthusiasts. (Microsoft was known as Micro-Soft at that time.)

JULY 2025

Ann.	Date	Event
50	2 Jul 1975	Death of James Robertson Justice, British film actor (*Doctor in the House, Doctor at Large, Doctor in Love, The Guns of Navarone, Chitty Chitty Bang Bang*, and many more).
50	5 Jul 1975	Cape Verde gained its independence from Portugal.
50	5 Jul 1975	American tennis player Arthur Ashe became the first black man to win Wimbledon.
50	6 Jul 1975	Comoros gained its independence from France.
50	8 Jul 1975	Bagan (also known as Pagan) earthquake, Burma. Many temples were damaged and the Bupaya Pagoda was completely destroyed. (It has now been rebuilt.)
50	12 Jul 1975	São Tomé and Príncipe gained its independence from Portugal.
50	15 Jul 1975	Death of Charles Weidman, American dancer, choreographer and teacher. One of the pioneers of modern dance in the USA.
50	17 Jul 1975	Apollo-Soyuz Test Project. A U.S. *Apollo* spacecraft and a Soviet *Soyuz* spacecraft docked in orbit – the first-ever docking by spacecraft from two countries. They remain docked for two days. This was the last *Apollo* mission, and the last U.S. manned space flight until the space shuttle programme began in 1981. It also marked the official end of the space race.
50	25 Jul 1975	The musical *A Chorus Line* opened on Broadway. It ran for 6,137 performances, setting a record for the longest-running Broadway production – until 1997 when it was overtaken by *Cats*.
50	25 Jul 1975	David Bowie's song *Fame* was released. It became his first #1 hit in the USA and Canada.
50	29 Jul 1975	The Organization of American States (OAS) lifted its sanctions against Cuba. The USA announced that it would review its own sanctions against Cuba, but chose to leave them in place.
50	29 Jul 1975	Gerald Ford became the first U.S. President to visit Auschwitz concentration camp in Poland.
50	30 Jul 1975	American trade union leader Jimmy Hoffa disappeared from a restaurant car park in Detroit, Michigan. He was never seen again. He was declared dead in July 1982.
40	2 Jul 1985	The European Space Agency (ESA) launched its *Giotto* spacecraft on a mission to fly by and study Halley's Comet. It was the first spacecraft to study a comet close up. It reached Halley's Comet in March 1986 and also flew by and studied Comet Grigg–Skjellerup in July 1992.
40	3 Jul 1985	The time-travel comedy film *Back to the Future* was released in the USA. (UK: 4th December.)
40	4 Jul 1985	British mathematics prodigy Ruth Lawrence graduated from Oxford University at the age of thirteen. She remains the youngest person in the UK to receive a first-class degree. (In 1994 ten-year-old Michael Kearney earned a degree in anthropology at the University of South Alabama in the USA.)

JULY 2025

Ann.	Date	Event
40	7 Jul 1985	German tennis player Boris Becker, aged seventeen, became the youngest-ever men's singles champion at Wimbledon. He was also the first unseeded player to win.
40	9 Jul 1985	Death of Charlotte, Grand Duchess of Luxembourg (1919–64).
40	9 Jul 1985	Death of Jimmy Kinnon, Scottish-born American founder of Narcotics Anonymous.
40	10 Jul 1985	The Greenpeace ship *Rainbow Warrior* was bombed and sunk in Auckland Harbour, New Zealand by French intelligence agents to prevent it from interfering with a planned nuclear test. One person was killed.
40	10 Jul 1985	Aeroflot Flight 7425 stalled and crashed near Uchkuduk, Uzbekistan. All 191 passengers and nine crew were killed. It was the Soviet Union's deadliest airline disaster. (Cause: crew fatigue.)
40	11 Jul 1985	The Coca-Cola Company announced that it would resume selling its original formula after a public backlash against New Coke.
40	13 Jul 1985	Live Aid. Two simultaneous concerts in London and Philadelphia, plus other venues including Sydney and Moscow, raised millions of pounds for famine victims in Africa.
40	15 Jul 1985	Aldus PageMaker, the first desktop publishing software application, was released. The first version was for Apple Macintosh computers. A version for IBM PCs was released in December. It was acquired by Adobe in 1994 and became Adobe PageMaker in 1995. It was discontinued in 2004 and replaced by Adobe InDesign.
40	19 Jul 1985	The Val di Stava dam in Italy collapsed. 268 people were killed.
40	19 Jul 1985	Christa McAuliffe of New Hampshire, USA was selected as the winner of NASA's Teacher in Space project. She was killed in the Space Shuttle *Challenger* disaster in January 1986.
40	20 Jul 1985	Andrei Gromyko became head of state of the Soviet Union.
40	20 Jul 1985	American treasure hunter Mel Fisher discovered the wreck of the Spanish galleon *Nuestra Señora de Atocha*, which sank off the Florida Keys in 1622. It was laden with gold, silver, emeralds and other artefacts worth an estimated $450 million.
40	23 Jul 1985	The Commodore Amiga 1000 personal computer was released. Its advanced graphics and audio capabilities led to it being called 'the first multimedia computer'.
40	23 Jul 1985	Death of Johnny Wardle, British cricketer (Yorkshire 1946–58, England 1948–57). A renowned spin bowler.
40	27 Jul 1985	The President of Uganda, Milton Obote, was overthrown in a military coup. He was succeeded by Tito Okello.
40	28 Jul 1985	Alan Garcia became President of Peru (until 1990). He was president again from 2006 until 2011.
40	31 Jul 1985	Death of Eugene Carson Blake, American Presbyterian Church leader and civil rights activist. General Secretary of the World Council of Churches (1966–72). He helped to organise the March on Washington.

JULY 2025

Ann.	Date	Event
30	1 Jul 1995	Death of Wolfman Jack, American radio disc jockey. Known for his gravelly voice and wolf howls.
30	3 Jul 1995	Death of Pancho Gonzales, American tennis player. World number 1 (1954–60).
30	4 Jul 1995	British Prime Minister John Major won the Conservative Party leadership election against John Redwood, and remained leader. He had resigned the party leadership in June after three years of verbal attacks, and had invited his critics to stand in an election against him.
30	4 Jul 1995	Death of Eva Gabor, Hungarian-born American actress, socialite and businesswoman. Known for her role in the sitcom *Green Acres* and as a voice artist in the Disney films *The Aristocats*, *The Rescuers* and *The Rescuers Down Under*. Sister of Zsa Zsa Gabor.
30	4 Jul 1995	Death of Bob Ross, American artist, teacher and host of the television series *The Joy of Painting*.
30	6 Jul 1995	IBM acquired Lotus Development, the developer of the Lotus 1-2-3 spreadsheet application, for $3.5 billion. It renamed the company Lotus Software and sold it to the Indian technology company HCL Technologies in 2018 for $1.8 billion.
30	9 Jul 1995	Navaly church bombing, Sri Lanka. The Church of Saint Peter and Saint Paul in Navaly was bombed by the Sri Lankan Air Force. 125 Tamil civilians who were sheltering inside were killed.
30	10 Jul 1995	Death of Hugh Dundas, British WWII fighter pilot and broadcasting executive. Chairman of Thames Television.
30	11 Jul 1995 to 22nd	Srebrenica Massacre. The Bosnian Serb Army seized control of Srebrenica and massacred 8,000 men and boys. Srebrenica was supposedly a United Nations safe area.
30	11 Jul 1995	The USA re-established full diplomatic ties with Vietnam.
30	13 Jul 1995	Death of Godtfred Kirk Christiansen, Danish toy manufacturer and businessman (Lego Group). He developed his father's business into an international sensation and built the first Legoland theme park.
30	14 Jul 1995	The MP3 digital audio format was officially named.
30	16 Jul 1995	French President Jacques Chirac admitted France's role in the Holocaust. The Vichy Government deported about 76,000 Jews during World War II. They were transported to Nazi concentration camps and death camps in Germany and Poland. He gave his speech on the anniversary of an event in 1942 when French police rounded up 13,000 Jews and held them at the Paris cycling stadium to be deported to Nazi death camps.
30	16 Jul 1995	Amazon.com opened its website to the public.
30	16 Jul 1995	Death of Sir Stephen Spender, British poet, novelist, essayist and critic. The first non-American poetry consultant to the U.S. Library of Congress.
30	17 Jul 1995	Death of Juan Manuel Fangio, Argentine racing driver. Formula One world champion five times (1951, 1954, 1955, 1956, 1957).

JULY 2025

Ann.	Date	Event
30	18 Jul 1995	The Soufriere Hills volcano on the Caribbean island of Montserrat began to erupt. Over the space of several years it devastated the island, destroyed the capital, and forced most of the population to flee.
30	18 Jul 1995	Barack Obama's memoir *Dreams from My Father* was published. At the time he was a professor of law and just beginning his campaign for the Illinois Senate. He became President of the USA in 2009.
30	21 Jul 1995 to 23 Mar 1996	The Third Taiwan Strait Crisis. China conducted a series of missile tests and military exercises in the waters around Taiwan, with the intention of intimidating the government and voters of Taiwan. The crisis ended in a cease-fire.
30	22 Jul 1995	Death of Harold Larwood, British cricketer. The main exponent of the controversial 'bodyline' bowling style, which was denounced as 'unsportsmanlike' and ended his career.
30	23 Jul 1995	Bosnian War: Britain sent 1,200 troops to help relieve the Bosnian capital, Sarajevo, which was under siege.
30	23 Jul 1995	Comet Hale–Bopp was discovered by two American astronomers, Alan Hale in New Mexico and Thomas Bopp in Arizona.
30	23 Jul 1995	Inventure Place opened in Akron, Ohio, USA as the new, much larger home of the National Inventors Hall of Fame.
30	25 Jul 1995	Bosnian Serb leader Radovan Karadžic was indicted for war crimes by the International Criminal Tribunal for the former Yugoslavia. He became a fugitive until 2008 when he was arrested in Belgrade, Serbia. In 2016 he was sentenced to forty years in prison – later increased to life imprisonment.
30	25 Jul 1995	The U.S. première of the cyber mystery thriller film *The Net*. (Released: 28th July. UK: 6th October.)
30	25 Jul 1995	Death of Charlie Rich, American country music singer and musician whose 'countrypolitan' sound combined country with jazz, blues, rockabilly, gospel and other genres. Best known for his hit songs *Behind Closed Doors* and *The Most Beautiful Girl*.
30	27 Jul 1995	The Korean War Veterans Memorial was dedicated in Washington, D.C., USA.
25	1 Jul 2000	The Øresund Bridge, linking Sweden and Denmark, was officially opened.
25	1 Jul 2000	Vermont became the first U.S. state to allow same-sex couples to form civil unions with the same rights and responsibilities as married couples. (Vermont legalised same-sex marriage in September 2009.)
25	1 Jul 2000	Goods and Services Tax (GST) was introduced in Australia.
25	1 Jul 2000	Death of Walter Matthau, American stage, film and television actor. Best known for his collaborations with Jack Lemon in films such as *The Odd Couple*.
25	1 Jul 2000	Death of Sarah Payne, eight-year-old British murder victim. She disappeared from Hersham, Surrey on 1st July. Her body found in a field in West Sussex on 17th July. In December 2001 Roy Whiting was convicted of killing her and was sentenced to life imprisonment.

JULY 2025

Ann.	Date	Event
25	2 Jul 2000	Death of Joey Dunlop, Northern Irish world motorcycling champion.
25	8 Jul 2000	J. K. Rowling's fantasy novel *Harry Potter and the Goblet of Fire* was published. It was the fourth book in the series.
25	10 Jul 2000	An oil pipeline in southern Nigeria exploded after it was punctured by fuel thieves. At least 250 people were killed. Similar incidents occurred in October 1998, 16th July 2000, November 2000, 2003, 2004, 2006 and 2008.
25	10 Jul 2000	Death of Hafez al-Assad, President of Syria (1971–2000 – died in office). Succeeded by his son, Bashar al-Assad, on 17th July.
25	11 Jul 2000	Microsoft introduced the C# (C Sharp) computer programming language.
25	11 Jul 2000	Death of Robert Runcie, Archbishop of Canterbury (1980–91).
25	12 Jul 2000	The U.S. première of the superhero film *X-Men*. (Released: 14th July. UK première: 15th August, released: 18th August.)
25	14 Jul 2000	A jury in a Miami-Dade court in Florida, USA ordered five major U.S. tobacco companies to pay $145 billion in punitive damages to 500,000 smokers whose health had been damaged by their products. It was the largest damage award in U.S. history. (Engle v. R. J. Reynolds Tobacco Co.)
25	20 Jul 2000	The discovery of the tau neutrino, a type of subatomic particle, was announced by scientists working at the U.S. Department of Energy's Fermi National Accelerator Laboratory (FermiLab).
25	23 Jul 2000	American golfer Tiger Woods, aged 24, became the youngest player to win the Grand Slam.
25	25 Jul 2000	An Air France Concorde crashed outside Paris shortly after taking off for New York. All 109 people on board and four people on the ground were killed.
25	26 Jul 2000	A U.S. federal judge approved a $1.25 billion settlement between Swiss banks and more than half a million plaintiffs. The plaintiffs alleged that the banks had hoarded money deposited by Holocaust victims.
25	29 Jul 2000	American actor Brad Pitt married actress Jennifer Aniston. They divorced in 2005.
20	1 Jul 2005	The last Ford Thunderbird (T-Bird) car was produced.
20	1 Jul 2005	Death of Luther Vandross, American soul and R&B singer, songwriter and producer.
20	2 Jul 2005	Live 8. Ten concerts were held simultaneously around the world in an effort to persuade G8 leaders to fight poverty in Africa. On 7th July, G8 leaders pledged to double the amount of aid to poor countries to $50 billion per year by 2010. Half of the money would go to Africa.
20	3 Jul 2005	Same-sex marriage was legalised in Spain.
20	4 Jul 2005 to 13th	Hurricane Dennis caused massive damage in Cuba, Haiti, the U.S. state of Florida, and other parts of the Caribbean. At least 89 people were killed.

JULY 2025

Ann.	Date	Event
20	4 Jul 2005	NASA's *Deep Impact* space probe released an impactor, which crashed into the comet Tempel 1. It created a crater and debris that revealed the interior of the comet's nucleus. A massive dust cloud obscured the view of the crater, but analysis of the debris showed that the nucleus was dustier and less icy than expected.
20	6 Jul 2005	The International Olympic Committee announced that London, UK would host the 2012 Olympic Games.
20	6 Jul 2005	Death of L. Patrick Gray III, American lawyer and government official. He was acting-director of the FBI during the Watergate Scandal, and was made a scapegoat and forced to resign. His innocence only became apparent in 2005 when Mark Felt (aka 'Deep Throat') admitted that he was the source of leaks to the press.
20	6 Jul 2005	Death of Ed McBain, American crime novelist and screenwriter. Best known for his *87th Precinct* series of police procedurals.
20	7 Jul 2005	7th July London bombings, UK. A coordinated series of four suicide bomb attacks on London's transport system during the morning rush hour. 56 people were killed, including the four bombers. More than 700 were injured. It was the worst-ever terrorist attack on Britain, and the country's first attack by suicide bombers. (See also: 21st July 2005.)
20	9 Jul 2005	American daredevil Danny Way became the first person to jump over the Great Wall of China on a skateboard.
20	10 Jul 2005	Death of A. J. Quinnell, British thriller novelist. Best known for *Man on Fire*.
20	11 Jul 2005	Death of Gretchen Franklin, British stage and television actress who worked in show business for nearly eighty years. Best known for her role as Ethel Skinner in the BBC TV soap opera *EastEnders*.
20	11 Jul 2005	Death of Frances Langford, American singer and film actress who entertained thousands of U.S. troops on Bob Hope's U.S.O. Tours.
20	12 Jul 2005	Prince Albert II was enthroned as the ruler of the Principality of Monaco.
20	13 Jul 2005	Ghotki rail crash, Pakistan. A train that had stopped at a station was hit from behind by another train, causing several carriages to derail. Those carriages were then hit by another train travelling in the opposite direction. Seventeen carriages were destroyed. Between 100 and 130 people were killed and more than 1,000 injured.
20	13 Jul 2005	The former CEO of WorldCom, Bernard Ebbers, was sentenced to 25 years in prison after being convicted of the largest accounting fraud in U.S. history (until 2008). He was released on health grounds after thirteen years, and died in 2020.
20	14 Jul 2005	Death of Dame Cicely Saunders, British physician and social worker who established the modern hospice movement.
20	16 Jul 2005	J. K. Rowling's fantasy novel *Harry Potter and the Half-Blood Prince* was released. It was the sixth book in the series.

JULY 2025

Ann.	Date	Event
20	17 Jul 2005	Death of Geraldine Fitzgerald, Irish-born American stage and film actress. Best known for her supporting roles (*The Mill on the Floss*, *Arthur*, *Wuthering Heights*, and more).
20	17 Jul 2005	Death of Sir Edward Heath, British Prime Minister (1970–74).
20	18 Jul 2005	American terrorist Eric Rudolph (the Olympic Park Bomber) was sentenced to two consecutive life terms for killing a police officer in 1998. On 22nd August he was sentenced to two further life terms for the Olympic Park bombing in Atlanta, Georgia in 1996.
20	18 Jul 2005	MySpace, the world's largest social networking website at that time, was acquired by News Corporation for $580 million. MySpace continued to grow for the next three years, but it was then overtaken by Facebook and it began to decline. NewsCorp sold it in 2011 for a reported $35 million, and it was acquired by Time, Inc. in 2016.
20	18 Jul 2005	Death of William Westmoreland, United States Army general. Commander of U.S. military operations during the Vietnam War.
20	20 Jul 2005	Same-sex marriage was legalised in Canada.
20	20 Jul 2005	Death of Charles Chibitty, Comanche code talker who relayed messages between U.S. Army units in Europe during WWII. He and his fellow code talkers spoke in their native language to prevent messages from being deciphered by the Germans.
20	20 Jul 2005	Death of James Doohan, Canadian actor. Best known for playing Montgomery ('Scotty') Scott, chief engineer of the starship *USS Enterprise*, in the *Star Trek* television series and films.
20	21 Jul 2005	21st July London bombings, UK. Four suicide bombers attempted to carry out a second attack on London's transport network, two weeks after the previous attack (see 7th July 2005). However, only the detonators exploded and the bombs failed to go off. One person was injured. A fifth bomber dumped his bomb without attempting to set it off.
20	21 Jul 2005	Death of Long John Baldry, British-born Canadian blues musician and voice artist.
20	22 Jul 2005	Death of Jean Charles de Menezes, Brazilian electrician. Shot dead by police in London, UK, aged 27, after being challenged and refusing to obey an order. The police were hunting fugitives from the previous day's failed bomb attacks (see 21st July above).
20	23 Jul 2005	Sharm el-Sheikh terrorist attacks, Egypt. Islamist terrorists carried out a series of bomb attacks on the resort city, killing 88 people and injuring about 200. It was the deadliest terrorist attack in Egyptian history.
20	24 Jul 2005	Death of Richard Doll, British epidemiologist who established the link between cigarette smoking and lung cancer.
20	26 Jul 2005 to 27th	Maharashtra floods, India. Large parts of the city of Mumbai were flooded following torrential rainfall. 1,094 people were killed.

JULY 2025

Ann.	Date	Event
20	26 Jul 2005	The U.S. Space Shuttle *Discovery* was launched on the first 'return to flight' mission following the *Columbia* Disaster of 2003. The problem of insulating foam being shed from the external fuel tank during launch occurred again, but this time it did not strike the shuttle.
20	26 Jul 2005	Death of Betty Astell, British actress. Best known for appearing with her husband, Cyril Fletcher, on his television series *The Cyril Fletcher Show*. She was also one of the first people to appear on John Logie Baird's experimental television broadcasts.
20	28 Jul 2005	The IRA ended its thirty-year armed campaign in Northern Ireland and ordered all units to dump their weapons. Its leadership stated that they would continue their campaign exclusively through peaceful means.
20	28 Jul 2005	A tornado hit the city of Birmingham, UK, injuring nineteen people and causing £40 million ($67.5 million) of damage.
20	31 Jul 2005	Death of Wim Duisenberg, Dutch economist. First president of the European Central Bank (1998–2003). He oversaw the introduction of the euro.
15	3 Jul 2010 to 4th	British man Raoul Moat shot his ex-girlfriend and her new partner in Tyne and Wear, Northumberland. Her partner died. He also shot a police officer, who was blinded in the attack and committed suicide in 2012. After the attack, Moat went on the run for six days. He was captured by police on 9th July after a massive manhunt. He then shot and killed himself.
15	7 Jul 2010 to 8th	The Swiss solar-powered plane *Solar Impulse* completed the first 24-hour flight using only solar power. In total it flew for 26 hours, including nine hours at night. In 2015–16, its successor, *Solar Impulse 2*, completed the first solar-powered round-the-world flight. The planned five-month journey actually took nearly sixteen months.
15	21 Jul 2010	The Dodd–Frank Wall Street Reform and Consumer Protection Act came into effect in the USA. It was the largest overhaul of U.S. financial regulations since the Great Depression in the 1930s.
15	23 Jul 2010	The largest hailstone ever recorded fell in Vivian, South Dakota, USA. It measured 8 inches (20 cm) in diameter.
15	26 Jul 2010 to Aug	2010 Pakistan floods. Monsoon rains caused flooding in the Indus River basin, flooding around twenty percent of the country and affecting 20 million people. At least 1,781 people were killed. The economic impact from the loss of property, infrastructure, crops and livelihoods was estimated to be up to $43 billion.
10	1 Jul 2015	Death of Val Doonican, Irish pop/easy listening singer and television presenter. Host of *The Val Doonican Show* (1965–86). Noted for his relaxed style.
10	10 Jul 2015	The U.S. state of South Carolina removed the Confederate flag from its Statehouse.
10	10 Jul 2015	Death of Omar Sharif, Egyptian film actor (*Lawrence of Arabia, Doctor Zhivago, Funny Girl*) and contract bridge player.

JULY 2025

Ann.	Date	Event
10	11 Jul 2015	Mexican drug trafficker Joaquín Guzmán ('El Chapo') escaped from a maximum-security prison through a mile-long tunnel that his associates had dug. After a massive manhunt he was recaptured after a shootout with police in January 2016. He was extradited to the USA in 2017 and sentenced to life imprisonment in 2019.
10	14 Jul 2015	NASA's *New Horizons* space probe, launched in 2006, completed the first-ever flyby of the dwarf planet Pluto and returned close-up photos.
10	20 Jul 2015	The USA and Cuba restored full diplomatic relations for the first time since 1961, and the U.S. Embassy in Havana, Cuba reopened. The USA continued to maintain its trade and financial embargo on Cuba.
10	21 Jul 2015	Death of E. L. Doctorow, American historical novelist, short story writer and educator. Best known for *Ragtime*, *Billy Bathgate* and *The March*. Several of his stories were adapted into films.
10	28 Jul 2015	Death of Edward Natapei, Prime Minister of Vanuatu (2001–04, 2008–10, 2011).

AUGUST 2025

Ann.	Date	Event
2000	5 Aug 25	Emperor Guangwu became Emperor of China (until 57 AD). He only ruled parts of China at first, but ruled the whole country by the end of his reign.
1700	25 Aug 325	The First Council of Nicaea ended with adoption of the Nicene Creed. It declared and summarised the Christian faith and established the doctrine of the Holy Trinity.
1000	28 Aug 1025	Birth of Emperor Go-Reizei, Emperor of Japan (1045–68).
750	15 Aug 1275	Death of Lorenzo Tiepolo, Doge (ruler) of Venice (1268–75).
400	13 Aug 1625	Birth of Rasmus Bartholin, Danish physician, mathematician, physicist and grammarian. Best known for discovering the double refraction (bifringence) of light by calcite.
400	20 Aug 1625	Birth of Thomas Corneille, French dramatist and lexicographer.
300	28 Aug 1725	Birth of Charles Townshend, British politician. Chancellor of the Exchequer (1766–67 – died in office.)
250	5 Aug 1775	The first Europeans to enter San Francisco Bay in California, USA: Spanish explorer Juan de Ayala and his crew on the ship *San Carlos* explored and mapped the bay. They named many of the geographical features and islands.
250	6 Aug 1775	Birth of Daniel O'Connell, Irish politician. Leader of Ireland's Roman Catholic majority. Member of Parliament for Clare (1828–30), Dublin City (1832–36, 1837–41), and Cork County (1841–47). Lord Mayor of Dublin (1841–42).
250	20 Aug 1775	The city of Tucson, Arizona, USA was established by the Spanish as a military fort.
250	21 Aug 1775 or 22nd	Death of Zahir al-Umar, Arab ruler of northern Palestine.
250	23 Aug 1775	American Revolution: King George III of Great Britain issued the Proclamation of Rebellion. It stated that the American colonies were in a state of open rebellion and should be suppressed.
200	4 Aug 1825	Birth of Arthur Haygarth, British cricketer (Marylebone 1844–61 and Sussex 1848–60), cricket writer and historian.
200	6 Aug 1825	Bolivia declared its independence from Spain, and the Bolivian War of Independence ended.
200	25 Aug 1825	Uruguay declared its independence from Brazil.
175	5 Aug 1850	Birth of Guy de Maupassant, French short story writer, novelist and poet.
175	17 Aug 1850	Death of José de San Martín, Protector (President) of Peru (1821–22).
175	18 Aug 1850	Death of Honoré de Balzac, French novelist and playwright.
175	26 Aug 1850	Death of Louis Philippe I, King of France (1830–48). The last king and the penultimate monarch of France.

AUGUST 2025

Ann.	Date	Event
150	4 Aug 1875	Death of Hans Christian Andersen, Danish writer. Best known for his fairy tales, including *The Emperor's New Clothes*, *The Little Mermaid*, *The Princess and the Pea*, *The Snow Queen*, *The Ugly Duckling*, *The Little Match Girl*, *Thumbelina*, and more.
150	8 Aug 1875	Birth of Arthur Bernardes, President of Brazil (1922–26).
150	25 Aug 1875	Captain Matthew Webb of the British Royal Navy became the first person to successfully swim the English Channel. He swam from Dover, England to Calais, France in 21 hours and 40 minutes.
150	26 Aug 1875	Birth of John Buchan, 1st Baron Tweedsmuir, Scottish novelist, historian, politician and diplomat. Governor General of Canada (1935–40). Best known for his novel *The Thirty-Nine Steps*.
150	27 Aug 1875	The chemical element gallium (Ga – atomic number 31) was discovered by French chemist Paul-Émile Lecoq de Boisbaudran. He also discovered samarium in 1879 and dysprosium in 1886.
150	27 Aug 1875	Birth of Katharine McCormick, American women's rights activist and philanthropist. As the heir to a substantial fortune, she funded much of the research that led to the development of the first birth control pill.
150	27 Aug 1875	Death of William Chapman Ralston, American businessman and financier. Founder of the Bank of California. (Drowned in San Francisco Bay, aged 49, the day after his financial empire collapsed.)
125	3 Aug 1900	The Firestone Tire and Rubber Company was founded in Akron, Ohio, USA. It was acquired by Bridgestone in 1988.
125	3 Aug 1900	Birth of Ernie Pyle, American journalist and WWII war correspondent. (Killed in action in Japan during WWII.)
125	3 Aug 1900	Birth of John T. Scopes, American teacher. Best known for violating Tennessee's Butler Act by teaching the theory of evolution to his students – and the subsequent court case (the Scopes Trial).
125	4 Aug 1900 to 16th	Second Boer War – the Battle of Elands River, Brakfontein Drift, Transvaal. British forces repulsed the Boer attack, and the thirteen-day siege on the British garrison and supply dump was successfully relieved.
125	4 Aug 1900	Birth of Queen Elizabeth, the Queen Mother. Queen consort of the United Kingdom (1936–52). Wife of King George VI. Mother of Queen Elizabeth II.
125	8 Aug 1900 to 10th	The first Davis Cup tennis competition was held, at the Longwood Cricket Club in Massachusetts, USA. The USA beat the British Isles 3 – 0. Dwight F. Davis, a member of the American team, purchased the trophy, and the competition was named in his honour.
125	10 Aug 1900	Birth of Arthur Porritt, Baron Porritt, Governor-General of New Zealand (1967–72).
125	11 Aug 1900	Birth of Charley Paddock, American athlete. Gold medallist at the 1920 Olympics (100 m and 4 x 100 m relay).

AUGUST 2025

Ann.	Date	Event
125	12 Aug 1900	Death of Wilhelm Steinitz, Austrian-born American chess player, chess writer and theoretician. The first official World Chess Champion (1886–94).
125	19 Aug 1900 to 20th	The first and only Olympic cricket match was played. Belgium, France, Great Britain and the Netherlands were scheduled to play in a knockout tournament, but Belgium and the Netherlands withdrew. France and Great Britain played each other in a two-day match. Great Britain won by 158 runs.
125	21 Aug 1900 to 27th	Second Boer War – the Battle of Bergendal, Belfast, South Africa. The last set-piece battle of the war. British victory.
125	25 Aug 1900	The first recorded use of the word 'television'. Russian scientist Constantin Perskyi used the word in a paper he presented at the first International Congress of Electricity, in Paris, France. The first recorded use of it in English was in 1907.
125	25 Aug 1900	Birth of Hans Adolf Krebs, German-born British biologist, biochemist and physician. Known for discovering cellular processes in organisms. Joint winner of the 1953 Nobel Prize in Physiology or Medicine for discovering the citric acid cycle.
125	25 Aug 1900	Death of Friedrich Nietzsche, German philosopher and philologist. His work had a major impact on modern intellectual history. One of his most prominent concepts was the 'will to power', which he believed was the main driving force in humans.
125	28 Aug 1900	Death of Henry Sidgwick, British utilitarian philosopher, economist and educator. Co-founder of Newnham College, a women-only college at the University of Cambridge. He also co-founded and led the Society for Psychical Research.
125	31 Aug 1900	Coca-Cola went on sale in the UK for the first time when the company founder's son, Charles Candler, brought five gallons of syrup with him on a visit to London. It was sold at a basement restaurant in London. It didn't officially go on sale in the UK until the early 1920s.
125	31 Aug 1900	Birth of Roland Culver, British stage, film and television actor.
100	2 Aug 1925	Birth of Jorge Rafael Videla, President/dictator of Argentina (1976–81). He was later convicted of large-scale human rights abuses and crimes against humanity that took place under his rule. He was sentenced to life imprisonment. (Died 2013.)
100	4 Aug 1925	U.S. highway route marker shields were approved by the Joint Board on Interstate Highways. The first route markers were installed in 1926.
100	5 Aug 1925	The Welsh nationalist political party Plaid Cymru was founded.
100	8 Aug 1925	The Ku Klux Klan held its first national March on Washington in the USA. Approximately 40,000 members took part.
100	8 Aug 1925	Birth of Alija Izetbegović, first President of Bosnia and Herzegovina (1996–98, 2000). (Died 2003.)
100	12 Aug 1925	Birth of Ross and Norris McWhirter, British writers, television presenters and political activists. Founders of *Guinness World Records*. (Ross was assassinated by the IRA in 1975. Norris died in 2004.)

AUGUST 2025

Ann.	Date	Event
100	14 Aug 1925	Norway officially gained sovereignty over Spitsbergen, as the Svalbard Treaty of 1920 came into effect.
100	15 Aug 1925	Birth of Oscar Peterson, Canadian jazz pianist, virtuoso and composer. Regarded as one of the greatest jazz pianists in history. (Died 2007.)
100	18 Aug 1925	Birth of Brian Aldiss, British science fiction novelist, short story writer and editor. His short story *Supertoys Last All Summer Long* was the basis for the film *A.I.: Artificial Intelligence*. (Died 2017.)
100	22 Aug 1925	Birth of Honor Blackman, British stage, film and television actress and singer. Best known for playing Cathy Gale in the TV series *The Avengers*, and Pussy Galore in the James Bond film *Goldfinger*. (Died 2020.)
100	27 Aug 1925	Birth of Nat Lofthouse, British footballer and manager. He played for Bolton Wanderers (1946–60) and England (1950–58) and managed Bolton Wanderers (1968–71). (Died 2011.)
90	13 Aug 1935	The first Transcontinental Roller Derby was held in Chicago Coliseum in Illinois, USA.
90	13 Aug 1935	Birth of Rod Hull, British television entertainer. Known for his appearances with Emu, an aggressive life-sized emu puppet. (Died 1999.)
90	14 Aug 1935	The Social Security Act came into effect in the USA. It created unemployment insurance, and pension plans for the elderly.
90	15 Aug 1935	Death of Wiley Post, American aviator. The first person to fly solo around the world. (Killed in a plane crash, aged 36, with Will Rogers – see below.)
90	15 Aug 1935	Death of Will Rogers, American cowboy performer, humourist and actor. (Killed in the same plane crash as Wiley Post, aged 55 – see above.)
90	15 Aug 1935	Death of Paul Signac, French neo-impressionist artist who helped develop pointillism with Georges Seurat.
90	21 Aug 1935	American musician Benny Goodman ('the King of Swing') and his big band performed at the Palomar Ballroom in Los Angeles, California. This event is often cited as the beginning of the Swing era. It might not have been the first swing performance, but it helped popularise swing music and brought it to the attention of the masses.
90	21 Aug 1935	Death of John Hartley, British tennis player. The world number 1 player in 1879 and 1880 – he won Wimbledon both years. He was also the only clergyman to win Wimbledon.
90	26 Aug 1935	Birth of Geraldine Ferraro, American politician. The first female vice-presidential nominee for a major party (Democrats, 1984) as the running mate of former Vice President Walter Mondale. (Died 2011.)
90	29 Aug 1935	Death of Astrid of Sweden, Queen consort of the Belgians (1934–35). Wife of King Leopold III. (Killed in a car crash, aged 29.)
90	30 Aug 1935	Birth of John Phillips, ('Papa John'), American singer, songwriter and guitarist (The Mamas & the Papas). (Died 2001.)
90	31 Aug 1935	With international tensions rising with Germany and Japan ahead of WWII, the USA passed the Neutrality Act of 1935. It prohibited the export of 'arms, ammunition, and implements of war' to foreign nations at war.

AUGUST 2025

Ann.	Date	Event
90	31 Aug 1935	Birth of Eldridge Cleaver, American writer and political activist who renounced his past as a member of the Black Panthers. Known for his collection of autobiographical essays *Soul On Ice*. (Died 1998.)
80	1 Aug 1945 to 2nd	World War II: the city of Toyama in Japan was almost completely destroyed by U.S. incendiary bombs.
80	2 Aug 1945	Death of Pietro Mascagni, Italian composer and conductor. Best known for his operas, especially *Cavalleria rusticana*.
80	6 Aug 1945	World War II – the Hiroshima atomic bomb. The U.S. Army Air Forces dropped an atomic bomb on the city of Hiroshima in Japan. The centre of the city was totally destroyed and approximately 80,000 people were killed immediately. A further 60,000 died by the end of the year from injury or radiation. Hiroshima was the first city in history to be hit by a nuclear weapon. (See also: 9th August 1945.)
80	8 Aug 1945	World War II: the Soviet Union entered the Pacific War exactly three months after the war in Europe ended, as agreed at the Yalta Conference in February. It declared war on Japan and (at one minute past midnight on 9th August) invaded the puppet state of Manchuria.
80	8 Aug 1945	World War II: the Nuremberg Charter (also known as the London Charter of the International Military Tribunal) was signed by the USA, Britain, France and the Soviet Union. It authorised the Nuremberg trials and stipulated the laws and procedures to be followed.
80	9 Aug 1945	World War II – the Nagasaki atomic bomb. The U.S. Army Air Forces dropped an atomic bomb on the city of Nagasaki in Japan. The north of the city was destroyed and approximately 40,000 people were killed immediately. A further 33,000+ died by the end of the year. It was the second (and last) city to experience a nuclear attack.
80	10 Aug 1945	World War II: following the bombing of Hiroshima and Nagasaki, Japan announced that it would be willing to surrender to the Allies to avoid further bloodshed. However, it would only do so if Emperor Hirohito's status remained unchanged. The following day (11th August) the Allies refused to accept Japan's terms of surrender, saying they would determine the Emperor's status after Japan had surrendered. (See also: 14th August 1945.)
80	10 Aug 1945 to 7 Dec 1949	The second phase of the Chinese Civil War. Chinese Communist Party victory. The third phase began in December 1949 and (officially) continues to the present day.
80	10 Aug 1945	Death of Robert H. Goddard, American engineer, physicist, inventor and educator. He built the first liquid-fuelled rocket and invented the multi-stage rocket. He has been called 'the man who ushered in the Space Age'. NASA's Goddard Space Flight Center was named in his honour.
80	12 Aug 1945	The Soviet Union occupied North Korea and established a communist government.

AUGUST 2025

Ann.	Date	Event
80	14 Aug 1945	The Kyujo Incident, Japan – an attempted military coup aimed at preventing Japan from surrendering in WWII. Two (failed) attempts were made to assassinate Prime Minister Kantaro Suzuki. The surrender went ahead, and the leaders of the coup committed suicide two days later.
80	14 Aug 1945	World War II: Japan's surrender and the end of the war. Japan announced its unconditional surrender, ending WWII in the Pacific. Japanese Emperor Hirohito publicly announced Japan's surrender on 15th August. The war officially ended on 2nd September when Japan signed the surrender document.
80	14 Aug 1945	World War II: American general Douglas MacArthur was appointed Supreme Command for the Allied Powers in Japan. He relocated from the Philippines to Tokyo, Japan on 18th September to begin his role. He held the post until 1951 when he was relieved of all his commands for making statements that contradicted U.S. policies.
80	14 Aug 1945 to 30th	August Revolution, Vietnam. Viet Minh victory. Emperor Bao Dai was persuaded to abdicate on 25th August, the empire was dissolved, and the Democratic Republic of Vietnam (North Vietnam) was established on 2nd September.
80	15 Aug 1945	World War II: following Japan's surrender, all Japanese forces in the Philippines surrendered and the Philippines Campaign ended. Allied victory. (Limited fighting continued until 2nd September.)
80	15 Aug 1945	World War II: the Allies liberated South Korea from the Japanese.
80	15 Aug 1945	World War II: gasoline and fuel oil rationing in the USA ended.
80	15 Aug 1945	Philippe Pétain, the leader of the Vichy France collaborationist regime during WWII, was convicted of treason and sentenced to death. His sentence was commuted to life imprisonment because of his advanced age and because he was a WWI national hero. He died in prison in 1951.
80	16 Aug 1945	The National Representatives' Congress convened in Vietnam. It supported the Viet Minh's uprising against French and Japanese forces in Vietnam, and appointed the National Liberation Committee as the provisional government of Vietnam. It was superseded by the National Assembly of Vietnam in March 1946.
80	16 Aug 1945	World War II: Emperor Puyi of Manchukuo was captured by the Soviet Red Army. He was the last Emperor of China and the Qing Dynasty.
80	16 Aug 1945	Death of Takijiro Ohnishi, Japanese admiral. Known as the father of the kamikaze – he sent around 4,000 pilots to their deaths. (Suicide, aged 54, after Japan surrendered at the end of WWII.)
80	17 Aug 1945	Indonesia declared its independence from the Netherlands and Sukarno became its first President. The Netherlands recognised Indonesia's independence in December 1949.
80	17 Aug 1945	Korea was divided along the 38th parallel into what would become North Korea and South Korea. U.S. forces occupied the southern area and Soviet forces occupied the northern area.

AUGUST 2025

Ann.	Date	Event
80	17 Aug 1945	George Orwell's satirical novella *Animal Farm* was published.
80	18 Aug 1945	Death of Subhas Chandra Bose, Indian nationalist. Leader of a WWII force that attempted (unsuccessfully) to liberate the Indian military from British rule.
80	25 Aug 1945	Death of John Birch, Indian-born American military intelligence officer and Baptist missionary in China. Killed by armed supporters of the Communist Party of China. He is considered to be the first victim of the Cold War. The anti-communist John Birch Society was formed in the USA in 1958 and named in his honour.
80	29 Aug 1945	The USA terminated its Lend-Lease programme, which had shipped $50 billion in aid to its allies during WWII.
80	30 Aug 1945	World War II: the Allied Control Council was established in Germany. It governed the Allied Occupation Zones in Germany and Austria after the war, replacing the German government, which had been dissolved.
80	30 Aug 1945	World War II: Hong Kong was liberated by British forces.
80	31 Aug 1945	The Liberal Party of Australia was founded.
75	1 Aug 1950	Guam became an unincorporated territory of the USA and its people became U.S. citizens.
75	1 Aug 1950	King Leopold III of Belgium announced that he would abdicate on 16th July 1951. He was succeeded by his son Baudouin on 17th July 1951.
75	3 Aug 1950	Korean War: the U.S. Congress removed the limit on the size of the U.S. armed forces. The U.S. Army immediately issued an involuntary recall of 30,000 enlisted men to active duty to fight in the war. The majority were members of the Organized Reserve Corps. They were ordered to report for duty in September.
75	4 Aug 1950 to 18 Sep	Korean War – the Battle of Pusan Perimeter, South Korea. One of the first major battles of the war. United Nations victory: the North Korean Army forces collapsed and were forced to retreat after the UN launched a counterattack at Incheon.
75	8 Aug 1950	American swimmer Florence Chadwick swam the English Channel from France to England, breaking the women's record. A year later she swam it again from England to France, breaking the women's record again and becoming the first woman to swim the Channel in both directions.
75	8 Aug 1950	The first Whataburger fast-food restaurant opened in Corpus Christi, Texas, USA. It has branches in Texas and the south-western and south-eastern U.S. states.
75	8 Aug 1950	Death of Fergus McMaster, Australian businessman and aviation pioneer. Co-founder of the Australian airline Qantas.
75	11 Aug 1950	Birth of Erik Brann, American rock guitarist and singer (Iron Butterfly). (Died 2003.)
75	12 Aug 1950	Korean War – the Battle of Pusan Perimeter – the Bloody Gulch massacre, South Korea. The North Korean Army murdered 75 American prisoners of war.

AUGUST 2025

Ann.	Date	Event
75	15 Aug 1950	Assam–Tibet Earthquake. The largest known earthquake to have been caused by two continental plates converging, rather than by an oceanic subduction. More than 1,500 people were killed and 30,000 injured.
75	15 Aug 1950	Birth of Anne, Princess Royal of the United Kingdom. Daughter of Queen Elizabeth II.
75	17 Aug 1950	The U.S. National Bureau of Standards' Standards Western Automatic Computer (SWAC) was dedicated at the Institute for Numerical Analysis in Los Angeles, California. It was the fastest computer in the world at that time, and operated until December 1967.
75	18 Aug 1950	Death of Julien Lahaut, Chairman of the Communist Party of Belgium. Noted for advocating the abolition of the monarchy. (Assassinated – possibly by Belgian royalists.)
75	19 Aug 1950	Saturday morning television programmes for children were first broadcast on ABC in the USA.
75	22 Aug 1950	The Brookhaven Graphite Research Reactor began operating at the Brookhaven National Laboratory in Upton, New York,USA. It was the first nuclear reactor developed to research peaceful applications of atomic energy. It operated until 1968.
75	22 Aug 1950	American tennis player Althea Gibson became the first black player to compete internationally.
75	27 Aug 1950 to May 1952	U.S. President Harry S. Truman put America's railroads under the control of the U.S. Army because of a national railroad strike. The strike lasted for 21 months.
75	27 Aug 1950	The first international television link. The BBC broadcast a live TV show across the English Channel. The two-hour show was transmitted from Calais in France across the Channel by microwave relays. It celebrated the centenary of the first cross-Channel telegraph transmission by undersea cable.
75	29 Aug 1950	Korean War: the first British troops arrived in Korea to bolster the U.S. presence there.
70	3 Aug 1955 to 15th	Hurricane Connie hit Puerto Rico, the eastern U.S. states and Ontario, Canada. 74 people were killed.
70	3 Aug 1955	The English-language première of Samuel Beckett's play *Waiting for Godot*, at the Arts Theatre in London, UK.
70	5 Aug 1955	Death of Carmen Miranda, ('the Brazilian Bombshell'), Portuguese-born Brazilian samba singer, dancer and Broadway actress. Noted for her signature Tutti Frutti hat, which she wore in many films, including *The Gang's All Here*.
70	7 Aug 1955	Bar-Ilan University opened in Ramat Gan, Israel. It is now the second-largest academic institution in Israel.
70	7 Aug 1955	Sony (then known as the Tokyo Telecommunications Engineering Corporation) released the first transistor radio made in Japan: the TR-55. It was also the first transistor radio in the world to use all-miniature components.

AUGUST 2025

Ann.	Date	Event
70	8 Aug 1955	The 26th of July Movement was founded in Mexico by a group of exiled revolutionaries including Fidel Castro and Che Guevara. They aimed to overthrow the Cuban dictator Fulgencio Batista – which they did in January 1959.
70	8 Aug 1955 to 20th	The Atoms for Peace Conference, Geneva, Switzerland. The first United Nations International Conference on Peaceful Uses of Atomic Energy.
70	12 Aug 1955	Death of Thomas Mann, German novelist, short story writer, essayist and social critic. Best known for his novels *Doctor Faustus* and *Death in Venice*. Winner of the 1929 Nobel Prize in Literature.
70	14 Aug 1955	Death of Herbert Putnam, American librarian. The longest-serving Librarian of the U.S. Congress (1899–1939). He built it into a world-renowned institution.
70	16 Aug 1955	The Italian automotive company Fiat ordered the world's first private nuclear reactor to power one of its manufacturing plants. It began operating in 1959 and ran until 1971.
70	17 Aug 1955 to 21st	Hurricane Diane struck North Carolina, the Mid-Atlantic U.S. states and New England, causing catastrophic flooding. At least 184 people were killed. It followed hard on the heels of Hurricane Connie (see 3rd August.)
70	20 Aug 1955	Algerian War – the Battle of Philippeville. Armed mobs of anti-French Berber insurgents raided several cities and towns in north-eastern Algeria, and other attacks occurred in Morocco. Hundreds of people were killed. Thousands may have been killed in the subsequent French reprisal attacks.
70	22 Aug 1955	The world's first computer users' group, SHARE, was founded in Los Angeles, California, USA by users of the IBM Model 701. The group is still running, and offers education, professional networking and industry influence to users of enterprise computer systems.
70	23 Aug 1955	Death of Reginald Tate, British stage, film and television actor. Best known for his role as Professor Bernard Quatermass in the science fiction TV series *The Quatermass Experiment*.
70	25 Aug 1955	Birth of John McGeoch, Scottish post-punk/new wave guitarist (Magazine, Siouxsie & the Banshees, Visage, Public Image Ltd.) (Died 2004.)
70	27 Aug 1955	The first edition of the *Guinness Book of Records* was published. It is now called *Guinness World Records*.
70	28 Aug 1955	Death of Emmett Till, African American teenager who was mutilated and killed in Mississippi after flirting with a white woman. His death was one of the key events that motivated the Civil Rights Movement.
70	31 Aug 1955	The 'Sunmobile', the world's first solar-powered car, was demonstrated at the General Motors Powerama show in Chicago, Illinois, USA. It was 15 inches (37.5 cm) long.

AUGUST 2025

Ann.	Date	Event
65	Aug 1960	The following countries gained their independence this month: Dahomey (Benin) Niger Upper Volta (Burkina Faso) Ivory Coast Chad Central African Republic Republic of the Congo (Brazzaville) Cyprus Gabon Senegal
65	5 Aug 1960	Death of Arthur Meighen, Prime Minister of Canada (1920–21, 1926).
65	6 Aug 1960	Cuban nationalised all American and foreign-owned property located within its borders in response to a U.S. embargo. The seizure included all American-owned oil refineries, sugar factories and mines. CUPET, Cuba's largest oil and gas company, was established from the nationalisation of Texaco and Shell.
65	6 Aug 1960	The Twist became a national sensation in the USA, and triggered one of the nation's biggest dance crazes, when singer Chubby Checker performed the song on Dick Clark's *American Bandstand*. The record, which was released in July, topped the charts in September.
65	7 Aug 1960	Several bishops from the Catholic Church in Cuba signed a joint letter condemning the rise of communism in Cuba and banning Catholics from joining the Communist Party. As a result, Cuban leader Fidel Castro cracked down on all church activities in Cuba. He initially banned religious TV and radio broadcasts, but later expelled Catholic priests, took over Catholic schools, and discouraged all forms of religion in the country. The discrimination against the Roman Catholic Church in Cuba began to ease following the collapse of the Soviet Union.
65	8 Aug 1960	The pop song *Itsy Bitsy Teenie Weenie Yellow Polkadot Bikini* by Brian Hyland became a worldwide hit. The record was released in June.
65	10 Aug 1960	The first successful recovery of a man-made object from orbit: a return capsule containing a package of instrumentation that was ejected from the U.S. reconnaissance satellite *Discoverer 13*.
65	12 Aug 1960	NASA launched the first successful communications satellite, *Echo 1*, into low Earth orbit, to relay telephone and television signals. The satellite's 30-metre (98-foot) shiny surface reflected signals from one point on the Earth to another. This satellite was officially named *Echo 1A*. It was a replacement for the first *Echo 1*, whose launch in May 1960 ended in failure and it ditched into the Atlantic.
65	17 Aug 1960	The Beatles gave their first live public performance, at the Indra Club in Hamburg, Germany. They performed there seven evenings a week. They relocated to the Kaiserkeller on 4th October after the Indra Club was closed down because of noise complaints.

AUGUST 2025

Ann.	Date	Event
65	18 Aug 1960	The first photo to be transmitted via satellite: Collins Radio of Cedar Rapids, Iowa, USA successfully transmitted a photo of U.S. President Dwight D. Eisenhower via the *Echo I* communications satellite.
65	18 Aug 1960	The U.S. Air Force launched *Discoverer 14*, a spy satellite. It took photographic images of military targets in the Soviet Union, and ejected them the following day, when they were successfully recovered in mid-air. This was the first successful recovery of photographic film from an orbiting satellite. It captured more images than all of the U-2 spy plane flights over the Soviet Union between 1956 and 1960.
65	19 Aug 1960	The Soviet Union launched *Sputnik 5* with the dogs Belka and Strelka on board (plus forty mice, two rats and a variety of plants). After a day in orbit they returned safely. They were the first animals to survive orbital flight.
65	19 Aug 1960	The Soviet Union convicted American U-2 spy plane pilot Gary Powers of espionage after shooting down his plane on 1st May. He was sentenced to three years in prison followed by seven years in a labour camp. He was released in a prisoner-exchange in February 1962.
65	20 Aug 1960	Regularly scheduled television programming began in Norway.
65	23 Aug 1960	Death of Oscar Hammerstein II, American lyricist, theatrical director and producer. Best known for his collaboration with the composer Richard Rodgers on musicals including *Oklahoma!*, *Carousel*, *South Pacific*, and *The Sound of Music*.
65	25 Aug 1960 to 11 Sep	The 1960 Summer Olympic Games were held in Rome, Italy. This was the first Olympics to be broadcast extensively in the USA, thanks to the advent of videotape.
65	27 Aug 1960	Ax Handle Saturday (also called the Jacksonville riot of 1960), Florida, USA. Two hundred members of the Ku Klux Klan, armed with axe handles and baseball bats, attacked African Americans who were holding a sit-in protest against racial segregation. The violence quickly spread and the group began attacking every African American in sight.
65	29 Aug 1960	Death of Hazza' Majali, Prime Minister of Jordan (1955, 1959–60). (Assassinated, aged 43, along with eleven others including senior government officials and Jordanian citizens.)
65	31 Aug 1960	The Agricultural Hall of Fame (now the National Agricultural Center and Hall of Fame) was established in Kansas, USA.
60	Aug 1965	Sony launched the CV-2000 home video recorder. It was one of the world's first consumer video recorders, and the first all-transistor model. It used open reel-to-reel tapes that could only be played back on the machine they were recorded on, as there was no tracking control.
60	1 Aug 1965	The advertising of cigarettes on British television was banned. (TV advertisements for cigars and loose tobacco were allowed until 1991.)
60	1 Aug 1965	Frank Herbert's epic science fiction novel *Dune* was published. Film adaptations were released in 1984 and 2021.

AUGUST 2025

Ann.	Date	Event
60	2 Aug 1965	Forest fires swept through the hills between Provence and St Tropez in southern France. Thousands of holiday makers abandoned campsites and fled to the coast, where they were rescued by ships. More than 30 square miles of forest was destroyed. At least two people were killed.
60	3 Aug 1965	Vietnam War – the Cam Ne incident. U.S. Marines destroyed 51 huts in the village of Cam Ne after being ordered to destroy any hamlet from which they received even a single burst of gunfire. A CBS war correspondent accompanied them, and his film report of Marines ignoring pleas from local residents and setting fire to their huts and destroying their personal possessions, even though no shots had been fired, was broadcast on the *CBS Evening News* on 5th August. The footage shocked the American public and sparked indignation.
60	4 Aug 1965	The Cook Islands became self-governing in free association with New Zealand.
60	5 Aug 1965 to 23 Sep	Indo–Pakistani War of 1965 (also known as the Second Kashmir War). The war began when between 26,000 and 33,000 Pakistani soldiers crossed the Line of Control disguised as Kashmiri locals. Indian forces, who had been tipped off by police, crossed the line on 15th August. India scored the most successes initially, but after a Pakistani counter-attack their progress stalled, and both sides made equal progress. The war ended in stalemate and a UN-mandated cease-fire, with both sides declaring victory.
60	6 Aug 1965	U.S. President Lyndon B. Johnson signed the Voting Rights Act of 1965 into law. It prohibited racial discrimination in voting and guaranteed every adult American the right to vote. The President called the day 'a triumph for freedom'.
60	6 Aug 1965	The Beatles' album *Help!* was released.
60	6 Aug 1965	Birth of Mark Speight, British television presenter. Best known for hosting the children's art series *SMart*. (Died 2008 – suicide.)
60	7 Aug 1965	American author Ken Kesey held an infamous party at his ranch in California, where his Merry Pranksters group of hippies introduced the Hells Angels motorcycle gang to psychedelic drugs.
60	8 Aug 1965	Death of Shirley Jackson, American novelist and short story writer. Best known for her short story *The Lottery* – one of the most famous short stories in the history of American literature. It was banned in South Africa.
60	9 Aug 1965	Singapore was expelled from Malaysia and became an independent country.
60	9 Aug 1965	53 maintenance workers were killed in a Titan II missile silo in Searcy, Arkansas, USA after workers accidentally cut through a high-pressure hydraulic line, causing a fire and loss of oxygen.
60	11 Aug 1965 to 17th	Watts Riots, Los Angeles, California. Six days of race riots erupted following an incident between a white member of the California Highway Patrol and an African American motorist. 34 people were killed, over 1,000 injured and more than 3,000 arrested. More than $40 million worth of damage was caused.

AUGUST 2025

Ann.	Date	Event
60	12 Aug 1965	Elizabeth Lane became Britain's first female High Court judge.
60	13 Aug 1965	The American rock band Jefferson Airplane gave their first public performance, at The Matrix nightclub in San Francisco, California.
60	13 Aug 1965	Death of Hayato Ikeda, Prime Minister of Japan (1960–64). He played a key role in Japan's economic growth after WWII.
60	15 Aug 1965	The birth of stadium rock. British rock group the Beatles played to more than 55,000 fans at Shea Stadium in New York City, USA. The famous event set attendance and revenue records that paved the way for future stadium rock concerts.
60	18 Aug 1965 to 24th	Vietnam War: Operation Starlite – the first major U.S. ground battle of the war. Result: indecisive.
60	19 Aug 1965	The Frankfurt Auschwitz Trials ended in Germany. 22 people were charged for their roles in the Holocaust. Seventeen of them received prison sentences, including six who were jailed for life.
60	20 Aug 1965	The song *(I Can't Get No) Satisfaction* by the Rolling Stones was released in the UK. (USA: 6th June. It was their first #1 hit in the USA.)
60	21 Aug 1965	NASA launched its *Gemini 5* spacecraft. The two-man crew set a new record for space flight duration (eight days), demonstrating that a return trip to the Moon was possible. They returned safely on 29th August.
60	22 Aug 1965	Death of Ellen Church, American airline stewardess. The world's first female flight attendant.
60	23 Aug 1965	Thurgood Marshall became Solicitor General of the United States. In August 1967 he became the first African American Supreme Court justice.
60	23 Aug 1965	Death of Jan Bata, Czech shoe manufacturer.
60	25 Aug 1965	Vietnam War: Henry Cabot Lodge Jr. became the U.S. Ambassador to South Vietnam for the second time (until 1967). He was also the U.S. Ambassador from August 1963 – June 1964.
60	27 Aug 1965	Death of Le Corbusier, Swiss-born French architect and city planner.
60	30 Aug 1965	Bob Dylan's album *Highway 61 Revisited* was released.
60	31 Aug 1965	Death of E. E. ('Doc') Smith, American science fiction writer. Known as 'the father of the space opera'. Best known for his *Skylark* and *Lensman* series.
50	1 Aug 1975	The Helsinki Accords were signed by 35 nations in an attempt to improve relations between the Communist Bloc and the West. The Conference for Security and Co-operation in Europe (now the Organisation for Security and Co-operation in Europe) was created.
50	3 Aug 1975	Two river boats collided and sank on the West River near Canton, China during a heavy storm. Up to 500 people are believed to have been killed, though few details were released by the Chinese authorities.
50	3 Aug 1975	The Louisiana Superdome (now the Caesars Superdome) opened in New Orleans, Louisiana, USA.

AUGUST 2025

Ann.	Date	Event
50	4 Aug 1975 to 5th	AIA Building hostage crisis, Kuala Lumpur, Malaysia. The Japanese Red Army (JRA), a communist militant organisation, took 53 hostages at the American Insurance Associates Building, which housed several international embassies. Hostages included the U.S. consul and the Swedish chargé d'affaires. All hostages were released unharmed after the Malaysian government released five JRA leaders from prison.
50	8 Aug 1975	The Banqiao Reservoir Dam in China collapsed during heavy flooding caused by Typhoon Nina. The surge of water caused 61 smaller dams to fail. 229,000 people were killed and 11 million made homeless.
50	8 Aug 1975	Death of Cannonball Adderley, American jazz saxophonist. (Cerebral haemorrhage, aged 46.)
50	9 Aug 1975	Death of Dmitri Shostakovich, Russian composer and pianist.
50	11 Aug 1975	East Timor coup. The Timorese Democratic Union (UDT) staged a coup against the Fretilin pro-independence party, forcing Governor Mário Lemos Pires to flee. This incident led to the Indonesian invasion of East Timor in December.
50	11 Aug 1975	Death of Anthony McAuliffe, U.S. Army general. Acting commander of the 101st Airborne Division during the WWII Battle of the Bulge. Known for his one-word reply 'Nuts!' in response to a Nazi order to surrender.
50	11 Aug 1975	Death of Howard Wendell, American stage, film and television actor.
50	15 Aug 1975	Military coup in Bangladesh. The President, Sheikh Mujibur Rehman, and most of his family were killed and a military government was established.
50	15 Aug 1975	British rock singer and musician Peter Gabriel quit the band Genesis.
50	16 Aug 1975	Aboriginal land rights: Australian Prime Minister Gough Whitlam gave the rights to a small piece of land in Northern Territory to the Gurindji people in a symbolic handover ceremony. This followed the Wave Hill walk-off, a seven-year strike by Gurindji workers. It led to the passing of the Aboriginal Land Rights (Northern Territory) Act 1976. In 2020 the traditional owners of the land were given the rights to 1,900 square miles of land in Wave Hill Station.
50	20 Aug 1975	NASA launched its *Viking 1* space probe on a mission to Mars. It became the first spacecraft to land successfully on Mars and complete its mission.
50	23 Aug 1975	Communist coup in Laos. King Savang Vatthana was forced to abdicate in December, the monarchy was abolished and the country became a republic. The country remains a single-party communist dictatorship, run by the Lao People's Revolutionary Party.
50	24 Aug 1975	Death of Charles Revson, American businessman. Co-founder of the Revlon cosmetics company.
50	25 Aug 1975	Bruce Springsteen's album *Born to Run* was released.
50	25 Aug 1975	Death of John R. Dunning, American physicist, engineer and educator whose experiments in nuclear fission led to the development of the atomic bomb.

AUGUST 2025

Ann.	Date	Event
50	27 Aug 1975	British cyclists Colin and Veronica Scargill completed the first round-the-world tandem bicycle ride. They began their journey in February 1974 and cycled 18,020 miles.
50	27 Aug 1975	Death of Haile Selassie, Emperor of Ethiopia (1930–74). (Strangled by former military officers.)
50	29 Aug 1975	The star V1500 Cygni in the constellation Cygnus became the second-brightest nova of the 20th century. It became the fourth brightest star in the sky, and could easily be seen with the naked eye. It remained visible for about a week before it faded.
50	29 Aug 1975	Death of Eamon de Valera, President of Ireland (1959–73).
40	2 Aug 1985	Delta Air Lines Flight 191 crashed on approach to Dallas/Fort Worth International Airport in Texas, USA after flying through a violent thunderstorm and losing control. 137 people were killed and 26 injured.
40	2 Aug 1985	The teen science-fiction comedy film *Weird Science* was released in the USA. (UK: 1st November.)
40	3 Aug 1985	American football player and actor O. J. Simpson was inducted into the Pro Football Hall of Fame. He was involved in two murder trials in 1994 and 1997 and later served a prison sentence for kidnapping and armed robbery.
40	6 Aug 1985	Death of Forbes Burnham, President of Guyana (1980–85).
40	8 Aug 1985	Death of Louise Brooks, American film actress and dancer. Best known for the film *Pandora's Box* and for her distinctive bobbed hairstyle.
40	10 Aug 1985	American pop singer Michael Jackson bought ATV Music Publishing for $47.5 million, giving him the rights to almost every song by the Beatles.
40	12 Aug 1985	Japan Airlines Flight 123 crashed into Mount Ogura, killing 520 people. It remains the world's worst single-plane air disaster.
40	13 Aug 1985	Whitney Houston's soul/R&B song *Saving All My Love for You* was released. It became a worldwide hit in October, and her first #1 hit in the USA and UK.
40	14 Aug 1985	Death of Gale Sondergaard, American stage and film actress. The first winner of the Academy Award for Best Supporting Actress. Her films include *Anthony Adverse*, *The Cat and the Canary*, *The Mark of Zorro*, and *Anna and the King of Siam*.
40	15 Aug 1985	British entrepreneur Richard Branson's speedboat *Virgin Atlantic Challenger* capsized off south-west England as he attempted the fastest-ever Atlantic crossing. In 1986 he successfully beat the record by two hours in *Virgin Atlantic Challenger II*.
40	16 Aug 1985	American pop singer Madonna married actor Sean Penn. They divorced in 1989.
40	17 Aug 1985	House of Hope was founded in Orlando, Florida, USA by former schoolteacher Sara Trollinger to help troubled teenagers. The organisation (later known as National House of Hope) now runs a network of Houses of Hope across the USA.

AUGUST 2025

Ann.	Date	Event
40	18 Aug 1985	Japan launched its *Suisei* spacecraft on a mission to fly past Halley's Comet (which it did successfully in March 1986).
40	19 Aug 1985	Hans Tiedge, the head of West German counter-intelligence, defected to East Germany and (on 23rd August) was unmasked as an East German spy. The revelation caused panic in West Germany and NATO.
40	20 Aug 1985 to 4 Mar 1987	The Iran–Contra affair. U.S. President Ronald Reagan's administration secretly facilitated the sale of arms to Iran, even though it was subject to an arms embargo. They planned to use the proceeds from the sale to fund the Contras in Nicaragua. The U.S. Congress and the Tower Commission investigated the affair, and concluded that the President was not aware of the extent of the programmes. Numerous officials were charged, and eleven were convicted. They were all eventually cleared or pardoned by President George H. W. Bush, who was Vice President at the time of the affair.
40	22 Aug 1985	Manchester air disaster, England. A British Airtours Boeing 737 burst into flames at Manchester Airport after an engine caught fire and a fuel tank ruptured. 55 people were killed.
40	22 Aug 1985	IBM and Microsoft signed a joint development agreement to develop a new operating system for personal computers. This led to the development of OS/2, which was released in 1987. The partnership broke up in 1990 and IBM released the last version of OS/2 in 2001. It then licensed it to other vendors.
40	23 Aug 1985	The coming-of-age romantic comedy film *Teen Wolf* was released in the USA. (UK: 24th January 1986.) A sequel was released in 1987, an animated TV series in 1986–87, and a live-action TV series in 2011–17.
40	25 Aug 1985	Death of Samantha Smith, American schoolgirl and goodwill ambassador. She wrote a letter to Soviet leader Yuri Andropov expressing her fear of a nuclear war, and he sent her a personal invitation to visit his country – which she accepted. (Killed in a plane crash, aged 13.)
40	27 Aug 1985	The Nigerian government was overthrown by Army Chief of Staff General Ibrahim Badamasi Babangida.
40	28 Aug 1985	The world première of the epic dark fantasy adventure film *Legend*, in France. (UK release: 13th December 1985. U.S. release: 18th April 1986.)
40	28 Aug 1985	Death of Ruth Gordon, American stage, film and television actress and writer. Her films include *Rosemary's Baby*, *Harold and Maude*, and *Every Which Way but Loose*.
40	30 Aug 1985	Death of Philly Joe Jones, American jazz drummer. One of the major percussionists of the bop era. Best known for his work with the Miles Davis Quintet.
40	31 Aug 1985	Richard Ramirez, the notorious 'Night Stalker' serial killer, was captured and beaten by a mob in Los Angeles, California, USA after being recognised from a police mug shot shown on TV and in newspapers.
40	31 Aug 1985	Death of Sir (Frank) Macfarlane Burnet, Australian physician, immunologist and virologist. Joint winner of the 1960 Nobel Prize in Physiology or Medicine for discovering acquired immunological tolerance, which is important in organ transplantation.

AUGUST 2025

Ann.	Date	Event
30	1 Aug 1995	The Westinghouse Electric Corporation purchased CBS for $5.4 billion. The company was subsequently bought by Viacom in 2000 for $37 billion. (Viacom was originally formed by CBS in 1952 as a spin-off company, then known as CBS Films.)
30	1 Aug 1995	The first Victoria's Secret Fashion Show was held, at the Plaza Hotel in New York City, USA.
30	4 Aug 1995 to 7th	Croatian War of Independence – Operation Storm. The last major battle of the war. Decisive Croatian victory.
30	9 Aug 1995	The computer services company Netscape went public and began trading its shares on the stock market. It was acquired by AOL in 1998 and was shut down in 2003.
30	9 Aug 1995	Death of Jerry Garcia, American rock guitarist, singer and songwriter (the Grateful Dead).
30	10 Aug 1995	Oklahoma City bombing: Timothy McVeigh and Terry Nichols were indicted for the bombing of the Alfred P. Murrah Federal Building in April. Their accomplice, Michael Fortier, pleaded guilty to his role and agreed to testify against them in a plea-bargain.
30	11 Aug 1995	U.S. President Bill Clinton banned all nuclear weapons testing by the USA, saying that the country's nuclear stockpile could be safely maintained without the need for any further testing. He made this statement ahead of signing the Comprehensive Nuclear-Test-Ban Treaty in September 1996.
30	13 Aug 1995	Death of Alison Hargreaves, British mountaineer. The first woman to climb Mount Everest solo and without the aid of supplementary oxygen. (Killed in a storm while descending K2, along with the American mountaineer Rob Slater and their Spanish and New Zealand team-mates.)
30	13 Aug 1995	Death of Mickey Mantle, American baseball player. One of the greatest players in baseball history.
30	14 Aug 1995	The Battle of Britpop. British bands Blur and Oasis released competing singles on the same day, launching a chart battle that was spurred on by the media. Blur won the battle, with their song *Country House* reaching #1 by the end of the week while Oasis's song *Roll With It* reached #2.
30	15 Aug 1995	Death of John Cameron Swayze, American news anchorman and television game show panellist in the 1950s.
30	16 Aug 1995	Bermuda independence referendum. The citizens of Bermuda voted against independence from the UK and decided to remain a British Dependent Territory.
30	17 Aug 1995	A bomb exploded at the Arc de Triomphe in Paris, France. Seventeen people were injured. The Algerian Armed Islamic Group (GIA) claimed responsibility. Three further bombs were planted over the following three weeks, only one of which exploded, injuring fourteen people at a Jewish school in Lyon.
30	17 Aug 1995	Death of Howard E. Koch, American playwright and screenwriter (*Casablanca, Shining Victory, Letter from an Unknown Woman, Mission to Moscow*). He was blacklisted by Hollywood in the 1950s for his outspoken leftist political views.

AUGUST 2025

Ann.	Date	Event
30	20 Aug 1995	Firozabad rail disaster, India. The Kalindi Express train hit a cow on the track and was unable to continue because its brakes were damaged. The Purushottam Express train then ran into the back of it. 358 people were killed.
30	24 Aug 1995	Microsoft released its Windows 95 operating system (with an extensive marketing campaign). On the same day, it also launched Microsoft Office 95, and Microsoft Network (MSN) – an online service designed to compete with AOL.
30	26 Aug 1995 or 27th	The International Rugby Board lifted all restrictions on payments in Rugby Union, allowing professional players to take part and ending its amateurs-only status.
30	26 Aug 1995	Death of Evelyn Wood, American teacher and businesswoman who coined the term 'speed reading' and developed and taught a speed-reading system called Reading Dynamics.
30	27 Aug 1995	Death of Carl Giles, British cartoonist. Best known for his work with the *Daily Express* newspaper. He was voted 'Britain's Favourite Cartoonist of the 20th Century'.
30	28 Aug 1995	Bosnian War – the Siege of Sarajevo – the second Markale market massacre. The Army of the Republika Srpska carried out a mortar attack on the crowded open-air market, killing 37 people and injuring more than 80. (The market was first attacked in February 1994, killing 68 people.)
30	28 Aug 1995	Fox television in the USA broadcast a seventeen-minute 'alien autopsy' film, which supposedly depicted the secret autopsy of an alien recovered from a spacecraft that crashed near Roswell, New Mexico in 1947. British entrepreneur Ray Santilli, who claimed to have discovered the film, later said most of it was a 'reconstruction' because the original film had deteriorated. The authenticity of the original film has never been confirmed.
30	28 Aug 1995	Death of Michael Ende, German children's writer. Best known for his fantasy stories including *The Neverending Story*, *Jim Button and Luke the Engine Driver* and *Momo*.
30	30 Aug 1995 to 20 Sep	NATO Intervention in Bosnia – Operation Deliberate Force. A sustained air campaign against the Army of the Republika Srpska (VRS) after it attacked UN-designated safe areas in Bosnia and Herzegovina.
30	30 Aug 1995	A key moment in the O. J. Simpson double-murder trial. Tape recordings of LAPD officer Mark Fuhrman were played in court, revealing that he repeatedly used racial slurs (which he had denied) and undermining his credibility as a witness. He was the officer who found the bloodied glove at the murder scene. When asked if he had planted or manufactured any evidence, he refused to answer, citing the Fifth Amendment. He retired from the LAPD soon afterwards, and was later charged with perjury.
30	31 Aug 1995	Ukraine's first satellite, *Sich-1*, and Chile's first satellite, *FASat-Alfa*, were launched.
30	31 Aug 1995	Death of J. Erik Jonsson, American businessman and philanthropist. Co-founder and president of Texas Instruments. Mayor of Dallas (1964–71).

AUGUST 2025

Ann.	Date	Event
25	4 Aug 2000	Queen Elizabeth, the Queen Mother celebrated her 100th birthday. (She died in March 2002, aged 101.)
25	5 Aug 2000	Death of Sir Alec Guinness, British stage and film actor (*Great Expectations, Oliver Twist, The Bridge on the River Kwai, Lawrence of Arabia, Doctor Zhivago, A Passage to India, Star Wars*, and more).
25	6 Aug 2000	Death of Sir Robin Day, British political commentator and broadcaster.
25	8 Aug 2000	The American Confederate submarine *H. L. Hunley* was raised from the sea bed in Charleston Harbor, South Carolina, USA. In 1864 it became the first submarine to sink an enemy warship in combat – though it apparently also sank itself in the process.
25	12 Aug 2000	The Russian nuclear submarine *Kursk* sank in the Barents Sea when its hull was damaged by a series of explosions. All 118 crew members were killed.
25	12 Aug 2000	Death of Loretta Young, American film and television actress.
25	15 Aug 2000	Death of Edward Craven Walker, British inventor of the lava lamp.
25	22 Aug 2000	Death of Abulfaz Elchibey, President of Azerbaijan (1992–93 – overthrown in a coup).
25	25 Aug 2000	Death of Jack Nitzsche, American rock/classical musician, composer, arranger and record producer. A close associate of producer Phil Spector in the 1960s. He later worked with bands including the Rolling Stones and worked on numerous film scores.
25	26 Aug 2000	Death of Bunny Austin, British tennis player. From 1938 until 2012 he was the last British male player to reach the final of Wimbledon. He was also the first tennis player to wear shorts.
25	28 Aug 2000	The first computer virus to target handheld devices was discovered. LibertyCrack attacked Palm OS-based devices, deleting applications and files. Two other Palm OS viruses, Vapor and Phage, were discovered on 21st and 22nd September respectively.
25	29 Aug 2000	In a speech at the Transplantation Society's international conference, Pope John Paul II endorsed voluntary organ donation and transplants but denounced the cloning of human embryos and stem cell research.
20	1 Aug 2005	Death of Fahd, King of Saudi Arabia (1982–2005). Succeeded by his half-brother Crown Prince Abdullah.
20	3 Aug 2005	The President of Mauritania, Maaouya Ould Sid'Ahmed Taya, was overthrown in a military coup while he was attending the funeral of King Fahd of Saudi Arabia (see 1st August above). He went into exile in Qatar. He was succeeded by Ely Ould Mohamed Vall.
20	3 Aug 2005	Mahmoud Ahmadinejad became President of Iran (until 2013).
20	3 Aug 2005	The Mozilla Corporation was established. It coordinates the development of internet-related software including the Firefox web browser and Thunderbird email client.

AUGUST 2025

Ann.	Date	Event
20	4 Aug 2005	A Russian mini-submarine carrying seven crew became caught on fishing nets and a military antenna 190 metres (620 feet) below the surface of the Pacific Ocean off the east coast of Russia. Russian attempts to release the submarine failed, but it was cut free on 7th August using a British-owned robotic craft. The crew were unharmed. (See also: 12th August 2000.)
20	5 Aug 2005	Death of Seungseop Lee, South Korean computer game addict. (Died of exhaustion, aged 28, after playing *StarCraft* continuously for about 50 hours in an internet café.)
20	6 Aug 2005	Death of Robin Cook, British politician. Foreign Secretary (1997–2001). Leader of the House of Commons (2001–03). (Heart attack, aged 59.)
20	7 Aug 2005	Death of Peter Jennings, Canadian-born American journalist and news anchor. Best known for ABC's *World News Tonight*.
20	8 Aug 2005	Death of Barbara Bel Geddes, American stage, film and television actress. Best known for her role as Miss Ellie in the TV series *Dallas*.
20	8 Aug 2005	Death of John H. Johnson, American publisher. Founder of the Johnson Publishing Company. The first African American to appear on the *Forbes 400* list of wealthiest Americans.
20	9 Aug 2005	Death of Matthew McGrory, American film and television actor (*Bubble Boy*, *Big Fish*, *Malcolm in the Middle*, *Charmed* and more). Noted for his great height. Listed in *Guinness World Records* as the world's tallest actor (7 feet 6 inches – 2.29 metres). (Heart failure, aged 32.)
20	12 Aug 2005	NASA's *Mars Reconnaissance Orbiter* spacecraft was launched. At the time of writing it is still operating, and is used as a high-speed data relay for other spacecraft and rovers on the surface of Mars.
20	12 Aug 2005	American communications companies Sprint and Nextel merged to form Sprint Nextel Corporation. In 2013 it dropped the Nextel branding and was renamed Sprint. In 2020 it merged with T-Mobile and the Sprint brand was discontinued.
20	13 Aug 2005	Death of David Lange, Prime Minister of New Zealand (1984–89).
20	15 Aug 2005	All remaining Israeli settlers in the Gaza Strip and the northern West Bank had to leave by this date, in exchange for government resettlement packages and compensation. Those who refused to leave were forcibly evicted by 23rd August. (See also: 22nd August 2005.)
20	15 Aug 2005	The Insurgency in Aceh ended after more than 28 years. The Free Aceh Movement had sought to make Aceh province independent from Indonesia. Following a military offensive and the 2004 Indian Ocean earthquake and tsunami, the two sides signed a peace agreement (the Helsinki Memorandum of Understanding) and Aceh was granted special autonomy.
20	15 Aug 2005	The Prime Minister of Japan, Junichiro Koizumi, issued an apology for Japan's actions during WWII and said the country would never again take the path to war. However, he was criticised for making several controversial visits to Yasukini Shrine, which honours Japan's war dead, including many convicted war criminals.

AUGUST 2025

Ann.	Date	Event
20	17 Aug 2005	Bangladesh bombings. Terrorists exploded more than 500 bombs at 300 locations across Bangladesh. Two people were killed and 50 injured. The two main perpetrators were captured in March 2006 and executed in May 2007.
20	18 Aug 2005	American serial killer Dennis Rader (the BTK killer) was sentenced to ten consecutive life terms – minimum 175 years without parole. He had been convicted of killing ten people in Kansas between 1974 and 1991.
20	19 Aug 2005	Southern Ontario Tornado Outbreak, Canada. A series of thunderstorms spawned several tornadoes and caused flash flooding in Toronto and the surrounding area. Around $500 million worth of damage was caused. No deaths or injuries were reported.
20	19 Aug 2005 to 25th	Peace Mission 2005 – the first joint military exercise between Russia and China.
20	19 Aug 2005	The U.S. pharmaceutical company Merck & Co. was found liable for the death of a Texas man who had taken the anti-inflammatory drug Vioxx. The jury awarded his widow $253 million in damages, later reduced to $26.1 million – the maximum allowed under Texas state law. This paved the way for thousands of similar claims. Vioxx, also known as Rofecoxib, was withdrawn in September 2004 over safety concerns.
20	19 Aug 2005	Death of Mo Mowlam, British politician. Secretary of State for Northern Ireland (1997–99). She played a key role in the successful peace negotiations which led to the Good Friday Agreement. (Brain tumour, aged 55.)
20	21 Aug 2005	Death of Robert Moog, American electrical engineer and electronic music pioneer. Inventor of the first commercial music synthesizer.
20	22 Aug 2005	The last Israeli settlers left the Gaza Strip, ending 38 years of occupation. Evacuees were given compensation totalling $870 million (£540 million) though it was several years before it was paid out. The legal hurdles claimants had to go through to get it was strongly criticised.
20	23 Aug 2005 to 30th	Hurricane Katrina hit the Bahamas, Cuba and the southern U.S. States. The city of New Orleans, Louisiana was particularly badly affected when the levee system failed, flooding 80 percent of the city for several weeks. Florida and Mississippi also suffered severe damage. More than 1,800 people were killed. It was the costliest natural disaster in U.S. history.
20	31 Aug 2005	Al-Aaimmah bridge stampede, Baghdad, Iraq. Rumours of a suicide bomber in a religious procession attended by 1 million people led to a stampede across the closed bridge. Nearly 1,000 people were killed in the crush, or drowned when the railings gave way and they fell into the river.
20	31 Aug 2005	Death of Michael Sheard, Scottish film and television actor. Best known for his roles as deputy headmaster Mr Bronson in the children's TV series *Grange Hill* and as Admiral Ozzel in the film *The Empire Strikes Back*.

AUGUST 2025

Ann.	Date	Event
15	5 Aug 2010	Copiapó mining accident, Chile. A cave-in at the San José copper and gold mine near Copiapó in northern Chile trapped 33 workers 700 metres (2,300 feet) underground. An international rescue operation was launched, and they were brought to the surface on 13th October after being trapped for 69 days. Around 1 billion people watched the rescue on television.
15	8 Aug 2010	Gansu mudslide, Zhouqu County, Gansu Province, China. More than 1,400 people were killed. The mudslide was part of the 2010 China floods and were triggered following decades of deforestation.
15	9 Aug 2010 to 10th	The Niger River in West Africa burst its banks after heavy rainfall, and caused serious flooding. 20,000 people were made homeless and 30,000 animals were killed. Further floods hit the region between 20th August and 19th September, when around 50,000 people were made homeless. Their clay houses simply dissolved in the flood water.
15	14 Aug 2010	The first Youth Olympic Games were held in Singapore, for athletes aged 14–18.
10	1 Aug 2015	Death of Cilla Black, British pop singer and television presenter. Known for her hit songs including *Anyone Who Had a Heart* and *You're My World*, and for hosting the TV series *Blind Date* and *Surprise Surprise*.
10	7 Aug 2015	Death of Louise Suggs, American golfer. Co-founder of the LPGA and modern ladies' golf.
10	8 Aug 2015	Death of David Nobbs, British comedy novelist and screenwriter. Best known for the TV series *The Fall and Rise of Reginald Perrin* and *A Bit of a Do*, which were both adapted from his novels.
10	12 Aug 2015	Death of Stephen Lewis, British stage, film and television actor, comedian, screenwriter and playwright. Best known for his TV roles as Blakey in *On the Buses* and Smiler in *Last of the Summer Wine*.
10	30 Aug 2015	Death of Wes Craven, American film director, producer, screenwriter, and actor. Best known for his horror films including *A Nightmare on Elm Street*, *Scream*, *The Hills Have Eyes*, and more.
10	30 Aug 2015	Death of Oliver Sacks, British-born American neurologist, science historian, writer, and educator.
10	31 Aug 2015	Death of Edward Douglas-Scott-Montagu, 3rd Baron Montagu of Beaulieu, British politician and founder of the National Motor Museum. He was imprisoned for homosexuality in 1954.

SEPTEMBER 2025

Ann.	Date	Event
1750	25 Sep 275	Tacitus became Roman emperor (until June 276) following Aurelian's assassination. This was the last time the Roman Senate elected an emperor.
1100	4 Sep 925	The coronation of Æthelstan, King of the Anglo-Saxons (924–927), King of England (927–939).
1000	17 Sep 1025	Death of Hugh Magnus, King of France (1017–25) – he was co-ruler with his father Robert II. Succeeded by Henry I (as Junior King) from May 1027.
900	13 Sep 1125	Lothair II became King of Germany, and King of Italy (as Lothair III).
750	24 Sep 1275	Death of Humphrey de Bohun, 2nd Earl of Hereford, Lord High Constable of England (1220–75). Succeeded by his grandson, Humphrey de Bohun, 3rd Earl of Hereford.
750	27 Sep 1275	Birth of John II, ('John the Peaceful'), Duke of Brabant, Lothier and Limburg.
600	8 Sep 1425	Death of Charles III, ('Charles the Noble'), King of Navarre (1387–1425). Succeeded by his daughter, Queen Blanche I.
500	11 Sep 1525	Birth of John George, Elector of Brandenburg (1571–98).
500	15 Sep 1525	Death of Jan de Bakker, Dutch Roman Catholic priest. Burned at the stake for heresy, aged 25 or 26. The first priest in the Northern Netherlands to be executed for his beliefs.
400	24 Sep 1625	Birth of Johan de Witt, Dutch statesman and political leader. Grand Pensionary (Prime Minister) of the Dutch Republic (1650–72). He was assassinated and his liver was eaten by a pro-monarchy mob.
300	3 Sep 1725	The Treaty of Hanover was signed by Great Britain, France, Hanover, and Prussia. The defensive alliance was established in response to the Austro–Spanish alliance that was established earlier in the year. (See also: 30th April 1725.)
300	29 Sep 1725	Birth of Robert Clive, 1st Baron Clive, (Clive of India), British general who helped found the British Empire in India.
250	8 Sep 1775	The Rising of the Priests (also known as the Maltese Rebellion of 1775). The Maltese clergy staged an uprising against the Order of Saint John, which ruled Malta. The uprising was quickly suppressed and the rebels were captured. Some were imprisoned or exiled, and three were executed.
250	8 Sep 1775	Birth of John Leyden, Scottish Indologist, writer, editor and translator.
250	16 Sep 1775	Death of Allen Bathurst, 1st Earl Bathurst, British politician and peer.
250	17 Sep 1775 to 4 Nov	American Revolutionary War – the Siege of Fort St. Jean, Quebec, Canada. The Continental Army attacked the British town and fort, and forced those defending it to surrender. This paved the way for the Continental Army to take Montreal in November. (See also: 25th September 1775.)
250	25 Sep 1775	American Revolution – the Battle of Longue-Pointe, Montreal, Quebec. American forces and Quebec militia led by Ethan Allen attempted to capture Montreal from the British. British victory – British forces (mostly made up of other Quebec militia) cut off the invaders' escape route, surrounded them, and captured them.

SEPTEMBER 2025

Ann.	Date	Event
200	4 Sep 1825	Birth of Dadabhai Naoroji, British Indian politician. One of the first Asians to become a British Member of Parliament (Finsbury Central, 1892–95). He also co-founded the Indian National Congress and was its president in 1886, 1893 and 1906.
200	27 Sep 1825	The world's first public railway opened: the Stockton and Darlington Railway in north-east England.
200	28 Sep 1825	Birth of Rafael Núñez, President of Colombia (1880–82, 1884–86, 1886–94).
175	9 Sep 1850	The U.S. Congress passed the Compromise of 1850. The package of five bills settled the status of territories acquired from Mexico in the Mexico–American War and established Texas's northern and western borders. Texas relinquished its claims to New Mexico and Utah, which became U.S. Territories. In exchange the U.S. government assumed responsibility for Texas's public debt. (See also: 18th September 1850.)
175	9 Sep 1850	California was admitted as the 31st state of the USA.
175	9 Sep 1850	Birth of Bharatendu Harishchandra, Indian poet, writer and playwright. Regarded as the father of Hindi literature and Hindi theatre.
175	18 Sep 1850	The U.S. Congress passed the Fugitive Slave Law as part of Compromise of 1850 (see 9th September above). Under the controversial law, all escaped slaves who were captured had to be returned to their slaveowners, even if they had escaped to one of the northern slave-free states. The law was a significant contributory factor to the American Civil War, and was one of the most-hated pieces of legislation in U.S. history.
175	20 Sep 1850	The District of Columbia in the USA abolished the slave trade (the sale of slaves) as part of the Compromise of 1850. However, slavery was allowed to continue until 1862.
175	23 Sep 1850	Death of José Gervasio Artigas, Uruguayan political leader, statesman and national hero. He played a key role in securing Latin America's independence from Spain, and established the Federal League. He is sometimes called the father of Uruguay.
175	24 Sep 1850	Pope Pius IX issued a papal bull (*Universalis Ecclesiae*) which restored and renamed the Roman Catholic dioceses in England. The earlier dioceses had been extinguished during the reign of Elizabeth I.
175	28 Sep 1850	The U.S. Navy abolished flogging as a punishment.
150	1 Sep 1875	Birth of Edgar Rice Burroughs, American novelist. Best known for creating the character Tarzan.
150	3 Sep 1875	Birth of Ferdinand Porsche, Austrian-born German automotive engineer. He designed the Volkswagen Beetle and Tiger tank, and founded the Porsche sports car company.
150	11 Sep 1875	The first comic strip to appear in a newspaper: *Professor Tidwissel's Burglar Alarm* was published in the *New York Daily Graphic* in the USA.
150	16 Sep 1875	Birth of James Cash Penney, American businessman who founded the J. C. Penney chain of department stores.
125	3 Sep 1900	Birth of Urho Kekkonen, President of Finland (1956–82).

SEPTEMBER 2025

Ann.	Date	Event
125	3 Sep 1900	The first car made in Flint, Michigan, USA made its debut in the city's Labor Day parade: Charles Wisner's 'Buzz-Wagon'. Flint later became a powerhouse of the American automobile industry.
125	5 Sep 1900	France proclaimed a military protectorate over Chad. It became an overseas territory in 1946 and gained its independence in 1960.
125	8 Sep 1900 to 13th	The Great Galveston hurricane, Texas, USA. The deadliest natural disaster in U.S. history. Between 6,000 and 12,000 people were killed (most sources give a figure of 8,000). 7,000 buildings were destroyed, including more than 3,600 houses, and every home in the city was damaged to some degree. It caused $35.4 million worth of damage – equivalent to more than $1 billion today.
125	9 Sep 1900	Birth of James Hilton, British novelist and screenwriter. Best known for *Goodbye Mr. Chips* and *Lost Horizon*.
125	13 Sep 1900	Philippine–American War – the Battle of Pulang Lupa. Filipino victory.
125	17 Sep 1900	The Philippine–American War – the Battle of Mabitac. Filipino victory.
125	17 Sep 1900	Birth of J. Willard Marriott, American businessman. Founder of the Marriott Corporation (now Marriott International), the world's largest hotel chain.
125	18 Sep 1900	Birth of Seewoosagur Ramgoolam, 1st Prime Minister of Mauritius (1968–82), Governor-General of Mauritius (1983–85 – died in office).
125	23 Sep 1900	Death of William Marsh Rice, American businessman. (Murdered by his valet in a plot to forge his will.) He bequeathed his fortune to found Rice University in Houston, Texas.
125	27 Sep 1900	The New Victory Theater, an off-Broadway theatre, opened in New York City, USA (as the Theatre Republic).
100	3 Sep 1925	The U.S. Navy's first rigid airship *USS Shenandoah* was torn apart and crashed during a storm over Ohio. Fourteen people were killed.
100	3 Sep 1925	The first international handball game was played, in Germany.
100	4 Sep 1925	Birth of Asa Earl Carter, American white supremacist, pro-segregationist and writer. He founded a Ku Klux Klan group, and wrote Governor of Alabama George Wallace's 'Segregation now, segregation tomorrow, segregation forever' speech. He later became a successful Western novelist (using the pen name Forrest Carter), best known for *The Outlaw Josey Wales*. (Died 1979.)
100	7 Sep 1925	Birth of Laura Ashley, Welsh designer and businesswoman. Known for her traditional printed fabrics, which she used to create soft furnishings and women's clothing. Co-founder (with her husband Bernard) of the Laura Ashley textile company and chain of shops. (Died 1985.) (The company filed for bankruptcy in 2020 and the shops closed in 2021. At the time of writing it continues to trade online.)
100	8 Sep 1925	Birth of Peter Sellers, British actor and comedian. Best known for the radio series *The Goon Show* and for his role as Inspector Clouseau in *The Pink Panther* film series. (Died 1980.)

SEPTEMBER 2025

Ann.	Date	Event
100	13 Sep 1925	Birth of Mel Tormé, American jazz singer, songwriter, musician, arranger, actor and writer. (Died 1999.)
100	16 Sep 1925	Birth of Charlie Byrd, American jazz guitarist. Associated with Brazilian music. He helped popularise the bossa nova. (Died 1999.)
100	16 Sep 1925	Birth of Charles Haughey, Taoiseach (Prime Minister) of Ireland (1979–81, 1982, 1987–92). (Died 2006.)
100	16 Sep 1925	Birth of B.B. King, American blues/R&B/rock and roll singer, songwriter, guitarist, and record producer. (Died 2015.)
100	20 Sep 1925	Birth of Rama VIII, King of Thailand (1935–46 – shot dead in mysterious circumstances).
100	26 Sep 1925	Birth of Marty Robbins, American country and western singer, songwriter, musician and NASCAR racing driver. (Died 1982.)
100	28 Sep 1925	Birth of Seymour Cray, American electronics engineer and computer designer. Known for his supercomputers. (Died 1996.)
90	Sep 1935	The use of eye prints (the pattern of capillaries on the retina) for identification purposes was first proposed by American ophthalmologist Isadore Goldstein and psychiatrist and criminologist Carleton Simon. Their paper was published in the *New York State Journal of Medicine*. The story also appeared in *Time* magazine in December 1935.
90	2 Sep 1935	Labor Day Hurricane, Florida Keys, USA. 423 people were killed.
90	3 Sep 1935	British driver Malcolm Campbell set a new world land speed record of 301.13 mph (484.62 km/h) in *Bluebird* at Bonneville Salt Flats, Utah, USA. He was the first person to break the 300-mph barrier.
90	8 Sep 1935	American singer Frank Sinatra made his radio debut, performing on the talent show *Major Bowes' Original Amateur Hour* as a member of The Hoboken Four. (They won.)
90	10 Sep 1935	Death of Huey Long, U.S. Senator and Governor of Louisiana. (Assassinated.)
90	11 Sep 1935	Birth of Gherman Titov, Soviet-Russian cosmonaut (*Vostok 2*). The second person to orbit the Earth and the first person to make more than one orbit. A Hero of the Soviet Union. (Died 2000.)
90	12 Sep 1935	American business magnate and aviator Howard Hughes set a new world landplane air speed record (352 mph) in his self-built *Hughes H-1 Racer*, in California, USA.
90	15 Sep 1935	The Nuremberg Laws were passed in Germany. Jews were no longer classed as German citizens, but were 'subjects of the state' without any rights of citizenship. Jews were not allowed to marry Germans. The Nazi flag was also adopted as the national flag of Germany.
90	15 Sep 1935	Birth of Mar Dinkha IV, Patriarch of the Assyrian Church of the East (1976–2015). He spent most of his life in exile in Chicago, Illinois, USA, and led the church from there.
90	17 Sep 1935	Birth of Ken Kesey, American novelist, short story writer and essayist. Associated with the counter-culture revolution. Best known for his novel *One Flew Over the Cuckoo's Nest*. (Died 2001.)

SEPTEMBER 2025

Ann.	Date	Event
90	18 Sep 1935	Birth of John Spencer, British world champion snooker player and broadcaster. (Died 2006.)
90	19 Sep 1935	Death of Konstantin Tsiolkovsky, Soviet-Russian research scientist. One of the founding fathers of rocketry and astronautics.
90	22 Sep 1935	The rank of Marshal of the Soviet Union was established.
90	28 Sep 1935	Death of William Kennedy Dickson, Scottish inventor who developed an early movie camera whilst working for Thomas Edison. He also invented the first practical celluloid film for movie cameras and chose the 35mm standard still used today. He appeared in one of Edison's first films, the *Dickson Greeting*, in 1891.
90	30 Sep 1935	The Hoover Dam was formally dedicated. It is on the Colorado River, on the border between the U.S. states of Arizona and Nevada.
90	30 Sep 1935	The première of George Gershwin's opera *Porgy and Bess*, in Boston, Massachusetts, USA. It opened on Broadway on 10th October.
80	2 Sep 1945	World War II: V-J Day (Victory over Japan Day). The war officially ended when representatives from Japan signed the formal instrument of surrender on board the U.S. battleship *USS Missouri* in Tokyo Bay. News of Japan's surrender took some time to reach Japanese forces in other countries, and some of them continued to fight for some months, or even years. The last confirmed holdout surrendered to the Indonesian Air Force in December 1974, 29 years after the war ended.
80	2 Sep 1945	The Democratic Republic of Vietnam (North Vietnam) was founded and declared its independence from France. Ho Chi Minh became its first President and Prime Minister.
80	5 Sep 1945	The Cold War began. Igor Gouzenko, a clerk at the Soviet Union embassy in Ottawa, Canada, defected to Canada. He brought with him more than 100 documents that detailed Soviet espionage activities in the West. This marked the beginning of the Cold War, as the people of North America became aware of the magnitude and dangers of Soviet espionage.
80	5 Sep 1945	Iva Toguri (better known as 'Tokyo Rose'), an American-born Japanese radio propaganda broadcaster during WWII, was arrested by U.S. forces in Yokohama.
80	6 Sep 1945	The People's Republic of Korea (PRK) was proclaimed following Japan's surrender in WWII. It was based on a network of people's committees. The USA, which occupied South Korea, banned the PRK in December. The Soviet Union then co-opted it into the structure of the Democratic People's Republic of Korea (North Korea), and established its first provisional government in February 1946.
80	8 Sep 1945	Following the partitioning of Korea on 15th August, U.S. forces arrived in South Korea to receive the Japanese surrender, while Japanese forces in North Korea surrendered to the Soviets. The U.S. occupied and governed South Korea until 1948.
80	8 Sep 1945	Bess Myerson became the first Jewish woman to be crowned Miss America.

SEPTEMBER 2025

Ann.	Date	Event
80	8 Sep 1945	Former Japanese Prime Minister Hideki Tojo shot himself in an attempted suicide bid, rather than face a WWII war crimes tribunal. (He survived, was convicted of war crimes, and was executed in December 1948.)
80	8 Sep 1945	Birth of Kelly Groucutt, British rock bassist and singer (Electric Light Orchestra – ELO). (Died 2009.)
80	8 Sep 1945	Birth of Ron 'Pigpen' McKernan, American rock singer and musician (the Grateful Dead). (Died 1973.)
80	9 Sep 1945	World War II: the Second Sino–Japanese War ended. Chinese victory.
80	10 Sep 1945	Former Norwegian Prime Minister Vidkun Quisling was convicted of collaborating with Nazi Germany during WWII, and numerous other crimes. He was sentenced to death, and executed on 24th October.
80	10 Sep 1945	Mike the Headless Chicken, an American Wyandotte chicken, was beheaded with the intention of killing him for the family's meal. He survived (the axe missed his jugular vein and brain stem) and he lived for another eighteen months, becoming a celebrity.
80	11 Sep 1945	World War II: U.S. President Harry S. Truman approved the joint recommendation of the U.S. Secretary of War and the U.S. Secretary of the Navy to call the war 'World War II'. The order was officially published on 19th September (War Department General Orders No. 80.)
80	13 Sep 1945 to 30 Mar 1946	War in Vietnam. This led to the First Indochina War (December 1946 –August 1954).
80	13 Sep 1945	World War II: the Burma Campaign in Burma and India ended. Allied victory. The State of Burma was dissolved and British Rule was restored.
80	14 Sep 1945 to 18th	The Homestead hurricane hit the Leeward Islands, the Turks and Caicos Islands, the Bahamas, and the U.S. states of Florida, Georgia, and North and South Carolina. It caused significant damage and flooding. 26 people were killed. 366 planes, 25 blimps, 150 cars and three hangars at the Naval Air Station Richmond in Florida were destroyed when the hurricane caused a fire on 15th September.
80	16 Sep 1945	World War II: Japanese occupying forces in Hong Kong officially surrendered to British forces.
80	19 Sep 1945	Nazi propaganda broadcaster William Joyce ('Lord Haw-Haw') was sentenced to death by a British court after being convicted of treason. He was executed on 3rd January 1946.
80	20 Sep 1945	The USA's Lend-Lease programme officially ended. Under the programme, the USA had supplied its WWII allies with food, oil, ships, planes and weapons.
80	20 Sep 1945	Operation Paperclip: the first seven German rocket scientists arrived in the USA after being recruited to help develop its ballistic missile and rocket programmes. Among them was Werner von Braun, the 'Father of Rocket Science'.

SEPTEMBER 2025

Ann.	Date	Event
80	24 Sep 1945	Death of Hans Geiger, German physicist. Best known for co-inventing the Geiger counter, which measures levels of ionising radiation.
80	26 Sep 1945	The first U.S. fatality in Vietnam: Lieutenant Colonel A. Peter Dewey from the Office of Strategic Services. He was shot dead by Viet Minh forces during the 1945 Vietnam uprising, in a case of mistaken identity.
80	26 Sep 1945	Death of Béla Bartók, Hungarian composer and pianist. One of the most important composers of the 20th century.
80	30 Sep 1945	Bourne End rail crash, Hertfordshire, UK. 43 people were killed when an express train derailed while travelling at excessive speed. (Cause: driver error.)
75	1 Sep 1950	The constitution of West Berlin came into effect. Although it was associated with West Germany it was not part of it, and was administered by the Western Allies. It was bordered by East Berlin and East Germany.
75	1 Sep 1950	Italian nuclear scientist Bruno Pontecorvo, who had been working in Britain, disappeared while on holiday in Italy. The British intelligence service launched a search for him. Several weeks later it was revealed that he had defected to the Soviet Union.
75	3 Sep 1950	Vietnam War: U.S. President Harry S. Truman sent the Military Assistance Advisory Group (MAAG) to Vietnam. They were not combat troops, but supported the French in the First Indochina War. Their role included training South Vietnamese forces, advising on strategy, and supervising U.S. military equipment.
75	3 Sep 1950	Italian racing driver Giuseppe ('Nino') Farina became the first-ever Formula One World Champion after winning the 1950 Italian Grand Prix.
75	4 Sep 1950	Korean War: the U.S. Air Force carried out the first helicopter rescue of a downed American pilot from behind enemy lines. Captain Robert E. Wayne was rescued after his plane was shot down by ground fire.
75	4 Sep 1950	The Southern 500, the first 500-mile NASCAR race, was held at Darlington Raceway in South Carolina, USA.
75	4 Sep 1950	The comic strip *Beetle Bailey* by Mort Walker was first published in the USA. (Mort Walker died in 2018. The comic strips are now produced by his sons Neal, Brian and Greg Walker.)
75	7 Sep 1950	The Knockshinnoch disaster, New Cumnock, Ayrshire, Scotland. A lake flooded a coal mine, trapping 129 miners underground. The rescue took three days. 116 miners were saved, but 13 died.
75	7 Sep 1950	The first episode of the television game show *Truth or Consequences* was broadcast on CBS in the USA. It later switched to NBC and continued (in various incarnations) until 1988. A radio version ran from 1940 to 1957.
75	9 Sep 1950	The first television show to use a laugh track (canned laughter): the sitcom *The Hank McCune Show* on NBC in the USA. The show was cancelled after three months.
75	10 Sep 1950 to 19th	Korean War – the Battle of Incheon, South Korea. United Nations victory. The United Nations staged a daring assault, landing thousands of troops behind enemy lines.

SEPTEMBER 2025

Ann.	Date	Event
75	10 Sep 1950	The first episode of the television variety show *The Colgate Comedy Hour* was broadcast on NBC in the USA. It ran for six seasons until 1955.
75	11 Sep 1950	Birth of Barry Sheene, British world champion motorcycle racer and broadcaster. (Died 2003.)
75	11 Sep 1950	Death of Jan Smuts, Prime Minister of South Africa (1919–24, 1939–48).
75	12 Sep 1950	The USA proposed rearming West Germany and incorporating it into NATO to help with the defence of Europe. West Germany joined NATO in 1955.
75	14 Sep 1950	Birth of Paul Kossoff, British blues/rock guitarist (Free). (Died 1976.)
75	22 Sep 1950 to 25th	Korean War – the Second Battle of Seoul. UN victory. The South Korean capital was liberated on 25th September (although fighting continued in the suburbs). It was officially returned to President Syngman Rhee on 29th September.
75	22 Sep 1950	American political scientist and diplomat Ralph Bunche became the first African American to win the Nobel Peace Prize. The prize, awarded on 10th December, recognised his efforts to resolve the Arab–Israeli conflict in Palestine.
75	23 Sep 1950	Korean War – the Battle of Hill 282. Result: stalemate. This battle also saw the first friendly fire incident of the war: U.S. Air Force planes mistook British forces on the hill for North Koreans, dropped napalm bombs on them, and attacked them with machine guns. Several British troops were killed and more than fifty wounded.
75	24 Sep 1950	Operation Magic Carpet ended after fifteen months. The British–American operation airlifted the majority of Yemeni Jews (around 47,000 people) from Yemen to the new state of Israel. Jews from other countries including Aden, Djibouti, Eritrea and Saudi Arabia were also transported.
75	24 Sep 1950	Death of Princess Victoria of Hesse and by Rhine. Granddaughter of Queen Victoria. Mother of Louis Mountbatten, 1st Earl Mountbatten of Burma.
75	28 Sep 1950	The BBC broadcast the first film made for television in the UK: *The Man who Walks By Night – A Dinner Date with Death*.
75	29 Sep 1950	The first automatic telephone answering machine was tested at Bell Telephone Laboratories in New York, USA.
70	4 Sep 1955	Kenneth Kendall became the first newsreader to appear on screen in the UK, reading the *BBC Television News*.
70	6 Sep 1955 to 7th	Istanbul Pogrom, Turkey. Tactical mobs and other groups organised by the ruling Democratic Party in Turkey attacked Istanbul's Greek minority. The revenge attacks were launched after the Party learned that Greeks had bombed the house where Turkey's founder, Mustafa Kemal Atatürk, was born. In fact, the bomb was planted by a Turkish employee at the consulate – and he confessed to it later. Between thirteen and thirty (possibly more) Greeks were killed.

SEPTEMBER 2025

Ann.	Date	Event
70	6 Sep 1955	Shukri al-Quwatli became President of Syria for the third time (until 1958).
70	10 Sep 1955	The first episode of the Western drama television series *Gunsmoke* was broadcast on CBS in the USA. It ran until 1975. It was based on the radio series of the same name, which ran from 1952 to 1961.
70	10 Sep 1955	Death of Robert Blackburn, British aviation pioneer. Founder of Blackburn Aircraft (now part of Hawker Siddeley). He introduced the first scheduled air service in Britain.
70	11 Sep 1955	The Bern Switzerland Temple was dedicated. It was the first temple of The Church of Jesus Christ of Latter-day Saints to be built outside North America.
70	13 Sep 1955 to 20th	Hurricane Hilda devastated Cuba's coffee crop and caused extensive damage and flooding in Mexico. 304 people were killed. (Mexico was also hit by Hurricane Janet ten days later. See 22nd September 1955.)
70	13 Sep 1955	Swiss electrical engineer George de Mestral was granted a U.S. Patent for his invention of Velcro. (U.S. Patent 2,717,437.)
70	15 Sep 1955	Vladimir Nabokov's controversial novel *Lolita* was first published in Paris, France. The publisher was best known for its pornographic works, and the book was littered with typographical errors. The many attempts to ban it only fuelled its popularity.
70	16 Sep 1955	Argentine President Juan Perón was overthrown in a military coup and forced into exile until 1973. Lieutenant General Eduardo Lonardi became president but was forced out of office after just two months by hardliners who disliked his conciliatory approach.
70	16 Sep 1955	The first submarine to launch a ballistic missile. The Soviet Union used a converted Zulu-IV class submarine to test launch a Scud missile. Following the successful test, six ballistic missile submarines entered service in the Soviet Union in 1956–57.
70	16 Sep 1955	The United States Auto Club (USAC) was founded. It is the sanctioning body for a number of racing series in the USA.
70	16 Sep 1955	Death of Leo Amery, British statesman and journalist. First Lord of the Admiralty (1922–24), Secretary of State for the Colonies (1924–29), Secretary of State for India and Burma (1940–45).
70	20 Sep 1955	The Soviet Union and East Germany signed and enacted the Treaty on Relations between the USSR and the GDR. It allowed the Soviet Union to maintain a military presence in East Germany following the end of Soviet occupation.
70	20 Sep 1955	The first episode of the television sitcom *The Phil Silvers Show* was broadcast on CBS in the USA. It featured comedy actor Phil Silvers as Sergeant Bilko. It ran for four seasons until 1959. For the first two months it was called *You'll Never Get Rich*.
70	21 Sep 1955	Britain annexed Rockall, an uninhabited granite islet in the North Atlantic, to prevent the Soviet Union from placing surveillance equipment there and spying on Britain's secret nuclear missile tests.
70	22 Sep 1955 to 30th	Hurricane Janet hit the Caribbean and Mexico, killing more than 1,000 people and causing over $65 million worth of damage.

SEPTEMBER 2025

Ann.	Date	Event
70	22 Sep 1955	Britain's first independent television channel, ITV, was launched. It ended the BBC's monopoly, and broadcast Britain's first TV advertisements. Initially only viewers in London could receive ITV. Regional franchises were gradually rolled out across the whole country by 1965.
70	22 Sep 1955	The first issue of *TV Times*, a television listings magazine, was published in the UK. It became a national publication in 1968.
70	24 Sep 1955	U.S. President Dwight D. Eisenhower suffered a serious heart attack and was hospitalised for six weeks. Richard Nixon became the first Vice-President to chair cabinet meetings while the president was recovering.
70	25 Sep 1955	The Royal Jordanian Air Force was founded.
70	25 Sep 1955	The CBS television variety show *Toast of the Town* was renamed *The Ed Sullivan Show*.
70	26 Sep 1955	Birds Eye frozen fish fingers went on sale in Britain.
70	28 Sep 1955	The World Series (baseball) was broadcast in colour for the first time, on NBC television in the USA.
70	29 Sep 1955	Arthur Miller's play *A View from the Bridge* was first performed, in New York City, USA.
70	30 Sep 1955	Death of James Dean, American film actor (*Rebel Without a Cause*, *East of Eden*, *Giant*). (Car crash, aged 24.)
65	2 Sep 1960	The Tibetan Parliament-in-Exile (based in India) held its first election for the Tibetan Assembly. It was the first time that Tibetans were able to elect their political leaders. The day is celebrated by Tibetans as 'Democracy Day'.
65	4 Sep 1960 to 12th	Hurricane Donna caused widespread devastation in the Caribbean, eastern USA and eastern Canada. 439 people were killed. Cost of damage: $980 million (equivalent to over $8 billion today).
65	5 Sep 1960	Congo crisis: the Prime Minister of the Republic of the Congo, Patrice Lumumba, was dismissed by President Joseph Kasa-Vubu. Parliament granted Lumumba emergency powers but on 14th September Army Chief of staff Mobutu Sese Seko launched a coup. Lumumba attempted to establish a new government but he was arrested. He was executed in January 1961.
65	5 Sep 1960	American boxer Cassius Clay (later known as Muhammad Ali) won the light heavyweight boxing gold medal at the 1960 Summer Olympic Games in Rome, Italy.
65	6 Sep 1960	Léopold Sédar Senghor became the first President of Senegal (until 1980).
65	7 Sep 1960	Death of Wilhelm Pieck, President of East Germany (1949–60).
65	8 Sep 1960	NASA's Marshall Space Flight Center in Huntsville, Alabama, USA was officially opened by U.S. President Dwight D. Eisenhower. It had been operating since 1st July.
65	8 Sep 1960	Death of Jussi Björling, Swedish operatic tenor. Known as the Swedish Caruso. One of the leading opera singers of the 20th century.

SEPTEMBER 2025

Ann.	Date	Event
65	10 Sep 1960	Abebe Bikila became the first Ethiopian to win an Olympic gold medal. He ran the marathon in bare feet and beat the world record. He also won the marathon at the 1964 Olympics in Tokyo, Japan, also in a world record time. He was paralysed in a car accident in 1969 and never walked again. He died in 1973.
65	13 Sep 1960	The U.S. Communications Act Amendments of 1960 banned deceptive practices in the broadcasting industry, including the rigging of television quiz shows, and payola (where record companies pay radio DJs to play particular records on their shows to help promote them).
65	14 Sep 1960	OPEC (the Organisation of Petroleum Exporting Countries) was founded by Iraq, Iran, Kuwait and Saudi Arabia.
65	17 Sep 1960	Cuba nationalised all U.S. banks located within its borders.
65	19 Sep 1960	Traffic wardens began operating in London. They issued 344 parking tickets on their first day.
65	22 Sep 1960	Mali gained its independence from France after Senegal withdrew from the Mali Federation.
65	24 Sep 1960	The International Development Association was established. It offers grants and low-cost loans to the poorest developing countries.
65	24 Sep 1960	The world's first nuclear-powered aircraft carrier, the *USS Enterprise*, was launched at Newport News in Virginia, USA.
65	25 Sep 1960	Death of Emily Post, American writer and authority on social etiquette.
65	26 Sep 1960	The first televised U.S. presidential debate took place, between Richard Nixon and John F. Kennedy, in Chicago, Illinois.
65	27 Sep 1960	Europe's first travellator (moving walkway/moving pavement) opened at Bank Station on the London Underground.
65	27 Sep 1960	Death of Sylvia Pankhurst, British suffragette leader. Daughter of Emmeline Pankhurst.
65	30 Sep 1960	American Mensa, the high-IQ society, was founded. It was the first Mensa group outside the UK, where it was founded in 1946.
65	30 Sep 1960	The first episode of the animated comedy television series *The Flintstones* was broadcast on ABC in the USA. It was the first animated prime time show.
60	3 Sep 1965	The First Treblinka Trial ended in Dusseldorf, Germany. Eleven staff members from the Treblinka extermination camp were tried for war crimes. Four of them received life sentences.
60	3 Sep 1965	Death of Otto Lederer, Austro–Hungarian/Czech-born American film actor. He appeared in 120 films between 1912 and 1933. Best known for his role as Moisha Yudelson in *The Jazz Singer*.
60	4 Sep 1965	Death of Albert Schweitzer, German-born French theologian, philosopher, organist, physician and missionary doctor in Africa. Winner of the 1952 Nobel Peace Prize.

SEPTEMBER 2025

Ann.	Date	Event
60	6 Sep 1965 to Dec 1966	Sobibór Trial, Hagen, Germany. Twelve staff members from the Sobibór extermination camp were tried for war crimes. One received a life sentence, four received shorter sentences, six were acquitted, and one committed suicide.
60	7 Sep 1965	Vietnam War – Operation Piranha: a U.S./South Vietnamese assault on the Batangan Peninsula. The Allied forces stormed a Viet Cong stronghold, killing about 200. But they failed to wipe out the Viet Cong 1st Regiment, the majority of whom had left the area before the operation began.
60	7 Sep 1965	Patricia R. Harris became the U.S. Ambassador to Luxembourg. She was the first African American woman to become a U.S. Ambassador.
60	8 Sep 1965 to 12th	Hurricane Betsy caused extensive damage in the Bahamas, and in southern Florida and Louisiana in the USA. 81 people were killed (mainly in Louisiana).
60	8 Sep 1965	Death of Dorothy Dandridge, American singer and film actress (*Carmen Jones, Island in the Sun, Porgy and Bess*). The first African American to be nominated for an Academy Award for Best Actress.
60	8 Sep 1965	Death of Hermann Staudinger, German chemist. Winner of the 1953 Nobel Prize in Chemistry for demonstrating that polymers are long-chain molecules. This led to the huge expansion of the plastics industry. He also discovered ketenes.
60	9 Sep 1965	Tibet became an autonomous region of China.
60	9 Sep 1965	The U.S. Department of Housing and Urban Development was established as part of President Lyndon B. Johnson's 'Great Society' programme.
60	9 Sep 1965	Death of Julián Carrillo, Mexican composer, conductor, violinist and music theorist. Best known for developing the theory of microtonal music, of which he was one of the 20th century's leading exponents.
60	10 Sep 1965	Death of Father Divine, American religious leader. Founder of the International Peace Mission – a precursor of the Civil Rights Movement.
60	11 Sep 1965	Death of Ralph C. Smedley, American founder of Toastmasters International.
60	13 Sep 1965	The Beatles' song *Yesterday* was released in the USA. (In the UK it was not released until 1976. The band blocked its release until then as Paul McCartney was the only band member to perform on it, and it was so different from their other songs.)
60	14 Sep 1965 to 19th	Indo–Pakistani War of 1965 – the Battle of Chawinda, Pakistan. One of the largest tank battles in history. The battle ended just before a United Nations-mandated ceasefire came into effect. Result: inconclusive.
60	14 Sep 1965	Vietnam War: the USA's 1st Cavalry Division arrived in Vietnam to provide air support to the South Vietnamese forces.
60	15 Sep 1965	The first episode of the science fiction television series *Lost in Space* was broadcast on CBS in the USA. It ran for three seasons until 1968.
60	15 Sep 1965	The first episode of the espionage adventure television series *I Spy* was broadcast on NBC in the USA. It ran for three seasons until 1968.

SEPTEMBER 2025

Ann.	Date	Event
60	16 Sep 1965	The first episode of the variety-comedy television series *The Dean Martin Show* was broadcast on NBC in the USA. It ran for nine seasons until 1974.
60	16 Sep 1965	Death of Fred Quimby, American animator and producer. Best known for producing the *Tom and Jerry* cartoons.
60	17 Sep 1965	The first episode of the WWII prisoner-of-war television sitcom *Hogan's Heroes* was broadcast on CBS in the USA. It ran for six seasons until 1971.
60	18 Sep 1965	Comet Ikeya-Seki was discovered independently by Japanese astronomers Kaoru Ikeya and Tsutomu Seki.
60	18 Sep 1965	The first episode of the fantasy television sitcom *I Dream of Jeannie* was broadcast on NBC in the USA. It ran for five seasons until 1970.
60	21 Sep 1965	Ted Erikson became the first American to swim a round trip of the English Channel (England–France–England). His record time of 30 hours and 3 minutes stood until 1975.
60	27 Sep 1965	Death of Clara Bow, (The 'It' Girl), American film actress. One of the leading film stars and sex symbols of the late 1920s.
60	28 Sep 1965 to 30th	Taal Volcano on the island of Luzon, Philippines erupted. About 200 people were killed.
60	29 Sep 1965	The National Endowment for the Humanities was established in the USA.
50	1 Sep 1975	All political parties and associations were outlawed in Bangladesh, and only four state-owned newspapers were allowed to continue publication.
50	4 Sep 1975	The Sinai Interim Agreement was signed by Egypt and Israel. It called for a diplomatic rather than military resolution to the Arab–Israeli conflict.
50	4 Sep 1975	The first episode of the science fiction television series *Space: 1999* was broadcast on ITV in the UK. It ran for two series until 1977.
50	5 Sep 1975	The attempted assassination of U.S. President Gerald Ford in Sacramento, California by Lynette ('Squeaky') Fromme, a follower of cult leader Charles Manson. The attack was thwarted by a Secret Service agent. Fromme was later sentenced to life imprisonment. (Released 2009.) There was a second attempt on the President's life on 22nd September 1975
50	5 Sep 1975	Hilton Hotel bombing, Park Lane, London, UK. An IRA bomb exploded in the hotel's lobby, killing two people and injuring 63.
50	5 Sep 1975	The U.S. Congress restored Confederate General Robert E. Lee's U.S. citizenship. He commanded the Confederate States Army in the American Civil War (1861–65) and died in 1870.
50	6 Sep 1975	Lice earthquake, Turkey. 2,311 people were killed and there was extensive damage in the towns of Hani, Lice, and Kulp and the surrounding villages.
50	6 Sep 1975	Czechoslovakian tennis player Martina Navratilova defected to the USA.
50	9 Sep 1975	NASA launched its *Viking 2* Mars probe. It reached Mars in August 1976. Its orbiter operated until July 1978 and returned almost 16,000 images, while its lander remained in operation until April 1980.

SEPTEMBER 2025

Ann.	Date	Event
50	10 Sep 1975	Death of Sir George Paget Thomson, British physicist. Joint winner of the 1937 Nobel Prize in Physics for demonstrating the wave properties of the electron.
50	12 Sep 1975	The city of Boston, Massachusetts, USA began a programme to integrate black and white students in previously segregated public schools. There were massive protests and violence, which continued for months, and many parents kept their children at home.
50	12 Sep 1975	Pink Floyd's prog rock album *Wish You Were Here* was released. It is frequently cited as one of the best albums of all time.
50	13 Sep 1975 to 24th	Hurricane Eloise hit the Caribbean and eastern USA, particularly Florida. Eighty people were killed and it caused extensive damage and flooding.
50	14 Sep 1975	The first U.S.-born saint, Elizabeth Ann Seton, was canonised by Pope Paul VI.
50	16 Sep 1975	Papua New Guinea gained its independence from Australia.
50	18 Sep 1975	American newspaper heiress Patty Hearst was arrested by the FBI in San Francisco, California. She had been kidnapped by the Symbionese Liberation Army in February 1974, and joined them in April 1974. In March 1976 she was sentenced to 35 years in prison – reduced to two years by U.S. President Jimmy Carter. She was released in February 1979, and pardoned by President Bill Clinton in 2001.
50	22 Sep 1975	The second attempted assassination of U.S. President Gerald Ford this month. Sara Jane Moore fired a shot at the President in San Francisco, California. She missed by a few inches and was pulled to the ground by a former FBI agent. She was later sentenced to life imprisonment. She was released in 2007. (See also: 5th September 1975.)
50	22 Sep 1975	The IRA detonated seventeen bombs across Northern Ireland, injuring twelve people.
50	22 Sep 1975	Enix, a Japanese video game publisher, was established. It merged with its rival Square in 2003 and became Square Enix.
50	24 Sep 1975	Dougal Haston and Doug Scott became the first Britons to reach the summit of Mount Everest. They were also the first climbers from any nation to conquer the south-west face.
50	27 Sep 1975	The last executions in Spain: five members of the armed Basque separatist organisation ETA and the Revolutionary Antifascist Front were executed for murder following a high-profile trial. They were sentenced to be strangled by garrotte, but there were no executioners available, so they were killed by firing squad instead. The last person killed by state-sanctioned garrotting was executed in 1974. Spain abolished capital punishment in 1978.
50	28 Sep 1975	The Spaghetti House siege, Knightsbridge, London, UK. An attempted armed robbery at the restaurant went wrong, leading to a six-day siege. Nine Italian staff members were held hostage. The hostages were eventually released unharmed and the robbers gave themselves up after becoming demoralised. They all received long prison sentences.

SEPTEMBER 2025

Ann.	Date	Event
50	29 Sep 1975	The first wholly African American-owned television station in the USA, WGPR, began broadcasting in Detroit, Michigan. It featured Sharon Dahlonega Raiford Bush as the first African American weather presenter in the USA. WGPR is now owned by CBS and is known as WWJ-TV.
50	29 Sep 1975	American R&B/soul singer Jackie Wilson suffered a heart attack and collapsed while performing. He lapsed into a nine-year coma which persisted until his death in 1984 (except for a short spell of consciousness in 1976).
50	29 Sep 1975	Death of Casey Stengel, American baseball player and manager.
50	30 Sep 1975	The Boeing AH-64 Apache attack helicopter made its first flight.
40	1 Sep 1985 or 2nd	Cambodian dictator Pol Pot officially retired as leader of the Khmer Rouge, and was succeeded by Son Sen. However, he continued as the de facto leader of the party until 1997.
40	1 Sep 1985	The wreck of the *RMS Titanic* was found in the Atlantic Ocean, 400 miles off the coast of Newfoundland, Canada, 73 years after it sank.
40	3 Sep 1985	Death of (Papa) Jo Jones, American jazz drummer. One of the most influential and admired jazz drummers of all time. Noted for his work with Count Basie and other artists of the swing era.
40	3 Sep 1985	Death of Johnny Marks, American songwriter. Best known for his Christmas songs, including *Rudolph, the Red-Nosed Reindeer*, *Rockin' Around the Christmas Tree*, *A Holly Jolly Christmas* and more.
40	4 Sep 1985	Buckminsterfullerene C60 (commonly known as the buckyball) was discovered by scientists at Sussex University in England and Rice University in Texas, USA. It was the first fullerene molecule of carbon to be discovered, and resembles a panelled soccer ball in shape. The scientists were awarded the 1996 Nobel Prize in Chemistry.
40	5 Sep 1985	The American computer hardware manufacturer Gateway, Inc. was founded (as Gateway 2000 – it changed its name in 1998). It was acquired by Acer in 2007, but continues to operate as a subsidiary company.
40	8 Sep 1985	Death of John Franklin Enders, ('the father of modern vaccines'), American microbiologist. Joint winner of the 1954 Nobel Prize in Physiology or Medicine for his role in cultivating the polio virus in tissue cultures. He also helped develop a vaccine against measles.
40	9 Sep 1985	U.S. President Ronald Reagan ordered limited sanctions against South Africa in a (failed) attempt to placate the anti-apartheid movement. In October 1986 the Senate overrode his veto and passed the Comprehensive Anti-Apartheid Act.
40	9 Sep 1985 to 11th	Handsworth riots, Birmingham, UK. Unemployment and racial tensions fuelled a mass riot following the arrest of a man in a café and a police raid on a public house. 45 shops were looted and burned, and at least two people were killed. Several riots occurred across England that autumn.
40	10 Sep 1985	Death of Jock Stein, Scottish football player and manager. Best known for his highly successful managerial career with Celtic and the Scottish national team.

SEPTEMBER 2025

Ann.	Date	Event
40	11 Sep 1985	NASA's *International Cometary Explorer* (ICE) (launched in 1978) became the first spacecraft to visit a comet (21P/Giacobini-Zinner). It passed within 4,800 miles of its nucleus and flew through its plasma tail.
40	11 Sep 1985	American baseball player Pete Rose broke Ty Cobb's 60-year record for career hits in Major League Baseball. When he retired in 1986 his final tally was 4,256 hits, which remains the record.
40	12 Sep 1985	Britain expelled 25 Soviet spies following the defection of KGB chief Oleg Gordievsky to the West. Two days later, on 14th September, the Soviet Union expelled 25 British nationals in a tit-for-tat row.
40	13 Sep 1985	Nintendo released the video game *Super Mario Bros.* in Japan. (USA: 18th October 1985. Europe: 15th May 1987.)
40	14 Sep 1985	The Penang Bridge opened in Malaysia. The 8.4-mile bridge connects Penang to the mainland.
40	15 Sep 1985	Death of Cootie Williams, American jazz/R&B trumpeter. Known for his distinctive sound. Noted for his work with Duke Ellington and Benny Goodman, as well as leading his own band.
40	16 Sep 1985	Apple Computer co-founder and chairman Steve Jobs resigned from the company over a power-struggle with the board of directors. He went on to found NeXT computers and co-founded Pixar Animation Studios before returning to rescue the near-bankrupt Apple in 1996.
40	17 Sep 1985	Death of Laura Ashley, Welsh designer and businesswoman. Known for her traditional-style printed fabrics, which she used to create soft furnishings and women's clothing. Co-founder (with her husband Bernard) of the Laura Ashley textile company and chain of shops. (Fell down stairs, aged 60.)
40	19 Sep 1985	Mexico City earthquake, Mexico. Large parts of the city were destroyed, between 5,000 and 45,000 people were killed, and 30,000 injured.
40	19 Sep 1985	American musicians Frank Zappa, John Denver and Dee Snider testified at U.S. Congressional hearings on obscenity in rock music. The Recording Industry Association of America (RIAA) agreed to put 'Parental Advisory' labels on selected releases.
40	19 Sep 1985	Death of Italo Calvino, Italian journalist, short story writer, novelist and essayist. One of the most important Italian fiction writers of the 20th century.
40	20 Sep 1985 to 22nd	North and South Korea's family reunion programme began. One hundred people, fifty from the north and fifty from the south, crossed the border for a brief visit with family members they had not seen since the end of the Korean War more than thirty years earlier. More than twenty reunions have been held since then, but only one hundred people are selected to take part each time.
40	22 Sep 1985	The first Farm Aid benefit concert was held, in Champaign, Illinois, USA. It was organised by Willie Nelson, John Mellencamp and Neil Young. The concerts became an annual event, raising money to help family farmers in the USA.

SEPTEMBER 2025

Ann.	Date	Event
40	22 Sep 1985	The Plaza Accord was signed in New York City, USA, by France, West Germany, Japan, the USA and the UK. Each country agreed to intervene in currency markets, leading to a depreciated U.S. dollar to improve international trade.
40	22 Sep 1985	The French Prime Minister, Laurent Fabius, admitted that French secret service agents were responsible for sinking the Greenpeace ship *Rainbow Warrior* in New Zealand in July.
40	22 Sep 1985	American boxer Michael Spinks beat the unbeaten Larry Holmes and became the world heavyweight boxing champion. Holmes had been one win away from tying Rocky Marciano's 49–0 record.
40	22 Sep 1985	Death of Axel Springer, German publisher. Founder of Axel Springer Verlag AG, one of the largest publishing companies in Europe.
40	26 Sep 1985 to 28th	Hurricane Gloria caused extensive damage along the east coast of the USA.
40	28 Sep 1985	Brixton riots, UK. Riots broke out on the streets of south London after a woman was shot and seriously injured during a house search by police.
40	29 Sep 1985	The first episode of the action-adventure television series *MacGyver* was broadcast on ABC in the USA. It ran for seven seasons until 1992.
40	30 Sep 1985	Death of Charles F. Richter, American physicist and seismologist. Best known for developing the Richter scale for measuring the magnitude of earthquakes.
40	30 Sep 1985	Death of Simone Signoret, French film actress. One of France's greatest film stars. The first French actor to win an Academy Award. Best known for *Room at the Top*. She controversially supported several left-wing causes.
30	1 Sep 1995	The Governor of New York, George Pataki, reinstated the death penalty, fulfilling an electoral campaign promise. In 2004 the New York Court of Appeals ruled that this violated the state's constitution. New York's death row was abolished in 2008.
30	2 Sep 1995	The Rock and Roll Hall of Fame museum opened in Cleveland, Ohio, USA.
30	2 Sep 1995	British boxer Frank Bruno beat the American WBC champion Oliver McCall to become the world heavyweight boxing champion. Bruno was beaten by Mike Tyson in his next fight, suffered a serious eye injury, and retired soon afterwards.
30	3 Sep 1995	The online auction site eBay was founded (as AuctionWeb). The first item sold was a broken laser pointer.
30	6 Sep 1995	American baseball player Cal Ripken Jr. beat Lou Gehrig's record of playing 2,131 consecutive baseball games. His run of 2,632 consecutive games ended when he sat out a game in September 1998.
30	7 Sep 1995	U.S. Senator Bob Packwood (from Oregon) announced his resignation. He was facing expulsion for sexual harassment.
30	9 Sep 1995	Sony's PlayStation game console was released in the USA. (Europe: 29th September.)

SEPTEMBER 2025

Ann.	Date	Event
30	12 Sep 1995	The Belarusian military shot down an American hydrogen-filled balloon when it entered Belarusian air space. The balloon was taking part in the Gordon Bennett Cup (the world's oldest gas balloon race), and two Americans on board were killed. Belarus had been informed of the race in May, and race organisers had filed a flight plan. Another of the balloons was forced to land, and another landed safely in Belarus two hours later. Their crews were fined for entering the country without a visa.
30	12 Sep 1995	Death of Jeremy Brett, British actor. Best known for his lead role in the television series *The Adventures of Sherlock Holmes*.
30	13 Sep 1995	Death of Walter Goetz, German-born British illustrator and cartoonist. Best known for his comic strips *Colonel Up and Mr Down* and *Dab and Flounder* in the *Daily Express* newspaper.
30	14 Sep 1995	Network Solutions, Inc. announced that the registration of internet domain names would no longer be free. New domains cost $100 for two years, and $50 a year to renew thereafter. The fee was reduced in 1997.
30	15 Sep 1995	The computer crime drama film *Hackers* was released in the USA. (UK: 3rd May 1996.)
30	15 Sep 1995	Death of Sam McCluskie, British Labour Party politician and trade union leader. General secretary of the National Union of Seamen (1986–90).
30	18 Sep 1995	Death of Doreen Cannon, American/British actress and teacher of method acting. Best known as the Head of Acting at Drama Centre London, where her students included Pierce Brosnan, Simon Callow, Colin Firth, Geraldine James, Frances de la Tour and Penelope Wilton. She later taught at RADA and other leading drama schools, where her students included Michael Sheen, Matthew Macfadyen, Ioan Gruffudd and Rachel Weisz.
30	19 Sep 1995	The *Unabomber's Manifesto* was published in *The New York Times* and *The Washington Post*. The terrorist listed everything that he thought was wrong with American society.
30	21 Sep 1995	The Hindu milk miracle, India. Statues of the elephant-headed Hindu god Ganesh began drinking milk when spoonfuls were placed near their mouths. The phenomenon ended after 24 hours.
30	22 Sep 1995	Nager Kovil school bombing, Sri Lanka. The Sri Lankan Air Force bombed the primary school, killing 39 Tamil children and injuring many more, several of whom later died.
30	22 Sep 1995	A U.S. Air Force Boeing E-3B Sentry (AWACS) aircraft crashed near Elmendorf Air Force Base in Alaska after a flock of geese were sucked into its two left-side engines. All 24 crew members on board were killed.
30	27 Sep 1995	The BBC began broadcasting its national radio stations on DAB (digital audio broadcasting).

SEPTEMBER 2025

Ann.	Date	Event
30	27 Sep 1995 to 4 Oct	Operation Azalee. French mercenary Bob Denard launched a coup in the Comoros and established a provisional government. This was his fourth (and last) coup attempt. The French military ended the coup on 4th October and arrested him. There have been more than twenty attempted coups in the Comoros since it gained its independence in 1975.
30	28 Sep 1995	Israel agreed to give Palestinians control of much of the West Bank, which Israel had occupied for 28 years.
25	6 Sep 2000 to 8th	The Millennium Summit was held at the United Nations headquarters in New York City, USA. It was the largest gathering of world leaders in history (until the World Summit in 2005). They discussed the UN's role in the 21st century.
25	8 Sep 2000 to 14th	UK fuel protests. Road hauliers blockaded oil refineries across the country in protest against the rising cost of fuel for vehicles. Within days, disruption was widespread and petrol stations ran out of fuel. The protest ended on 14th September and fuel supplies began to be restored on 16th September.
25	9 Sep 2000	Death of Julian Critchley, British Conservative politician and journalist.
25	10 Sep 2000	Sierra Leone Civil War – Operation Barras. A daring British Army operation to rescue five British soldiers and a Sierra Leone Army liaison officer. They had been captured by the West Side Boys – a militia group. British victory, though one British paratrooper was killed and twelve were wounded.
25	12 Sep 2000	Death of Gary Olsen, British stage, film and television actor. Best known for his role as Ben Porter in the TV sitcom *2point4 Children*. (Cancer, aged 42.)
25	14 Sep 2000	Microsoft launched Windows ME (aimed at home users).
25	15 Sep 2000 to 1 Oct	The 2000 Olympic Games were held in Sydney, Australia.
25	17 Sep 2000	Death of Paula Yates, British television presenter (*The Tube*, *The Big Breakfast*). Wife of the musician Bob Geldof. Also noted for her relationship with the musician Michael Hutchence. Daughter of Hughie Green, host of the talent show *Opportunity Knocks* – though she didn't discover this until late in life. (Heroin overdose, aged 41.)
25	20 Sep 2000	The Whitewater investigation ended after seven years. Independent Counsel Robert Ray said there was insufficient evidence to determine whether U.S. President Bill Clinton or his wife Hillary had knowingly participated in any criminal conduct. Fifteen other people, including several Clinton aides and supporters, were convicted of more than forty crimes. The Governor of Arkansas, Jim Guy Tucker, was convicted of fraud and was removed from office.
25	20 Sep 2000	Death of Gherman Titov, Soviet/Russian cosmonaut. The second person to orbit the Earth, and the first to orbit it multiple times.

SEPTEMBER 2025

Ann.	Date	Event
25	23 Sep 2000	British rower Steve Redgrave won a gold medal at his fifth consecutive Olympic Games, in Sydney, Australia.
25	27 Sep 2000	Anti-globalisation/anti-capitalist protests, Prague, Czech Republic. Thousands of activists travelled to Prague from all over the world to protest during the International Monetary Fund/World Bank summit. They clashed with police, attacked shops and journalists, and tried to prevent the summit from opening. Around 900 people were arrested. 84 were injured, including 64 police officers.
25	28 Sep 2000 to 8 Feb 2005	Israeli–Palestinian conflict – the Second Intifada (also known as the Al-Aqsa Intifada). A Palestinian uprising against Israel. Israel eventually suppressed the uprising, built the Israeli West Bank barrier, and withdrew from the Gaza Strip.
25	28 Sep 2000	The Federal Drug Administration (FDA) approved the use of Mifepristone (also known as RU-486) in the USA. It induces abortion. It was first used in France in 1987.
25	28 Sep 2000	Death of Pierre Trudeau, Prime Minister of Canada (1968–79, 1980–84). Father of Prime Minister Justin Trudeau.
25	29 Sep 2000	Maze Prison in County Down, Northern Ireland closed down. The high-security prison housed paramilitary prisoners during the Troubles.
20	2 Sep 2005	The world première of the Western romantic drama film *Brokeback Mountain*, at the Venice Film Festival in Italy. (U.S. première: 29th November, limited release: 9th December, full release: 13th January 2006. UK limited release: 6th January 2006, full release: 13th January 2006.)
20	2 Sep 2005	Death of Bob Denver, American television actor (*Gilligan's Island* and *The Many Loves of Dobie Gillis*).
20	3 Sep 2005	The U.S. government and local/state officials along the Gulf Coast were criticised for their slow response to Hurricane Katrina. Although federal funds were released quickly, many people in New Orleans were left without food or water for up to five days. Mike Brown, the director of the Federal Emergency Management Agency (FEMA), resigned on 12th September after being removed from his post as coordinator of the federal relief efforts.
20	3 Sep 2005	Death of William Rehnquist, Chief Justice of the United States (1986–2005).
20	6 Sep 2005	Death of Eugenia Charles, Prime Minister of Dominica (1980–95). The first female lawyer in Dominica, and its first female Prime Minister.
20	7 Sep 2005	Egypt held its first multi-candidate presidential election. Incumbent Hosni Mubarak was re-elected amid widespread reports of vote-rigging and corruption. In December, the runner-up D. Ayman Nour was convicted of forgery and sentenced to five years' hard labour after contesting the results and calling for the election to be re-run.
20	7 Sep 2005	Apple introduced the iPod Nano portable music player.

SEPTEMBER 2025

Ann.	Date	Event
20	9 Sep 2000	The Netherlands Antilles was dissolved. All of the island territories remain part of the Netherlands, though their legal status now differs.
20	12 Sep 2005	The evacuation of all Israeli security forces and Israeli civilian settlements from the Gaza Strip in the state of Palestine was completed. Israel had occupied the Gaza Strip for 38 years.
20	12 Sep 2005	Hong Kong Disneyland opened.
20	13 Sep 2005	Death of Julio César Turbay Ayala, President of Colombia (1978–82).
20	14 Sep 2005	A U.S. District Judge in Sacramento, California ruled that reciting the Pledge of Allegiance in public schools was unconstitutional as the phrase 'under God' violated children's rights.
20	14 Sep 2005	Death of Robert Wise, American film director, producer and editor (*West Side Story, The Sound of Music, Citizen Kane, The Day the Earth Stood Still, The Andromeda Strain, Star Trek: The Motion Picture*, and more).
20	15 Sep 2005	Death of Sidney Luft, American film producer. Husband of the actress Judy Garland.
20	16 Sep 2005	Death of Gordon Gould, American physicist. Credited (though not by everyone) with inventing the laser. At the very least he played a key role in its early development and coined the term 'laser'.
20	19 Sep 2005	The terrorist organisation Al-Qaeda claimed responsibility for the 7th July bombings in London, UK in which 52 people (plus four suicide bombers) were killed. A number of other organisations with links to Al-Qaeda have also claimed responsibility.
20	19 Sep 2005	The former CEO of Tyco International, Dennis Kozlowski, and the former Chief Financial Officer, Mark Swartz, were sentenced to up to 25 years in prison for looting hundreds of millions of dollars from the company. They were released on parole in Jan 2014.
20	20 Sep 2005 to 26th	Hurricane Rita caused devastation and flooding across the southern U.S. states. 120 people were killed.
20	20 Sep 2005	Death of Simon Wiesenthal, Austrian Holocaust survivor and Nazi hunter. Founder of the Jewish Documentation Centre in Vienna.
20	24 Sep 2005	The IRA decommissioned the last of its weapons in front of independent inspectors.
20	25 Sep 2005	Death of M. Scott Peck, American psychiatrist and writer. Best known for his book *The Road Less Traveled*, which revolutionised the self-help genre.
20	26 Sep 2005	Death of Helen Cresswell, British children's writer and television scriptwriter. Best known for the *Lizzie Dripping* series and *The Bagthorpe Saga*.
20	27 Sep 2005	Michaëlle Jean became the first black Governor-General of Canada.
20	28 Sep 2005	Death of Constance Baker Motley, American lawyer, judge and civil rights activist. The first African American woman to become a federal judge.
20	29 Sep 2005	John Roberts became Chief Justice of the United States.

SEPTEMBER 2025

Ann.	Date	Event
20	29 Sep 2005	Death of Patrick Caulfield, British artist and printmaker.
20	29 Sep 2005	Death of Austin Leslie, American chef. Internationally renowned for his 'Creole Soul' food. Known as 'the Godfather of Fried Chicken'.
20	30 Sep 2005	The Danish newspaper *Jyllands-Posten* published twelve editorial cartoons featuring the Islamic prophet Muhammad. It sparked international protests and violent demonstrations and riots in some Muslim countries. At least 140 people were reportedly killed as a direct result.
15	4 Sep 2010	2010 Canterbury earthquake (also known as the Darfield earthquake), South Island, New Zealand. Two people were killed and around 100 injured. An aftershock in February 2011 (the 2011 Christchurch earthquake) killed 185 people.
15	6 Sep 2010	Aweil flood, Northern Bahr el Ghazal, South Sudan. Flooding caused massive destruction in the region and destroyed homes, crops, animals and livelihoods. Many people subsequently suffered from waterborne diseases.
15	7 Sep 2010	Bauchi prison break, northern Nigeria. About fifty members of the Islamist militant sect Boko Haram attacked the prison and freed 721 inmates, about 150 of whom were affiliated with the sect. Five people were killed, including a police officer.
15	19 Sep 2010	The *Deepwater Horizon* oil spill in the Gulf of Mexico was finally sealed after gushing oil for almost five months. It was the largest marine oil spill in history. In 2016, BP agreed to pay fines of $20.8 billion – the largest corporate settlement in U.S. history. It also paid over $65 billion in clean-up costs. (An investigation in 2018 found that oil was still seeping from the well.)
15	23 Sep 2010	Blockbuster, the video rental service, went out of business in the USA. Its stores were purchased by Dish Network in 2011 and the last Blockbuster stores closed in 2014. Its UK subsidiary went out of business in 2013.
10	3 Sep 2015	Death of Judy Carne, British actress. Best known as the 'Sock it to me!' girl in the American television comedy series *Rowan & Martin's Laugh-In*. Wife of the actor Burt Reynolds.
10	13 Sep 2015	Death of Brian Close, British cricket player (Yorkshire 1949–70, Marylebone Cricket Club 1950–67, Somerset 1971–77, England 1949–76).
10	14 Sep 2015	The first direct observation of gravitational waves was made by the Laser Interferometer Gravitational-Wave Observatory (LIGO) in the USA and the Virgo interferometer in Italy. Their observation was officially announced on 11th February 2016.
10	19 Sep 2015	Death of Jackie Collins, British romantic novelist (*The World Is Full of Married Men*, *The Stud*, *Hollywood Wives*, *Lady Boss*, and many more). Sister of the actress Joan Collins.
10	22 Sep 2015	Death of Yogi Berra, American baseball player, coach and manager (New York Yankees, New York Mets, Houston Astros).

SEPTEMBER 2025

Ann.	Date	Event
10	24 Sep 2015	2015 Mina stampede. More than 2,000 people were killed in a crush and stampede during the annual Hajj pilgrimage in Mecca, Saudi Arabia.

OCTOBER 2025

Ann.	Date	Event
1700	18 Oct 325	Death of Ming, Emperor of the Jin dynasty in China (323–325). Succeeded by his four-year-old son, Emperor Cheng.
1600	23 Oct 425	Valentinian III became Roman Emperor in the West (until 455). He was six years old.
1400	25 Oct 625	Death of Pope Boniface V. Succeeded by Honorius I, who was excommunicated after his death for monothelitism.
750	27 Oct 1275	The city of Amsterdam in the Netherlands was traditionally founded on this date.
400	4 Oct 1625	Birth of Jacqueline Pascal, French nun and writer. Sister of the mathematician and physicist Blaise Pascal. She joined Jansenism, a Catholic theological movement, but all nuns were later forced to recant it. She was so distraught by this that it ruined her health and she died on her 36th birthday.
300	22 Oct 1725	Death of Alessandro Scarlatti, Italian Baroque composer.
250	12 Oct 1775	Birth of Lyman Beecher, American Presbyterian clergyman. Father of several notable figures, including the writer and abolitionist Harriet Beecher Stowe.
250	13 Oct 1775	The Second Continental Congress established the Continental Navy. It became the United States Navy in 1794.
250	16 Oct 1775	American Revolutionary War – the Burning of Falmouth (now Portland, Maine). A British Royal Navy fleet attacked the town, then landed with the intention of destroying it. More than 400 homes were damaged or destroyed and 1,000 people (out of a population of around 2,500) were left homeless.
250	22 Oct 1775	Death of Peyton Randolph, first and third President of the Continental Congress (1774, 1775) and arguably the first President of the USA.
200	9 Oct 1825	The Norwegian ship *Restauration* arrived in New York Harbor, USA after a three-month voyage. It carried the first organised group of immigrants from Norway to the USA. The ship has been nicknamed the 'Norse *Mayflower*'.
200	10 Oct 1825	Birth of Paul Kruger, President of the South African Republic (1883–1902).
200	13 Oct 1825	Birth of Charles Frederick Worth, British fashion designer. Founder of the House of Worth, one of the leading fashion houses of the 19th and early 20th centuries. Regarded as the 'father of haute couture'.
200	13 Oct 1825	Death of Maximilian I Joseph, King of Bavaria (1806–25), Elector of Bavaria (1799–1806).
200	15 Oct 1825	Birth of Marie of Prussia, Queen consort of Bavaria (1848–64). Wife of Maximilian II of Bavaria. Mother of the Bavarian kings Ludwig II and Otto.
200	25 Oct 1825	Birth of Johann Strauss II, ('the Waltz King'), Austrian composer. Best known for his waltzes, including *The Blue Danube*.

OCTOBER 2025

Ann.	Date	Event
200	26 Oct 1825	The Erie Canal opened in the USA. It links the Great Lakes to the Atlantic Ocean via the Niagara River and the Hudson River.
175	2 Oct 1850	Death of Sarah Biffen, British artist. She was born without arms, and painted miniatures using her mouth.
175	10 Oct 1850	The Chesapeake & Ohio Canal in the USA was fully completed and opened for trade along its entire length of 184.5 miles. It operated until 1924.
175	23 Oct 1850 to 24th	The first National Women's Rights Convention was held in Worcester, Massachusetts, USA.
150	10 Oct 1875	Death of Aleksey Konstantinovich Tolstoy, Russian poet, novelist and playwright. Regarded as the most important Russian dramatist of the 19th century. Cousin of the writer Leo Tolstoy.
150	12 Oct 1875	Birth of Aleister Crowley, British occultist, ceremonial magician and writer. Known as 'the wickedest man in the world' and 'the Great Beast'.
150	16 Oct 1875	Brigham Young University was founded in Provo, Utah, USA (as the Brigham Young Academy).
150	25 Oct 1875	Tchaikovsky's *Piano Concerto No. 1 in B♭ minor* (Opus 23) was performed for the first time, in Boston, Massachusetts, USA.
150	28 Oct 1875	Birth of Gilbert H. Grosvenor, American geographer and editor. President of the National Geographic Society (1920–54). He built its magazine *National Geographic* into a world-renowned publication. He is also regarded as the father of photojournalism.
150	29 Oct 1875	Birth of Marie of Romania, Queen consort of Romania (1914–27). Wife of King Ferdinand I. A member of the British royal family. Daughter of Prince Alfred, Duke of Edinburgh.
125	3 Oct 1900	Birth of Thomas Wolfe, American novelist, short story writer and playwright. His work influenced several later writers including Jack Kerouak, Ray Bradbury, and Philip Roth. He died of tuberculosis in 1938, aged 37.
125	7 Oct 1900	Birth of Heinrich Himmler, German politician and Nazi party official. Reichsführer-SS (1929–45), Chief of German Police (1936–45). The main architect of the Holocaust. He was fired from all his positions after he realised that Germany had lost WWII and attempted to open peace talks with the Allies. He committed suicide in 1945, aged 44, after being captured by the British.
125	9 Oct 1900	Britain annexed the Cook Islands – at its own request – to prevent the French from seizing it. It became a self-governing state in free association with New Zealand in 1965.
125	9 Oct 1900	Birth of Alastair Sim, Scottish stage and film actor.
125	10 Oct 1900	Birth of Helen Hayes, (the 'First Lady of the American Theatre'), American stage and film actress.
125	16 Oct 1900	Birth of Goose Goslin, American baseball player (Washington Senators, St. Louis Browns, Detroit Tigers).

OCTOBER 2025

Ann.	Date	Event
125	19 Oct 1900	German theoretical physicist Max Planck announced the first version of his black-body radiation law. He revised it to incorporate energy quantisation and statistical mechanics, and presented the final version on 14th December. He was awarded the 1918 Nobel Prize in Physics for his discovery.
125	20 Oct 1900	American aviation pioneers the Wright Brothers made their first untethered glider flight at Kill Devil Hills in North Carolina, USA. They made their first successful powered flight in December 1903.
125	23 Oct 1900	Birth of Douglas Jardine, British cricketer. Captain of England's national team during the infamous 'bodyline' tour of Australia in 1932–33. He was responsible for implementing the bodyline bowling tactics devised by batsman Don Bradman.
125	26 Oct 1900	Birth of Ibrahim Abboud, military ruler of Sudan. First President and fourth Prime Minister of Sudan (1958–64).
125	28 Oct 1900	Death of Max Müller, German-born British philologist, Orientalist, writer and scholar. Known for his studies of Indian history, culture, language and literature. He also directed the translation of the fifty-volume *Sacred Books of the East*.
125	31 Oct 1900	Birth of Carl Hubbard, American football player (New York Giants, Green Bay Packers, Pittsburgh Pirates). He was one of the inventors of the linebacker position in American football. He later became a Major League Baseball umpire.
100	2 Oct 1925	Scottish engineer John Logie Baird performed the first successful test of a working television system. His system used a mechanical spinning disc. He gave the first public demonstration in January 1926.
100	3 Oct 1925	Birth of Gore Vidal, American postmodernist novelist, political commentator and essayist. (Died 2012.)
100	4 Oct 1925	The New York Giants American football team played their first game. They beat New Britain, Connecticut 26–0.
100	6 Oct 1925	Xavier University of Louisiana was founded in New Orleans, USA as a Catholic university for black students. It was the first Catholic university founded by a saint – Katharine Drexel, who was canonised in 2000.
100	11 Oct 1925	Birth of Elmore Leonard, American novelist, short story writer and screenwriter. Best known for his crime fiction and suspense thrillers. (Died 2013.)
100	13 Oct 1925	Birth of Lenny Bruce, American stand-up comedian, satirist and free speech activist. Noted for his black humour and controversial comedy routines that were punctuated by obscenity. (Died 1966.)
100	13 Oct 1925	Birth of Margaret Thatcher, Baroness Thatcher, British Prime Minister (1979–90). (Died 2013.)
100	15 Oct 1925	Birth of Tony Hart, British artist and children's television presenter (*Vision On*, *Take Hart*, *Hartbeat*). (Died 2009.)
100	16 Oct 1925	The Texas State Textbook Commission in the USA ordered that all mention of evolution should be deleted from school textbooks.

OCTOBER 2025

Ann.	Date	Event
100	17 Oct 1925	Birth of Harry Carpenter, British radio and television sports broadcaster. Best known for his boxing commentaries. (Died 2010.)
100	18 Oct 1925	Birth of Ramiz Alia, first President of Albania (1991–92). (Died 2011.)
100	20 Oct 1925	Birth of Art Buchwald, American humourist, newspaper columnist and writer. (Died 2007.)
100	21 Oct 1925	Birth of Celia Cruz, (the 'Queen of Salsa'), Cuban-born American singer and actress. (Died 2003.)
100	23 Oct 1925	Birth of Johnny Carson, American television host and comedian. Best known for *The Tonight Show* (1962–92). (Died 2005.)
100	25 Oct 1925	The American Negro Labor Congress was founded. In 1930 it was renamed the League of Struggle for Negro Rights. It was dissolved in 1935 when the National Negro Congress was founded.
100	27 Oct 1925	The first U.S. patent for water skis was granted to Fred Waller of New York. (U.S. Patent 1,559,390.) Water skiing was invented by Ralph Samuelson in Minnesota in 1922.
100	27 Oct 1925	Birth of Warren Christopher, U.S. Secretary of State (1993–97). (Died 2011.)
100	29 Oct 1925	Birth of Dominick Dunne, American writer, investigative journalist, and film and television producer.
100	29 Oct 1925	Birth of Robert Hardy, British stage, film and television actor. Best known for his role as Siegfried Farnon in the TV series *All Creatures Great and Small*. He also played Cornelius Fudge in the *Harry Potter* films, and British Prime Minister Winston Churchill in several TV productions. (Died 2017.)
90	3 Oct 1935 to May 1936	Second Italo–Ethiopian War. Italian victory.
90	8 Oct 1935	Birth of Albert Roux, French-born British restaurateur and chef. His restaurant, Le Gavroche, in London (which he ran with his brother Michel and is now run by his son Michel Roux Jr.) was the first in the UK to be awarded three Michelin stars. He trained several chefs who also won Michelin stars. (Died 2021.)
90	10 Oct 1935	Georgios Kondylis became Prime Minister of Greece after ousting Panagis Tsaldaris in a royalist coup. He ended the Second Hellenic Republic, and the Greek monarchy was restored in November.
90	10 Oct 1935	George Gershwin's opera *Porgy and Bess* opened on Broadway. It is regarded as the first great American opera.
90	12 Oct 1935	Birth of Luciano Pavarotti, Italian operatic tenor. Considered one of the finest tenors of the 20th century, and one of the most commercially successful of all time. (Died 2007.)
90	20 Oct 1935	The Long March ended in China. Communist leader Mao Zedong and 8,000 followers arrived in Yan'an after a year-long 6,000-mile march. He established the People's Republic of China in 1949.

OCTOBER 2025

Ann.	Date	Event
90	20 Oct 1935	Birth of Jerry Orbach, American stage, film and television actor and singer. Best known for the films *Dirty Dancing* and *Beauty and the Beast*, the stage shows *The Fantasticks*, *Promises, Promises*, *42nd Street* and *Chicago*, and the TV series *Murder, She Wrote* and *Law & Order*. (Died 2004.)
90	20 Oct 1935	Death of Arthur Henderson, British politician, leader of the Labour Party (1908–10, 1914–17, 1931–32). The first Labour cabinet minister. Winner of the 1934 Nobel Peace Prize.
90	25 Oct 1935	A hurricane struck Haiti. More than 2,000 people were killed.
90	28 Oct 1935	Birth of Alan Clarke, British stage, film and television director. Noted for his stark and often controversial plays and films including *Scum*, *Made in Britain*, *The Firm*, and *Rita, Sue and Bob Too*.
90	30 Oct 1935	Birth of Michael Winner, British film director, producer and screenwriter, restaurant critic and media personality. Best known for his films *Death Wish* and *The Big Sleep*. (Died 2013.)
80	3 Oct 1945	The World Federation of Trade Unions was founded.
80	4 Oct 1945	Pierre Laval, the Prime Minister of Vichy France during WWII, went on trial for treason. He was found guilty and sentenced to death. He was executed by firing squad on 15th October.
80	5 Oct 1945	The Indonesian Army was founded (as the People's Security Army).
80	5 Oct 1945	Hollywood Black Friday: a six-month strike by set decorators developed into a riot at the gates of Warner Brothers' studios. More than 40 people were injured. The strike ended a month later, but the Conference of Studio Unions was soon broken up.
80	5 Oct 1945	Birth of Brian Connolly, Scottish singer, songwriter, musician and actor. Lead singer of The Sweet. (Died 1997.)
80	8 Oct 1945	U.S. President Harry S. Truman announced that Britain and Canada were the USA's only partners in the development of the atomic bomb. He said the secrets would be shared between them, but not divulged to any other country. In 1950, Klaus Fuchs, who worked on the Manhattan Project, was convicted of relaying atomic bomb secrets to the Soviet Union. There is considerable debate about whether the information he passed to them was of value, as he was only involved at an early stage. (See also: 18th October 1945.)
80	10 Oct 1945	The Double Tenth Agreement was signed by the Chinese Communist Party (CCP) and the Kuomintang (KMT – the Chinese Nationalist Party). The agreement recognised the KMT as the legitimate government of China and the CCO as the legitimate opposition party.
80	12 Oct 1945	World War II: U.S. Army combat medic Desmond Doss became the first conscientious objector in U.S. history to receive a Medal of Honor for his actions. He saved the lives of 75 men during the Battle of Okinawa.
80	13 Oct 1945	Death of Milton S. Hershey, American confectioner and philanthropist. Founder of the Hershey chocolate company and the company town of Hershey, Pennsylvania.

OCTOBER 2025

Ann.	Date	Event
80	15 Oct 1945	Death of Pierre Laval, Prime Minister of Vichy France during WWII. (Executed for treason.)
80	16 Oct 1945	The Food and Agriculture Organisation of the United Nations was founded.
80	17 Oct 1945	Loyalty Day in Argentina. A mass demonstration demanded the release of Juan Perón, who had been forced to resign as Vice President (on 8th October) by opponents in the military, and was then imprisoned. He was released later that day. He became President of Argentina in June 1946. (See also: 21st October 1945.)
80	18 Oct 1945	The President of Venezuela, Isaías Medina Angarita, was overthrown in a military coup. He was succeeded by Rómulo Betancourt.
80	18 Oct 1945	German theoretical physicist Klaus Fuchs, working at the Los Alamos National Laboratory in the USA, supplied the Soviet Union with detailed technical information from the Manhattan Project which developed the first nuclear weapons. He continued to pass information to Soviet authorities until early 1949. He was convicted in 1950 and served nine years in prison in the UK. He then resumed his scientific career in East Germany.
80	19 Oct 1945	Birth of Divine, (Harris Glenn Milstead), American actor, singer and drag artist. Known for the song *You Think You're a Man*. (Died 1988.)
80	19 Oct 1945	Death of Plutarco Elías Calles, President of Mexico (1924–28).
80	21 Oct 1945	French women were allowed to vote in a national election for the first time, in the French legislative election.
80	21 Oct 1945 or 22nd	Argentine military officer and politician Juan Perón married actress Eva Duarte ('Evita').
80	24 Oct 1945	The United Nations was formally established and began operating. It replaced the League of Nations.
80	24 Oct 1945	Death of Vidkun Quisling, Norwegian politician and Nazi collaborator who seized power of German-occupied Norway in a Nazi-backed coup. Minister President of Norway (1942–45). His name became a synonym for 'traitor'. (Executed for treason and other crimes.)
80	25 Oct 1945	Taiwan Retrocession Day. The Republic of China took over the administration of Taiwan following Japan's surrender.
80	27 Oct 1945 to 20 Nov	World War II – the Battle of Surabaya (Indonesia). British victory. The heaviest fighting occurred on 10th November – now celebrated as Heroes Day in Indonesia.
80	27 Oct 1945	The first issue of *Elsevier Weekblad* was published. It is the Netherlands' most popular news magazine.
80	27 Oct 1945	Birth of Carrie Snodgress, American film and television actress. Best known for her role in the film *Diary of a Mad Housewife*. (Died 2004.)

OCTOBER 2025

Ann.	Date	Event
80	29 Oct 1945	The President of Brazil, Getúlio Vargas, resigned. He was succeeded by José Linhares. He became President again in January 1951.
80	29 Oct 1945	The first commercially successful ballpoint pen went on sale at Gimbels department store in New York City, USA. (Ballpoint pens were launched in the UK in December 1945.)
80	30 Oct 1945	World War II: shoe rationing ended in the USA.
75	1 Oct 1950	The first live television broadcast from an aircraft in flight. The BBC broadcast aerial views of central London from a specially outfitted plane as it flew over the city.
75	2 Oct 1950	The *Peanuts* comic strip by Charles M. Schulz was first published in nine U.S. newspapers (as *Li'l Folks*). It ran until February 2000.
75	3 Oct 1950	Indonesia invaded the self-proclaimed Republic of South Maluku following its declaration of independence in April. Fighting continued until 1963 when the republic was disestablished.
75	3 Oct 1950	American researchers John Bardeen, Walter Brattain and William Shockley of AT&T Bell Laboratories were granted a U.S. patent for their invention of the transistor. (U.S. Patent 2,524,035.) They were also awarded the 1956 Nobel Prize in Physics for their work.
75	5 Oct 1950	The first episode of the television quiz show *You Bet Your Life*, hosted by Groucho Marx, was broadcast on NBC in the USA. It ran until 1961. The radio version began in 1947 and ran until 1960.
75	5 Oct 1950	Birth of 'Fast' Eddie Clarke, British rock guitarist (Motörhead, Fastway). (Died 2018.)
75	6 Oct 1950 to 23 May 1951	The annexation of Tibet by the People's Republic of China. The annexation began with a military conflict – the Battle of Chamdo (6th – 24th October). (See also: 7th October 1950.) In May 1951, Tibet was pressured into accepting the Seventeen Point Agreement, and it became Tibet Autonomous Region, China.
75	7 Oct 1950	China invaded Tibet. Tibetan forces were overcome by 19th October, and Tibet despatched a delegation to China to agree terms for China's annexation of Tibet.
75	7 Oct 1950	Mother Teresa founded what would become the Missionaries of Charity, in Calcutta (now Kolkata), India.
75	9 Oct 1950	Korean War: United Nations (mainly U.S.) forces crossed the 38th parallel into North Korea. On 19th – 20th October they captured and occupied the North Korean capital, Pyongyang.
75	9 Oct 1950 to 31st	The Goyang Geumjeong Cave massacre, South Korea. South Korean police killed 153 unarmed civilians who were suspected of sympathising with North Korea. In 2006–07 the Truth and Reconciliation Commission found that most of those killed were not connected to the sympathisers, and demanded that the government apologise, pay reparations and erect a memorial. The Seoul Central Court enforced the order in 2011.

OCTOBER 2025

Ann.	Date	Event
75	12 Oct 1950	The first episode of the television sitcom *The George Burns and Gracie Allen Show* (also known as *The Burns and Allen Show*) was broadcast on CBS in the USA. It ran for eight seasons until 1958.
75	15 Oct 1950	The world's first radio paging service began operating at the Jewish Hospital in New York City, USA. It had a range of 30 miles. The first page was sent to a doctor who was playing golf 25 miles away.
75	17 Oct 1950 to 19th	Korean War – the Battle of Pyongyang, North Korea. United Nations victory. Shortly afterwards, China joined the war in support of North Korea, and recaptured Pyongyang on 5th December.
75	17 Oct 1950	Birth of Howard Rollins, American stage, film and television actor. (Died 1996.)
75	18 Oct 1950	American baseball team manager Connie Mack retired as manager of the Philadelphia Athletics after fifty years. He is the longest-serving manager in baseball history.
75	19 Oct 1950	The USA's Point Four Program began. Iran became the first country to accept U.S. technical assistance to improve its economy and agricultural output.
75	19 Oct 1950	Britain's Chancellor of the Exchequer, Stafford Cripps, resigned due to ill health. (He died 18 months later.) He was succeeded by Hugh Gaitskell.
75	20 Oct 1950	Birth of Tom Petty, American singer, songwriter, guitarist and record producer. He was a member of Tom Petty and the Heartbreakers, and the Traveling Wilburys, and also enjoyed a successful solo career. (Died 2017.)
75	20 Oct 1950	Death of Henry L. Stimson, U.S. Secretary of State (1929–33), U.S. Secretary of War (1911–13, 1940–45), Governor-General of the Philippines (1927–29).
75	21 Oct 1950 to 22nd	Korean War – the Battle of Yongju, North Korea. United Nations (U.S./UK/Australia) victory.
75	21 Oct 1950	Birth of Ronald McNair, American astronaut and physicist. (Killed in the Space Shuttle *Challenger* disaster in 1986.)
75	23 Oct 1950	Death of Al Jolson, Russian-born American singer, stage and film actor, and comedian. The most famous American entertainer of the 1930s. Best known for the film *The Jazz Singer*.
75	25 Oct 1950 to 4 Nov	Korean War – the Battle of Unsan, North Korea. Chinese victory. China's first battle of the war, which they joined as allies of North Korea. U.S. forces made a rapid retreat.
75	28 Oct 1950	The first televised episode of *The Jack Benny Program* was broadcast on CBS in the USA. It was a seamless continuation of the radio series and ran until 1965.
75	29 Oct 1950	Death of Gustaf V, King of Sweden (1907–50). Succeeded by his son Gustaf VI Adolf.
75	30 Oct 1950	Pope Pius XII witnessed the Miracle of the Sun from the Vatican gardens. (He witnessed it again on 31st October, 1st November and 8th November.)

OCTOBER 2025

Ann.	Date	Event
75	31 Oct 1950	Earl Lloyd became the first African American to play in the National Basketball Association (NBA).
75	31 Oct 1950	Birth of John Candy, Canadian film actor and comedian. Known for the films *Splash*, *Cool Runnings*, *Spaceballs*, *Uncle Buck*, *Planes, Trains and Automobiles*, and many more. (Died 1994.)
70	1 Oct 1955	The first episode of the television sitcom *The Honeymooners* was broadcast on CBS in the USA. It only ran for one series, then continued as one-off specials and as a series of sketches on *The Jackie Gleason Show*.
70	2 Oct 1955	The first episode of the literary anthology television series *Alfred Hitchcock Presents* was broadcast on CBS in the USA. It ran until 1965. (It was revived in 1985.)
70	3 Oct 1955	The first episode of the children's television show *The Mickey Mouse Club* was broadcast on ABC in the USA. It ran (intermittently) until 1996, moving to The Disney Channel from 1989.
70	3 Oct 1955	The first episode of the children's television show *Captain Kangaroo* was broadcast on CBS in the USA. It ran for 38 seasons until 1984.
70	7 Oct 1955	American beat poet Allen Ginsberg read his poem *Howl* for the first time, at a poetry reading at the Six Gallery in San Francisco, California, USA. It was an immediate success, but he was later accused of obscenity. Copies of it were seized in March 1957, a bookstore owner was arrested and jailed for selling it in June, and there was a widely publicised obscenity trial. The judge ruled it was 'not obscene' and was of 'redeeming social importance'. It is now considered one of the great works of American literature and helped establish the Beat Generation.
70	8 Oct 1955	The U.S. Navy supercarrier *USS Saratoga* was launched. It was in service from April 1956 until August 1994. It was involved in the Vietnam War, the Gulf War, and numerous other assignments, particularly in the Mediterranean.
70	13 Oct 1955	Death of Manuel Ávila Camacho, President of Mexico (1940–46).
70	19 Oct 1955	The discovery of the antiproton was announced by Emilio Segrè and Owen Chamberlain from the University of California, Berkeley in the USA. They were awarded the 1959 Nobel Prize in Physics.
70	20 Oct 1955	Egypt and Syria signed a mutual defence treaty, pledging to support each other in any conflict against Israel.
70	20 Oct 1955	*The Return of the King*, the third and final part of J. R. R. Tolkein's *The Lord of the Rings*, was published.
70	20 Oct 1955	Little Richard's pioneering rock and roll song *Tutti Frutti* was released. It became his first major hit, and was a model for future rock songs.
70	22 Oct 1955 to 26 Nov	The science fiction television serial *Quatermass II* was broadcast on the BBC in the UK.
70	23 Oct 1955	In a referendum, the citizens of the Saar Protectorate voted not to become independent in an economic union with France, but to reunite with West Germany. Saarland became a state of Germany on 1st January 1957.
70	25 Oct 1955	The first microwave oven for domestic use went on sale in the USA. It was manufactured by Tappan, was very expensive, and did not sell well.

OCTOBER 2025

Ann.	Date	Event
70	25 Oct 1955	The Buraimi dispute, in what is now the United Arab Emirates and western Oman, ended after almost three years. Saudi Arabia had invaded the territory as it was suspected to contain significant reserves of oil. The United Arab Emirates and British troops forced the Saudis to withdraw. This later led to the Saudi Arabia–United Arab Emirates border dispute.
70	25 Oct 1955	Death of Sadako Sasaki, twelve-year-old Japanese victim of the atomic bomb dropped on Nagasaki. She famously tried to fold 1,000 origami cranes before she died of leukaemia. She is reported to have folded 1,300 cranes.
70	26 Oct 1955	The Prime Minister of the State of Vietnam, Ngo Dinh Diem, proclaimed the Republic of Vietnam (South Vietnam), with himself as its first president. He remained in office until November 1963 when he was captured and assassinated during a military coup.
70	26 Oct 1955	Austria declared its permanent neutrality after regaining its sovereignty in May. (See also: 15th May 1955.)
70	26 Oct 1955	The first edition of the weekly newspaper *The Village Voice* was published in New York City, USA.
70	27 Oct 1955	Egypt and Saudi Arabia signed a joint defence agreement in Cairo.
70	31 Oct 1955	Princess Margaret of the United Kingdom announced that she had cancelled her plans to marry Group Captain Peter Townsend. Their relationship was controversial because he was divorced and she would have had to renounce her royal status to marry him. She married Antony Armstrong-Jones, the Earl of Snowdon, in 1960. In 1978 she became the first member of the royal family to divorce since Henry VIII in 1540.
65	1 Oct 1960	Nigeria gained its independence from the UK.
65	3 Oct 1960	The first episode of the television sitcom *The Andy Griffith Show* was broadcast on CBS in the USA. It ran for eight seasons.
65	4 Oct 1960	The U.S. Army and ARPA launched *Courier 1B*, the first successful active repeater satellite. The experimental satellite received teletype messages, stored them, and then retransmitted them when it was in sight of a ground station. It operated for seventeen days, then stopped responding.
65	7 Oct 1960	The first episode of the crime-adventure television series *Route 66* was broadcast on CBS in the USA. It ran for four seasons until 1964.
65	10 Oct 1960	East Pakistan was hit by a cyclone that killed 6,000 people and devastated coastal communities, leaving 100,000 homeless. An even more devastating cyclone hit the same area on 31st October.
65	12 Oct 1960	Cold War: Nikita Khrushchev's shoe-banging incident. At a meeting of the United Nations General Assembly, Soviet leader Nikita Khrushchev is reported to have removed his shoe and pounded his table with it in protest against a speech by the Philippine delegate, which criticized Soviet policy in Eastern Europe. (Some sources say he brandished his shoe, but didn't pound the table.)

OCTOBER 2025

Ann.	Date	Event
65	17 Oct 1960	Birth of Bernie Nolan, Irish-born British singer and actress. Best known as the lead singer of the Nolans. (Died 2013.)
65	19 Oct 1960	The USA imposed an embargo on exports to Cuba. All goods were prohibited, except medicines and certain foods. (See also: 6th August and 24th October 1960.)
65	21 Oct 1960	Britain's first nuclear submarine, *HMS Dreadnought*, was launched.
65	24 Oct 1960	Cuba nationalised all remaining U.S.-owned property in Cuba, completing a nationalisation program that began on 6th August in response to the U.S. embargo. (See also: 19th October 1960.)
65	24 Oct 1960	Nedelin catastrophe, Baikonur Cosmodrome, Kazakhstan, Soviet Union. A prototype R-16 intercontinental ballistic missile exploded on the launch pad due to a short circuit. The Soviet Union suppressed news of the explosion for many years, and did not acknowledge it until 1989. The exact death toll is unknown – various sources give figures between 54 and 300. The head of the Soviet Union's Strategic Rocket Forces, Mitrofan Ivanovich Nedelin, was among those killed, and the disaster was named after him.
65	25 Oct 1960	Bulova launched the Accutron 214, the world's first electronic watch. It was guaranteed accurate to within two seconds per day. (This is not the same as an *electric* watch, the first of which was sold by Hamilton in 1957.)
65	25 Oct 1960	Death of Harry Ferguson, British agricultural equipment manufacturer who helped to develop the modern tractor. He also built his own plane and the first four-wheel-drive Formula One car. The company he founded is now part of Massey Ferguson, Ltd.
65	29 Oct 1960	American boxer Cassius Clay (later known as Muhammad Ali) won his first professional fight, in Louisville, Kentucky.
65	30 Oct 1960	Birth of Diego Maradona, Argentine football player, manager and coach. Regarded as one of the greatest football players in history. (Died 2020.)
65	31 Oct 1960	East Pakistan was hit by a second cyclone and tidal surge, three weeks after the previous one devastated the area (see 10th October). 14,000 people were killed and 200,000 left homeless.
60	1 Oct 1965	The 30th September Movement staged an attempted coup in Indonesia. Six Indonesian Army generals were assassinated. This led to an anti-communist purge in which more than 500,000 people were killed.
60	4 Oct 1965	The Soviet Union launched its *Luna 7* spacecraft on a mission to soft land on the Moon. The landing systems failed and it crashed on the Moon on 7th October.
60	4 Oct 1965	Pope Paul VI became the first pope to visit the USA.
60	6 Oct 1965	Patricia Roberts Harris became the U.S. Ambassador to Luxembourg. She was the first African American U.S. Ambassador.
60	8 Oct 1965	The Post Office Tower (now the BT Tower) in London was officially opened. It was the tallest building in the UK until 1980.

OCTOBER 2025

Ann.	Date	Event
60	11 Oct 1965	The Vinland Map was first displayed to the public at Yale University, Connecticut, USA. It is claimed to be a 15th century map of the world which shows that America was visited by Norse explorers in the 11th century. Its authenticity is disputed.
60	11 Oct 1965	Death of Dorothea Lange, American documentary photographer and photojournalist. Best known for her images of the Great Depression.
60	11 Oct 1965	Death of Walther Stampfli, President of the Swiss Confederation (1944).
60	12 Oct 1965	Death of Paul Hermann Müller, Swiss chemist. Winner of the 1948 Nobel Prize in Physiology or Medicine for discovering the insecticidal properties of DDT. This led to significant increases in world food production and the reduction of insect-borne diseases. DDT was banned in many countries by 1970 and replaced by less toxic substances.
60	14 Oct 1965	Death of Randall Jarrell, American poet and literary critic. Consultant in Poetry to the Library of Congress (1956–58).
60	15 Oct 1965	Vietnam War: the first public burning of a draft card in the USA took place at a student-led anti-war demonstration in New York City. Destruction or mutilation of draft cards had been made illegal in August. The protester, David Miller, was sentenced to two years in prison.
60	17 Oct 1965	The musical *On a Clear Day You Can See Forever* opened on Broadway. It ran until June 1966. It was not well received. A revised version opened on Broadway in 2011.
60	18 Oct 1965	Death of Henry Travers, British stage and film actor. Best known for his role as the angel Clarence Odbody in the film *It's a Wonderful Life*.
60	19 Oct 1965 to 25th	Vietnam War – the Siege of Plei Me, South Vietnam. The first major confrontation between U.S. forces and the North Vietnamese People's Army. The U.S. supported the South Vietnamese forces with air power, and the siege was successfully lifted.
60	22 Oct 1965	The Vivian Beaumont Theater opened in New York City, USA. It is the only Broadway theatre located outside of New York's theatre district.
60	22 Oct 1965	The Highway Beautification Act was signed into law in the USA. It placed limits on outdoor advertising and signage, required junkyards to be screened or removed, and encouraged the scenic enhancement and development of roadsides. It was a pet project of the First Lady, Lady Bird Johnson.
60	22 Oct 1965	The rock song *Get Off of My Cloud* by the Rolling Stones was released in the UK. (USA: 25th September.)
60	23 Oct 1965 to 20 Nov	Vietnam War – Operation Silver Bayonet. The U.S. 1st Cavalry Division joined forces with the South Vietnamese to seek and destroy North Vietnamese regiments in western Pleiku Province. The operation included the Battle of Ia Drang Valley (see 14th November).
60	26 Oct 1965	British rock band the Beatles were presented with their MBEs by Queen Elizabeth II at Buckingham Palace. (John Lennon returned his in 1969.)

OCTOBER 2025

Ann.	Date	Event
60	28 Oct 1965	Pope Paul VI absolved the Jews of their collective guilt for the crucifixion of Jesus Christ, as part of his decree *Nostra Aetate* (meaning: In Our Time).
60	28 Oct 1965	The Gateway Arch in St. Louis, Missouri, USA was completed. It was dedicated in March 1968.
60	28 Oct 1965	Death of Earl Bostic, American jazz/rhythm and blues saxophonist.
60	30 Oct 1965	Death of Arthur M. Schlesinger Sr., American historian, writer, educator and intellectual. Closely associated with Harvard University. Father of the historian Arthur M. Schlesinger Jr.
50	1 Oct 1975	Following a referendum in 1974, the Gilbert and Ellice Islands, a British colony, split into two separate colonies. The Gilbert Islands became Kiribati and the Ellice Islands became Tuvalu. They became independent countries on 1st January 1978.
50	1 Oct 1975	The Thrilla in Manila. Muhammad Ali knocked out Joe Frazier to win the World Heavyweight Championship in boxing.
50	1 Oct 1975	Death of Al Jackson Jr., American R&B/soul/funk drummer (Booker T. & The MG's). (Shot dead.)
50	2 Oct 1975	Japanese Emperor Hirohito made his first visit to the USA. He met U.S. President Gerald Ford at the White House.
50	7 Oct 1975	U.S. President Gerald Ford signed Public Law 94-106, which required the U.S. military to open its academies to women. The first women were admitted in September 1976 and graduated in 1980.
50	9 Oct 1975	The IRA detonated a bomb near the Ritz Hotel in Piccadilly, London. One person was killed and at least twenty injured.
50	9 Oct 1975	Soviet nuclear physicist and dissident Andrei Sakharov won the Nobel Peace Prize. He advocated civil liberties and civil reforms in the Soviet Union, and was persecuted by the state as a result. His prize was presented on 10th December, but the Soviet Union prevented him from travelling to Norway to accept it. His wife accepted it on his behalf.
50	10 Oct 1975	British-American film actress Elizabeth Taylor remarried Welsh actor Richard Burton, sixteen months after they divorced.
50	11 Oct 1975	The first episode of the sketch/comedy/variety television show *Saturday Night Live* was broadcast on NBC in the USA (as *NBC's Saturday Night*).
50	11 Oct 1975	Future U.S. President Bill Clinton married Hillary Rodham.
50	12 Oct 1975	The 17th century Irish archbishop Oliver Plunkett was canonised. He was the first new Irish saint for 700 years.
50	14 Oct 1975 to 1976	Operation Savannah, Angola. A covert South African intervention in the Angolan Civil War. Part of the South African Border War.
50	15 Oct 1975	Iceland extended its international boundary from 50 miles from its coastline to 200 miles. This led to the Third Cod War with Britain (November 1975 – June 1976).

OCTOBER 2025

Ann.	Date	Event
50	16 Oct 1975	The Balibo Five, a group of Australian television journalists, were killed during an Indonesian incursion into East Timor.
50	16 Oct 1975	Rahima Banu, a two-year-old Pakistani girl, became the last-known person to contract naturally occurring smallpox. She was treated by a team from the World Health Organisation and made a full recovery. The last person to die from smallpox was British medical photographer Janet Parker, who was exposed to it in a laboratory accident in 1978.
50	20 Oct 1975	The U.S. Supreme Court ruled that corporal punishment (spanking) was permissible in schools, even if the student's parents objected to it. Corporal punishment could only be administered if students were aware that it was a possibility for certain types of behaviour, if other disciplinary measures had been tried, and if the punishment was witnessed by a named official from the school. (Baker v. Owen). The case was upheld in 1977 (Ingraham v. Wright). Some U.S. states have banned it in public schools, but it is still legal in all private schools. It is illegal in 128 countries including the UK, Europe, Canada and New Zealand.
50	21 Oct 1975	Mexico City subway crash. Twenty people were killed when a stationary train was hit by another train which failed to stop in time. Automatic traffic lights were installed following this incident.
50	22 Oct 1975	The 'Guildford Four' were convicted of planting IRA bombs in two pubs in Guildford, Surrey, UK, which killed five people. They were sentenced to life imprisonment. Their convictions were reversed in 1989 and they were released.
50	22 Oct 1975	The Soviet Union's *Venera 9* landed on Venus and became the first spacecraft to send back images from the surface of another planet. Its orbiter began surveying Venus on 26th October. *Venera 10* also reached Venus on 23rd October and landed on 25th October.
50	22 Oct 1975	The World Football League went out of business midway through its second season. (In 2008 a minor American football league acquired the rights and began playing under the same name.)
50	22 Oct 1975	Sergeant Leonard Matlovich was discharged from the U.S. Air Force after appearing on the cover of *Time* magazine with the headline 'I Am a Homosexual'. He then spent years fighting for acceptance and pursuing a legal case to be reinstated. He became a well-known figure in the media, and was recognised as a leader of the LGBT community.
50	22 Oct 1975	Death of Arnold Toynbee, British historian, philosopher of history, and writer. Best known for his twelve-volume work *A Study of History*.
50	24 Oct 1975	Women's Day Off, Iceland. The women of Iceland went on strike for a day to protest against pay discrepancy and unfair employment practices. They wanted to show that women were an indispensable part of Iceland's economy and society. Ninety percent of Iceland's female population took part. Iceland passed a law guaranteeing equal pay in 1976.

OCTOBER 2025

Ann.	Date	Event
50	26 Oct 1975	Anwar Sadat became the first Egyptian president to make an official visit to the USA.
50	27 Oct 1975	Death of Rex Stout, American writer of detective fiction. Best known for his series of novels featuring the detective Nero Wolfe.
50	28 Oct 1975	Death of Georges Carpentier, French world light-heavyweight boxing champion (1920–22).
50	29 Oct 1975	U.S. President Gerald Ford gave a speech in which he said he would not grant federal assistance to New York City to save it from bankruptcy. The following day, 30th October, the *New York Daily News* ran the headline 'Ford to City: Drop Dead'. Ford later said the headline was a key factor when he lost the 1976 presidential election. He granted the city a $2.3 billion seasonal loan on 9th December 1975.
50	30 Oct 1975	British serial killer Peter Sutcliffe (the Yorkshire Ripper) killed his first victim, in Leeds, West Yorkshire. He had attacked at least four women prior to this. In 1981 he was convicted of murdering thirteen women.
50	30 Oct 1975	Death of Gustav Hertz, German physicist. Joint winner of the 1925 Nobel Prize in Physics for discovering the laws governing the impact of an electron upon an atom. Nephew of the physicist Heinrich Hertz.
50	31 Oct 1975	Irish rock band the Boomtown Rats played their first concert (as the Nightlife Thugs – they changed their name to the Boomtown Rats during the interval).
40	1 Oct 1985	Riots broke out in Toxteth in Liverpool and Peckham in London, UK.
40	1 Oct 1985	Israeli–Palestinian conflict – Operation Wooden Leg. The Israeli Air Force bombed the Palestine Liberation Organisation's headquarters near Tunis, Tunisia.
40	1 Oct 1985	Death of E. B. White, American writer and children's author. Best known for *The Elements of Style* (Strunk & White), and the children's stories *Charlotte's Web* and *Stuart Little*.
40	2 Oct 1985	Death of Rock Hudson, American film and television actor. One of the most popular film stars of his era. The first major celebrity to die from AIDS.
40	3 Oct 1985	The USA renamed the position of *'Consultant in Poetry to the Library of Congress'* to *'Poet Laureate Consultant in Poetry to the Library of Congress'* (more commonly known as the U.S. Poet Laureate). Robert Penn Warren became the first U.S. Poet Laureate in February 1986.
40	3 Oct 1985	Death of Charles Collingwood, American television journalist and news anchor (CBS).
40	4 Oct 1985	The terrorist organisation Islamic Jihad announced that they had executed William Buckley, a U.S. Army officer and the CIA's station chief in Beirut, Lebanon. In fact, he is believed to have died from a heart attack while being tortured five months earlier, on 3rd June.
40	4 Oct 1985	The Free Software Foundation was formed.

OCTOBER 2025

Ann.	Date	Event
40	5 Oct 1985 to 7th	Puerto Rico floods and Mameyes landslide. At least 180 people were killed. The Mameyes landslide was the worst in North American history.
40	6 Oct 1985	Broadwater Farm housing estate riot, Tottenham, London, UK. Metropolitan Police constable Keith Blakelock was killed – the first British constable to be killed in a riot since 1833.
40	6 Oct 1985	Death of Nelson Riddle, American popular music composer and arranger. He worked with many top artists including Frank Sinatra, Nat King Cole, Dean Martin, Judy Garland, Rosemary Clooney, Peggy Lee, Johnny Mathis and Ella Fitzgerald.
40	7 Oct 1985	Palestinian terrorists seized the Italian ship *MS Achille Lauro* in the Mediterranean with about 440 passengers on board. They threatened to blow it up unless Israel freed 50 Palestinian prisoners. The killed a disabled American passenger and threw his body overboard.
40	7 Oct 1985	American basketball player Lynette Woodard became the first woman to join the Harlem Globetrotters.
40	8 Oct 1985	The musical *Les Misérables* opened at the Barbican Theatre in London, UK for its first English-language production and its first West End production.
40	9 Oct 1985	Strawberry Fields, a memorial to the British musician John Lennon (the Beatles), was dedicated in Central Park, New York City, USA.
40	9 Oct 1985	Death of Emílio Garrastazú Médici, President of Brazil (1969–74).
40	10 Oct 1985	Death of Yul Brynner, Russian-born American stage and film actor (*The King and I, The Ten Commandments, The Magnificent Seven, Westworld*, and many more).
40	10 Oct 1985	Death of Orson Welles, American stage, film and radio actor, director, writer and producer (*The War of the Worlds, Citizen Kane, The Magnificent Ambersons, Touch of Evil*, and more).
40	11 Oct 1985	Death of Tex Williams, American country/western swing singer and songwriter. Best known for the novelty song *Smoke! Smoke! Smoke! (That Cigarette)*.
40	12 Oct 1985	Death of Ricky Wilson, American rock/new wave musician and songwriter (The B-52's). (AIDS, aged 32.)
40	13 Oct 1985	Scientists at the Fermi National Accelerator Laboratory in Illinois, USA observed the first proton-antiproton collisions, using the Tevatron collider.
40	14 Oct 1985	Death of Emil Gilels, Soviet pianist. Considered one of the greatest pianists of the 20th century.
40	15 Oct 1985	IBM launched its Token Ring local area networking (LAN) system for personal computers, mid-range computers and mainframes. It was a competitor to Xerox's Ethernet system. Ethernet eventually became the industry standard.
40	17 Oct 1985	Intel launched the 80386 32-bit microprocessor, commonly known as the 386.

OCTOBER 2025

Ann.	Date	Event
40	17 Oct 1985	Britain's House of Lords ruled that doctors could prescribe contraceptives to girls aged under sixteen without parental consent. (The Gillick case.)
40	18 Oct 1985	Nintendo released the Nintendo Entertainment System (NES) in the USA. (Europe: 1st September 1986.)
40	19 Oct 1985	The first Blockbuster Video store opened, in Dallas, Texas, USA.
40	25 Oct 1985	Death of Morton Downey, American singer and entertainer. Father of the talk show host Morton Downey Jr.
40	25 Oct 1985	Death of Gary Holton, British actor and rock singer. Best known for his role as Wayne in the television comedy drama series *Auf Wiedersehen, Pet*. (Morphine/alcohol overdose, aged 32.)
40	26 Oct 1985	The Australian government returned the ownership of Uluru / Ayers Rock to the local Pitjantjatjara people, on condition that they lease it to the National Parks and Wildlife Agency for 99 years, and allow it to be jointly managed.
40	27 Oct 1985 to 1 Nov	Hurricane Juan hit Louisiana, Florida and the Mid-Atlantic U.S. states, causing devastating floods. At least twelve people were killed.
30	1 Oct 1995	Death of Margaret Gorman, American beauty queen. The first Miss America (1921).
30	3 Oct 1995	The O. J. Simpson murder trial ended. The American actor and former football star was found not guilty of killing his ex-wife Nicole Brown Simpson and her friend Ronald Goldman.
30	6 Oct 1995	The first extrasolar planet was discovered by astronomers in Geneva, Switzerland. It orbits the star 51 Pegasi, and is 47.9 light-years from Earth. Thousands of extrasolar planets have been discovered since then.
30	7 Oct 1995	Death of Louis Meyer, American racing driver. Three-times winner of the Indianapolis 500.
30	8 Oct 1995	Death of John Cairncross, British civil servant and Soviet spy. The 'fifth man' in the Cambridge spy ring. During WWII he passed the Soviet Union information that it used to win the Battle of Kursk against Germany.
30	8 Oct 1995	Death of Christopher Keene, American conductor, musician and arts administrator. Head of the New York City Opera.
30	9 Oct 1995	Death of Alec Douglas-Home, Baron Home of the Hirsel of Coldstream, British Prime Minister (1963–64).
30	9 Oct 1995	Death of John A. Scali, American television news reporter (ABC) and diplomat. He acted as an intermediary in the 1962 Cuban missile crisis, and was the U.S. Ambassador to the United Nations (1973–75).
30	10 Oct 1995	Death of John Rodolph, American athlete. The world record holder in wheelchair racing. (Hit by two trucks after they collided, aged 31.)
30	14 Oct 1995	Death of Ellis Peters (pen name of Edith Pargeter), British historical/mystery novelist. Best known for the *Brother Cadfael* series.
30	16 Oct 1995	The Million Man March took place in Washington, D.C., USA.

OCTOBER 2025

Ann.	Date	Event
30	16 Oct 1995	The Skye Bridge in Scotland opened. It connects the Isle of Skye to the mainland via the island of Eilean Bàn.
30	16 Oct 1995	Death of Linda Goodman, American astrologer and writer. Best known for her 1968 book *Linda Goodman's Sun Signs*, which achieved unprecedented success and is considered to have accelerated the growth of the New Age movement.
30	18 Oct 1995	Europe's *Astra 1E* satellite was launched. It was the first digital communications satellite in Europe, and carried the first digital television channels for the UK, France, Germany and other countries, as well as a broadband internet service. It operated until 2015.
30	19 Oct 1995	Death of Don Cherry, American jazz trumpeter. A pioneer of free jazz and world music.
30	20 Oct 1995	The Secretary General of NATO, Willy Claes, resigned after the Belgian Parliament decided he should stand trial for his role in a bribery scandal.
30	21 Oct 1995	Death of Maxene Andrews, American singer (The Andrews Sisters).
30	21 Oct 1995	Death of Shannon Hoon, American rock singer, songwriter and musician (Blind Melon). (Drug overdose, aged 28.)
30	22 Oct 1995	Death of Sir Kingsley Amis, British novelist, poet, scriptwriter, critic and teacher. Best known for his novel *Lucky Jim*. Father of the writer Martin Amis.
30	23 Oct 1995	The first court-ordered computer network wiretap. A U.S. federal judge authorised Harvard University's Faculty of Arts and Sciences to carry out electronic surveillance on its computer network after someone was suspected of hacking into it in order to break into military computers across the country. 21-year-old Julio Cesar Ardita from Argentina was convicted in March 1996. He was fined $5,000.
30	24 Oct 1995	Death of Émile Jonassaint, President of Haiti (1994 for five months).
30	25 Oct 1995	The musical *Victor/Victoria* opened on Broadway. It ran until July 1997. It was based on the 1982 musical comedy film of the same name.
30	25 Oct 1995	Death of Bobby Riggs, American tennis player. World number 1 in 1939 and 1946–47.
30	26 Oct 1995	Death of Georgia Neese Clark Gray, the first female Treasurer of the United States (1949–53).
30	26 Oct 1995	Death of Fathi Shikaki, founder and leader of the Islamic Jihad Movement in Palestine. (Assassinated by Mossad agents in Malta.)
30	27 Oct 1995	Former Italian Prime Minister Bettino Craxi was convicted (in his absence) of corruption. He was in Tunisia where he had fled to avoid a prison sentence. He remained there until his death in January 2000.
30	28 Oct 1995	Baku Metro fire, Azerbaijan. About 300 people were killed and 265 injured in the world's deadliest subway fire. It was blamed on an electrical fault caused by outdated equipment, but some commentators say it was sabotage.

OCTOBER 2025

Ann.	Date	Event
30	29 Oct 1995	Death of Terry Southern, American satirical novelist, screenwriter and educator. Noted for his work on films including *Dr. Strangelove*, *The Cincinnati Kid*, *Barbarella* and *Easy Rider*.
30	30 Oct 1995	Quebec independence referendum. The citizens of Quebec narrowly voted to remain part of Canada.
30	31 Oct 1995	Death of Rosalind Cash, American singer and stage, film and television actress. Best known for her roles as Lisa in the science fiction film *The Omega Man* and Mary Mae Ward in the soap opera *General Hospital*.
30	31 Oct 1995	Death of Sir Wallace Edward (Bill) Rowling, Prime Minister of New Zealand (1974–75).
25	1 Oct 2000	Death of Reginald ('Reggie') Kray, British gangster (the Kray twins).
25	3 Oct 2000	Death of Benjamin Orr, American rock bassist and singer (the Cars).
25	4 Oct 2000	Death of Yu Kuo-hwa, Premier of the Republic of China (1984–89)
25	7 Oct 2000	Vojislav Koštunica became President of Yugoslavia (until 2003) after beating Slobodan Milošević in a run-off election. Milošević had disputed the results of the presidential election, held on 24th September, and declared a run-off, leading to mass protests. Koštunica became Prime Minister of Serbia in 2004.
25	7 Oct 2000	The last football match was played at the old Wembley Stadium in London, UK. The match was a 2002 World Cup qualifying game between England and Germany. The stadium was closed after the match and demolished in 2003. The new Wembley Stadium opened on the same site in 2007.
25	10 Oct 2000	Death of Sirimavo Bandaranaike, Prime Minister of Sri Lanka (1960–65, 1970–77, 1994–2000). The world's first female prime minister.
25	11 Oct 2000	Death of Donald Dewar, Scottish politician. First Minister of Scotland (1999–2000).
25	12 Oct 2000	The American destroyer *USS Cole* was badly damaged in Aden, Yemen, when two suicide bombers rammed the ship in a boat laden with explosives. Seventeen crew members were killed. The bombers were members of the terrorist organisation Al-Qaeda.
25	15 Oct 2000	Death of Konrad Emil Bloch, German-born American biochemist. Joint winner of the 1964 Nobel Prize in Physiology or Medicine for his discoveries relating to the regulation and synthesis of cholesterol and fatty acids.
25	17 Oct 2000	Hatfield rail crash, Hertfordshire, UK. A high-speed passenger train derailed because of a cracked rail. Four people were killed. The spiralling cost of the subsequent national rail replacement programme forced the railway infrastructure organisation Railtrack into administration.
25	18 Oct 2000	Death of Julie London, American singer and actress.
25	22 Oct 2000	The U.S. première of the action-comedy film *Charlie's Angels*. (Released 3rd November. UK première: 22nd November, released: 24th November.)

OCTOBER 2025

Ann.	Date	Event
25	26 Oct 2000	Laurent Gbagbo became President of the Ivory Coast (until 2010/11) following a popular uprising against the military ruler Robert Guéï.
25	26 Oct 2000	The BSE Inquiry Report (also known as the Phillips Report) was published in the UK. It concluded that the BSE (mad cow disease) epidemic was caused by the use of infected meat and bone meal in cattle feed. It criticised agriculture officials, scientists and government ministers, who it said had misled the public.
25	26 Oct 2000	Sony's Playstation 2 video games console was released in North America. (Japan: 4th March. Australia: 17th November. Europe: 24th November.)
25	30 Oct 2000	Death of Steve Allen, American television entertainer, comedian, writer, composer and pianist. The host of several game shows and talk shows, and the first host of *The Tonight Show*. He composed more than 14,000 songs.
25	31 Oct 2000	Russia launched its *Soyuz TM-31* spacecraft, carrying the first resident crew to the International Space Station (ISS). It docked with the ISS on 2nd November.
25	31 Oct 2000	Death of Ring Lardner Jr., American screenwriter. He was blacklisted by Hollywood during the Red Scare of the 1940s and 50s.
20	1 Oct 2005	Bali bombings, Indonesia. Terrorists attacked tourist areas of Bali using suicide bombers and car bombs. 23 people were killed (including three bombers) and more than 100 injured.
20	2 Oct 2005	*Ethan Allen* boating accident, Lake George, New York, USA. Twenty people were killed when the overloaded tour boat capsized.
20	2 Oct 2005	Death of Nipsey Russell, American comedian and actor. Best known for his many appearances as a panellist on television game shows. Noted for his humorous poems, which he recited on each show.
20	3 Oct 2005	Death of Ronnie Barker, British television comedian, actor and writer (*The Frost Report, The Two Ronnies, Porridge, Going Straight, Open All Hours*).
20	7 Oct 2005	Death of Charles Rocket, American film and television actor. Best known as a cast member on *Saturday Night Live* and for his roles as Nicholas Andre in the film *Dumb and Dumber* and Dave Dennison in the Disney film *Hocus Pocus*.
20	8 Oct 2005	Kashmir earthquake. The earthquake affected Kashmir, Pakistan, India, Afghanistan, western China and Tajikistan. About 100,000 people were killed, 138,000 injured and 3.5 million made homeless.
20	10 Oct 2005	Death of Milton Obote, President of Uganda (1966–71, 1980–85).
20	12 Oct 2005	The European Union (EU) agreed to legally require telecommunications companies to retain records of phone and email traffic for one year. The law was introduced as part of the EU's anti-terrorism campaign, particularly in response to the London bombings on 7th and 21st July 2005.
20	12 Oct 2005	The Large Binocular Telescope at Mount Graham International Observatory in Arizona, USA saw first light. It became fully operational in January 2008.

OCTOBER 2025

Ann.	Date	Event
20	17 Oct 2005	The first episode of the late-night television talk show *The Colbert Report* was broadcast on Comedy Central in the USA.
20	17 Oct 2005	Death of Ba Jin (pen name of Li Yaotang), Chinese anarchist novelist and short story writer. One of the most widely read Chinese writers of the 20th century.
20	18 Oct 2005 to 26th	Hurricane Wilma, the most intense Atlantic hurricane ever recorded, hit the Caribbean, Central America and the eastern USA. 63 people were killed. It caused massive damage worth $29 billion (£18.1 billion).
20	19 Oct 2005	The former President of Iraq, Saddam Hussein, went on trial in Baghdad for crimes against humanity. He was convicted on 5th November 2006, sentenced to death, and hanged on 30th December 2006.
20	22 Oct 2005 to 24th	Tropical Storm Alpha hit the Dominican Republic and Haiti. 26 people were killed. It was the first tropical storm to be given a letter from the Greek alphabet because all the designated names for that year had been used. 2005 was the most-active Atlantic hurricane season on record.
20	22 Oct 2005	Busch Memorial Stadium in St. Louis, Missouri, USA closed down. It was demolished in November-December. The new Busch Stadium opened on part of the same site in April 2006.
20	22 Oct 2005	Death of Tony Adams, Irish stage and film producer. Best known for producing six *Pink Panther* films, the film *10*, and the film and Broadway musical *Victor/Victoria*.
20	24 Oct 2005	Death of José Azcona del Hoyo, President of Honduras (1986–90).
20	24 Oct 2005	Death of Rosa Parks, American civil rights activist. She famously refused to give up her bus seat to a white man, which led to the Montgomery bus boycott in Alabama in 1955–56.
20	28 Oct 2005	Scooter Libby, chief of staff to U.S. Vice-President Dick Cheney, was indicted for interfering with the criminal investigation of the Plame affair. He immediately resigned. In March 2007 he was convicted of perjury, obstruction of justice, and making false statements. He was sentenced to 30 months in prison (later commuted) and fined $250,000.
20	28 Oct 2005	Iran's first satellite, *Sina-1* (a reconnaissance satellite) was launched.
20	28 Oct 2005	Death of Richard Smalley, American chemist, physicist and educator. Joint winner of the 1996 Nobel Prize in Chemistry for co-discovering buckminsterfullerene (C60) – a new form of carbon.
20	29 Oct 2005	Delhi bombings, India. 62 people were killed and over 200 injured when Kashmir separatist/Islamist terrorists exploded bombs at two markets and on a bus.
15	1 Oct 2010	Sky TV launched Sky 3D in the UK. It was the first dedicated 3D television channel in Europe. It closed down in June 2015.
15	6 Oct 2010	Instagram, the photo- and video-sharing social networking service was launched. It was acquired by Facebook (now Meta) in April 2012.

OCTOBER 2025

Ann.	Date	Event
15	13 Oct 2010	33 Chilean miners who had been trapped underground for 69 days following the collapse of the San José copper–gold mine were rescued. Around 1 billion TV viewers around the world watched them being pulled to the surface one-by-one in a specially designed capsule.
15	17 Oct 2010	The Chancellor of Germany, Angela Merkel, said attempts to build a multicultural society in Germany had 'failed utterly'.
15	17 Oct 2010	Australia's first saint, Mary MacKillop, was canonised by Pope Benedict XVI. She became Saint Mary of the Cross.
10	3 Oct 2015	Death of Denis Healey, British politician. Chancellor of the Exchequer (1974–79), Secretary of State for Defence (1964–70).
10	5 Oct 2015	Death of Henning Mankell, Swedish crime novelist, children's writer, playwright and screenwriter. Best known for his series of novels featuring Inspector Kurt Wallander.
10	6 Oct 2015	Death of Árpád Göncz, first President of Hungary (1990–2000).
10	8 Oct 2015	Death of Paul Prudhomme, American celebrity chef, restaurateur and cookbook writer. Known for popularising Cajun and Louisiana Creole cuisine.
10	9 Oct 2015	Death of Geoffrey Howe, British Conservative politician. A leading figure in Margaret Thatcher's cabinet. Chancellor of the Exchequer (1979–83), Foreign Secretary (1983–89), Deputy Prime Minister and Leader of the House of Commons (1989–90).
10	21 Oct 2015	Death of Michael Meacher, British Labour politician. He served various roles in the cabinets of Harold Wilson, James Callaghan and Tony Blair, including Environment Secretary (1997–2003).
10	22 Oct 2015 to 24th	Hurricane Patricia struck the Pacific coast of Mexico. Eight people were killed, plus a further five indirectly, and it caused more than $450 million worth of damage. It produced the lowest sea-level air pressure ever recorded in the Western Hemisphere, and the second-lowest globally (872 millibars, 25.75 inHg).
10	24 Oct 2015	Death of Maureen O'Hara, Irish-born American film actress and singer. One of the last surviving stars of Hollywood's Golden Age. Noted for her portrayals of wilful women.
10	26 Oct 2015	October 2015 Hindu Kush earthquake, South Asia. The earthquake affected Afghanistan, India and Pakistan. At least 399 people were killed and 2,536 injured – mostly in Pakistan.

NOVEMBER 2025

Ann.	Date	Event
500	17 Nov 1525	Death of Eleanor of Viseu, Queen consort of Portugal (1481–95). Wife of King John II of Portugal.
400	1 Nov 1625	Birth of Saint Oliver Plunkett, Irish archbishop, martyr and saint. Archbishop of Armagh and Primate of All Ireland. The last victim of the Popish Plot. Executed for treason in 1681 for promoting the Catholic faith. Canonised in 1975 – the first new Irish saint for nearly 700 years.
250	7 Nov 1775	American Revolutionary War: Dunmore's Proclamation. John Murray, the 4th Earl of Dunmore (also known as Lord Dunmore), Governor of the Province of Virginia, issued a proclamation declaring martial law and offering freedom to any male slaves who left their provincial masters and joined the British Army. Between 800 and 2,000 slaves are reported to have taken up his offer.
250	10 Nov 1775	The Continental Marines was established in Philadelphia, Pennsylvania. It became the United States Marine Corps in 1798.
250	12 Nov 1775	General George Washington declared that negroes, children and old men were forbidden from enlisting in the Continental Army.
250	13 Nov 1775	American Revolutionary War: U.S. forces captured Montreal in Canada.
250	17 Nov 1775 to 25 Jan 1776	American Revolutionary War – the noble train of artillery (also known as the Knox Expedition). Continental Army Colonel Henry Knox led a 70-day expedition to collect sixty tons of British heavy weapons that had been captured at Fort Ticonderoga, New York in May. He reached the Fort on 5th December, then transported the weapons to Continental Army camps near Boston, Massachusetts. The weapons were used in the Fortification of Dorchester Heights in March 1776, as a result of which the British were forced to withdraw from Boston.
250	29 Nov 1775	American Revolutionary War: the Second Continental Congress established the Committee of Secret Correspondence. Its stated aim was to correspond with 'our friends in Great Britain and other parts of the world'. But it put most of its resources into forging alliances with other European countries that would be sympathetic to the North Americans' cause.
200	4 Nov 1825	The Wedding of the Waters. Following the opening of the Erie Canal on 26th October 1825, the Governor of New York, DeWitt Clinton, made the ten-day journey to New York Harbor. When his boat anchored off Sandy Hook, he poured a barrel of water from Lake Erie into the Atlantic Ocean to celebrate the Wedding of the Waters.
200	6 Nov 1825	Birth of Charles Garnier, French architect. Best known for the Palais Garnier opera house in Paris, France and the Opéra de Monte-Carlo opera house in Monaco.
200	26 Nov 1825	The oldest still-existing college fraternity, Kappa Alpha, was founded at Union College in Schenectady, New York, USA.

NOVEMBER 2025

Ann.	Date	Event
200	29 Nov 1825	The first opera to be performed in Italian in the USA: Rossini's *The Barber of Seville*, at the Park Theatre in New York City.
175	13 Nov 1850	Birth of Robert Louis Stevenson, Scottish novelist, poet and travel writer. Best known for his novels *Treasure Island*, *The Strange Case of Dr Jekyll and Mr Hyde*, and *Kidnapped*.
175	16 Nov 1850	Death of George Wombwell, British menagerie proprietor. Founder of Wombwell's Travelling Menagerie, which was famous in Britain during the Regency and early Victorian eras.
175	19 Nov 1850	Alfred, Lord Tennyson became Poet Laureate of the UK (until 1892).
175	19 Nov 1850	American inventor Frederick Langenheim was granted the first U.S. patent for magic lantern slides made of glass. (U.S. Patent 7,784.)
175	19 Nov 1850	Death of Richard Mentor Johnson, Vice President of the United States (1837–41).
150	16 Nov 1875	Ethiopian–Egyptian War – the Battle of Gundet. Egyptian forces invaded Ethiopia, but they were vastly outnumbered and swiftly repelled by the Ethiopians.
150	19 Nov 1875	Birth of Mikhail Kalinin, Head of State of Russia (1919–38) and the Soviet Union (1938–46).
150	22 Nov 1875	Death of Henry Wilson, Vice President of the United States (1873–75 died in office). The vice presidency remained vacant until March 1877.
125	3 Nov 1900 to 9th	The first major automobile show in the USA was held at Madison Square Garden in New York City.
125	3 Nov 1900	Birth of Adolf 'Adi' Dassler, German businessman. Founder of the sportswear and sporting equipment company Adidas. His brother Rudolf founded the rival company Puma after a family feud.
125	6 Nov 1900	Second Boer War – the Battle of Bothaville. British victory.
125	7 Nov 1900	Second Boer War – the Battle of Leliefontein. A tactical victory for the Boers, and the British–Canadian forces were forced to withdraw. A Canadian rear-guard unit repelled several Boer assaults, allowing for a successful withdrawal. Three members of the Royal Canadian Dragoons were awarded the Victoria Cross for their actions.
125	8 Nov 1900	Birth of Margaret Mitchell, American novelist and journalist. Known for her only novel, *Gone with the Wind*. (She was killed in 1949 when she was hit by a car.)
125	8 Nov 1900	Birth of Charlie Paddock, American athlete. 2x gold medallist at the 1920 Olympics (100 m and 4 x 100 m relay).
125	14 Nov 1900	Birth of Aaron Copland, American composer, conductor and educator. His best-known works include *Appalachian Spring* and *Fanfare for the Common Man*.
125	20 Nov 1900	Birth of Chester Gould, American cartoonist. Creator of the *Dick Tracy* comic strip.

NOVEMBER 2025

Ann.	Date	Event
125	22 Nov 1900	Death of Arthur Sullivan, British composer. Best known for his collaborations with the dramatist W. S. Gilbert on operas including *H.M.S. Pinafore*, *The Pirates of Penzance* and *The Mikado*. He also wrote the hymn *Onward, Christian Soldiers*.
125	29 Nov 1900	Birth of Mildred Gillars, ('Axis Sally'), American radio broadcaster of Nazi propaganda during WWII. She was captured in Germany after the war and became the first person to be convicted of treason against the USA. She served 12 years in prison.
125	30 Nov 1900	Death of Oscar Wilde, Irish playwright, short story writer and poet. Known for his novel *The Picture of Dorian Gray*, his play *The Importance of Being Earnest*, and his poem *The Ballad of Reading Gaol*. He was convicted of gross indecency (homosexual acts) and served two years in prison. (Meningitis, aged 46.)
100	10 Nov 1925	Birth of Richard Burton, Welsh stage and film actor (*Cleopatra*, *Who's Afraid of Virginia Woolf?*, *The Taming of the Shrew*, and many more). Fifth and sixth husband of the actress Elizabeth Taylor. (Died 1984.)
100	11 Nov 1925	Birth of June Whitfield, English radio, television and film actress. She appeared in numerous sitcoms including *Beggar My Neighbour*, *Happy Ever After*, *Terry and June*, *Absolutely Fabulous*, *Last of the Summer Wine*, and four *Carry On…* films. (Died 2018.)
100	11 Nov 1925	Birth of Jonathan Winters, American comedian, actor, writer, artist and television host. He appeared in hundreds of TV shows and films, and was known for playing eccentric characters. (Died 2013.)
100	13 Nov 1925	The world's first exhibition of Surrealist art opened at Galerie Pierre in Paris, France. It included works by Max Ernst, Joan Miró, Pablo Picasso and Man Ray.
100	17 Nov 1925	Birth of Rock Hudson, American film and television actor. One of the most popular film stars of his era. The first major celebrity to die from AIDS. (Died 1985.)
100	20 Nov 1925	Birth of Robert F. ('Bobby') Kennedy, American politician, U.S. Attorney General (1961–64). Senator from New York (1965–68). Brother of President John F. Kennedy. (Assassinated 1968.)
100	20 Nov 1925	Death of Queen Alexandra of the United Kingdom, Empress of India. Queen consort of King Edward VII (1901–10). Formerly Princess Alexandra of Denmark (1844–63) and Princess of Wales (1863–1901).
100	22 Nov 1925	Birth of Jerrie Mock, American aviator. The first woman to fly solo around the world (1964). (Died 2014.)
100	23 Nov 1925	The world première of British playwright Noël Coward's play *Easy Virtue*, in Newark, New Jersey, USA. It opened on Broadway in December.
100	23 Nov 1925	Birth of José Napoleón Duarte, President of El Salvador (1984–89). (Died 1990.)
100	24 Nov 1925	The Eugene O'Neill Theatre, a Broadway theatre, opened in New York City, USA (as the Forrest Theatre, later known as the Coronet Theatre).

NOVEMBER 2025

Ann.	Date	Event
100	24 Nov 1925	Birth of William F. Buckley Jr., American writer, publisher, intellectual, and host of the public affairs television show *Firing Line*. Founder of *National Review* magazine. (Died 2008.)
100	27 Nov 1925	Birth of Ernie Wise, British television comedian and actor. Best known for his comedy partnership with Eric Morecambe (Morecambe and Wise). (Died 1999.)
100	28 Nov 1925	The first Grand Ole Opry country music concert was held in Nashville, Tennessee, USA, and also broadcast on the radio.
90	3 Nov 1935	The Greek monarchy was restored and King George II regained the throne. Greece had been a republic since 1924. The monarchy was abolished again in 1973.
90	5 Nov 1935	The board game Monopoly was launched by Parker Brothers. Its inventor, Charles Darrow, was awarded a U.S. Patent for it design on 31st December. (U.S. Patent 2,026,082.) He assigned it to Parker Brothers.
90	6 Nov 1935	American electrical engineer Edwin H. Armstrong announced his development of FM radio broadcasting. He presented his paper 'A Method of Reducing Disturbances in Radio Signaling by a System of Frequency Modulation' to the New York section of the Institute of Radio Engineers.
90	6 Nov 1935	Britain's Hawker Hurricane fighter plane made its first flight. It played a major role in WWII, especially during the Battle of Britain.
90	7 Nov 1935	The Royal National Institute for the Blind (RNIB) in the UK launched the first Talking Books (specially adapted gramophone records and players). Each record played for 25 minutes per side, and the average novel would fit onto ten records. Each set was returned to the RNIB after it had been played, and it was then sent out to another subscriber.
90	9 Nov 1935	The Congress of Industrial Organizations (CIO), a federation of trade unions, was founded in the USA. In 1955 it joined with the American Federation of Labor (AFL) and became the American Federation of Labor and Congress of Industrial Organizations (AFL–CIO).
90	12 Nov 1935	Portuguese neurologist (António) Egas Moniz performed the world's first leukotomy (also called a lobotomy) on a mentally ill patient at the Hospital Santa Marta in Lisbon. He declared the procedure a success and the patient cured – though she was never discharged from the hospital. He was awarded the 1949 Nobel Prize in Physiology or Medicine for his work – though the award is considered controversial.
90	13 Nov 1935	Anti-British riots broke out in Egypt. Two people were killed and 175 injured.
90	14 Nov 1935	Holocaust: the Nazis began implementing the Nuremburg Laws, stripping German Jews of their German citizenship. The laws were extended to cover gypsies and negroes on 26th November.
90	14 Nov 1935	Birth of Hussein, King of Jordan (1952–99).
90	15 Nov 1935	The Commonwealth of the Philippines was established. It governed the Philippines until 1946 when it gained its full independence from the USA. Manuel L. Quezon became President (until 1944).

NOVEMBER 2025

Ann.	Date	Event
90	20 Nov 1935	Death of John Rushworth Jellicoe, 1st Earl Jellicoe, British admiral of the fleet. He commanded the Grand Fleet at the Battle of Jutland during WWI.
90	22 Nov 1935	The first Trans-Pacific airmail service began as the Pan American flying boat *China Clipper* left San Francisco, California, USA for Manila in the Philippines.
90	23 Nov 1935	American polar explorer Lincoln Ellsworth discovered the Ellsworth Mountains – the highest mountain ranges in Antarctica.
90	23 Nov 1935	Birth of Vladislav Volkov, Soviet cosmonaut who flew on the *Soyuz 7* and *Soyuz 11* missions. He and his two colleagues were found dead in their capsule when *Soyuz 11* returned to Earth in June 1971. (Cause: decompression due to a hatch being improperly closed.)
80	1 Nov 1945	The North Korean daily newspaper *Rodong Sinmun* (meaning: Workers' Newspaper) was first published (as *Chongro*). It is the official newspaper of the Central Committee of the Workers' Party of Korea.
80	1 Nov 1945	The first issue of *Ebony*, an African American-focused monthly magazine, was published in the USA.
80	1 Nov 1945	Happy Chandler became the 2nd Commissioner of Baseball in the USA.
80	6 Nov 1945	The first jet-powered plane (a Ryan FR-1 Fireball) to land on an aircraft carrier (the *USS Wake Island*), in San Diego, California, USA.
80	11 Nov 1945	Death of Jerome Kern, American composer. Known for his musical comedies and film music.
80	16 Nov 1945	UNESCO, the United Nations Educational, Scientific and Cultural Organisation, was founded.
80	18 Nov 1945	Birth of Wilma Mankiller, American tribal leader, social worker and activist. The first female Principal Chief of the Cherokee Nation (1985–95). (Died 2010.)
80	20 Nov 1945	Russian composer Dmitri Shostakovich's *Symphony No. 9* (Opus 70) was performed for the first time, in Leningrad. It was intended to celebrate the Soviet Union's victory over Germany in WWII, but it was not well received as its light mood failed to reflect the character of the war or the spirit of the people.
80	21 Nov 1945	Russian composer Sergei Prokofiev's ballet *Cinderella* (Opus 87) was performed for the first time, in Moscow.
80	23 Nov 1945 to 1 Oct 1946	The first Nuremberg trial was held in Germany. 23 of the most important political and military leaders of the Third Reich were tried for war crimes. Twelve of the defendants were sentenced to death, and ten were executed on 16th October 1946. (The other two were already dead.)
80	23 Nov 1945	Wartime food rationing ended in the USA.
80	23 Nov 1945	Birth of Tony Pond, British rally driver. (Died 2002.)

NOVEMBER 2025

Ann.	Date	Event
80	27 Nov 1945	Care International was founded (as CARE – the Cooperative for American Remittances to Europe, later renamed the Cooperative for Assistance and Relief Everywhere). It was originally intended to be a temporary organisation to send food packages to Europe following the end of WWII.
80	29 Nov 1945	Yugoslavia abolished its monarchy and became the Federal People's Republic of Yugoslavia.
75	1 Nov 1950	The attempted assassination of U.S. President Harry S. Truman by two Puerto Rican nationalists from the Armed Forces of National Liberation (FALN), in Washington, D.C. The President was not hurt.
75	1 Nov 1950	Pope Pius XII dogmatically defined the doctrine of the Assumption of the Virgin Mary into Heaven (commonly known as The Assumption).
75	1 Nov 1950	Basketball player Chuck Cooper became the first African American to play in the NBA (for the Boston Celtics).
75	2 Nov 1950	Death of George Bernard Shaw, Irish playwright and literary critic. Best known for *Pygmalion*. Winner of the 1925 Nobel Prize in Literature. Co-founder of the London School of Economics. The only person to win both an Academy Award and the Nobel Prize in Literature.
75	8 Nov 1950 ?	Korean War: the first all-jet aerial dogfight in history took place, with U.S. jets taking on North Korea's Chinese-supplied MiG-15s. (Some sources report that the first all-jet dogfight took place a week earlier on 1st November.)
75	13 Nov 1950 to 16th	The first contract bridge world championship – the Bermuda Bowl – was held at the Castle Harbor Hotel in Bermuda. Teams from the USA, UK and Europe entered, and the USA won. The competition continues to run in odd-numbered years.
75	13 Nov 1950	Death of Carlos Delgado Chalbaud, President of Venezuela (1948–50). (Assassinated.)
75	15 Nov 1950	Arthur Dorrington became the first African American to join a professional ice hockey team (the Atlantic City Seagulls).
75	16 Nov 1950	Death of Bob Smith, American physician and surgeon. Co-founder of Alcoholics Anonymous.
75	17 Nov 1950	Tenzin Gyatso, aged 15, was enthroned as the 14th Dalai Lama.
75	22 Nov 1950	Kew Gardens train crash, Queens, New York City, USA. Two commuter trains collided on the Long Island Railroad's Main Line. 79 people were killed and 363 injured. (Cause: the train in front had broken down with seized brakes. A misunderstanding meant that the rear of the train was left unlit. The driver of the following train misread signs and failed to see the stationary train until the last second, colliding with it at 30 mph.)
75	22 Nov 1950	The lowest-scoring game in the NBA (National Basketball Association) in the USA. The Fort Wayne Pistons (later the Detroit Pistons) beat the Minneapolis Lakers (later the Los Angeles Lakers) 19–18 – a combined total of 37 points.

NOVEMBER 2025

Ann.	Date	Event
75	24 Nov 1950	The Great Appalachian Storm (also known as The Great Thanksgiving Storm or the Storm of the Century) hit eastern USA and Canada. More than 300 people were killed.
75	24 Nov 1950	Korean War: U.S. forces launched the Home-by-Christmas Offensive. It failed and they were forced to retreat. The war continued until July 1953. (See also: 25th November 1950.)
75	24 Nov 1950	The musical *Guys and Dolls* opened on Broadway.
75	25 Nov 1950 to 2 Dec	Korean War – the Battle of the Ch'ongch'on River, North Korea. China launched its first counter-offensive of the war against the UN and Allied forces, forcing them to retreat from North Korea. Chinese victory.
70	1 Nov 1955	Vietnam War: the first official U.S. involvement in the war. U.S. President Dwight D. Eisenhower deployed the Military Assistance Advisory Group to train the Army of the Republic of Vietnam (South Vietnam).
70	1 Nov 1955	United Airlines Flight 629 exploded over Longmont, Colorado, USA. All 39 passengers and five crew were killed. (Cause: a bomb planted in the suitcase of one of the passengers by her son, who wanted to kill her for the insurance money. Jack Gilbert Graham was convicted in May 1956 and executed in January 1957.)
70	1 Nov 1955	Death of Dale Carnegie, American writer and lecturer. Known for his courses on self-improvement, salesmanship and the psychology of success. Best known for his book *How to Win Friends and Influence People*.
70	3 Nov 1955	David Ben-Gurion became Prime Minister of Israel for the second time.
70	3 Nov 1955	The U.S. première of the musical film *Guys and Dolls*. (Released: 23rd December. UK première: 20th September 1956.)
70	4 Nov 1955	Death of Cy Young, American baseball player.
70	5 Nov 1955	The Vienna State Opera reopened in Austria. The original building was demolished and rebuilt after being severely damaged by U.S. incendiary bombs during WWII.
70	5 Nov 1955	Death of Maurice Utrillo, French artist. Known for his street scenes of the Montmartre quarter of Paris.
70	12 Nov 1955	Birth of Les McKeown, Scottish pop/rock singer. Lead singer of the Bay City Rollers. (Died 2021.)
70	12 Nov 1955	Death of Alfréd Hajós, Hungarian swimmer and architect. The first Olympic swimming champion (1896).
70	13 Nov 1955	Pedro Aramburu became President of Argentina (until 1958). He was a major figure in the military coup that had ousted Juan Perón in June.
70	15 Nov 1955	The Saint Petersburg Metro in Russia opened.
70	15 Nov 1955	Death of Lloyd Bacon, American actor and film director who made films in almost every genre. His films include *42nd Street*, *A Slight Case of Murder*, *The Oklahoma Kid*, *Knute Rockne: All American*, and *It Happens Every Spring*.

NOVEMBER 2025

Ann.	Date	Event
70	18 Nov 1955	The Bell X-2 experimental rocket plane made its first powered flight.
70	19 Nov 1955	The first issue of the conservative magazine *National Review* was published in the USA.
70	20 Nov 1955	American rock and roll singer Bo Diddley made his national television debut on *The Ed Sullivan Show* in the USA, and became the first African American to appear on the show. He was supposed to perform the song *Sixteen Tons*, but when he saw the words 'Bo Diddley' on a cue card, he performed his self-titled song *Bo Diddley* as well – reportedly infuriating Sullivan.
70	20 Nov 1955	Death of Tomasz Arciszewski, Prime Minister of the Polish Government in Exile (1944–47).
70	21 Nov 1955	RCA Victor acquired Elvis Presley's recording contract with Sun Records for $40,000. (Elvis's father signed the contract, as Elvis was under 21.)
70	22 Nov 1955	Death of Shemp Howard, American actor and comedian (The Three Stooges).
70	23 Nov 1955	Control of the Cocos (Keeling) Islands in the Indian Ocean was transferred from the UK to Australia.
70	25 Nov 1955	Civil Rights: the U.S. Interstate Commerce Commission banned the segregation of black passengers travelling on buses that crossed state lines.
70	25 Nov 1955	Former British Prime Minister Clement Atlee retired as leader of the Labour Party. He was succeeded by Hugh Gaitskell (on 14th December).
70	26 Nov 1955	A state of emergency was declared in Cyprus following an uprising against British rule. (Cyprus gained its independence in October 1960.)
70	27 Nov 1955	Death of Arthur Honegger, French-Swiss composer. Best known for his orchestral work *Pacific 231*.
65	1 Nov 1960	The Benelux Customs Union (made up of Belgium, the Netherlands and Luxembourg) was superseded by the Benelux Economic Union.
65	2 Nov 1960	A British jury cleared Penguin Books of obscenity for publishing D. H. Lawrence's novel *Lady Chatterley's Lover*. This is often considered the beginning of the permissive society in Britain.
65	3 Nov 1960	Félix Houphouët-Boigny became the first President of the Ivory Coast. He remained in office until 1993.
65	3 Nov 1960	The musical *The Unsinkable Molly Brown* opened on Broadway. It ran until February 1962. It was adapted into a film in 1964.
65	5 Nov 1960	Death of Mack Sennett, Canadian-born American comedy film producer and director during the silent era. Best known for the *Keystone Kops* series.
65	8 Nov 1960	John F. Kennedy was elected as the 35th President of the USA. (Inaugurated 4th March 1961. Assassinated 22nd November 1963.)
65	15 Nov 1960	Inventors from Union Carbide in Ohio, USA were granted a U.S. patent for the alkaline dry-cell battery. (U.S. Patent 2,960,558.) The team was led by Austrian chemist Karl Kordesch, who had moved to the USA as part of Operation Paperclip at the end of WWII. The battery became the Eveready Energizer D-sized battery.

NOVEMBER 2025

Ann.	Date	Event
65	16 Nov 1960	British engineer Christopher Cockerell was granted a British patent for his invention of the hovercraft. (British Patent 854,211.)
65	16 Nov 1960	Death of Clark Gable, American film actor. Best known for his role as Rhett Butler in *Gone with the Wind*.
65	19 Nov 1960	Birth of Miss Elizabeth, American professional wrestler, wrestling manager and television announcer. (Died 2003.)
65	24 Nov 1960	Death of Grand Duchess Olga Alexandrovna of Russia. Daughter of Emperor Alexander III of Russia. Sister of Emperor Nicholas II.
65	25 Nov 1960	The Mirabal sisters (Patria, Miverva and Maria Teresa) were assassinated in the Dominican Republic for opposing Rafael Trujillo's dictatorship. They became symbols of the resistance. In 1999 the United Nations designated 25th November as the International Day for the Elimination of Violence against Women.
65	25 Nov 1960	Birth of John F. Kennedy Jr., American lawyer, journalist, and magazine publisher. Son of U.S. President John F. Kennedy. (Killed in a plane crash in 1999.)
65	28 Nov 1960	Mauritania gained its independence from France.
60	2 Nov 1965	American Quaker Norman Morrison set himself on fire outside the Pentagon to protest against the USA's involvement in the Vietnam War. Roger Allen LaPorte, a member of the Catholic Worker Movement, did the same thing outside the United Nations building in New York City on 9th November. They both died.
60	4 Nov 1965	American racing driver Lee Breedlove became the first woman to exceed 300 mph. She drove her husband's car *Spirit Of America – Sonic 1* at 308.56 mph at Bonneville Salt Flats in Utah. Her husband, Craig Breedlove, broke the land speed record several times and was the first person to exceed 500 mph and 600 mph.
60	5 Nov 1965 to 8th	Vietnam War – Operation Hump. U.S. and Australian forces launched a search and destroy mission to drive out Viet Cong from their positions on key hills north of Bien Hoa. Allied victory. The mission included the Battle of Gang Toi, in which Australian forces were forced to withdraw after a fierce battle, as they lacked sufficient combat power to launch an assault.
60	6 Nov 1965	Freedom Flights between Cuba and the USA began. The USA began airlifting Cuban refugees to Miami, Florida. The flights ended in 1973, by which time 300,000 Cubans had been relocated. (Little Havana in Miami was established as a result of this.)
60	7 Nov 1965	The Pillsbury Doughboy (also known as Poppin' Fresh) made his first appearance in a U.S. television commercial for the Pillsbury Company.
60	8 Nov 1965	The British Indian Ocean Territory (also known as the Chagos Islands) was established as a joint military facility of the UK and USA.
60	8 Nov 1965	The first episode of the television soap opera *Days of Our Lives* was broadcast on NBC in the USA.

NOVEMBER 2025

Ann.	Date	Event
60	9 Nov 1965	The death penalty was abolished in the United Kingdom.
60	9 Nov 1965	The Northeast blackout of 1965 – the biggest power failure in U.S. history. More than 30 million people were left without power for thirteen hours in New York state, parts of seven neighbouring states, and eastern Canada. (Cause: a circuit breaker tripped at a power plant on the Niagara River and sent a chain reaction of power surges down the line to other power plants along the east coast.)
60	10 Nov 1965	The Manneken Pis statue in Brussels, Belgium was stolen. A replica now stands in its place. The original was later recovered but it was damaged. It was restored and is now kept at the Maison du Roi (King's House).
60	11 Nov 1965	Rhodesia (now Zimbabwe) issued a Unilateral Declaration of Independence from Britain. The move was widely condemned, and the United Nations imposed economic sanctions on 20th November.
60	12 Nov 1965	The Soviet Union launched its *Venera 2* space probe to Venus. It flew past Venus in February 1966 but failed to return any data. It was declared lost in March. (See also: 16th November 1965.)
60	14 Nov 1965 to 18th	Vietnam War – Operation Silver Bayonet – the Battle of the Ia Drang. The first major battle between regular U.S. Army forces and the North Vietnamese. One of the first battles where the U.S. used body-count to measure success. Result: inconclusive – both sides claimed victory.
60	15 Nov 1965	American racing driver Craig Breedlove set a new land speed record of 600.601 mph, becoming the first person to reach 600 mph. He was also the first person to reach 400 mph and 500 mph.
60	15 Nov 1965	Walt Disney announced the Experimental Prototype Community of Tomorrow (EPCOT). It was planned to be a real city in Florida, USA that would be a 'living blueprint of the future'. The project was abandoned after Disney's death the following year.
60	16 Nov 1965	The Soviet Union launched its *Venera 3* space probe to Venus. It is thought to have crashed on Venus in March 1966 – its communications system had failed prior to its arrival.
60	18 Nov 1965	Death of Henry A. Wallace, Vice President of the United States (1941–45).
60	23 Nov 1965	Death of Elisabeth of Bavaria, Queen consort of Belgium (1909–34). Wife of King Albert I. Mother of King Leopold III of Belgium and Queen Marie-José of Italy.
60	24 Nov 1965	Mobuto Sese Seko became President of the Democratic Republic of the Congo after seizing power in a coup. He renamed the country Zaire in 1971. He was a notoriously corrupt ruler and embezzled billions of dollars of public funds for his personal use. He was overthrown in 1997, and the country reverted to its previous name.
60	24 Nov 1965	Death of Abdullah III, the last Sheikh and first Emir of Kuwait (1950–65).
60	25 Nov 1965	Death of Dame Myra Hess, British pianist.
60	26 Nov 1965	France became the world's third space power when it successfully launched its first satellite *Astérix* into orbit from Algeria.

NOVEMBER 2025

Ann.	Date	Event
60	27 Nov 1965	Vietnam War – the 'More Flags' programme. U.S. President Lyndon B. Johnson called on other countries to join the war and help support South Vietnam. The President-elect of the Philippines, Ferdinand Marcos, announced the following day, 28th November, that he would send forces to help.
60	29 Nov 1965	Canada's research satellite *Alouette 2* was launched in California, USA.
60	30 Nov 1965	American consumer advocate Ralph Nader's book *Unsafe at Any Speed* was published. In the book, he stated that car manufacturers were reluctant to spend money on car safety features such as seat belts. The book became a best-seller and led to the creation of the U.S. Department of Transportation, the National Highway Traffic Safety Administration, and the first federal seat belts laws.
50	3 Nov 1975	Military coup in Bangladesh. Several leading politicians were killed. Brigadier General Khaled Mosharraf illegally installed himself as Army Chief. He was ousted and assassinated in an uprising on 7th November.
50	3 Nov 1975	Britain's first North Sea oil pipeline was officially opened.
50	5 Nov 1975	Death of Annette Kellerman, American swimmer and actress. She popularised the one-piece bathing costume and synchronised swimming, and was the first major actress to appear nude in a Hollywood film.
50	5 Nov 1975	Death of Edward L. Tatum, American biochemist and geneticist. Joint winner of the 1958 Nobel Prize in Physiology or Medicine for discovering that genes act by regulating chemical events.
50	6 Nov 1975	The Green March, Morocco. About 350,000 Moroccans advanced into the Western Sahara in an effort to force Spain to hand over the disputed Province of Sahara. This led to the fifteen-year Western Sahara War – see 14th November 1975.
50	6 Nov 1975	British punk rock group the Sex Pistols gave their first public performance, at St Martin's College of Art in London. The performance was cut short after ten minutes and a fight broke out.
50	6 Nov 1975	The first episode of the television show *Good Morning America* was broadcast on ABC in the USA.
50	10 Nov 1975 to 1991	Cuban intervention in the Angolan Civil War (See also: 11th November 1975).
50	10 Nov 1975	The United Nations General Assembly adopted Resolution 3379, which determined that Zionism is a form of racism and racial discrimination. It was revoked in 1991.
50	10 Nov 1975	The American freighter *SS Edmund Fitzgerald* sank in Lake Superior during a storm. All 29 crew members were killed.
50	11 Nov 1975	Angola gained its independence from Portugal following the thirteen-year Angolan War of Independence. It immediately began a civil war, which continued (with some interludes) until April 2002.

NOVEMBER 2025

Ann.	Date	Event
50	11 Nov 1975	Australian constitutional crisis. The Governor-General of Australia dismissed Prime Minister Gough Whitlam, replaced him with opposition leader Malcolm Fraser, and called for a general election to be held in December. (Fraser won the election and remained PM until 1983.)
50	12 Nov 1975	U.S. Supreme Court Justice William O. Douglas retired after more than 36 years – the longest term in the history of the Supreme Court. He was succeeded by John Paul Stevens on 17th December.
50	14 Nov 1975	Spain signed an agreement with Morocco and Mauritania (the *Madrid Accords*) and relinquished its control of Western Sahara. Algeria objected to the agreement and began a fifteen-year war. Much of the territory is now administered by Morocco, though its status remains in dispute. (See also: 6th November 1975.)
50	16 Nov 1975 to Jun 1976	The Third Cod War between Iceland and Great Britain. Icelandic victory. Iceland retained its recently introduced 200-mile exclusion zone, severely damaging the British fishing industry which was already in decline.
50	19 Nov 1975	Lynette 'Squeaky' Fromme, a member of the Manson Family cult, was convicted of the attempted assassination of U.S. President Gerald Ford on 5th September. During her trial, President Ford gave a videotaped testimony, and became the first U.S. President to testify in a criminal trial. Fromme was sentenced to life imprisonment. (Paroled 2009.)
50	20 Nov 1975	Death of General Francisco Franco, Spanish dictator (1939–75).
50	21 Nov 1975	American mass murderer Ronald DeFeo Jr. was convicted of the Amityville murders in Long Island, New York in November 1974. He shot and killed his mother, father, two brothers and two sisters. The case inspired the novel and film *The Amityville Horror*. He received six sentences of 25 years to life in prison. He died in 2021.
50	21 Nov 1975	Death of Gunnar Gunnarsson, Icelandic novelist. One of the most popular novelists in Denmark and Germany during the first half of the 20th century, and thought to be the only Icelander to meet Adolf Hitler.
50	22 Nov 1975	Juan Carlos became King of Spain following the death of dictator Francisco Franco (on 20th November).
50	25 Nov 1975	Suriname gained its independence from the Netherlands.
50	25 Nov 1975	American radiologist Robert Ledley was granted a U.S. patent for his invention of the whole-body CT scanner. (U.S. Patent 3,922,552.)
50	27 Nov 1975	Death of Ross McWhirter, British writer, television presenter and political activist. Co-founder of *Guinness World Records* with his twin brother Norris. (Assassinated by the IRA.)
50	28 Nov 1975	East Timor declared its independence from Portugal. Indonesia invaded it on 7th December and annexed it as a province of Indonesia in July 1976. The United Nations took control of it in 1999 and restored its independence in 2002.
50	29 Nov 1975	Death of Graham Hill, British racing driver. Formula 1 world champion (1962 and 1968), Indianapolis 500 champion (1966). One of Britain's greatest racing drivers. Father of Damon Hill. (Plane crash, aged 46.)

NOVEMBER 2025

Ann.	Date	Event
50	30 Nov 1975	Dahomey was renamed Benin (officially the People's Republic of Benin – it became the Republic of Benin in 1990).
40	1 Nov 1985	Quantum Link (also known as Q-Link), an online service for Commodore personal computers, began operating. In 1989, the service was renamed America Online (AOL) and was made available to users of other computers, including the IBM PC.
40	1 Nov 1985	Death of Phil Silvers, American actor and comedian. Best known for playing Sergeant Bilko in *The Phil Silvers Show*.
40	5 Nov 1985	Death of Spencer W. Kimball, President of The Church of Jesus Christ of Latter-day Saints (1973–85).
40	6 Nov 1985	An exploratory oil well at Ranger, Texas, USA exploded. 6.3 million gallons of oil were spilled – the fourth-largest oil spill in U.S. history.
40	6 Nov 1985 to 7th	Palace of Justice siege, Bogotá, Colombia. Guerrillas belonging to the 19th of April Movement took control of the building and held the Supreme Court hostage. Eleven Supreme Court Justices were killed, as were 48 Colombian soldiers and all 35 guerrillas. Eleven others (mostly palace staff) were declared missing after the siege. The building was left in ruins. It was demolished in 1989 and rebuilt.
40	13 Nov 1985	The Nevado del Ruiz volcano in Colombia erupted, triggering a mudslide that buried the city of Armero and killed 23,000 people.
40	15 Nov 1985	The Anglo–Irish Agreement was signed by British Prime Minister Margaret Thatcher and Irish President Garret Fitzgerald. It gave the Irish government a consultative role in the affairs of Northern Ireland.
40	17 Nov 1985	Death of Jimmy Ritz, American singer, dancer, comedian and actor (the Ritz Brothers).
40	18 Nov 1985	The comic strip *Calvin and Hobbes* by Bill Watterson was first published. (It ended in December 1995.)
40	19 Nov 1985	U.S. President Ronald Reagan and Soviet leader Mikhail Gorbachev met for the first time at a superpower summit in Geneva, Switzerland.
40	19 Nov 1985	A jury in Texas, USA awarded the oil company Pennzoil $10.53 billion in a settlement against Texaco. Pennzoil had entered an agreement to buy Getty Oil, but Texaco jumped in and bought Getty Oil for itself. The award was the largest in U.S. history, but it was eventually settled for $3 billion after Texaco filed for bankruptcy.
40	19 Nov 1985	Death of Stepin Fetchit, American comedian and film actor.
40	20 Nov 1985	Microsoft Windows 1.0 was released.
40	21 Nov 1985	American intelligence analyst Jonathan Pollard was arrested for selling classified information about Arab nations, Pakistan and the Soviet Union to Israel. In 1987 he was sentenced to life imprisonment. (He was released in 2015 and now lives in Israel.)
40	22 Nov 1985 to 27th	The largest series of naturalisation ceremonies ever held in the USA took place in Los Angeles, California. 38,648 people became U.S. citizens during six days of ceremonies at the LA Convention Center.

NOVEMBER 2025

Ann.	Date	Event
40	22 Nov 1985	Two French secret service agents were found guilty of bombing the Greenpeace ship *Rainbow Warrior* in Auckland Harbour, New Zealand. They were sentenced to ten years in prison for manslaughter and arson.
40	23 Nov 1985	Palestinian gunmen hijacked EgyptAir Flight 648 en route from Athens to Cairo and forced it to land in Malta. Egyptian commandos stormed the plane on 24th November. Dozens of passengers were killed.
30	1 Nov 1995	The first all-race municipal elections were held in South Africa following the end of apartheid.
30	2 Nov 1995	Death of Florence Greenberg, American record company founder and producer (Tiara Records, Scepter Records and Wand Records).
30	4 Nov 1995	Death of Marti Caine, British singer, comedian and television presenter who found fame after winning the TV talent show *New Faces*. (Cancer, aged 50.)
30	4 Nov 1995	Death of Paul Eddington, British television actor. Best known for his roles as Jerry Leadbetter in *The Good Life* (USA: *Good Neighbors*), and Jim Hacker in *Yes, Minister* and *Yes, Prime Minister*.
30	4 Nov 1995	Death of Eddie Egan, American police officer who helped break up an organised crime ring in New York City in 1961. His story is told in the film *The French Connection*, in which he is played by Gene Hackman.
30	4 Nov 1995	Death of Yitzhak Rabin, Prime Minister of Israel (1974–77, 1992–95). Joint winner of the 1994 Nobel Peace Prize. (Assassinated at a peace rally.)
30	10 Nov 1995	Death of Ken Saro-Wiwa, Nigerian writer and environmental/human rights activist. (Executed for opposing Nigeria's military regime.)
30	11 Nov 1995	Death of Charles Scribner Jr., American publisher. Head of the Charles Scribner's Sons book publishing company (1952–84). The company was founded by his great-grandfather.
30	12 Nov 1995	The Croatian War of Independence ended with the signing of the Erdut Agreement.
30	12 Nov 1995	Death of Jackie Mann, British RAF Spitfire pilot in the Battle of Britain who was kidnapped in Lebanon in 1989 and held hostage by Islamic terrorists for more than two years.
30	12 Nov 1995	Death of Sir Robert Stephens, British actor. One of the most respected actors of his era. Closely associated with the National Theatre. Husband of the actress Dame Maggie Smith.
30	13 Nov 1995	Mozambique joined the Commonwealth of Nations. It was the first country to join that was not previously a part of the British Empire. (It had gained its independence from Portugal in 1975.)
30	14 Nov 1995 to 19th	U.S. President Bill Clinton blocked two temporary funding measures in a dispute with Congress over the 1996 budget. As a result, national parks and museums were forced to close and government offices ran reduced services. There was another shutdown between 16th December 1995 and 6th January 1996 when temporary finance provisions expired.

NOVEMBER 2025

Ann.	Date	Event
30	14 Nov 1995	Death of Jack Finney, American novelist, short story writer and playwright. Best known for his novels *The Body Snatchers* (also called *Invasion of the Body Snatchers*) and *Time and Again*.
30	15 Nov 1995	British computer programmer Christopher Pile (aka the Black Baron) was sentenced to eighteen months in prison for writing and distributing computer viruses. He was the first person to be jailed for this offence.
30	16 Nov 1995	Death of Leah Betts, eighteen-year-old British girl who fell into a coma after taking an ecstasy tablet and then drinking twelve pints (seven litres) of water in ninety minutes. She died three days later. Her death was covered extensively in the media. Her death was caused by the excessive amount of water she drank, not the drug itself, but the drug was a contributory factor.
30	17 Nov 1995 to 5 Dec	Sri Lankan Civil War – Operation Riviresa. The Sri Lankan Armed Forces recaptured the city of Jaffna and the Jaffna peninsula from the Tamil Tigers, and drove them out of their heartland.
30	17 Nov 1995	Death of Alan Hull, British folk-rock singer and songwriter (Lindisfarne).
30	19 Nov 1995	The U.S. première of the film *Toy Story*. It was the first feature-length computer-generated film, and the first full-length film made by Pixar. (Released USA: 22nd November. UK: 22nd March 1996.)
30	20 Nov 1995	Princess Diana admitted that she had committed adultery, and spoke openly about her separation from the Prince of Wales in a frank interview for the BBC. In 2021, BBC journalist Martin Bashir was accused of using deception, including fake bank statements, to persuade her to give the interview.
30	20 Nov 1995	Death of Sergei Grinkov, Russian figure skater. He and his wife Ekaterina Gordeeva were Olympic pairs champions in 1988 and 1994, and four-times world champions. (Heart attack, aged 28.)
30	21 Nov 1995	The civil war in Bosnia and Herzegovina ended with the signing of the Dayton Peace Agreement in Ohio, USA. It was ratified in Paris, France on 14th December.
30	21 Nov 1995	Death of Peter Grant, British rock music manager (The Yardbirds, Led Zeppelin, Bad Company) and record company executive. Noted for his shrewd management skills and ruthlessness. He helped gain significant improvements to musicians' pay and conditions for live performances.
30	22 Nov 1995	British serial killer Rose West, wife of serial killer Fred West, was sentenced to life imprisonment for murdering ten young women and girls.
30	23 Nov 1995	Death of Louis Malle, French film director, screenwriter and producer.
30	23 Nov 1995	Death of Junior Walker, American saxophonist (Junior Walker and the All Stars – a popular Motown group).
30	24 Nov 1995	In a referendum, the citizens of Ireland narrowly voted in favour of legalising divorce.
30	24 Nov 1995	Death of Stuart Henry, Scottish radio DJ. Best known for his work on BBC Radio 1 and Radio Luxembourg. (Multiple sclerosis, aged 53.)

NOVEMBER 2025

Ann.	Date	Event
30	26 Nov 1995	Death of Charles Warrell, ('Big Chief I-Spy'), British writer, publisher and teacher. Known for his popular series of *I-Spy* spotters' guides for children.
30	28 Nov 1995	The 55-mph federal speed limit in the USA was abolished (effective from 8th December). Individual states became free to set their own maximum speed limits – typically 65 or 70 mph, but 75 mph in a few states. (The 55-mph limit was introduced during the 1974 Middle East oil embargo.)
30	30 Nov 1995	Bill Clinton became the first serving U.S. President to visit Northern Ireland.
25	1 Nov 2000	Chhattisgarh became India's 26th state. It was previously part of Madhya Pradesh. (See also: 9th and 15th November 2000.)
25	2 Nov 2000	The first crew moved into the International Space Station. It has remained permanently staffed ever since.
25	2 Nov 2000	The Chief Inspector of Schools in England, Chris Woodhead, resigned. He had been a controversial figure, who attacked schools and teachers for being 'mediocre' and overruled his inspectors. This sometimes had catastrophic results for the schools, teachers and students. Teachers' unions had demanded that he be replaced.
25	7 Nov 2000	George W. Bush was elected as the 43rd President of the USA. The result of the election would not be known for more than a month because of disputed votes in Florida.
25	7 Nov 2000	Hillary Clinton became the first former First Lady to be elected to the U.S. Senate.
25	7 Nov 2000	Death of Ingrid of Sweden, Queen consort of Denmark (1947–72). Wife of King Frederick IX. Mother of Queen Margrethe II of Denmark.
25	9 Nov 2000	Uttarakhand became India's 27th state. It was previously part of Uttar Pradesh.
25	9 Nov 2000	Pets.com ceased trading just two years after its launch. It was one of the most high-profile failures of the dot-com bubble.
25	9 Nov 2000	Death of Eric Morley, British television host. He established the ballroom dancing competition show *Come Dancing* (1949–98) and founded the Miss World beauty pageant. As a director of Mecca, he also helped popularise bingo in the UK. *Come Dancing* was succeeded by a celebrity version, *Strictly Come Dancing*, in 2004.
25	9 Nov 2000	Death of Hugh Paddick, British actor. Best known for his sketches (such as 'Julian and Sandy') on the 1960s BBC radio show *Round the Horne*.
25	11 Nov 2000	Kaprun disaster, Austria. A funicular railway car caught fire while being pulled through an Alpine tunnel. 155 skiers and snowboarders were killed.
25	15 Nov 2000	Jharkhand became India's 28th state. It was previously part of Bihar.
25	15 Nov 2000	The Southern Cross Cable began operating. The high-speed data network links Australia, New Zealand, Fiji and Hawaii to the west coast of the USA.

NOVEMBER 2025

Ann.	Date	Event
25	15 Nov 2000	Madame Tussauds waxwork museum opened in New York City, USA. Marie Tussaud opened her first waxwork museum in London in 1835, and there are now museums in seventeen cities around the world.
25	16 Nov 2000	Bill Clinton became the first U.S. President to visit Vietnam since the end of the Vietnam War.
25	17 Nov 2000	Log pod Mangartom Landslide, Slovenia. Heavy rain caused a major landslide on the slopes of Mount Mangart. The upper section of the village of Log pod Mangartom was swept away and seven people were killed. The affected part of the village was rebuilt in a safer location.
25	17 Nov 2000	The President of Peru, Alberto Fujimori, resigned (by fax from Japan). His resignation was rejected and he was instead dismissed for being 'morally unfit'. He was succeeded by Valentín Paniagua.
25	18 Nov 2000	American actor Michael Douglas married Welsh actress Catherine Zeta-Jones.
25	22 Nov 2000	Death of Emil Zátopek, Czech long-distance runner and inventor of interval training. One of the greatest runners of the 20th century. 3x gold medallist at the 1952 Olympics (5000 m, 10,000 m, and marathon).
25	24 Nov 2000	The Sony PlayStation 2 games console was released in Europe. (Japan: 4th March. North America: 26th October. Australia: 17th November.)
25	25 Nov 2000	Baku earthquake, Azerbaijan. 26 people were killed and 412 injured. More than ninety buildings were seriously damaged.
25	27 Nov 2000	Nigerian schoolboy Damilola Taylor, aged ten, died after being stabbed in the leg by a gang of hooded attackers near his home in south London, UK.
25	27 Nov 2000	Death of Sir Malcolm Bradbury, British writer and academic. Best known for his novel *The History Man*.
25	27 Nov 2000	Death of Len Shackleton, British footballer (Newcastle United and Sunderland). Known as the 'Clown Prince of Football' and regarded as one of the most entertaining players in English football.
25	30 Nov 2000	The Countryside and Rights of Way Act 2000 came into effect in the UK. It included the controversial 'right to roam' which had been long sought by ramblers. Several disputed areas became accessible as a result.
20	5 Nov 2005	Death of John Fowles, British novelist (*The French Lieutenant's Woman*).
20	5 Nov 2005	Death of Link Wray, American rock and roll guitarist. Inventor of the power chord. Noted for his fuzzy, feedback-laden electric guitar sound. Best known for his instrumental hit *Rumble*, which was banned by several radio stations for inciting violence.
20	6 Nov 2005	The UK première of the fantasy film *Harry Potter and the Goblet of Fire*. The fourth film in the series. (Released: 18th November. U.S. première: 12th November, released: 18th November.)

NOVEMBER 2025

Ann.	Date	Event
20	7 Nov 2005	India and Pakistan opened the disputed Kashmir border between the two countries to allow aid from India to reach victims of the 8th October earthquake. Other crossing points were opened over the following days. Initially only aid workers were allowed to cross, angering civilians. 24 civilians were allowed to cross on 19th November.
20	9 Nov 2005	Amman hotel bombings, Jordan. Suicide bombers attacked three hotels that were often used by foreign diplomats. 60 people were killed (plus the three bombers) and 115 injured. Among those killed were 38 guests at a wedding party.
20	9 Nov 2005	The European Space Agency's *Venus Express* spacecraft was launched. It went into polar orbit around Venus in April 2006 and returned data about its atmospheric dynamics. It ceased operating in 2014, and is believed to have burnt up in Venus's atmosphere in early 2015.
20	9 Nov 2005	Death of K. R. Narayanan, President of India (1997–2002).
20	11 Nov 2005	Death of Patrick Lichfield, 5th Earl of Lichfield, British photographer. One of Britain's best-known photographers. The official photographer for several notable Royal events. (His real surname was Anson. He used Lichfield as his professional name.)
20	18 Nov 2005	A civil jury in Los Angeles, California found American actor Robert Blake liable for the wrongful death of his wife, Bonnie Lee Bakley. He was ordered to pay her family $30 million. A criminal trial jury had acquitted him in March.
20	22 Nov 2005	Angela Merkel became the first female Chancellor of Germany.
20	22 Nov 2005	Microsoft released the Xbox 360 video games console in the USA. (Europe: 2nd December.)
20	23 Nov 2005	Death of Constance Cummings, American-born British stage and film actress whose career spanned nearly seventy years.
20	24 Nov 2005	The Licensing Act 2003 came into effect in England and Wales. It introduced flexibility to pub opening hours, with the potential for 24-hour opening.
20	24 Nov 2005	Death of Pat Morita, American film and television actor. Best known for playing Arnold in the TV sitcom *Happy Days* and Mr Miyagi in the film series *The Karate Kid*.
20	25 Nov 2005	Death of George Best, Northern Irish footballer. European Footballer of the Year (1968). Also known for his long battle with alcoholism, which eventually led to his death.
20	26 Nov 2005	Death of Stan Berenstain, American children's author and illustrator who created *The Berenstain Bears* series of books with his wife Jan.
20	27 Nov 2005	The world's first partial face transplant was carried out in France. The patient, Isabelle Dinoire, had been mauled by her pet dog in May. Her body rejected the transplant in 2015, and her daily regimen of immunosuppressive drugs left her vulnerable to cancer. She died in April 2016.

NOVEMBER 2025

Ann.	Date	Event
20	28 Nov 2005	Canada's three opposition parties claimed that the Liberal government was corrupt, and the House of Commons passed a vote of no confidence. Parliament was dissolved the following day, forcing a federal election, which was held on 23rd January 2006.
20	28 Nov 2005	The first Cyber Monday was held. It was created by retailers to encourage people to shop online, and is held annually, worldwide, on the first Monday after the USA's Thanksgiving Day. It is now the busiest day of the year for online shopping.
20	30 Nov 2005	John Sentamu became Archbishop of York (until 2020). He was the first black archbishop in the Church of England.
15	17 Nov 2010	Researchers at CERN in Switzerland announced that they had trapped antimatter for the first time. They held 38 single atoms of antihydrogen in a magnetic trap for more than 170 milliseconds using the Antihydrogen Laser Physics Apparatus (ALPHA).
10	10 Nov 2015	Death of Pat Eddery, Irish jockey and horse trainer. British flat racing champion eleven times, and 3x winner of the Derby.
10	10 Nov 2015	Death of Helmut Schmidt, Chancellor of West Germany (1974–82).
10	10 Nov 2015	Death of Allen Toussaint, American R&B/soul/funk/blues/jazz songwriter, musician and record producer. His songs have been recorded by numerous artists and he produced hundreds of recordings.
10	13 Nov 2015	November 2015 Paris attacks, France. Suicide bombers and armed terrorists from the militant organisation Islamic State (IS) attacked a football stadium, rock concert, cafés and restaurants. 130 people were killed and 416 injured. Seven attackers were also killed. IS said the attacks were in retaliation for French air-strikes on IS targets in Syria and Iraq.
10	14 Nov 2015	Death of Warren Mitchell, British radio, television, stage and film actor. Best known for his role as Alf Garnett in the sitcoms *Till Death Us Do Part* and *In Sickness and in Health*.
10	15 Nov 2015	Death of Saeed Jaffrey, British-Indian stage, film, radio and television actor (*My Beautiful Laundrette, The Jewel in the Crown, Tandoori Nights*, and many more).
10	16 Nov 2015	Same-sex marriage was legalised in Ireland following a referendum held in May.
10	18 Nov 2015	Death of Jonah Lomu, New Zealand rugby player. The youngest-ever All Black. (Kidney disease/heart attack, aged 40.)
10	20 Nov 2015	Death of Keith Michell, Australian stage, film and television actor. He worked primarily in the UK, and is best known for playing King Henry VIII in several productions. He also sang the hit song *Captain Beaky and His Band*.
10	22 Nov 2015	Death of Kim Young-sam, President of South Korea (1993–98).

DECEMBER 2025

Ann.	Date	Event
1000	15 Dec 1025	Death of Basil II, senior Byzantine emperor (976–1025). Succeeded by his brother Constantine VIII, who became sole emperor after sharing the crown for 63 years (since he was three-years old).
1000	25 Dec 1025	The Coronation of Mieszko II Lambert, King of Poland (1925–31).
800	31 Dec 1225	The 216-year Lý Dynasty in Vietnam ended when the Empress Lý Chiêu Hoàng was married and forced to cede the throne to her husband. They were both seven years old. Trần Thái Tông became the first emperor of the Trần Dynasty on 11th January 1226.
600	9 Dec 1425	The Old University of Leuven was established in Brabant (now in Belgium) (as the Studium Generale). It closed in 1797.
500	1 Dec 1525	Birth of Tadeáš Hájek, Czech astronomer, physician, mathematician and naturalist. The personal physician of the Holy Roman Emperor Rudolph II. The most important Czech astronomer of his era – though he was regarded as an occultist rather than a scientist until recently.
250	3 Dec 1775	The Continental Navy warship *USS Alfred* became the first ship to fly the Grand Union Flag (the precursor to the Stars and Stripes).
250	9 Dec 1775	American Revolutionary War – the Battle of Great Bridge (now Chesapeake), Virginia. Colonial victory. The British Governor of Virginia, Lord Dunmore, and his staff, left Virginia immediately afterwards.
250	14 Dec 1775	Birth of Philander Chase, American bishop, educator and pioneer. Presiding Bishop of the Episcopal Church (1843–52 – his death).
250	14 Dec 1775	Birth of Thomas Cochrane, 10th Earl of Dundonald and Marquess of Maranhão. Scottish admiral in the British Royal Navy. He was highly successful in the Napoleonic Wars. He also helped Chile and Brazil gain their independence from Portugal after he was dismissed from the Navy for fraud (he was later pardoned). He was the inspiration for the fictional characters Horatio Hornblower, created by C. S. Forester, and Jack Aubrey, created by Patrick O'Brian.
250	16 Dec 1775	Birth of Jane Austen, British novelist (*Sense and Sensibility*, *Pride and Prejudice*, *Mansfield Park*, *Emma*, *Northanger Abbey*, *Persuasion*).
250	31 Dec 1775	American Revolutionary War – the Battle of Quebec, Canada. British victory – the first major defeat for the Americans.
250	31 Dec 1775	Death of Richard Montgomery, Irish-born American soldier. A major general in the Continental Army during the American Revolutionary War. He led the unsuccessful invasion of Quebec (see above).
200	1 Dec 1825	Death of Alexander I, Emperor of Russia (1801–25). (Typhus, aged 47.) Succeeded by brother, Nicholas I.
200	2 Dec 1825	Birth of Pedro II (Pedro the Magnanimous), Emperor of Brazil (1831–89).

DECEMBER 2025

Ann.	Date	Event
200	26 Dec 1825	The Decembrist revolt, Saint Petersburg, Russia. A military uprising against Emperor Nicholas I after his brother Constantine declined the throne following the death of their father Alexander I. Loyalist forces opened fire on the rebels, and they fled. Many were later executed, imprisoned, or exiled in Siberia.
200	30 Dec 1825	The Treaty of St. Louis was proclaimed between the USA and the Shawnee Nation. Peace and friendship between the two nations was renewed, and the Shawnee ceded land near Cape Girardeau, Missouri to the USA.
175	4 Dec 1850	Death of William Sturgeon, British physicist, electrical engineer and inventor. He created the first electromagnets and invented the first British electric motor.
175	16 Dec 1850	Canterbury Province was founded in New Zealand by British settlers (the Canterbury Pilgrims) who arrived on the immigrant ships *Charlotte Jane* and *Randolph*. Two more ships arrived over the following days, and others soon followed. The settlers built the city of Christchurch.
175	21 Dec 1850	Hawaii's first post office opened in Honolulu.
175	22 Dec 1850	Birth of Victoriano Huerta, President of Mexico (1913–14).
175	27 Dec 1850	The Honolulu Fire Department was established. It was the first fire department in Hawaii.
175	30 Dec 1850	Birth of John Milne, British geologist, mining engineer, inventor, anthropologist and educator. Co-founder of the Seismological Society of Japan. He invented the horizontal pendulum seismograph for detecting earthquakes, and established monitoring stations around the world.
150	4 Dec 1875	Corrupt American politician 'Boss' Tweed, the former head of the Tammany Hall political machine in New York City, escaped from prison and fled to Spain. He was recaptured and returned to prison in November 1876. He died in prison in 1878.
150	6 Dec 1875	Birth of Evelyn Underhill, British writer and pacifist. Best known for her works on religion and Christian mysticism, particularly her book *Mysticism*.
150	17 Dec 1875	Montreal bread riots, Canada. 2,000 unemployed labourers marched to the city hall to demand work or bread. The desperate and distressed men turned violent – and the mayor said they had every right to demonstrate their anger. Over the next few days, he organised a relief plan that provided work for around 1,300 men. The sewer system was extended, roads resurfaced, and landfill projects were authorised.
150	19 Dec 1875	Birth of Carter G. Woodson, ('the father of black history'), American historian, writer and journalist. Founder of the Association for the Study of African American Life and History, *The Journal of Negro History*, and Negro History Week (now Black History Month).
125	3 Dec 1900	Birth of Richard Kuhn, Austrian-born German biochemist. Winner of the 1938 Nobel Prize in Chemistry for his work on carotenoids and vitamins.

DECEMBER 2025

Ann.	Date	Event
125	6 Dec 1900	Birth of Agnes Moorehead, American stage, film, radio and television actress. Best known for her role as Endora in the TV series *Bewitched*. She also had major roles and supporting roles in several films including *Citizen Kane, Show Boat, The Magnificent Ambersons, Johnny Belinda*, and more, and is known for the radio play *Sorry, Wrong Number*.
125	9 Dec 1900	Birth of Joseph Needham, British biochemist, sinologist and historian. Noted for his scientific work on embryology, and for his major study of Chinese science and technology. He co-founded the United Nations Educational, Scientific, and Cultural Organisation (UNESCO), and received several notable awards. He was also noted for his controversial lifestyle and unorthodox political views, and was blacklisted by the U.S. government for supporting the Chinese and being a communist sympathiser.
125	12 Dec 1900	Second Boer War: Field Marshal Herbert Kitchener, 1st Earl Kitchener, became Commander-in-Chief of British Forces in South Africa. He succeeded Frederick Roberts, and held the position until the end of the war in June 1902.
125	12 Dec 1900	Birth of Sammy Davis Sr., American dancer. Father of the entertainer Sammy Davis Jr.
125	16 Dec 1900	Birth of V. S. Pritchett, British short story writer, literary critic and educator.
125	17 Dec 1900	The second Ellis Island Immigration Station opened in New York Harbor, USA. The original immigration station opened in 1892 but was destroyed by fire. The station processed around 12 million immigrants between 1892 and 1954. It is now a museum.
125	17 Dec 1900	The Prix Guzman (aka the Pierre Guzman Prize) was announced in France. A prize of 100,000 francs (about $580,000 or £430,000 today) would be awarded to anyone who succeeded in communicating with extra-terrestrials from another celestial body (except Mars, which was considered to be inhabited and therefore too easy). Until someone won the prize, smaller prizes would be awarded every five years to those who made significant progress in astronomy and medicine.
125	18 Dec 1900	The Puffing Billy Railway opened in Victoria, Australia. It closed in 1958, but reopened in stages from 1962 when the Puffing Billy Preservation Society took it over as a narrow gauge heritage railway.
125	20 Dec 1900	The comet 21P/Giacobini-Zinner was discovered by French astronomer Michel Giacobini. It became the first comet to be visited by a spacecraft: the *International Cometary Explorer* passed through its tail in September 1985.
125	20 Dec 1900	Birth of Gabby Hartnett, American baseball player and manager (Chicago Cubs, New York Giants). One of the greatest catchers in the National League.
125	22 Dec 1900	The first Mercedes car was produced. It became known as the Mercedes 35 HP and entered full production in 1901. It is regarded as the first modern car. (The brand name Mercedes was not registered until June 1902.)

DECEMBER 2025

Ann.	Date	Event
125	23 Dec 1900	Canadian-born inventor Reginald Fessenden became the first person to transmit speech by radio. He transmitted the signal over a distance of 1 mile on Cobb Island in Maryland, USA. The received signal was too distorted to be of practical use, but it proved that audio transmission was possible, and paved the way for later developments.
100	1 Dec 1925	The Locarno Treaties were signed in London, UK. They settled territorial boundaries and normalised relations between countries following the end of WWI. (Effective from 14th September 1926.)
100	6 Dec 1925	The border between Egypt and Libya was formally established when Egypt and Italy signed the Jaghbub treaty, which finalised its position.
100	7 Dec 1925	The Samuel J. Friedman Theatre opened on Broadway, New York City, USA (as the Biltmore Theatre).
100	8 Dec 1925	The musical *The Cocoanuts* by Irving Berlin and George S. Kaufman opened on Broadway. It was adapted into a 1929 film starring the Marx Brothers.
100	8 Dec 1925	Birth of Sammy Davis Jr., American singer, dancer, actor and entertainer. (Died 1990.)
100	10 Dec 1925	Irish playwright George Bernard Shaw received the 1925 Nobel Prize in Literature.
100	12 Dec 1925	The world's first motel opened in San Luis Obispo, California, USA. Originally named the Milestone Mo-Tel, it is now known as the Motel Inn of San Luis Obispo. (It closed down in 1991. Earlier motels dating back to 1915 have been discovered, though they did not use the name motel.)
100	15 Dec 1925	The Shah of Iran, Ahmad Shah Qajar, was deposed in a coup. He was the last Shah of the Qajar Dynasty. He was succeeded by Reza Shah Pahlavi (until 1941).
100	15 Dec 1925	The third Madison Square Garden indoor arena opened in New York City, USA. The opening event was an ice hockey game: the Montreal Canadiens beat the New York Americans 3 – 1. It was the first hockey match to be played at Madison Square Garden. The arena closed in 1968 and the fourth and current Madison Square Garden opened on another site.
100	16 Dec 1925	The Sri Lanka Broadcasting Corporation was founded (as Colombo Radio, later named Radio Ceylon).
100	16 Dec 1925	The silent film *Wolf Blood* (also known as *Wolfblood: A Tale of the Forest*) was released. It is the earliest surviving werewolf film. (The first-known werewolf film, *The Werewolf*, was released in 1913, but it is considered lost.)
100	17 Dec 1925	The Soviet Union signed a non-aggression pact with Turkey.
100	21 Dec 1925	The première of Sergei Eisenstein's silent film *Battleship Potemkin*, in Moscow, Russia. (Released: Russia: 24th December. USA: 5th December 1926.)
100	26 Dec 1925	The Communist Party of India was founded.
100	26 Dec 1925	Turkey adopted the Gregorian Calendar.

DECEMBER 2025

Ann.	Date	Event
100	26 Dec 1925	Death of Jan Letzel, Czech architect and diplomat. Best known for designing the Japanese Chamber of Commerce and Industry in Hiroshima, Japan. It was one of the few buildings to survive the atomic bomb attack in 1945, and its ruins are now the Hiroshima Peace Memorial. Many of his other buildings in Japan were destroyed by an earthquake in 1923.
100	28 Dec 1925	George and Ira Gershwin's musical *Tip-Toes* opened on Broadway. It was moderately successful, ran for 192 performances, and was adapted into a silent film.
100	28 Dec 1925	Birth of Milton Obote, President of Uganda (1966–71, 1980–85). Both of his terms in office were ended by coups. After the second coup he left the country and spent the rest of his life in exile. (Died 2005.)
100	30 Dec 1925	Birth of Ian MacNaughton, Scottish film and television director and producer. Best known for directing and producing the TV series *Monty Python's Flying Circus* and the film *And Now for Something Completely Different*. (Died 2002.)
90	1 Dec 1935	The first air route traffic control centre opened in Newark, New Jersey, USA. It directs the movement of aircraft from their departure to their destination.
90	1 Dec 1935	Death of Bernhard Schmidt, German optician. Inventor of the Schmidt telescope. Its high-quality corrective optics enabled astronomers to photograph large areas of the sky using very large wide-angled cameras.
90	3 Dec 1935	Death of Princess Victoria of the United Kingdom. Daughter of King Edward VII. Sister of King George V.
90	5 Dec 1935	The National Council of Negro Women was founded in the USA.
90	5 Dec 1935	The world's first commercial-scale hydroponic plant culture operation was established in Montebello, California, USA.
90	6 Dec 1935	Michael Joseph Savage became the first Labour Prime Minister of New Zealand. (He died in office in 1940.)
90	8 Dec 1935	The Second Oomoto Incident, Japan. Japanese military police launched a violent suppression of the Oomoto religious sect, which it accused of worshipping figures other than Amaterasu (a major Shinto deity from whom the Emperor of Japan is said to be descended).
90	9 Dec 1935	Death of Walter Liggett, American journalist. Best known for investigating and exposing organised crime and political corruption in Minneapolis and Saint Paul, Minnesota. (Shot dead, aged 49.)
90	11 Dec 1935	Birth of Pranab Mukherjee, President of India (2012–17). (Died 2020.)
90	12 Dec 1935	The Lebensborn project was established in Germany to counteract falling birth rates and promote Nazi eugenics.
90	14 Dec 1935	Thomas Masaryk, the founder and first president of Czechoslovakia, resigned due to ill health. He was succeeded by Edvard Beneš on 18th December.

DECEMBER 2025

Ann.	Date	Event
90	14 Dec 1935	Birth of Lewis Arquette, American film and television actor, writer and producer. Best known for his role as J. D. Pickett in the TV series *The Waltons*. Father of the actors Rosanna, Patricia, Alexis and David Arquette. (Died 2001.)
90	14 Dec 1935	Birth of Lee Remick, American film and television actress (*Anatomy of a Murder*, *Days of Wine and Roses*, *The Omen*, and more). (Died 1991.)
90	17 Dec 1935	The Douglas DC-3 airliner made its first flight.
90	17 Dec 1935	Death of Juan Vicente Gómez, President/dictator of Venezuela (1908–35).
90	17 Dec 1935	Birth of Cal Ripken Sr., American baseball player, coach and manager (Baltimore Orioles). Father of the baseball players Cal Ripken Jr. and Billy Ripken. (Died 1999.)
90	18 Dec 1935	Birth of Rosemary Leach, British stage, film and television actress. Known for her roles in the films *84, Charing Cross Road*, *That'll Be the Day* and *A Room with a View*, and the TV series *The Jewel in the Crown*, *The Charmer*, *The Buccaneers*, *Berkley Square*, and the sitcom *My Family*. (Died 2017.)
90	21 Dec 1935	Birth of Yusuf Bey, American Black Muslim activist and baker. (Died 2003.)
90	23 Dec 1935	Birth of Johnny Kidd, British rock and roll singer and songwriter (Johnny Kidd and the Pirates). Best known for his hit song *Shakin' All Over*. (Died 1966 – car crash, aged 30.)
90	23 Dec 1935	Birth of Esther Phillips, American R&B/blues singer. (Died 1984.)
90	24 Dec 1935	Death of Alban Berg, Austrian composer. Noted for his atonal and 12-tone compositions and the operas *Wozzeck* and *Lulu*.
90	27 Dec 1935	Regina Jonas of Berlin, Germany became the first woman to be ordained as a rabbi. She was persecuted by the Nazis and died in Auschwitz concentration camp in 1944.
90	30 Dec 1935	Second Italo–Abyssinian War – the Dolo hospital airstrike, Ethiopia. The Italian Air Force bombed a Swedish Red Cross hospital. It was reportedly a reprisal attack after Ethiopians killed an Italian prisoner of war. Between 22 and 30 people were killed.
90	30 Dec 1935	Birth of Omar Bongo, President of Gabon (1967–2009 – died in office).
80	Dec 1945	Ballpoint pens were launched in the UK by the Miles-Martin Pen Company.
80	5 Dec 1945	Flight 19, a squadron of five U.S. Navy bombers, disappeared over the Bermuda Triangle during a training flight. They were never seen again.
80	7 Dec 1945	The monster/horror film *House of Dracula* was released. It was a sequel to *House of Frankenstein*.
80	11 Dec 1945	Death of Charles Fabry, French physicist who discovered the Earth's ozone layer.

DECEMBER 2025

Ann.	Date	Event
80	12 Dec 1945	The People's Republic of Korea (PRK), established in September 1945, was outlawed by the U.S. military government in South Korea. The Soviet Union subsequently co-opted the PRK's committees into the Democratic Republic of Korea (North Korea).
80	13 Dec 1945	Death of Josef Kramer, ('the Beast of Belsen'), German Nazi concentration camp commandant. (Executed along with ten other concentration camp staff who were found guilty of the ill treatment of inmates.)
80	15 Dec 1945	The Allied occupying authorities in Japan issued the *Shinto Directive* which abolished state support for the Shinto religion.
80	16 Dec 1945	Death of Giovanni Agnelli, Italian industrialist. Founder of the Fiat car company.
80	16 Dec 1945	Death of Fumimaro Konoe, Prime Minister of Japan (1937–39, 1940–41).
80	20 Dec 1945	Leopold Figl became Chancellor of Austria (until 1953). Karl Renner, the former Chancellor became President (until 31st December).
80	21 Dec 1945	The musical *Billion Dollar Baby* by Morton Gould, Betty Comden and Adolph Green opened on Broadway. It ran for 220 performances, but was not well received.
80	21 Dec 1945	Death of George S. Patton, U.S. Army general who commanded the 3rd and 7th U.S. Armies in Europe during WWII. A highly regarded tank commander. (Car crash in Germany.)
80	24 Dec 1945	Birth of Lemmy, British rock/heavy metal singer, songwriter and bassist. A member of the bands Motörhead and Hawkwind. Noted for his distinctive appearance, gravelly voice and overpowered bass guitar sound. (Died 2015.)
80	25 Dec 1945	Birth of Noel Redding, British bass guitarist (the Jimi Hendrix Experience). (Died 2003.)
80	27 Dec 1945	The World Bank, the International Monetary Fund, and the International Bank for Reconstruction and Development were founded. They had been created at the Bretton Woods Conference in July 1944.
80	28 Dec 1945	The U.S. Congress formally recognised the *Pledge of Allegiance*. It was written in 1892. Before 1945 it was known as the *Pledge to the Flag*. It was revised in 1954 when the words 'under God' were added.
80	28 Dec 1945	Birth of Birendra, King of Nepal (1972–2001 – shot dead by his son, Crown Prince Dipendra, who also shot himself and died three days later).
80	28 Dec 1945	Death of Theodore Dreiser, American novelist. A leading exponent of Naturalism in fiction. Known for *Sister Carrie* and *An American Tragedy*.
80	30 Dec 1945	Birth of Davy Jones, British singer, songwriter and actor (the Monkees). (Died 2012.)
80	31 Dec 1945	World War II: tyre rationing ended in the USA. Rationing began on 5th January 1942 because the Japanese had captured the rubber production regions of south-east Asia. Other rubber products were also rationed during the war.

DECEMBER 2025

Ann.	Date	Event
75	5 Dec 1950	Korean War: the North Koreans and their Chinese allies recaptured the North Korean capital, Pyongyang, from UN forces.
75	8 Dec 1950	Birth of Dan Hartman, American pop singer, musician, songwriter and record producer. Best known for his songs *Relight My Fire* and *Instant Replay*. (Died 1994.)
75	10 Dec 1950	Dr Ralph Bunche became the first African American to receive the Nobel Peace Prize, for his efforts to mediate between Israel and nearby Arab states.
75	11 Dec 1950	Birth of Christina Onassis, American heiress and businesswoman. Daughter of the shipping magnate Aristotle Onassis. (Died 1988.)
75	12 Dec 1950	The first woman in the USA to perform rabbinical functions: Paula Ackerman was appointed interim spiritual leader of Temple Beth Israel in Meridian, Mississippi, USA following the death of her husband, who was the rabbi there. She remained in the role for three years.
75	13 Dec 1950	American actor James Dean made his first television appearance, in a commercial for Pepsi Cola.
75	14 Dec 1950	The United Nations High Commissioner for Refugees (also known as the UN Refugee Agency) was established.
75	16 Dec 1950	Korean War: U.S. President Harry S. Truman declared a national state of emergency in order to fight 'Communist imperialism' after China entered the war in support of North Korea.
75	19 Dec 1950	General Dwight D. Eisenhower (later U.S. President) was appointed NATO's first Supreme Commander, with responsibility for the Allied forces in Europe. He took up his post on 2nd April 1951.
75	21 Dec 1950	Cole Porter's musical *Out of This World* opened on Broadway following tryouts in Philadelphia and Boston in November. It ran until May 1951.
75	25 Dec 1950	The Stone of Scone, the coronation stone of British monarchs, was taken from Westminster Abbey in London by four Scottish students. They transported it to Scotland, but broke it. It was later returned to London and used in the coronation of Queen Elizabeth II. Since 1996 it has been kept in Edinburgh Castle, Scotland, with the agreement that it will be transported to Westminster Abbey when needed for coronations.
75	31 Dec 1950	Death of Karl Renner, President of Austria (1945–50), Chancellor of Austria (1918–20, 1945).
70	1 Dec 1955	African American civil rights activist Rosa Parks refused to give up her bus seat to a white man in Montgomery, Alabama, USA, violating the city's racial segregation laws. This led to the Montgomery bus boycott (5th December 1955 – 20th December 1956) and the birth of the modern American civil rights movement.
70	4 Dec 1955	Death of Glenn L. Martin, American aviation pioneer and manufacturer whose aircraft company is now part of Lockheed Martin.
70	5 Dec 1955	The American Federation of Labor and Congress of Industrial Organizations (AFL–CIO) was formed when the two trade unions merged.

DECEMBER 2025

Ann.	Date	Event
70	6 Dec 1955	Death of Honus Wagner, ('the Flying Dutchman'), American baseball player. One of the first five members inducted into the Baseball Hall of Fame.
70	8 Dec 1955	The Flag of Europe was adopted by the Council of Europe.
70	10 Dec 1955	The first episode of the animated television series *Mighty Mouse Playhouse* was broadcast on CBS in the USA. It popularised Mighty Mouse and the tradition of Saturday morning cartoons.
70	15 Dec 1955	The Tappan Zee Bridge, the longest bridge in the state of New York, USA, opened.
70	15 Dec 1955	Jens Olsen's World Clock was officially started by King Frederick IX at Copenhagen City Hall, Denmark. The advanced astronomical clock has over 14,000 parts and took more than ten years to build.
70	16 Dec 1955	The Queen's Building at London Airport was officially opened. The airport was renamed Heathrow Airport in 1965 and the Queen's Building became part of Terminal 2. It was replaced by a new Terminal 2 in June 2014.
70	20 Dec 1955	Cardiff was proclaimed the capital city of Wales.
70	24 Dec 1955	The *NORAD Tracks Santa* service was launched. It began by accident when a Sears department store advertisement in the USA invited children to phone Santa Claus but gave the wrong number. Calls went to NORAD instead, where staff gave Santa's 'current location' so as not to disappoint callers.
65	3 Dec 1960	The musical *Camelot* by Alan Jay Lerner and Frederick Loewe opened on Broadway. It ran until January 1963. It became closely associated with U.S. President John F. Kennedy's administration – sometimes referred to as the 'Camelot era'.
65	9 Dec 1960	The first episode of the television soap opera *Coronation Street* was broadcast on ITV in the UK.
65	14 Dec 1960	UNESCO adopted the Convention against Discrimination in Education. It came into effect on 22nd May 1962.
65	15 Dec 1960	Nepal coup d'état: King Mahendra imposed direct rule and took charge of the country under emergency powers. He suspended the constitution, dissolved parliament, and dismissed and imprisoned the Prime Minister. He then instituted a system of local, district and national councils.
65	16 Dec 1960	New York air disaster. Two airliners collided over Staten Island, New York City, USA. 128 passengers and crew were killed, plus six people on the ground.
65	19 Dec 1960	The U.S. Navy supercarrier *USS Constellation* caught fire while under construction in Brooklyn Navy Yard, New York. Fifty shipbuilders were killed. The ship, which was almost complete, was badly damaged. It cost $75 million to repair, and the commissioning date was set back by seven months. (Cause: a forklift operator accidentally knocked 500 gallons of diesel into the lower part of the ship, where it was ignited by welders' torches.)

DECEMBER 2025

Ann.	Date	Event
65	20 Dec 1960	The Vietnamese National Liberation Front of South Vietnam (also known as the Viet Cong) was established by North Vietnam. The armed communist political revolutionary organisation fought alongside North Vietnam in the Vietnam War. It aimed to reunify North and South Vietnam – which it achieved in 1976.
65	31 Dec 1960	Britain's farthing coin ceased to be legal tender. It had been in use since the 13th century.
65	31 Dec 1960	Birth of John Allen Muhammad, American murderer who carried out the Washington D.C./Beltway sniper attacks in 2002. (Executed 2009.)
60	1 Dec 1965 to 1973	Freedom Flights carrying Cuban refugees to the USA began operating. It was the largest airborne operation in U.S. history. The flights brought around 300,000 refugees to Miami, Florida. The flights followed the Camarioca boatlift, which began in September 1965 and saw thousands of boats attempt to traverse the Florida Straits and enter the USA illegally.
60	1 Dec 1965	India's Border Security Force was established.
60	3 Dec 1965	In a landmark trial in the USA, an all-white jury convicted three members of the Ku Klux Klan of killing a white civil rights activist, Viola Liuzzo, in Alabama in March 1965. The FBI then released defamatory disinformation about her to deflect attention from the fact that one of the perpetrators was an undercover informant they had employed.
60	3 Dec 1965 to 12th	The Beatles' played their last tour of Britain. They only played two more concerts in Britain after this, at the Empire Pool (now Wembley Arena) in London in May 1966 and their final live performance on the roof of Apple Records' headquarters in January 1969.
60	3 Dec 1965	The Beatles' album *Rubber Soul* was released.
60	4 Dec 1965	The USA launched its *Gemini 7* manned spacecraft. Astronauts Frank Borman and James A. Lovell remained in space for almost fourteen days and achieved the first manned space rendezvous (with *Gemini 6A*) on 15th December. The two craft manoeuvred to within 12 inches (30 cm) of each other.
60	4 Dec 1965	The American rock band the Grateful Dead played their first official concert, in San Francisco, California. (They actually played their first concert in May 1965, but at that time they were known as the Warlocks.)
60	5 Dec 1965 to 11 Nov 1968	Vietnam War – Operation Tiger Hound. The U.S. Air Force and U.S. Navy launched a covert campaign to halt the flow of North Vietnamese military supplies through south-eastern Laos into South Vietnam. The operation was followed by Operation Commando Hunt (November 1968 – March 1972). Both operations are regarded as U.S. strategic failures.
60	7 Dec 1965	Pope Paul VI and Ecumenical Patriarch Athenagoras I withdrew the mutual excommunication that had existed between the Catholic and Orthodox Churches since 1054.
60	8 Dec 1965	The Second Vatican Council ended.

DECEMBER 2025

Ann.	Date	Event
60	8 Dec 1965	The Race Relations Act (1965) went into effect in the UK. It banned racial discrimination in public places. Critics said it did not go far enough.
60	9 Dec 1965	Nikolai Podgorny became Head of State of the Soviet Union (until 1977).
60	9 Dec 1965	Kecksburg UFO incident, Pennsylvania, USA. A large, bright fireball was seen from six U.S. states and was reported to have crashed in woods near Pittsburgh. Numerous theories and conspiracy theories have been put forward.
60	9 Dec 1965	The world première of the fourth James Bond film *Thunderball*, in Tokyo, Japan. (U.S. première: 21st December, released 22nd December. UK première: 29th December, released: 30th December.)
60	9 Dec 1965	The animated television special *A Charlie Brown Christmas* was first broadcast in the USA. It was based on Charles M. Schulz's *Peanuts* comic strip and continues to be broadcast annually.
60	9 Dec 1965	Death of Branch Rickey, American baseball executive. He developed the farm system for training players, and broke the colour barrier by hiring the first black players.
60	15 Dec 1965	Cyclone 13B hit East Pakistan. Around 10,000 people were killed. It was the third major cyclone to hit the region that year. (See also: 11th May 1965 and 1st June 1965.)
60	15 Dec 1965	Vietnam War: U.S. Air Force bombers attacked industrial targets in North Vietnam for the first time. The first attack destroyed the Uong Bi power plant, which supplied power to Haiphong and the capital, Hanoi. Five U.S. planes were shot down during the attack.
60	15 Dec 1965	Zeeland Bridge, the longest bridge in the Netherlands, was officially opened.
60	15 Dec 1965	The musical *Charlie Girl* by David Heneker and John Taylor opened in London, UK. It was one of the most successful shows of that time, and ran until March 1971.
60	16 Dec 1965	NASA launched its *Pioneer 6* space probe to measure solar wind, the solar magnetic field and cosmic rays. It remained in operation until 1995.
60	16 Dec 1965	Death of W. Somerset Maugham, British novelist, short story writer and playwright. One of the most popular writers of his era. Best known for his novels *Of Human Bondage*, *The Moon and Sixpence*, *Cakes and Ale* and *The Razor's Edge*.
60	16 Dec 1965	Death of Queen Salote Tupou III of Tonga. Succeeded by her son Taufa'ahau Tupou IV.
60	17 Dec 1965	The first musical artists to play at the Houston Astrodome in Texas, USA: Judy Garland and the Supremes. The Astrodome opened on 9th April 1965 and closed in 2008. Various plans to renovate it have not come to fruition.
60	20 Dec 1965	The first episode of the television game show *The Dating Game* was broadcast on ABC in the USA. It ran until 1973. It has been revived since then as *The New Dating Game*, *The All-New Dating Game* and *The Celebrity Dating Game*. In the UK it was known as *Blind Date* (1985–2003, 2017–19).

DECEMBER 2025

Ann.	Date	Event
60	22 Dec 1965	A maximum speed limit of 70 mph was introduced on previously unrestricted roads in Britain. The limit was introduced on a trial basis but it was made permanent in July 1967.
60	22 Dec 1965	The U.S. première of the film *Dr. Zhivago*. (UK: 26th April 1966.)
60	22 Dec 1965	Death of Richard Dimbleby, British journalist and radio/television broadcaster. The BBC's first war correspondent. One of the greatest figures in British broadcasting history. Father of the television presenters David Dimbleby and Jonathan Dimbleby.
60	22 Dec 1965	Death of Al Ritz, American singer, dancer, comedian and actor (the Ritz Brothers).
60	24 Dec 1965	The Barwell meteorite. Two villages in Leicestershire, England were showered with thousands of fragments from a meteorite. The largest weighed about 2 pounds (1 kg). No one was hurt.
60	27 Dec 1965	*Sea Gem* oil rig disaster, North Sea. Britain's first oil rig capsized due to metal fatigue after being moved to a new site. Thirteen crew were killed.
60	30 Dec 1965	Ferdinand Marcos became President of the Philippines (until 1986).
60	31 Dec 1965 to 1 Jan 1965	Military coup in the Central African Republic. President David Dacko was ousted by army leader Jean-Bédel Bokassa, who took over the presidency. In 1976 Bokassa proclaimed himself Emperor. He was overthrown in 1979, and Dacko was restored as president until 1981.
50	1 Dec 1975	Lambda Theta Phi, the first officially recognised Latino fraternity, was established at Kean College, Union, New Jersey, USA.
50	1 Dec 1975	Death of Nellie Fox, American baseball player (Philadelphia Athletics, Chicago White Sox, Houston Astros). (Cancer, aged 47.)
50	1 Dec 1975	Death of Ernesto Maserati, Italian racing driver and engineer. One of the Maserati brothers, who founded the Maserati sports car company. From 1932 to 1937 he was the company's director, chief engineer and racing driver. He continued as a designer and engineer after the company was sold in 1937, and founded the racing/sports car company O.S.C.A. in 1947.
50	2 Dec 1975	The sixteen-year Laotian Civil War ended when the communist political group Pathet Lao seized power, abolished the monarchy, and established the Lao People's Democratic Republic.
50	6 Dec 1975 to 12th	Balcombe Street siege, Marylebone, London, UK. Four IRA members entered an apartment while fleeing from police, and took the two residents hostage. A six-day stand-off ended after the police broadcast false information via the BBC to make the gang surrender.
50	7 Dec 1975 to 17 Jul 1976	East Timor was invaded and annexed by Indonesia, just days after it declared its independence from Portugal (see 28th November 1975).
50	7 Dec 1975	Death of Thornton Wilder, American playwright and novelist. Best known for his plays *Our Town* and *The Skin of Our Teeth*, and his novel *The Bridge of San Luis Rey*.

DECEMBER 2025

Ann.	Date	Event
50	8 Dec 1975	The world's first computer retail store, the Byte Shop, opened in Mountain View, California, USA. It helped popularise the personal computer, and was the first retailer to sell an Apple computer (the Apple I). Founder Paul Terrell's order for the first fifty units helped fund Apple in its early days and convinced Apple's co-founder Steve Jobs that there was a market for personal computers.
50	11 Dec 1975	Third Cod War: one of the most serious incidents of the Cod Wars occurred when an Icelandic ship opened fire on three unarmed British tugboats. No one was hurt.
50	12 Dec 1975	Robert Muldoon became Prime Minister and Minister of Finance of New Zealand (until 1984). He was the last person to hold both positions simultaneously.
50	16 Dec 1975	The first episode of the television sitcom *One Day at a Time* was broadcast on CBS in the USA. It ran for nine seasons until 1984.
50	17 Dec 1975	John Paul Stevens becomes an Associate Justice of the U.S. Supreme Court (until 2010).
50	21 Dec 1975	OPEC siege, Vienna, Austria. Six militants led by Ilich Ramírez Sánchez ('Carlos the Jackal') stormed an OPEC meeting, calling for the liberation of Palestine. They took sixty people hostage, and killed three of them. The remaining hostages were released unharmed on 22nd December.
50	23 Dec 1975	The Metric Conversion Act was signed into law in the USA. It declared the metric system to be the preferred system of measurement in business, but permitted the use of customary units of measurement in non-business activities. Participation was voluntary.
50	23 Dec 1975	Death of Richard Welch, American intelligence officer. The CIA's station chief in Athens, Greece. (Assassinated, aged 46, after his identity as a CIA agent was disclosed.)
50	24 Dec 1975	Death of Bernard Herrmann, American film composer (*Psycho, North by Northwest, The Man Who Knew Too Much, Vertigo, Citizen Kane, The Ghost and Mrs. Muir, Cape Fear, Taxi Driver, The Twilight Zone* [TV series], and many more).
50	26 Dec 1975	The Soviet Union's Tupelov Tu-144 supersonic airliner went into service. Its passenger service was retired three years later, after two of the planes crashed and the others suffered from reliability problems and rising fuel costs. It remained in service as a cargo plane until 1983, and was then used for research and training until 1999.
50	27 Dec 1975	Chasnala mining disaster, Jharkhand, India. An explosion caused the roof of the mine to collapse, and it then flooded. 372 miners were killed.
50	27 Dec 1975	Birth of Heather O'Rourke, American child actress. Best known for her role as Carol Anne in the *Poltergeist* film series. (Died 1988, aged 12, from a congenital bowel disorder and septic shock.)
50	29 Dec 1975	LaGuardia Airport bombing, New York City, USA. Eleven people were killed and 74 injured when a bomb exploded near the TWA baggage reclaim terminal. The perpetrators and motive are unknown.

DECEMBER 2025

Ann.	Date	Event
50	29 Dec 1975	The Sex Discrimination Act and the Equal Pay Act came into effect in the UK. It prevents women from being paid less than their male counterparts when they perform the same roles.
40	2 Dec 1985	The musical *The Mystery of Edwin Drood* by Rupert Holmes opened on Broadway. It is based on an unfinished novel by Charles Dickens. It ran until May 1987.
40	2 Dec 1985	Death of Philip Larkin, British poet, librarian and jazz critic.
40	6 Dec 1985	Death of Burr Tillstrom, American puppeteer who created *Kukla, Fran and Ollie*.
40	7 Dec 1985	Death of Robert Graves, British poet, novelist, critic, translator and classical scholar. Known for his historical novel *I, Claudius*, his WWI memoir *Good-Bye to All That* and his scholarly work *The White Goddess: A Historical Grammar of Poetic Myth*.
40	7 Dec 1985	Death of Potter Stewart, Associate Justice of the U.S. Supreme Court (1958–81).
40	8 Dec 1985	The South Asian Association for Regional Cooperation was established. It promotes economic development and regional integration.
40	12 Dec 1985	Arrow Air Flight 1285 crashed after taking off from Newfoundland, Canada. All 248 passengers and eight crew were killed. The passengers were members of the U.S. Army's 101st Airborne Division who were returning from a six-month peacekeeping mission in Sinai.
40	12 Dec 1985	Death of Ian Stewart, Scottish keyboard player and road manager. Co-founder of the Rolling Stones. (Heart attack, aged 47.)
40	14 Dec 1985	Wilma Mankiller became the Principal Chief of the Cherokee Nation of Oklahoma – the first woman to lead a major American Indian tribe.
40	14 Dec 1985	Death of Roger Maris, American baseball player.
40	15 Dec 1985	Death of Seewoosagur Ramgoolam, first Prime Minister of Mauritius (1968–82), Chief Minister of Mauritius (1961–68), Governor-General of Mauritius (1983–85 – died in office).
40	16 Dec 1985	Mafia mobsters Paul Castellano and Thomas Bilotti were shot dead in a gangland slaying in New York City, USA.
40	19 Dec 1985	Mary Lund of Kensington, Minnesota, USA became the first woman to receive an artificial heart. She received a human heart transplant 45 days later, but died in October 1986.
40	23 Dec 1985	Two young American men, James Vance, aged 20, and Raymond Belknap, aged 18, shot themselves in a playground in Nevada. Belknap died instantly, but Vance was disfigured and died from complications from his injuries three years later. An inquest found that they had been drinking, smoking marijuana, and listing to an album by the rock band Judas Priest. This led to an infamous trial in August 1990 in which the band was accused of planting subliminal messages in its songs. The case was dismissed by the judge, who said there were no hidden messages. The so-called subliminal phrases were simply a coincidence caused by guitar chords converging with the singer's breathing pattern.

DECEMBER 2025

Ann.	Date	Event
40	26 Dec 1985	Death of Dian Fossey, American zoologist. The world's leading authority on mountain gorillas. Known for her book *Gorillas in the Mist*. (Murdered in Rwanda, aged 53, possibly by poachers.)
40	27 Dec 1985	Palestinian guerrillas mounted twin terrorist attacks at airports in Rome, Italy and Vienna, Austria. Eighteen people were shot dead and 120 wounded.
40	31 Dec 1985	Death of Ricky Nelson, American rock and roll/rockabilly/pop singer, songwriter, musician and actor. (Plane crash, aged 45.)
40	31 Dec 1985	Death of Sam Spiegel, Austrian-born American film producer (*The African Queen*, *On the Waterfront*, *The Bridge on the River Kwai*, *Suddenly Last Summer*, *Lawrence of Arabia*, and more).
30	1 Dec 1995	The first version of the Apache HTTP Server (version 1.0) was released. The free, open-source, cross-platform web server software currently serves around 35 percent of the world's websites.
30	2 Dec 1995	British 'rogue trader' Nick Leeson was jailed for 6½ years in Singapore for fraudulent financial dealings which led to the fall of Barings Bank.
30	2 Dec 1995	Death of Robertson Davies, Canadian novelist, playwright and educator. One of Canada's best-known and most popular authors.
30	3 Dec 1995	The former President of South Korea, Chun Doo-hwan, was arrested for his role in the 1979 military coup. In August 1996 he was sentenced to death for leading the insurrection. It was commuted to life imprisonment in December, and he was pardoned and released in December 1997. He was ordered to pay a massive fine, but he said he did not have enough money and only paid a quarter of it.
30	3 Dec 1995	Death of Jimmy Jewel, British stage, radio, television and film comedian and actor. Known for his double-act with Ben Warriss. He also starred in the sitcom *Nearest and Dearest* and other TV episodes.
30	4 Dec 1995	Bosnian War: the first NATO troops landed in Sarajevo to begin setting up a peace mission. Peacekeeping operations began on 20th December.
30	4 Dec 1995	The first version of the computer programming language JavaScript was released. It enabled the development of interactive web pages, and is now used by over 97 percent of websites.
30	4 Dec 1995	Death of Itzhak Rabin, Prime Minister of Israel (1974–77, 1992–95). The first native-born Prime Minister of Israel. (Assassinated.) Succeeded by Shimon Peres.
30	7 Dec 1995	NASA's *Galileo* spacecraft reached Jupiter after a six-year journey. It remained in the Jovian system for eight years, studying the planet, its moons, and other bodies. It was deliberately crashed into Jupiter in 2003 to prevent it from contaminating Jupiter's moons with bacteria from Earth. In July 1995 it also released a probe, which entered Jupiter's atmosphere on 7th December and sent back data on its structure and composition before being destroyed by the pressure just under an hour later.
30	8 Dec 1995	British head teacher Philip Lawrence was stabbed to death outside his west London school while trying to protect a student who was being assaulted by a gang of youths.

DECEMBER 2025

Ann.	Date	Event
30	9 Dec 1995	Death of Douglas 'Wrong Way' Corrigan, American aviator and folk hero. He famously made a solo flight across the Atlantic 'by accident' in 1938 when his request to do so was turned down by aviation authorities. He filed a flight plan for a trip from New York to California but flew in the opposite direction and landed in Ireland, claiming he had misread his compass.
30	11 Dec 1995	Death of Arthur Mullard, British film and television comedy actor. A well-known figure in British comedy films and sitcoms of the 1960s – 70s.
30	12 Dec 1995	Death of David Marshall, first Chief Minister of Singapore (1955–56).
30	13 Dec 1995	Brixton riot, south London, UK. Hundreds of youths rioted on the streets of Brixton following the death of a black man in police custody.
30	14 Dec 1995	The Bosnian War ended with the ratification of the Dayton Accords in Paris, France. Operation Joint Endeavour, a NATO-led international peacekeeping force, began operating in Bosnia and Herzegovina on 20th December, and remained there for a year.
30	14 Dec 1995	American AIDS patient Jeff Getty received the first bone-marrow transplant from a baboon in an experiment to find a treatment for the disease. The transplant failed to take, but he reported a reduction in his symptoms. He died in 2006.
30	15 Dec 1995	The European Council announced that the new European currency would be called the euro.
30	15 Dec 1995	The internet search engine AltaVista was launched. It was highly popular at first, but was soon overtaken by Google when it launched in 1997. It was acquired by Yahoo! in 2003 and shut down in 2013.
30	15 Dec 1995	The fantasy adventure film *Jumanji* was released in the USA. (UK: 16th February 1996.) Two sequels were released in 2017 and 2019.
30	18 Dec 1995	Death of Konrad Zuse, German engineer who built the world's first digital computer, the Z3.
30	19 Dec 1995	Death of Dame Nita Barrow, the first female Governor-General of Barbados (1990–95).
30	20 Dec 1995	Queen Elizabeth II urged the Prince and Princess of Wales (Charles and Diana) to seek an early divorce.
30	21 Dec 1995	The city of Bethlehem passed from Israeli to Palestinian control. On 26th December, Israel also passed dozens of West Bank villages over to the Palestinian Authority.
30	23 Dec 1995	Dabwali fire, India. Between 400 and 540 people were killed (including 170 children) when tent fabric caught fire during an end-of-year school function at the Rajiv Marriage Palace.
30	23 Dec 1995	The charred remains of sixteen members of the Solar Temple religious cult were found in a clearing near Grenoble, France following a mass suicide.

DECEMBER 2025

Ann.	Date	Event
30	23 Dec 1995	Aleksander Kwaśniewski became President of Poland (until 2005) after narrowly defeating former president Lech Wałęsa in an election held on 5th and 19th November.
30	25 Dec 1995	Death of Dean Martin, American singer, film actor, comedian and television host. Known for his partnership with Jerry Lewis as well as for his solo work. One of the most popular entertainers of the 20th century. A member of the Rat Pack.
30	29 Dec 1995	Death of Nello Celio, President of Switzerland (1972).
30	29 Dec 1995	Death of Lita Grey, American actress. Second wife of the comedy actor Charlie Chaplin. He married her to avoid a scandal when she became pregnant at the age of sixteen.
30	30 Dec 1995	Death of Doris Grau, American script supervisor, actress and voice actress. Best known as the voice of Lunchlady Doris in the animated television series *The Simpsons*.
30	30 Dec 1995	Death of Heiner Müller, German playwright, poet and theatre director. One of the most important German dramatists of the 20th century.
30	31 Dec 1995	The comic strip *Calvin and Hobbes* by Bill Watterson ended after ten years, and Watterson completely withdrew from public life. *Calvin and Hobbes* continues in newspapers worldwide as reruns.
25	1 Dec 2000	Vicente Fox became President of Mexico (until 2006). He was the first Mexican president to be elected from an opposition party after 71 years of rule by the Institutional Revolutionary Party (PRI).
25	1 Dec 2000	JPMorgan Chase, the largest bank in the USA (and the third-largest in the world), was formed when Chase Manhattan acquired J. P. Morgan.
25	3 Dec 2000	Death of Gwendolyn Brooks, American poet. U.S. Poet Laureate (1985–86). The first African American to win a Pulitzer Prize (1950).
25	4 Dec 2000	Death of Henck Arron, Surinamese politician. First Prime Minister of Suriname (1973–80 – overthrown in a coup). First Vice President of Suriname (1988–90 – overthrown in a coup).
25	6 Dec 2000	Death of Werner Klemperer, German-born American stage, film and television actor. Best known for his role as Colonel Klink in the TV sitcom *Hogan's Heroes*.
25	10 Dec 2000	Israeli Prime Minister Ehud Barak announced his resignation. This triggered an election, held on 6th February 2001, in which he was defeated by Ariel Sharon.
25	13 Dec 2000	George W. Bush finally claimed the U.S. presidency, 36 days after the election was held. The result was delayed by disputed votes in Florida.
25	13 Dec 2000	The Texas Seven escaped from the John B. Connally Unit, a maximum-security prison near Kenedy, Texas, USA. After escaping, they committed a robbery in which a police officer was shot dead. Six of the prisoners were recaptured in January, and the other committed suicide before he could be arrested. The surviving six were sentenced to death for killing the police officer. At the time of writing, four of them had been executed.

DECEMBER 2025

Ann.	Date	Event
25	14 Dec 2000	America Online and Time Warner merged. The company was known as AOL Time Warner until 2003 when it dropped the name AOL and became Time Warner. AOL was later spun off as a separate company, which was purchased by Verizon in 2015, and by Apollo Global Management in 2021.
25	15 Dec 2000	The last reactor (Reactor 3) at Chernobyl Nuclear Power Plant in Kiev, Ukraine, was shut down. It was unaffected by the Chernobyl disaster in 1986, and had continued generating electricity. The disaster only affected Reactor 4. Reactor 2 was shut down following a fire in 1991, and Reactor 1 was decommissioned in 1996.
25	16 Dec 2000	U.S. President-elect George W. Bush chose Colin Powell as the first African American secretary of state.
25	16 Dec 2000	NASA announced that its *Galileo* space probe had detected a liquid saltwater ocean beneath the icy surface of Jupiter's moon Ganymede. Another study in 2014 suggested that Ganymede may have a stack of several oceans, separated by different phases of ice.
25	18 Dec 2000	Death of Kirsty MacColl, British singer and songwriter. Best known for the songs *There's a Guy Works Down the Chip Shop Swears He's Elvis*, *A New England*, *Days*, *They Don't Know*, and *Fairytale of New York* (with The Pogues). (Hit by a speedboat while diving in Mexico, aged 41.)
25	19 Dec 2000	The UN Security Council imposed an arms embargo on Taliban-controlled Afghanistan. It also extended financial sanctions imposed in October 1999 unless Afghanistan handed over wanted terrorist Osama bin Laden and shut down Al-Qaeda's terrorist training camps.
25	19 Dec 2000	Death of Robert Buck, American rock guitarist and songwriter (10,000 Maniacs). (Liver disease, aged 42.)
25	21 Dec 2000	The Children's Internet Protection Act was signed into law in the USA. It limits children's exposure to pornography and other explicit content online.
25	22 Dec 2000	American pop singer Madonna married British film director Guy Ritchie. They divorced in 2008.
25	23 Dec 2000	Death of Victor Borge, Danish-born American pianist and comedian.
25	24 Dec 2000	Death of John Cooper, British racing driver, engineer and businessman. Co-founder of the Cooper Car Company with his father, Charles.
25	25 Dec 2000	Luoyang Christmas fire, Henan Province, China. The Dongdu building caught fire while construction workers were carrying out welding work in the basement. Other workers on the second and third floor were trapped, as were people attending a Christmas celebration in a nightclub on the fourth floor. 309 people were killed.
25	26 Dec 2000	Death of Jason Robards, American stage and film actor.
25	27 Dec 2000	British pharmaceutical companies Glaxo Wellcome and SmithKline Beecham merged, creating the world's largest pharmaceutical company, GlaxoSmithKline (GSK).

DECEMBER 2025

Ann.	Date	Event
25	28 Dec 2000	U.S. retail giant Montgomery Ward announced that it was going out of business after 128 years, and closed all of its stores.
25	30 Dec 2000	Rizal Day Bombings, Metro Manila, Philippines. Islamist terrorists detonated a series of bombs, killing 22 people and injuring more than 100.
20	1 Dec 2005	South Africa voted to legalise same-sex marriage (effective from 30th November 2006).
20	1 Dec 2005	Death of Mary Hayley Bell, Chinese-born British stage actress, playwright and novelist. Wife of the actor Sir John Mills. Best known for her novel *Whistle Down the Wind*, which was adapted into a film starring her daughter Hayley Mills, and a stage musical by Andrew Lloyd Webber.
20	5 Dec 2005	The first same-sex civil partnership in Britain was formed in Worthing, West Sussex. The Civil Partnership Act was not due to come into effect until 19th December, but an exception was made in this case as one of the partners was terminally ill. He died the following day.
20	6 Dec 2005	David Cameron became leader of Britain's Conservative Party. He became Prime Minister in May 2010.
20	6 Dec 2005	Death of Devan Nair, President of Singapore (1981–85).
20	7 Dec 2005	South Korean regulators fined Microsoft $32 million (£18 million) following an antitrust ruling. They said that by bundling its media player and instant messaging service with Windows it was creating a monopoly that prevented other software companies from selling their own versions. The regulators ordered Microsoft to separate its instant messaging service from all copies of Windows sold in South Korea.
20	7 Dec 2005	The first complete genome sequence of a dog was mapped. Geneticists from the Broad Institute in Cambridge, Massachusetts, USA mapped the genome of a female boxer dog named Tasha. Boxers are easier to sequence than other dogs because they are highly inbred and the differences in their paired chromosomes are smaller.
20	8 Dec 2005	Death of Rose Heilbron, British High Court judge. The first female judge at the Old Bailey, and the first female judge to lead a murder case. She also achieved several other notable 'firsts' for women.
20	9 Dec 2005	Death of György Sándor, Hungarian-born American pianist. Noted for his performances of works by East European composers, particularly Bela Bartok, whose works he sometimes premièred.
20	9 Dec 2005	Death of Robert Sheckley, American science fiction novelist and short story writer. His work is noted for its dark humour.
20	10 Dec 2005	Death of Eugene McCarthy, American Congressman and Senator from Minnesota (1949–71). An outspoken opponent of the Vietnam War. He sought presidential nomination several times. In 1968 he influenced President Lyndon B. Johnson's decision to drop his bid for re-election.
20	10 Dec 2005	Death of Richard Pryor, American stand-up comedian and film actor.

DECEMBER 2025

Ann.	Date	Event
20	11 Dec 2005	Buncefield Oil Depot fire, Hertfordshire, UK. An oil storage tank exploded when an unconfined vapour cloud ignited, causing nearby tanks to explode. 43 people were injured. The explosion was so loud that it was heard in France, Belgium and the Netherlands.
20	11 Dec 2005	Cronulla riots, Sydney, Australia. Thousands of people gathered on the beach to protest against ethnic attacks on local people. The gathering turned into a riot, with retaliatory riots taking place on subsequent nights.
20	13 Dec 2005	U.S. President George W. Bush admitted that much of the intelligence the USA had used as a basis for invading Iraq had been wrong. But he defended the invasion because it had led to the removal of Iraqi President Saddam Hussein.
20	13 Dec 2005	Death of Stanley Williams, American gangster. Co-founder and leader of the Crips in Los Angeles, California – the first major African American street gang. He was convicted of murdering four people during two robberies. (Executed, aged 51.)
20	15 Dec 2005	A (mostly peaceful) general election was held in Iraq. Incumbent Prime Minister Ibrahim al-Jaafari's United Iraqi Alliance (UIA) won the most seats but failed to reach a majority. A coalition government led by Nouri al-Maliki took office on 20th May 2006.
20	15 Dec 2005	Latvia amended its constitution to ensure that same-sex couples could not marry.
20	15 Dec 2005	The video-sharing website YouTube was officially launched.
20	15 Dec 2005	Death of William Proxmire, American Senator from Wisconsin. Known for his annual Golden Fleece Award which highlighted wasteful government spending. He halted numerous scientific projects that were (in his opinion) of little value, and infamously withdrew NASA's budget for research into space colonisation.
20	17 Dec 2005	U.S. President George W. Bush acknowledged the existence of the National Security Agency's Terrorist Surveillance Program, which monitored certain international communications. The Attorney General later revealed that other intelligence-gathering operations (collectively known as the President's Surveillance Program) had been authorised by the President as part of the same package, but details remained classified.
20	17 Dec 2005	Death of Jack Anderson, American journalist. Regarded as one of the fathers of modern investigative journalism. Known for his column *Washington Merry-Go-Round* which exposed political corruption in Washington, D.C.
20	18 Dec 2005 to 15 Jan 2010	The Chadian Civil War. Chadian Government victory. The war began when Chadian rebels (allegedly supported by Sudan) attacked the border town of Adré, killing about 100 people. The rebels were repulsed by Chadian government forces, aided by France.
20	19 Dec 2005	Afghanistan's first democratically elected parliament since 1973 convened in Kabul.

DECEMBER 2025

Ann.	Date	Event
20	19 Dec 2005	The Civil Partnership Act came into effect in the UK. The first civil partnership under the act was formed in Belfast, Northern Ireland that day. The first in Scotland was on 20th December, and the first in England and Wales were on 21st December. (See also: 5th December 2005.)
20	19 Dec 2005	Death of Keith Duckworth, British mechanical engineer who designed the Cosworth DFV engine, which revolutionised Formula One racing.
20	20 Dec 2005	The President of Iran, Mahmoud Ahmadinejad, banned western music from being played on state-run radio and television stations.
20	22 Dec 2005	NASA's Hubble Space Telescope discovered two new moons and a second ring system around the planet Uranus.
20	26 Dec 2005	Death of Kerry Packer, Australian media magnate and creator of World Series Cricket. The richest man in Australia at the time of his death.
20	27 Dec 2005	The Free Aceh Movement in Indonesia abolished its thirty-year armed struggle for independence, disbanded its military wing, and confirmed its commitment to peace.
20	28 Dec 2005	The first satellite (*GIOVE-A*) in Europe's *Galileo* network of global positioning satellites was launched. Its purpose was to test the technology. It was retired in 2012.
20	31 Dec 2005	SBC Communications acquired its former parent company AT&T for $16 billion and took on AT&T's name and branding. SBC was formerly Southwestern Bell Corporation – one of the seven regional Bell companies formed in 1983 when AT&T was split up following an antitrust lawsuit.
15	3 Dec 2010	The Nissan Leaf, one of the first mass-market electric cars, was launched. It went on sale in the USA on 11th December, in Japan on 22nd December, and in the UK in March 2011.
15	8 Dec 2010	SpaceX launched the Dragon – a partially reusable cargo spacecraft – and became the first private company to successfully launch a spacecraft into orbit and recover it. In 2012, the Dragon became the first commercial spacecraft to successfully rendezvous with the International Space Station.
15	16 Dec 2010	Ireland was granted a €67.5 billion bailout from the European Union to prevent its banks and other financial institutions from collapsing.
15	17 Dec 2010 to Dec 2012	Arab Spring in North Africa and the Middle East. The Tunisian Revolution (18th January 2010 – 14th January 2011) spread and became a wave of demonstrations, protests, riots, coups, foreign interventions, and civil wars in North Africa and the Middle East. The leaders and governments of several countries were overthrown and ousted, and Libyan leader Muammar Gaddafi was killed in October 2011.
15	26 Dec 2010	Israeli archaeologists announced the discovery of 400,000-year-old human remains (eight teeth) in the Qesem Cave near Tel Aviv in Israel. The controversial discovery challenges the theory that humans originated in Africa.

DECEMBER 2025

Ann.	Date	Event
10	18 Dec 2015	The last deep-pit coal mine in the UK closed: Kellingley Colliery in North Yorkshire.
10	19 Dec 2015	Death of Jimmy Hill, British football player (Brentford, Fulham), manager (Coventry City), and sports broadcaster. Host of the BBC football television series *Match of the Day* (1973–88).
10	27 Dec 2015	Death of Meadowlark Lemon, American basketball player (the Harlem Globetrotters) and Christian minister.
10	28 Dec 2015	Death of Lemmy, British hard rock singer, bassist and songwriter (Motörhead, Hawkwind).
10	31 Dec 2015	Death of Natalie Cole, American R&B/soul/pop/jazz singer, songwriter and actress. Daughter of the jazz singer and pianist Nat King Cole.

To purchase more copies or other editions visit ideas4writers.com

The next edition will be **The Date-A-Base Book 2026**. Expected release date: 1st March 2022.

Have you checked out our other books yet?

- Our 35 **'ideas for writers'** books cover numerous genres, characters, plots, description, dialogue, storylines, and more. There are more than 5,000 ideas in total, so you'll always have something amazing to write about – and no more writer's block!

- **How to Win Short Story Competitions** tells you everything you need to know, including how judges score each story, and how to get the highest scores in each category. It's packed with hints, tips and insider secrets that will get you onto the shortlist every time.

- **The Fastest Way to Write Your Book** walks you through the whole process of writing a full length novel or non-fiction book in less than a month. You'll come up with your great idea, expand it into a full-length outline, and write your entire first draft – all in just twenty to thirty days, and with no loss of quality. It's packed with tried-and-tested tips that will enable you to complete each step in the fastest time possible. Why write one book a year when you can write twelve? *(Expanded second edition.)*

- **The Fastest Ways to Edit, Publish and Sell Your Book** continues where *The Fastest Way to Write Your Book* ends. It's packed with ideas and tips to get your book polished, printed and into your readers' hands in the fastest time possible. It covers traditional publishing, self-publishing, printed books and e-books, and walks you through the fastest approaches for each of them.

You'll find full details on all of these at ideas4writers.com

Printed in Great Britain
by Amazon